# Social Movements, Mobilization, and Contestation in the Middle East and North Africa

**SECOND EDITION**

Edited by Joel Beinin and Frédéric Vairel

Stanford University Press
Stanford, California

Stanford University Press
Stanford, California

Printed in the United States of America on acid-free, archival-quality paper.

Library of Congress Cataloging-in-Publication Data

Social movements, mobilization, and contestation in the Middle East and North Africa /
edited by Joel Beinin and Frédéric Vairel.--Second Edition.
    pages cm--(Stanford studies in Middle Eastern and Islamic societies and cultures)
    Includes bibliographical references and index.
    ISBN 978-0-8047-8568-6 (cloth : alk. paper)--ISBN 978-0-8047-8569-3 (pbk. : alk. paper)
    1. Social movements--Political aspects--Middle East--Case studies. 2. Social movements--
Political aspects--Africa, North--Case studies. 3. Political participation--Middle East--Case
studies. 4. Political participation--Africa, North--Case studies. 5. Middle East--Politics
and government--1979- 6. Africa, North--Politics and government. 7. Arab Spring, 2010-
I. Beinin, Joel, 1948- editor of compilation. II. Vairel, Frédéric, 1977- editor of compilation.
III. Series: Stanford studies in Middle Eastern and Islamic societies and cultures.
    HN656.A8S63 2013
    323.0956--dc23                                                          2013018891

    ISBN 978-0-8047-8803-8 (electronic)

Typeset by Bruce Lundquist in 10/14 Minion

à Alice

# CONTENTS

Preface   ix

Contributors   xiii

Introduction: The Middle East and North Africa
Beyond Classical Social Movement Theory   1
Joel Beinin and Frédéric Vairel

**PART 1. AUTHORITARIANISMS AND OPPOSITIONS**

1   Protesting in Authoritarian Situations:
Egypt and Morocco in Comparative Perspective   33
Frédéric Vairel

2   Egyptian Leftist Intellectuals' Activism from the Margins:
Overcoming the Mobilization/Demobilization Dichotomy   49
Marie Duboc

3   Leaving Islamic Activism Behind:
Ambiguous Disengagement in Saudi Arabia   68
Pascal Menoret

4   Hizbullah's Women:
Internal Transformation in a Social Movement and Militia   86
Anne Marie Baylouny

**PART 2. MOBILIZING FOR RIGHTS**

5   Three Decades of Human Rights Activism in the Middle East
and North Africa: An Ambiguous Balance Sheet   105
Joe Stork

6   Unemployed Moroccan University Graduates and
Strategies for "Apolitical" Mobilization   129
Montserrat Emperador Badimon

7   Presence in Silence: Feminist and Democratic
Implications of the Saturday Vigils in Turkey                        149
Zeynep Gülru Göker

8   Mobilizations for Western Thrace and Cyprus in Contemporary
Turkey: From the Far Right to the Lexicon of Human Rights        167
Jeanne Hersant

PART 3. HOW ARABS BECAME REVOLUTIONARY

9   Becoming Revolutionary in Tunisia, 2007–2011                    185
Amin Allal

10  A Workers' Social Movement on the Margin
of the Global Neoliberal Order, Egypt 2004–2012                  205
Joel Beinin and Marie Duboc

11  Dynamics of the Yemeni Revolution:
Contextualizing Mobilizations                                    228
Laurent Bonnefoy and Marine Poirier

12  "Oh Buthaina, Oh Sha'ban—the Hawrani Is Not Hungry,
We Want Freedom!": Revolutionary Framing and Mobilization
at the Onset of the Syrian Uprising                              246
Reinoud Leenders

Notes                                                            265

Bibliography                                                     289

Index                                                            323

## PREFACE

Despite the plentiful evidence of lively political contestation and challenges to constituted power, nothing in the first edition of this book was intended to or could have predicted the insurrectionary movements that erupted in Tunisia in December 2010 and spread to Egypt and the rest of the Arab world throughout 2011. This should not be considered unusual. Predictions in the social sciences are incorrect as often as they are correct, and such prognostication is not their most useful preoccupation. Even the organizers of the mass demonstrations that led to the unceremonious ouster of Tunisian President Zine el-Abidine Ben Ali and Egyptian President Hosni Mubarak did not anticipate the extent of their success. As the second edition of this book goes to press two years later, it is still too soon to judge if these massive explosions of popular anger against decades of autocratic rule, corruption, systematic abuse of human rights, and economic deprivation will be consolidated as democratic regimes providing "Bread, Freedom, and Social Justice"—as one of the movement's most popular slogans demanded. De Tocqueville's remark about the French Revolution is apt: "elle dure encore" (it still continues).

With Saudi assistance, the movement for a constitutional monarchy in Bahrain was brutally repressed. But in mid-2012 popular demonstrations revived, albeit with a more pronounced Shi'i character than a year earlier. In Saudi Arabia itself, oppositional mobilization was preempted by massive state expenditures. In late 2012, opposition to hereditary rule in Kuwait and Jordan crossed previously established red lines. In Algeria, the movement for democracy stalled. A mild constitutional reform left the Moroccan monarchy with most of its powers intact. Islamists, albeit ones prepared to collaborate with the king, won a plurality in the parliamentary elections of late 2011, and for the first time the parliament, not the king, selected the prime minister. Despite the emergence of a revolutionary movement, a similar compromise leaving most elements of the old regime in place was negotiated in Yemen under the patronage of Saudi Arabia and the United States. Libya experienced the most thorough regime change and held reasonably democratic elections. But the government is far from having established a monopoly of force throughout the entire country. In Syria, the outcome of the increasingly violent confrontation between the regime and the opposition is uncertain.

In Bahrain, Libya, Yemen, and Syria, the revolutionary movements were indigenous creations, but foreign intervention became a potent factor. In Tunisia and Egypt the uprisings were entirely home grown. The latter two held free elections that brought Islamists to power, but they provoked violent confrontations by claiming a mandate beyond what was justified by their electoral pluralities. The new governments' utter failure to address the social and economic discontent that undermined the legitimacy of the old regimes rapidly diminished their popularity.

These movements differ not only in their outcomes as of this writing. Perhaps analytically more important is the "erruption of the unexpected" in Tunisia, Egypt, Syria, Libya, and Bahrain in contrast to movements deploying routine repertoires of contention in Morocco, Algeria, Jordan, and Kuwait, again, as of this writing. This variety does not diminish the utility of speaking of a "revolutionary movement for democracy and social justice" that enveloped the Arab world in 2011 on a scale comparable to Latin America in the 1820s and Europe in 1848 and 1989. While the Arab movement could not be anticipated, the pre-2011 histories and contexts of mobilization and contestation examined in this book are essential to understanding these political and social processes.

The editors and authors of this book believe that the value of social science is primarily in its capacity to understand the past, which is and always will be contested. Good scholarship about the past may also help us understand the present. The most dramatic political development in the Middle East since the 1970s—the 1979 Iranian revolution—was completely unpredicted. On New Year's Eve 1977, a little more than a year before the shah was compelled to leave Iran by the most broad-based revolutionary movement in the twentieth-century Middle East, President Jimmy Carter toasted him at a state dinner in Tehran saying, "Under the shah's brilliant leadership, Iran is an island of stability in one of the most troublesome regions of the world." No Western social scientist could claim to have been any more prescient. A month before the fall of the shah, the Hoover Institution published a lavish and admiring volume entitled *Iran Under the Pahlavis*, edited by the late George Lenczowski, with a full-color portrait of the shah as its frontispiece.

Rather than prediction, the continuity between the contents of the first edition of this book and the new chapters on Syria, Tunisia, and Yemen and the updates and revisions of the chapters on Egypt and Morocco in the current edition is their emphasis on the fine-grained dynamics of contentious mobilizations of secular movements of the working classes, the intelligentsia, unemployed degree holders, human rights and democracy activists, and unexpected forms of Islamist mobilization (and demobilization). Islamists were not necessarily the most active oppositional forces throughout the 2000s. Their historical longevity, superior organization, mobilizational capacity, populist appeal, and a certain "revolutionary fatigue" allowed them to reap the harvest of the revolutionary movements. Ultimately, our processual, dynamic, and historicized approach to social movements, mobilization, and contestation in hostile and repressive contexts focusing on precise contexts, informal social networks, and repertoires of contentious practices, offers a method of analyzing the emergence and development of collective action that contributes to understanding the events in the Arab world in a more substantive manner than instant analysis focusing on Facebook, the domino effect, and, more recently, the "Islamist hijacking" of democratic movements.

Like any successful mobilization, the preparation of this book relied on the support of both institutions and people. The idea for the project emerged during a seminar funded by the Ford Foundation and hosted by the Middle East Studies Center of the American University in Cairo during the academic year 2007–2008. Jack Brown was the graduate assistant for that seminar. The editors then organized a workshop entitled "Social Movements in the Middle East and North Africa: Shouldn't We Go a Step Further?" at the Tenth Annual Mediterranean Research Meeting of the European University Institute's Robert Schuman Centre for Advanced Studies at Montecatini Terme, Italy, March 25–28, 2009. We thank the scientific coordinators of that event, Imco Brouwer and Aleksandra Djajic-Horvath, for providing the opportunity to assemble most of the authors in this volume for an intense and productive discussion. Monique Cavallari, Angela Conte, Laura Jurisevic, Valerio Pappalardo, and Elisabetta Spagnoli—members of the staff of the Schuman Centre—were very helpful during the meeting. We would like to thank warmly Najat Abdulhaq, Diana Keown Allan, Abdelilah Bouasria, Kevin Koehler, Henri Onodera, Nicola Pratt, and Jana Warkotsch for their valuable contributions to the workshop and their thoughtful insights and comments on the papers at Montecatini Terme. Funding for the translations of the chapters by Amin Allal and Laurent Bonnefoy and

Marine Poirier from French was provided by the Croyance, Histoire, Espace, Régulation Politique et Administrative (CHERPA) research center of the Institut d'Études Politiques d'Aix-en-Provence and the Department of History and the Dean of Humanities and Sciences of Stanford University. We thank Larry Cohen for the two chapters' translation. We thank Christophe Traïni, Richard Saller, Debra Satz, and Kären Wigen for making this possible. The three new chapters in this edition that address the Arab uprisings of 2011 have replaced the chapters by Roel Meijer and Emre Öngün in the first edition; we thank them for their graciousness and understanding in this respect.

Two leading scholars of Social Movement Theory, Doug McAdam and Sidney G. Tarrow, read drafts of parts of this book and shared their incomparable knowledge of the field and its internal history. They were extraordinarily generous with us—investing considerable time and encouraging our project even though we have not been uncritical of some of their work. Their exemplary scholarly and human graciousness is matched only by their well-deserved eminence and outstanding contributions to social science.

We thank the anonymous reviewers for Stanford University Press for engaging with the ambitions of this volume. Their comments and criticisms improved and sharpened our arguments.

The index to the second edition was prepared by Vladimir Troyansky.

From our earliest correspondence on the idea for this book and its second edition, Kate Wahl at Stanford University Press has shown an encouraging and highly professional interest in the project. She has been supportive at all stages of its elaboration. Mariana Raykov was the able and cheerful production editor for both editions of the book.

*Joel Beinin*
*Frédéric Vairel*

# CONTRIBUTORS

Amin Allal is a PhD candidate at the Institut d'Études Politiques d'Aix-en-Provence and a researcher at CHERPA. He is coeditor, with Thomas Pierret, of *Devenir révolutionnaires, Au coeur des révoltes arabes* (Armand Colin/Recherches, 2013) and the author of two articles on the Tunisian popular uprisings of 2011 in *Politique Africaine* (vols. 117 and 121) and, with Youssef El Chazli, "Figures du déclassement et passage au politique dans les situations révolutionnaires égyptienne et tunisienne," in Ivan Sainsaulieu and Muriel Surdez, eds., *Sens politiques du travail* (Armand Colin/Recherches, 2012).

Montserrat Emperador Badimon is lecturer of comparative politics at the Université Lumière-Lyon 2. She received her PhD in political science from the Institut d'Études Politiques d'Aix-en-Provence. Her dissertation deals with the collective action of the unemployed graduates in Morocco, its internal organization and public management.

Anne Marie Baylouny is associate professor of national security affairs at the Naval Postgraduate School, where she specializes in Middle East politics, social organizing, and Islamism. Her book *Privatizing Welfare in the Middle East: Kin Mutual Aid Associations in Jordan and Lebanon* (Indiana University Press, 2010) analyzes social and political organizing resulting from new economic policies. Her current research is on Hizbullah's constituencies and its media.

Joel Beinin is the Donald J. McLachlan Professor of History and professor of Middle East history at Stanford University. He is the author or coeditor of nine books, including *Workers and Peasants in the Modern Middle East* (Cambridge University Press, 2001) and *The Struggle for Worker Rights in Egypt* (Solidarity Center, 2010).

Laurent Bonnefoy is a CNRS researcher at the CERI-Sciences Po focusing on political dynamics in Yemen, Islamist movements, and politicization of

Salafism. He previously held research positions at the CEFAS in San'a' and at the IFPO in the Levant. He is the author of *Salafism in Yemen: Transnationalism and Religious Identity* (Hurst/Columbia University Press, 2011) and coeditor, with Franck Mermier and Marine Poirier, of *Yemen, Le tournant révolutionnaire* (Karthala/CEFAS, 2012).

Marie Duboc is a postdoctoral researcher at the Middle East Institute, National University of Singapore. She received a PhD in sociology from the School of Advanced Social Science Studies (EHESS) in Paris. In 2010–11 she was a Besse scholar at the University of Oxford. Her recent publications include "Where Are the Men? Here Are the Women! Surveillance, Gender, and Strikes in Egyptian Textile Factories," *Journal of Middle East Women Studies* and "La contestation sociale en Egypte depuis 2004: entre précarité et mobilisation locale," *Revue Tiers-Monde.*

Zeynep Gülru Göker is a doctoral candidate in the Department of Political Science at the City University of New York Graduate Center. Her dissertation explores the concept of silence in democratic theory. Her research interests include democratic theory, feminist theory, language and power, and the links between gender, militarism, and democracy.

Jeanne Hersant is associate professor at the Universidad Andres Bello, Facultad de Ciencias Sociales, Escuela de Sociología in Viña del Mar, Chile. Her recent publications include "Souveraineté et gouvernementalité: la rivalité gréco-turque en Thrace occidentale," *Critique Internationale* no. 45 (2009).

Reinoud Leenders is reader in international relations with a focus on Middle East studies in the Department of War Studies at King's College, London. He is the author of *Spoils of Truce: Corruption and State-Building in Postwar Lebanon* (Cornell University Press, 2012) and coeditor of *Middle East Authoritarianisms: Governance, Contestation and Regime Resilience in Syria and Iran* (Stanford University Press, 2012).

Pascal Menoret is assistant professor of Middle Eastern Studies at New York University, Abu Dhabi. He was previously a postdoctoral fellow at Princeton's Institute for the Transregional Study of the Middle East, North Africa, and Central Asia and at the Harvard Academy for International and Area Studies. He is currently completing *Kingdom Adrift: Urban Spaces and Youth Rebellion in Saudi Arabia* (Cambridge University Press, forthcoming) and is the author of *The Saudi Enigma: A History* (Zed Books, 2005) and *L'Arabie, des routes de l'encens à l'ère du pétrole* (Gallimard, 2010).

Marine Poirier is a PhD candidate and assistant lecturer in political science at the Institut d'Études Politiques d'Aix-en-Provence. Based on her fieldwork in Yemen from 2007 to 2011, she has published articles on political parties, mobilizations, and elections as well as the revolutionary process begun in 2011. She is the coeditor, with Laurent Bonnefoy and Franck Mermier, of *Yémen, Le tournant révolutionnaire* (Karthala/CEFAS, 2012).

Joe Stork is deputy director of Human Rights Watch's Middle East and North Africa division. Prior to joining HRW in 1996, he was editor of *Middle East Report*, a bimonthly (now quarterly) magazine published by the Middle East Research and Information Project (MERIP).

Frédéric Vairel is assistant professor in the School of Political Studies at the University of Ottawa. He has coedited, with Myriam Catusse, "Le Maroc de Mohammed VI: mobilisations et action publique," *Politique africaine* 120 (2010) and, with Florian Kohstall, *Fabrique des élections* (Le Caire, CEDEJ, 2011).

Social Movements, Mobilization, and Contestation
in the Middle East and North Africa

# INTRODUCTION

The Middle East and North Africa
Beyond Classical Social Movement Theory

## Joel Beinin and Frédéric Vairel

EVEN BEFORE THE ARAB POPULAR UPRISINGS OF 2011, the Middle East and North Africa had been catapulted from relatively unknown regions in Anglo-American intellectual and journalistic discourse to places that almost everyone "knew" something about. The conventional wisdom about these regions was that they are culturally defined by "Islam," that this culture has a strong anti-Western and antimodern component (or simply, "they hate us"), and that it is uniquely susceptible to irrational political radicalism, authoritarianism, and terrorism. This book offers a different view, emphasizing the contentious politics of the working classes, the dissident intelligentsia, and unexpected forms of Islamism: a complex collage of striking workers, unemployed university graduates demanding work, human rights and democracy activists, demobilized leftists and Islamists, and an Islamic movement encouraging women to expand their public roles and professional skills.

These phenomena challenge much of the conventional wisdom about the Middle East and North Africa and emphasize that they are regions rich with political contestations and mobilizations of all sorts, which, while not leading inexorably toward the expansion of civil society or democratization, do not necessarily degenerate into violence and social anarchy. Moreover, we argue that many of the contentious episodes described and analyzed in this book can be understood as social movements, although they do not necessarily resemble the paradigmatic movements—the civil rights movement in the American South (Morris 1984; McAdam 1982, 1986, 1988a), student activism (McAdam 1988) and the international feminist upsurge of the 1960s and 1970s (Evans 1980; Rupp and Taylor 1987), mobilizations for gay and lesbian rights (Engel 2001), the French revolutions and their aftermaths (Traugott 1985; Tilly 1986), or the Polish Solidarity trade union of the 1980s (Mason 1989)—that provided the original empirical basis for the development of Social Movement Theory (SMT).

We believe that the Middle East and North Africa can be understood using the tools that social science has developed for the rest of the world. And we argue that the Middle East and North Africa provide a complex and fascinating laboratory, not only to confirm the applicability of SMT but also to enrich our theoretical knowledge of social movements and other forms of political contestation.

The study of social movements reveals how the production of social sciences in European or North American contexts has proceeded mostly without reference to Middle Eastern and North African cases. Decades after its first formal articulations, Social Movement Theory is now a mainstream and often routinized subfield of social science. During the last ten years, SMT and the broader study of contentious politics have become internationalized—as the tables of contents of the journal *Mobilization* clearly demonstrate. But the Middle East has largely been on the sidelines of this intellectual trend. Again, the tables of contents of some of the outstanding social science journals are quite revealing. Even with an expansive definition of processes of mobilization—such as the definition adopted by McAdam, Tarrow, and Tilly (2001) over the last decade, which includes lobbies and interest groups and ranges from political parties to ethnic struggles, from peaceful social movements to revolutions—the disinterest of the dominant currents in comparative politics or sociology in collective action and social movements in the Middle East and North Africa is striking.[1]

Due to a combination of implicit or explicit exceptionalism, training focused on mastering difficult languages, and a sense that at least until September 11, 2001, these regions were on the margin of global developments (except for oil, which is usually not integrated into social analysis other than as an impediment to democracy), studies of the Middle East and North Africa that have employed SMT have usually limited themselves to using these regions as a source of case studies to validate the classical concepts of *political opportunity structure, collective action frames, mobilizing structures, and repertoires of contention*.[2] While the forefathers of SMT have been self-critically discussing the limits of their earlier formulations for over a decade (McAdam, Tarrow, and Tilly 2001; Aminzade et al. 2001; Tilly 2008), this has had little impact on the limited literature on social movements in the Middle East and North Africa.

When deployed in the Middle East and North Africa, SMT has most often been used in studying modern Islamic social movements.[3] In the introduction to his influential edited volume, Quintan Wiktorowicz notes that "scholarship has tended to ignore developments in social movement research that could provide theoretical leverage over many issues relevant to Islamic activism" (2004, 3). The use of SMT in understanding Islamic activism is a salutary development in rendering the region legible using standard social science categories. This is all the more important because many of those whose work on Islamic activism is best known to nonspecialist audiences are uninterested in social science.[4]

However, the contribution of the authors in this volume, and others as well, to the interpretation and explanation of Islamic movements is paradoxical. They introduced a major methodological insight and broke with neo-Orientalism by empathically considering Islamic activists as "normal" social actors having resources, strategies, and practices that are comprehensible using the tools of social science. But their deployment of SMT is limited and instrumental rather than an effort to participate in the general discourse of social science.

The most common conclusion of SMT studies of modern Islamic activism is that the theory's classical concepts also "work" for the Middle East and North Africa. Consequently, despite their empirical richness and their aspiration to normalize the study of Islam in these regions—in particular by asserting the rationality of even the most violent actors—many such studies tend to limit themselves to the assertion that these cases confirm the theory's predictions. Thus, Janine Clark notes, "According to SMT/resource mobilization theory . . . these findings are confirmed in Egypt, Jordan, and Yemen" (2004a, 21, 25). Clark's book is based on excellent fieldwork and engages with SMT, but it does not aim to contribute to or to reformulate aspects of the theory by building on the strength of its important empirical observation, which we would characterize as the construction of an Islamic *mouvance* including the middle classes active in Islamic charitable institutions and the poor. Likewise, Wiktorowicz's edited volume (2004), whose contributors include most of those currently applying SMT to study Islamic movements, does not go beyond summarizing the literature on SMT and arguing for its applicability to Islamic activism. A similar limitation applies to Mohammed Hafez's comparative study, *Why Muslims Rebel* (2003). The book's ambition does not go beyond demonstrating the rationality of Muslim rebellions. It is helpful to point out Arab and Muslim rebels' rationality and their use of repertoires to mobilize and contest, just as European or North American contentious actors do. But Hafez's objective of normalizing these mobilizations is undermined by his focus on cases of violent uprisings only.

The conclusion that Islamic movements are rational is undoubtedly correct up to a point. But because the overarching purpose of most studies of Islamic movements is to demonstrate the applicability of SMT, many scholars, like Hafez, tend to embrace uncritically aspects of the theory that do not adequately explain these cases and, we suggest, many others as well. This promotes the further routinization of SMT and misses an opportunity to contribute to the larger world of social science and historical scholarship through the study of the Middle East and North Africa. Moreover, the focus on specifically Islamic social movements has allowed even proponents of SMT who have encouraged expanding its geographic ambit to once again relegate the Middle East and North Africa to the margins of social science with the exceptionalist claim that these regions are a locus of "ugly movements" (Tarrow 1998, 8, 194, 203), although this judgment will likely be revised following the Arab popular uprisings of 2011.

The Iranian revolution of 1979 inspired three paradigmatic exceptions to this trend. Misagh Parsa (1989) proposes a structuralist explanation of the revolution, emphasizing the politicized and highly visible role of the state in capital accumulation. The rising price of petroleum allowed the state to invest in the modern sector at the expense of the bazaar. Rapidly increasing petroleum revenues led to inflation, which the state tried to stop through policies detrimental to the bazaar classes. Bazaaris mobilized, utilizing the national network of mosques to build a coalition including other adversely affected classes—industrial and white-collar workers and professionals—against the perceived injustices of the state (an example of resource mobilization). Parsa's analysis—emphasizing an emerging threat and the use of mosques as mobilizing structures—is both highly original and compatible with the Political Process Model (PPM) version of SMT.

Charles Kurzman's account of the revolution falls on the opposite end of the analytical spectrum. He adopts a social constructionist perspective emphasizing the agency and perceptions of contentious actors, even if their perceptions of their environment and their "self-understandings and activities" are counterintuitive and mismatch the "objective" situation and the balance of forces with state authorities (2003, 312). So despite their belief that no new opportunity was available and that the limited liberalizing measures of the regime were a sham, masses of Iranians followed the call of the revolutionaries among the leading clerics and joined the cycle of demonstrations that resulted in the fall of the Shah. Kurzman (2004, 2004a) calls this an "anti-explanation" because it rejects attempts to theorize general patterns in social life and foregrounds subjectivities, conjunctures, and accidents.

Mansoor Moaddel's (1992, 1993) account of the Iranian revolution emphasizes the "broad episodic context" (1992, 375) in which a revolutionary discourse emerged and the specific character of revolutions as modes of mobilization. This can be understood as an effort to bring together structural and ideological factors. Moaddel's theoretical approach underscores the importance of detailed empirical work, knowledge of the relevant languages, and precise analyses of both historical and contemporary contexts. Indeed this is the necessary foundation that enables all three of these authors to normalize one of the most "exceptional" regimes in the Middle East as well as to contribute to the understanding of social movements and revolutions.

Most of the contributions to this volume belong to the relatively small body of scholarship on social movements in the Middle East and North Africa not framed in Islamic terms—clumsy terminology to be sure, but "secular" would be inappropriate. Disproportionately focused on Israel/Palestine, that literature includes the works of Alimi (2006, 2007, 2009), Marteu (2009), Norman (2010), and Pearlman (2011). While more analytical than the copious descriptive literature on social movements in Israel/Palestine, they are informed by the classical concepts of SMT without taking any distance from or critically engaging with them.

Pearlman's *Violence, Nonviolence, and the Palestinian National Movement* (2011), perhaps the most notable among these works, contends that "movement cohesion" is the key variable explaining whether movements can successfully employ nonviolent tactics. Greater discipline, cohesion, and a hegemonic leadership are necessary for nonviolence. While this apparently fits the cases of the "self-determination" movements she examines—Palestine, South Africa, and Ireland—it does not apply to most of the movements discussed in this book. The movements to overthrow the dictatorships in Tunisia, Egypt, Syria, and Yemen were not characterized by a high degree of cohesion or formal institutionalization. This does not explain the difference between the relatively nonviolent uprisings in the former two and the violence in the latter. In Syria and Yemen the incumbent regimes first resorted to violence, as Reinoud Leenders and Laurent Bonnefoy and Marine Poirier demonstrate, while protesters devoted considerable energy to defining themselves as peaceful actors and demarcating themselves from armed actors.

"Social movements" and "movements for self-determination" are not homogeneous categories. Likewise, despite their temporal and thematic connections and common contextual factors—authoritarian rule, contempt for human dignity, economic misery, a growing gap between the rich and the poor, widespread corruption, and a youth bulge—the Arab uprisings of 2011 were not a single movement. But the differences between the mostly nonviolent movements in Tunisia and Egypt and the protracted violence in Syria, Libya, and Yemen are due to factors more complex than the degree of movement cohesion. The length of the conflict, the modes of contentious interaction before the introduction of violence, the extent of repression or tolerance by the incumbent regime, and the origins and histories of the populations (urban, tribal) that join mobilizations should all be considered. We would suggest that good social analysis requires restraining the nomothetic urge.

## BEYOND CLASSICAL SOCIAL MOVEMENT THEORY

Kurzman (1996) anticipated Goodwin and Jasper's (1999) radical critique of the structuralist bias of classical SMT and proposed a social constructionist approach to understanding emotions, perceptions, and the meanings of actors engaged in contention. Goodwin and Jasper are the primary critics of the concept of Political Opportunity Structures (POS), which they argue, along with many of the contributors to this volume, tends to have a rigid and objectivist understanding of contexts. As they put it, "An extraordinarily large number of processes and events, political and otherwise, potentially influence movement mobilization, and they do so in historically complex combinations and sequences. . . . Such opportunities, when they are important, do not result from some invariant menu of factors, but from situationally specific combinations and sequences of political processes—none of which, in the abstract, has determinate consequences" (1999, 36, 39).

In *Dynamics of Contention*, McAdam, Tarrow, and Tilly acknowledge that they "come from a structuralist tradition" (2001, 22; see also Tarrow 2003). Although the original formulation of PPM tended to have a culturalist orientation (McAdam 1982), in their work from the 1970s through the 1990s, as well as that of many other SMT scholars whom they inspired in that period and beyond, there is no shortage of overly structuralist formulations of the concept of POS, suggesting that "opportunities" are confined to a closed list of variables relevant to any mobilization and are the most important factors in sparking contentious episodes that may develop into social movements.[5] Conceptualizations of POS tend to vary from one author to another, which is an indirect way of recognizing that contexts are never equivalent. For over a decade, Tarrow's own usage of the term has scaled back considerably its explanatory claims (Tarrow 1998, 200; 2011, 32–33). Similarly, mobilizing structures were often considered to be preexisting rather than dynamically created and appropriated;

collective action frames, a later addition to PPM, were sometimes regarded as concepts proposed by leaders to their followers rather than established through a dialectical interaction of leaders and followers by trial and error.

In response to the criticism of Goodwin and Jasper (1999) and others (Gamson and Meyer 1996, 275; Tarrow 1988, 430) directed especially at overly rigid understandings of POS, *Dynamics of Contention* repudiates structuralism and advocates transcending much of the research agenda and radically revising many of the concepts of classical SMT, and PPM as well (22, 41–50). In their place, McAdam, Tarrow, and Tilly propose a "relational" perspective, which makes "interpersonal networks" central to a dynamic model of mobilization. Their new orientation emphasizes challengers' "perceptions of opportunities and threats" (Kurzman's point); "active appropriation of sites for mobilization" rather than preexisting mobilizing structures; dynamic construction of framing among challengers; innovation in repertoires of contention; the description and analysis of "contentious performances" rather than stable repertoires of collective action; and a broad processual understanding of mobilization and linkages of mechanisms rather than a search for the precise origins of contentious episodes.

This method is conceptually innovative and highly sophisticated, even if sometimes overly complex. One may or may not be convinced by the several technical distinctions introduced by the authors—for example, the difference between processes and mechanisms—and their high degree of abstraction. Designating processes and mechanisms as distinct concepts while leaving their explication and practical functioning underdeveloped is perhaps the salient weakness of this ambitious intellectual endeavor (Koopmans 2003, 117); Tarrow (2011) has recently attempted to rectify this lacuna with mixed results.

The authors of *Dynamics of Contention* appear not to have completely changed their minds about the categories they helped to establish. They transform, reuse, or adjust them by modifying their meaning (Tarrow and Tilly 2006; Tilly 2008, 88–115). Sometimes they more or less reassert them in synthesizing the common knowledge of the field (McAdam, Tarrow, and Tilly 2007; Tarrow 2011).

Nevertheless, McAdam, Tarrow, and Tilly's revised conceptual model is far better suited to studying social and political mobilizations and contestations in the Middle East and North Africa than classical SMT and PPM. Most of the social movements examined in this volume operate in the interstices of persisting authoritarianisms that subject them to varying degrees of coercion and offer them few openings for mobilization. Many of them have very limited resources and weak formal organizations. They typically rely on informal networks and innovative repertoires to mobilize. Several chapters in this book do discuss appeals to the absolute rights of autonomous individual subjects distinct from their social worlds, but in at least some instances it seems that deploying the discourse of human rights is merely instrumental. Therefore, studying social movements in these regions allows us to expand and enrich SMT by considering such cases.

The contributions in this volume demonstrate a variety of ways and contexts in which a more processual, dynamic, and historicized approach to social movements, mobilization, and contestation can be developed, building on Middle Eastern and North African cases, by analyzing the emergence and development of collective action in hostile and repressive contexts, including Bahrain, Egypt, Lebanon, Morocco, Tunisia, Turkey, Saudi Arabia, Syria, and Yemen. In seeking to understand how Arabs and Muslims disobey and challenge authority, we self-consciously oscillate between the classical questions of comparative politics and comparative historical sociology: What can Middle Eastern and North African cases bring to mainstream social theory? And in turn, what new insights can such a discussion bring to our knowledge of these regions? We suggest that this inquiry can be developed by focusing on three axes: contexts, networks, and practices.

## CONTEXTS

The so-called Arab spring of 2005 generated great excitement among many pundits who imagined it was "the first bloom of democracy in Iraq, Lebanon, Egypt, Palestine, and throughout the greater Middle East" (Krauthammer 2005). While Egypt and several other Arab states in which there were no popular democratic upsurges in 2005 enjoy somewhat more credible formal democratic procedures today than then, substantive democracy remains an aspiration. There have been no democratic transformations in the other states noted by Krauthammer: the "prospects for democracy" in Palestine, and arguably also Iraq, are worse than in 2005; Lebanon has seen no real change. What we can learn from this premature spring fever is the importance of detailed knowledge of local contexts. The Iraqi legislative elections of January 30, 2005, the demonstrations of the Egyptian intelligentsia for democratic reform, the mobilization, led mainly by Christians, to demand withdrawal of the Syrian occupation of Lebanon, and the victories of Hamas in the 2004–5 municipal elections in the West Bank and the Gaza Strip have only the most superficial similarities.

We should not reconstruct the meanings of the mobilizations (and demo-bilizations) analyzed in the first two parts of this edition of the book looking backward from the popular uprisings of 2011. This would distort the under-standings of earlier episodes of political contention for both the insurgents and the incumbent regimes, neither of which anticipated the ouster of the auto-crats in Egypt, Tunisia, Libya, and Yemen. Those events, and the movements in Morocco, Algeria, Jordan, and Bahrain, which were contained, repressed, or did not achieve their goals despite their unexpected strength, have (once again) misleadingly been dubbed the "Arab spring" or the "Arab awakening"—as though these societies were frozen in a long winter or slumber during which there had been no history of social movements, mobilization, and contention in the region. What is required is a contextually informed and nonteleological understanding of politics in the Middle East and North Africa.

The first edition of this book proposed that these regions inspired the socio-logical imagination because they provided cases where mobilizations emerged in the absence of "opening opportunities" or when they were highly restricted or uncertain. "Tak[ing] protesters' beliefs seriously" (Kurzman 2004, 115), several of the mobilizations analyzed in this volume describe the development of collec-tive action despite high risks and repression. The chapters by Amin Allal, Mont-serrat Emperador Badimon, Joel Beinin and Marie Duboc, Zeynep Gülru Göker, Reinoud Leenders, and Frédéric Vairel dealing with Tunisia, Egypt, Morocco, Syria, and Turkey emphasize the importance of a perceived collective threat, rather than an "opportunity," as the impetus for action, another element in the revisionist positions of the leading lights of SMT (Goldstone and Tilly 2001).

The historical specificities that inform any situation are never entirely re-producible. Comparison is always a hazardous undertaking. Kurzman en-gages in a comparative step by systematically introducing a critical perspective into debates of the last decade—a contribution warmly welcomed by the most prominent figures of SMT and by their sharper critics. He also advocates an "anti-explanation" approach to social and historical phenomena, which makes comparison, and therefore understanding beyond the idiographic, difficult or impossible. We favor his comparative efforts and keep our distance from his more nominalist propositions.

Large-scale social and historical structures can be useful heuristic devices (Tilly 1985). But categories like "nation," "class," and even "Islam" have no "ob-jective" existence or transhistorical essence. They are inherently problematic and should always be disaggregated, localized, and contextualized. Since sociological concepts are produced in relation to a sociohistorical context, they are not automatically reproducible from one case to another (Passeron 1991; Kalberg 1994).

Insofar as the past and the present have any meaning, that meaning must be established through a dynamic exchange among social actors (living or deceased) and those who seek to understand them. There is no a priori prescription determining which social actors, and therefore whose perspective, should be privileged in understanding a place and a situation and how these change over time. But we believe that empathic foregrounding of social movements, networks, and contentious practices that are typically marginalized or demonized, combined with the intimate familiarity acquired through intensive original research and fieldwork, can yield new understandings that are relevant to those interested in SMT and contentious politics beyond the Middle East and North Africa as well as to specialists in these regions.

Determining useful categories requires detailed knowledge of cases and their historical formation. Taking this into account, the contributors to this book aim to provide precise descriptions of the contexts of the mobilizations they study. The contributions explicate the different matrices of constraints imposed on contentious activities, their diverse resources, and how both are perceived by the actors and their opponents. Such close attention to contexts comes from a strong belief in the importance of the historical dimension in understanding social and political processes.

## NETWORKS

Snow, Zurcher, and Ekland-Olson (1980) were pioneers in arguing for the importance of networks for the mobilization of social movements. PPM emerged as a critique of the tendency of Resource Mobilization Theory (RMT) to focus only on formal organizational networks and emphasized the importance of social settings that were relatively free of state control (McAdam 1986, 1988a; Gould 1991). Several scholars have recognized the role of informal networks in contention, especially the role of micromobilization processes (Snow et al. 1986) and of "social movement communities" (Buechler 1990; Taylor and Whittier 1992). They move us away from the "'immaculate conception' view of [social movements] origins" (Taylor 1989, 761), reminding us that mobilizations never emerge in a state of social and political weightlessness. These approaches avoid the organizational fetishism of earlier RMT formulations by focusing on people, mutual knowledge, social ties, and informal organizational structures preexisting social movement organizations. Such informal factors always nurture and shape mobilizations and help us to explain the evolving form of a social movement across time.

However, the notion of social movement communities tends to present a romantic view of collective action outside formal, institutionalized organizations (Fantasia 1988). While the notion "is potentially very useful in analyzing both how movements emerge within cycles of protest and how some movements maintain themselves beyond the decline of a protest cycle" (Staggenborg 1998, 181), it may overestimate the extent of shared interests, values, and goals inside a movement. By emphasizing common cultures and identities inside communities, this approach underappreciates the extent to which the definition of a movement, its public face, and its tactics are stakes in the struggle.

Attention to this range of phenomena is important for understanding politics in the global South, which often takes place below the radar screen of the formal terrain that political science usually studies. But it may still be inadequate to understanding the myriad silent refusals, bypassing of authority, day-to-day forms of resistance, evasion of power practices, or other behavior in the authoritarian states of the Middle East and North Africa that does not fit neatly into the binary categories of resistance or collaboration. These behaviors are more common than the open contestations that have typically been the subject of SMT and that are more common in the global North (Bayat 1997, 2010; Bennani-Chraïbi and Fillieule 2003; Robinson 2006; Zaki 2007). James Scott's (1985) conception of "weapons of the weak" can be used to explain not only the behavior of individuals but also certain social mobilizations in the South that seek to bypass, accommodate, or co-opt rather than openly confront constituted authority.

Guilain Denoeux (1993, 1993a) was among the first to apply SMT in Middle Eastern and North African contexts using the concept of "informal networks." This promising development was not followed up as energetically as it might have been. Diane Singerman's (1995) analysis of informal networks in Cairo was an important effort to redirect the study of politics to the only institutions that actually work and matter to most Egyptians—family and neighbors—rather than distant and ineffectual formal state apparatuses, political parties, and even many NGOs. Homa Hoodfar (1997) adopted a similar approach in her study of marriage in low-income Cairene households. Jenny White's (2002) exploration of neighborhood-level mobilizations in Istanbul relying on "vernacular politics" and Carrie Rosefsky Wickham's (2002) elaboration of the "lumpen intelligentsia" as a social category and the carrier of the Islamist message (*da'wa*) are important insights that explain the success of Islamic mobilizations in Turkey and Egypt.

It is not only that informal networks and indirect or minimalist forms of contesting constituted authority are prevalent in the Middle East and North Africa. The character of informal networks and the social processes through which individuals become embedded in these networks and may be mobilized through them must be understood. All but one of the chapters of Diani and McAdam's *Social Movements and Networks* (2003) examine Western societies, where it may make sense to pose the question of joining a movement in terms of individual calculations and decisions (although even in these cases we are not entirely willing to concede this point). The exception in that volume is Broadbent's chapter, which argues that "thick networks" of social relations are key to understanding the mobilization of Japan's environmental protest movement. He avoids both individual rational calculation and explanations emphasizing Japan's "deferential political culture" and proposes that "the final necessary ingredient was a protest leader from within the community who enjoyed high status there" (Broadbent 2003, 225). Focusing "on the *social* aspect of power"—the social context of networks and the power relations they embody—can overcome the unsatisfactory options of individual rationality based either on material factors or on subjective, culturalist factors as competing explanations of mobilization.

Broadbent suggests that his emphasis on the "ontological context" and the central importance of "social hegemony via networks" may render establishing universal theories of social movements impossible. We do not believe that social theory must be universal to have value. Like Broadbent, we reject both the notion of the universality of "individual economic rationality" as well as any sort of Arab or Muslim cultural exceptionalism as explanations for social movements, mobilization, and contestation in the Middle East and North Africa. Instead we adopt a midrange approach, which takes context, more or less as Broadbent understands it, as central to understanding how informal networks in the Middle East and North Africa operate and how actors among them calculate, when they do so. The implication that Japan and the Middle East and North Africa may share comparable forms of local networking does not mean that there is an essential East/West divide on this or other matters. Rather, we suggest that the West may not be as rational and instrumentalist as many have imagined it to be. Boltanski and Thèvenot (2006) discuss the plurality of social worlds and polities in which actors are involved and the plurality of modes of justification or criticism they use during various courses of action.

The particular character of informal networks, the forms of hierarchy and status they embody, and their social context matter. Montserrat Emperador Badimon shows how the self-limiting character of the mobilizations of Moroccan unemployed degree-holders protects them from certain forms of repression. Zeynep Gülru Göker demonstrates the power of silence and nonhierarchical feminine presence in diffusing repression of the Saturday vigils of mothers in Turkey. Joel Beinin and Marie Duboc explain how Egyptian workers' reliance on local networks simultaneously enables and limits the extent of their mobilization; it helps to sustain even protracted local strikes, while at the same time it impedes workers' coordination or unification on a national basis. The local character of the mobilizations also protected them from being perceived by the Mubarak regime as an intolerable threat. Amin Allal and Reinoud Leenders highlight that networks in different social milieus were differentially politicized in Tunisia and Syria. Such contextualizations of calculus are critical and highlight the importance of integrating history into the analysis of social movements.

We further propose that informal networks may be a key to understanding both the quotidian struggles for survival and social reproduction that absorb the energies of the vast majority of the population in the region, as well as how undercurrents of anger and dissatisfaction may be mobilized, the conditions that render mobilization possible, and why, despite the same levels of anger and dissatisfaction, mobilization is an episodic phenomenon and only in exceptional cases is sustained over a long period with a strategic objective like "democratization," "dignity," or regime change. The sustained mobilization of Egyptian workers persisted for over a decade without articulating a common strategic objective.

Conversely, through field research on Saudi Islamists and Egyptian leftists, Pascal Menoret and Marie Duboc show how persisting informal networks can facilitate subtle forms of disengagement. They explore the various reorientations actors give to their activism, converting it into diverse forms of commitment, without necessarily fully abandoning all forms of political activity. Here, networks are useful, not because they sustain or explain involvement but because changes in their form and density reflect and sustain the redirections of activism. Considering networks in this light allows us to examine the transformations of involvements in social movements in a way that avoids a binary understanding—involvement or apathy—of their functioning, one that usually relies on a switch-on, switch-off metaphor.

Finally, as Joe Stork, Zeynep Gülru Göker, Frédéric Vairel, and Jeanne Hersant note, throughout the Middle East and North Africa networks of former political activists, notwithstanding their past political positions, have adopted the global discourse of human rights, which both they and incumbent regimes perceive as a less direct form of contestation sanctioned by the neoliberal global order and which often, but not always, entails a lower risk of violent repression. The redeployment of networks of former political comrades in the arena of human rights advocacy suggests that under certain conditions—whether repression by authoritarian regimes or approval by NGOs based in the global North—networks can be reformed to pursue objectives very different from and even ideologically opposed to those for which they were initially formed.

## CONTENTIOUS PRACTICES

McAdam, Tarrow, and Tilly's *Dynamics of Contention* (2001) abandons the classical PPM approach to SMT in favor of investigating what people do when they protest and contest. By doing so, they return to a major insight of the late Charles Tilly (1986, 1995, 2008)—the study of repertoires of collective action. We embrace this development and seek to advance it through describing and explaining the internal structures of protest movements in the Middle East and North Africa and how they behave or conduct their affairs. These questions are related to the meaning of contentious action and to its very possibility. Contention is never self-evident, especially in authoritarian contexts.

Tilly's notion of a repertoire of collective action links best the logics of action and the logics of context. At any given time in a society there are a limited number of ways to have one's voice heard, consisting of "a rather small number of alternative ways to act collectively" (Tilly 1995, 26). However, over a longer time frame, the methods of protest are more varied: political struggles offer opportunities for learning and experimentation, as they provide the occasions for sedimenting these experiences. As Traugott (1995, 2) suggests:

> The metaphor of the repertoire allowed him [Tilly] to stress, without unnecessary teleological implications, both the great continuity that collective action exhibits over many generations and the sweeping changes in the accepted form of protest that occur only at long intervals.

Our interest in the repertoire of collective action is not only to underline the scarcity of methods of protest or the instrumental dimension of protest.

The concept of repertoire "also assumes a universe of shared meaning, prior to mobilization" (Siméant 1993, 315). It includes "routines that are learned, shared and acted out through a relatively deliberate process of choice," in Tilly's (1986, 26) words. But those routines may also be disputed. The repertoire is also a "'tool kit' of symbols, stories, rituals, and world-views, which people may use in varying configurations to solve different kinds of problems" (Swidler 1986, 273).

Analyzing repertoires allows us to examine anticipations, perceptions, and self-definitions of contentious actors and how they take up a position in the political field. In the contributions to this book, the description of repertoires of collective action brings us to reflect on the identity of political causes and on the vocabulary of motives people use: elitist or populist, oppositional or radical. Contentious practices are strongly related to how actors define the political situation. At the same time, a shared contentious practice allows the reformulation of actors' interests and values in relation to their political stances. A given means of contention gathers different actors: entrepreneurs of mobilization and conscientious supporters of social movement organizations who may not benefit directly from their accomplishments ("conscience constituents"), sympathizers, activists, and "fellow travelers." Repertoires of contention become the subject of struggles when actors define and implement tactics and gauge their potential efficacy in the political environment. Conversely, these struggles are part of activist groups' processes of identity formation. Finally, modes of action provide the occasion and are a means for protesters to bring all their influence to bear on the definition of social and political reality.

Because it attends to a fundamental variable in the modalities and dynamics of contention—the authorities—the notion of a repertoire of collective action facilitates adopting a relational perspective on contentious politics. It is all the more important in authoritarian situations where activists feel more heavily the authorities' arbitrary behavior and violence. Avoiding binary concepts traditionally used in political sociology, the notion leads to a dynamic perspective on collective action.

By taking into account logics of action and logics of situation—in other words, the practical reasons why actors choose one means of protesting over others—we avoid the structuralist tendency in the notion of repertoire, which may focus on modes of protest in synchronic case studies while inadequately examining the practical dilemmas actors face in actual mobilizations (Dobry 1986, 361). With this precaution taken, the notion of a repertoire permits us to bypass the binary alternative of macrosociology—how authorities discipline contention—and microsociology—actors' calculations. It offers the advantage of considering pragmatically these processes: between routine and reinvention, between the constraints and the resources available to activists.

Finally, because it reveals strategic actors depending on traditions, activist legacies, and political histories, contention seen through the prism of repertoires appears to be situated at the crossroads of the different rationalities of identity and strategy. Thus we are able to observe at the same time forces that are too often separated: authorities and contentious actors, structures and calculations, immediate actions and histories of methods of protest. Several of the chapters in this book (Allal, Beinin and Duboc, Bonnefoy and Poirier, Duboc, Göker, Leenders, Menoret, Stork, Vairel) describe the dialectical interaction of contentious actors and states and the consequent changes in the forms, methods, and intensities of social protest. The mobilizations of the Egyptian intelligentsia during 2005 and 2006 and the Moroccan Justice and Development Party and human rights campaigners discussed in Frédéric Vairel's chapter, and the Moroccan unemployed degree-holders described in Montserrat Emperador Badimon's chapter, all demonstrate how contentious actors may carefully limit their challenges to authoritarian regimes to avoid repression and how they strategically proportion their levels and means of contesting authorities.

## AN "AWAKENING CIVIL SOCIETY"?

Some of those who have applied classical SMT to the Middle East and North Africa have linked it to the assumption that an "awakening of civil society" was underway, and that social movements were both a sign and a development of this trend and would bring democratization to the region (Norton 1995; Ibrahim 1998; Ben Nefissa et al. 2005; Howard 2010). The term "civil society" is widely used in the Middle East and North Africa (Browers 2006). Political theorists, scholars, activists, experts, donors, incumbents, and their opponents employ the term. Therefore, civil society exists as a polysemic practical concept (Camau 2002) or a theory-in-use (Giddens 1984). But these "actually existing" civil societies, while they reflect the expansion of associational life in the region, have not led to democratization and did not play a major role in mobilizing the Arab popular uprisings of 2011.

Moreover, as Bruce Cummings has argued, the concept of civil society is often based on a false imagination of "a Western civil society where well-informed citizens debate the important questions of politics and the good life without fear or favor, in contrast to the limited democracies, authoritarian systems, and general illiberalism of East Asia" (2002, 92). This contrast applies equally to the Middle East and North Africa. In fact, what passes for political debate in the United States is an embarrassment to the Habermasian ideal of a rational public sphere; most US cities and their public institutions are in decay, while the "safe" suburbs are structured not by the "public square" but by strip malls, megaplexes, and downtowns that house the same globally branded coffee shops and boutiques. Since the nineteenth century the public space between ruling elites and private life in the global North has not been constructed through open debate but, as Habermas suggested, by deal making of corporate and political elites to the exclusion of the interests of the majority, with some periods of limited exceptions (Cummings 2002, 109).

Gramsci argues that civil society is the space where ruling elites, by establishing their ideological hegemony, win the consent of the ruled rather than rule by naked coercion. Following this understanding, constructing a civil society in authoritarian states of the Middle East and North Africa would not necessarily mean empowering the majority of the people. The same or other elites with authoritarian inclinations might rule by relying more on ideological hegemony than coercion. While this might be an improvement, it should not be surprising that it does not inspire the imaginations of the popular strata of society. They understand intuitively that procedural democracy without substantive democracy—social justice and alleviating the most egregious economic inequalities—would not meet their real needs. This accounts for the persisting popularity of idealized memories of Nasserist-style authoritarian populism or of Islamist promises of a moral economy. Consequently, elites are understandably nervous about the upheavals that a transition to this new mode of rule might entail.

Several of the contributions to this volume demonstrate that despite the popularity of the term "civil society," its uses are unstable. Contentious actors include or exclude allies and rivals according to the logic of their political and social positions and their perceptions of what regimes may tolerate. Some secular proponents of "civil society" in Egypt or Turkey agree with the regimes and their secularist oppositions that Islamists of any kind are not qualified for inclusion in this category; others hold the opposite view. Anne Marie Baylouny's and Frédéric Vairel's chapters demonstrate that the common Western view of Islamic movements, which classifies them on the basis of foreign policy interests, misperceives what is happening on the ground and lacks the appropriate categories to interpret their mobilizations.

Thus, Baylouny's chapter investigating Hizbollah's approach to gender relations based on an analysis of the content and style of its television station, al-Manar, reveals the inadequacy of the terms "moderate" and "radical" as analytical categories for Islamic (and, in fact, many other) movements and parties. The US State Department classifies al-Manar as simply the mouthpiece of a terrorist organization. In contrast, Baylouny demonstrates that its women's programming, contrary to what might be expected of a so-called Islamic fundamentalist movement, promotes what many Westerners would regard as progressive gender relations. Al-Manar programs directed toward women encourage them to pursue education and careers, while female presenters and (sometimes unveiled) guests provide positive role models for such aspirations. Men are encouraged to treat their wives as equals and share in housework. Problems and questions posed by the programs are resolved pragmatically and with reference to Western expertise when appropriate, not on the basis of an exclusive, rigid interpretation of *shari'a*. This certainly does not mean that Hizbollah has embraced the liberal values Euro-American societies claim to promote. The gender relations advocated by al-Manar must be understood in terms of the internal sociological logic of Hizbollah and its positioning in the Lebanese political context.

Similarly, Vairel argues that while the Moroccan Jama'at al-'adl w'al-ihsan (Justice and Spirituality) is commonly regarded as "radical" and the Justice and Development Party as "moderate," this is not the real distinction between them. It is rather that the former challenges the legitimacy of the Moroccan king's claim to the title of "commander of the faithful," whereas the latter does not. Only a very convoluted logic could argue that a movement rejecting the oversized claim of a hereditary monarch is somehow more radical and less democratic than one accepting it.

The concept of an expanding civil society also turns our attention away from a prominent phenomenon in the Middle East and North Africa: the fatigue and demobilization of social movements, both before and after the uprisings of 2011. There are many reasons for fatigue and demobilization. But we should not disregard the role of naked repression. Several of the chapters in this volume argue that repression of overtly political dissent was a factor in former leftists, Islamists, and Kurdish nationalists adopting the discourse of human rights and international law or the civil society repertoire.

The instrumental (at least initially) emergence of human rights and international law as themes in dissident discourse in the Middle East and North Africa may be one of the factors that raise questions about the capacity of this discourse to mobilize social movements, as Stork observes. It is not even certain that contentious actors who publicly deploy this discourse have adopted the values traditionally associated with it. As highlighted by the Turkish mobilizations for the recovery of Western Thrace presented by Jeanne Hersant, using the discourse of human rights does not necessarily lead to internalizing liberal values by either contentious actors or states.

## CYCLES OF CONTENTION WITHOUT STRUCTURALISM AND TELEOLOGY

Tarrow (1989, 1995a) is generally credited with coining the phrase "cycles of contention"—a structured process by which social movements formed, mobilized, and declined due to political opportunities, innovations in forms of contention, successful articulation of collective action frames, coexistence of organized and unorganized activists, and increased interaction between challengers and constituted authority. In elaborating the term Tarrow sought to provide a link between unusual moments of "madness," when everything seems possible, and the slower pace of "normal" contentious action, providing both a description and a model (1998, 149). "Cycles of contention" became a building block of classical SMT. Following Koopmans (2003a), Tarrow's reformulations in the third edition of *Power in Movement: Social Movements and Contentious Politics* (2011, 199–201) modify this approach by considering a wide range of dynamic interactions among multiple political contenders. However, other parts of the book retain the structuralist inclinations of its earlier editions despite his announced (2003) "recovery" from structuralism.

While it would be difficult to discern any obvious political opportunity at their onset, the emergent mobilizations in December 2010 in Tunisia led to a new cycle of contention, operating on both a regional and national scale. This process remains in motion as we write, complicating the task of interpretation.

As both McAdam (1983) and Tarrow (2011, 133–35, 197) suggest, a simple tactical innovation enabled the unexpectedly large turnout for the demonstration in Cairo on January 25, which initiated the eighteen-day occupation of Tahrir Square that culminated in Hosni Mubarak's ouster. We regard this as more important than the innovations of Facebook and other social-networking media because it reached beyond the circles of the computer-literate middle classes. Instead of calling on people to gather in Tahrir Square, assembly points were organized in several peripheral neighborhoods. By the time demonstrators converged on larger squares on the way to Tahrir, their numbers overwhelmed security forces. Surprised by their own numbers, and angered by the security forces' attempts to remove them, the demonstrators spontaneously decided to remain occupying the square. (Tahrir had previously been briefly occupied in solidarity with the second Palestinian intifada and in opposition to the US invasion of Iraq in 2003.) The violence of the security forces prompted much larger demonstrations on January 28 in Cairo, Alexandria, and Port Said with overtly insurrectionary orientations exemplified by the torching of the headquarters of the ruling National Democratic Party overlooking Tahrir Square.

One of the characteristics of this cycle is the demand for dignity and the removal of entrenched autocrats. Even in Morocco, Algeria, and Jordan, where ousting the incumbents was not at stake, protesters articulated economic grievances and demands for profound political reforms. In Egypt, Tunisia, Morocco, Bahrain, Jordan, Yemen, and Algeria, there were cycles of contentious collective action preceding December 2010. Although they do not constitute a teleological trajectory culminating in the Arab popular uprisings, they are nonetheless critical components of their social and historical context. We agree with Tarrow and Taylor (1989) that even "failed" movements leave a cumulative residue that can be taken up in subsequent cycles of protest (see also Giugni, Bandler, and Eggert 2006, 3, 12). But it is too soon to know if this cycle will follow the stages Tarrow has modeled.

Those cycles of contention and the popular slogans of "democracy, freedom, human dignity" and "bread, freedom, social justice" raised in the Arab uprisings—albeit approximately and crudely—expressed the different priorities of the middle classes and the poor and working classes. While somewhat more credible formal democratic procedures have been achieved in Egypt, Tunisia, Morocco, Libya, and Yemen, a largely unreformed military remains a powerful political factor in Egypt and Yemen, while local militias are powerful in Libya. Social justice is not at the top of the agenda in any of these countries. The influence of the "unholy trinity" (Peet 2009)—the International Monetary Fund, the World Bank, and the World Trade Organization—remains powerful. However, the authority of the "Washington Consensus" has been diminished, allowing post-2011 Arab regimes to be more selective in applying their prescriptions. The international financial institutions allowed regimes that desired to do so to buy off their populations with "social" expenditures and to postpone resuming "structural adjustment."

The international financial institutions as well as postmodern radical democratic theory, despite their divergent perspectives, share the view that workers' mobilization is an idea whose time has passed and that the working class as an organizing principle or class solidarity as a slogan are no longer fashionable. Nevertheless, the economic reasons for mobilization that informed the previous constructions of the working class as a political category have not disappeared. The orthodoxy (perhaps soon passé) of neoliberal development promoted by the international financial institutions has not improved the living conditions for most people in the region. Cuts in public expenditures, reduced employment in the public and state sectors, rising unemployment, inflation, and diminished job security have been salient consequences of neoliberal development everywhere it has been implemented. The trend toward privatization of public enterprises undermined the authoritarian-populist social contract (Heydemann 2007). This contributed substantially to the delegitimization of the Ben Ali and Mubarak regimes, leading many protesters to believe that they had nothing to lose but their lives, and undermined the stability of the monarchies in Morocco and Jordan.

As Amin Allal demonstrates, the 2008 "revolt of the Gafsa phosphate-mining basin" was the biggest protest in Tunisia since the anti-IMF "bread revolt of January 1984." Despite strong repression, support for the people of Gafsa grew into an unprecedented eight-month-long social movement that drew support from the coastal intelligentsia and even Tunisians in France and Canada. The difference was that in 1984 the Tunisian trade union federation, the Union Générale Tunisienne du Travail (UGTT), supported the protest. In 2008, both the UGTT and the regime were targets of the protest (Allal 2010). But before 2011, the pro-democracy movement existed mainly in exile or as small, Tunis-based, counter-elite circles.

In Morocco there were anti-IMF strikes by workers and students in 1981, riots in poor areas of Casablanca in 1990, and a general strike of textile workers in Fes in 1990 that forced the government to moderate its economic policies. After 2006, peaceful demonstrations were organized by coordination committees (*tansiqiyyat*) against the rise in the prices of water, electricity, and food supplies and to demand salary increases. While they were informally linked on a national basis, protests remained localized (Zaki 2008, 87). As Montserrat Emperador-Badimon shows, the movement of unemployed graduates framed its demands in apolitical terms and deployed moderate tactics. It kept its distance from the February 20th movement for democracy. By contrast, the Democratic Labor Federation (CDT), and sections of the largest federation, the Moroccan Union of Labor (UMT), supported the February 20th movement.

The chapters by Frédéric Vairel and by Joel Beinin and Marie Duboc demonstrate that there were two largely disconnected social movements in Egypt during the decade of the 2000s—one of the urban intelligentsia and another of workers. While the intelligentsia made increasingly bold calls for democracy, most workers did not. Neither believed that toppling Mubarak or a more extensive regime change was a realistic possibility until after January 25, 2011, though the demise of Tunisia's Zine el-Abidine Ben Ali two weeks earlier inspired hope and perhaps, for optimists, anticipation.

Although it was not unprecedented (Messadi et al. 1998),[6] Mohamed Bouazizi's self-immolation on December 17, 2010, (subsequently imitated by several Egyptians before the demonstration of January 25, 2011) was a tactical innovation, a local tipping point, in that his family held the authorities responsible for his death and protested publicly to obtain reparations. Thus, what began as an individual protest over economic misery and humiliation ignited a prairie fire of popular contentious collective action across the Arab region. Earlier economic protests, while not overtly political and not sharing a common collective action frame with pro-democracy activists, and not even necessarily with other groups of economic protesters, gradually delegitimized regimes over the course of decades so that the demands for regime change and democracy ultimately became, in Gramscian terms, "common sense."

## THE ARAB UPRISINGS AND THE ELEMENT OF SURPRISE

The powerful mobilizations beginning in Tunisia in December 2010–January 2011 opened a large-scale, and yet uncompleted, trend of political changes in the region, varying across national contexts. They invite us to reconsider the paradoxes of collective actions that are accentuated by their authoritarian context. The literature on revolutions inspired by the seminal work of Barrington Moore (1966) and Theda Skokpol (1979) sought to uncover the causal processes or "recurring conditions that lead to revolutions" (Tarrow 1998, 147). The evolution from the first generation of theories of revolution (Goldstone 1980) to the fourth (Foran 1993) led to ever-more sophisticated models, aggregating various factors (Goodwin 1994; Emirbayer and Goodwin 1996).

In its most sophisticated and ambitious versions, this research program aimed to foresee revolutions (Goldstone 1995). In the predictive perspective, revolutions are the outcome of grievances, deprivations, and various political and social dysfunctions. This contradicts a key insight of SMT: "Grievances alone cannot explain mobilization" (Tarrow 1998, 16).

Long ago Isaiah Berlin (1966) warned of the impossibility of such political forecasts. In fact, the only rule about revolutions is that they conform to no rules (Tilly 1993). Therefore, unlike the broad and abstract question posed by Gurr (1970) or Hafez (2003), "why (wo/men or Muslims) rebel?" we find it more fruitful to ask how popular uprisings occur. How, in some situations, do people raise their heads and their voices? How do they dissent and collectively publicize their opposition?

By focusing on identifying regularities in "what happens before revolutions (the preconditions) and on what follows them" (Chazel 1985, 680) or the "revolutionary outcomes" (Tilly 1978, 193–200), causal models of revolution risk separating the broad historical and sociological factors in the making of revolutions from revolutionary processes in their own right—"the chain of underlying processes," or the unfolding of events and the social mechanisms in motion during revolutions, not least of which are the processes of mobilization (Chazel 2003a, 135). This may divert attention from the particular ways that powerful popular mobilizations can rupture the relationships and linkages among the component elements constituting a regime and how this affects the calculations, evaluations, and self-understandings of ruling elites (Dobry 1986). Focusing on the dynamics of revolutionary processes (Chazel 1989) avoids resorting to binary oppositions: agency/structure, macro/micro, individual/collective, strategy/identity (Corcuff 1995). It enables an integrated perspective on contentious politics—from social movements to revolutions (Dobry 1986; McAdam, Tarrow, and Tilly 2007).

The chapters added or updated for the second edition of this book (Allal, Beinin and Duboc, Emperador Badimon, Bonnefoy and Poirier, Leenders) demonstrate the benefits of this approach to revolutions. Although they are "dated" in the sense that their perspective is linked to the beginning of a process that is still unfolding, this enables them to focus on understanding how mobilizations leading to revolutionary situations take off. Despite a hostile context with no apparent "political opportunities," mobilizations developed into nationwide contention in Tunisia, Egypt, and other Arab countries. Allal and Beinin and Duboc show how in Tunisia and Egypt the previously routine activities of relatively anonymous actors became "revolutionary" and the numbers who mobilized unexpectedly and quickly multiplied many fold while the oppositional elites of so-called civil society—members of NGOs and legal oppositional parties—played only a small role in the movement. In such cases, actors' perceptions are central, especially when they are mismatched with the "objective" political contexts (Kurzman 1996).

The linkages from one locality to another and from one country to another also merit consideration. In McAdam's auto-critique of the Political Process Model (1995, 220) he focuses attention on "movements developmentally dependent on another" and the social preconditions for diffusion mechanisms. However, because the PPM, like other versions of SMT, is framed as a universal explanation of social movements, studies in that tradition do not extend beyond identifying factors like the "attribution of similarity," the presence of links between sites or causes, critical mass, preference falsification processes, and the bandwagon effect (Beissinger 2011). "Diffusion" imperfectly describes mechanisms of mass protest, nationalization of collective action, and unifying slogans. Undeniably, the "power of example" (Beissinger 2007) exerts an effect. It remains necessary to explain how and for what reasons, and why, in some cases, the "power of example" is deployed to change the meaning, size, and scope of mobilizations. For example, while protestors unequivocally demanded regime change in Tunisia and Egypt, in Algeria, Morocco, Jordan, and Bahrain they demanded reform (a constitutional monarchy in the latter three). A useful approach to these questions might be to analyze the alleged role of new information technologies (Lecomte 2011).

The modes of diffusion of contention, as Bonnefoy and Poirier and Leenders show, should be problematized in inquiries into the Arab uprisings. It is necessary to pay attention to actors' practices: What exactly do they do when, while putting their lives at risk, they make demands, gather, demonstrate, or take up arms? During the uprisings new modes of action were likely learned more quickly than the typical pace of change in repertoires of contention (Tilly 1984; Traugott 1995). Allal follows how ordinary people, routinely engaged in activities far from political opposition, become revolutionaries.

Finally, the modular phenomenon of occupying squares in capital cities invites us to examine the strategic and symbolic dimensions of "place." Laurent Bonnefoy and Marine Poirier demonstrate how the occupation of University Square in San'a' linked modes of action, tactics, and slogans, diffusion processes, and the effect of numbers. From Tunis and Cairo to San'a', Manama, Amman, and beyond for activists and incumbents, urban squares became the emblematic site of change—simultaneously, a stake and the symbol of the struggle.

## OUTLINE OF THE VOLUME

The aims of this edited volume are both empirical and theoretical. We offer an array of "state of the art" studies of social movements in the Middle East and North Africa based on new empirical, field-based research. While answering the simple question—What do people do when they gather, contest, and protest?—the studies presented in the book demonstrate the diversity and complexity of contention in the region (from professional, Western-style NGOs to militant street protests). Some of these mobilizations are related to the deep social transformations of urbanization, privatization, and the shattering of the old social compact. This collection clearly exemplifies that Arab and Muslim protests are far more diverse than the stereotypical and contradictory images provided by al-Qa'ida on the one hand and the "participation of civil society through NGOs" mantra on the other (P. Chatterjee 2004, 69). The authors demonstrate the need to question the dominance of an abstract "Islam" as the principal prism through which the region is viewed. The book is divided into the following themes.

### Authoritarianisms and Oppositions

The Middle East and North Africa are excellent sites for studying collective action under authoritarianism. To complement the literature focused on structural processes at the state or regime level, it is necessary to pay attention to "politics under the threshold" (Heydemann 2002): opportunities and constraints for collective action in authoritarian regimes and their effects on the reconfiguration of such regimes. This helps in understanding regime transformations through the social and political relations that underlie them and not simply through the democracy-authoritarianism lens or normative promotion of civil society as a panacea for the ills of the region. It also allows us to understand how protests function in political settings where repression and violence have deeply left their mark: in such settings contention faces huge constraints, the collective dimension of protest is far from given, and the security apparatuses are omnipresent.

### Mobilizing for Rights

Since the 1980s human rights have become part of the repertoire of social mobilization in the region. The importation of this concept gave birth to a considerable literature, most of it inquiring how human rights discourse could and would undermine authoritarian regimes. The diverse uses of this rather elitist discourse by poor people or dominated actors have been less explored. The

Turkish case, for example, suggests that the capacity of human rights as an oppositional discourse may be at least partly undermined as it is institutionalized.

### How Arabs Became Revolutionary

The popular uprisings beginning in Tunisia in December 2010–January 2011 opened a new, regionwide cycle of collective action. The element of surprise and the end of political apathy of large sectors of the population have embodied and set in motion dynamics of political change, varying from one country to another. The essays collected here prefer the "how" question, when inquiring into revolutionary processes, to the "why" question, which would focus on the causes of the uprisings. The chapters detail "the emergence of the unexpected" and its repercussions for individuals—both contesters and incumbents—their practices, and the meanings they invest in their activities. They also address the emergence of violence and its impact on contention. Moreover, the authors show how revolutionary dynamics take root in disparate, sometimes very local, contexts. Revolutionary moments also create new contexts, while their strength and staying power can draw in people beyond the social milieus that mobilized initially.

### CONCLUSION

What then are the contributions to SMT that emerge from this volume? We believe that social movements, political mobilizations, and contentious politics in the Middle East can be understood in rational terms. But this does not mean a resuscitation of earlier versions of SMT that emphasized economically motivated or other methodologically individualist forms of calculation. Rather, rationality must be understood in its historical and social context. We do not regard these contexts as entirely "other," because Western culture (to the extent that such a thing exists) is not as calculating or as individualistic as many imagine it to be. Moreover, we believe that people in the Middle East and North Africa inhabit the same present as we do.

Contextually conditioned rationality helps explain how informal networks recruit and mobilize adherents. These networks are embedded in a local social structure of power. Members of such networks typically do not envision themselves as autonomous individuals whose rights and obligations can be disconnected from these networks. This is not because they have a "different" culture from the West, but because the combination of poverty, states with limited capacity to provide essential services, and authoritarianism makes these networks essential for survival and simultaneously enhances their power over individuals.

These same networks are also relevant to explaining how activists become demobilized. Through them activists maintain contacts that allow them to re-engage when they choose to and to feel righteous in their inaction when they do not. Such networks also help us to understand how former activists redeploy their competences and reorganize their lives alongside the political realm. The demobilization of activists highlights the capacity of authoritarian regimes to reinvent themselves, persist, and regroup in the face of demands for democracy, human rights, and social justice.

As a result of the neoliberal structural transformation of the region, the struggles of workers and of unemployed or underemployed professionals—the "lumpen intelligentsia"—are particularly salient. Mobilizations of workers are largely secular in character; those of the "lumpen intelligentsia" can be either secular or Islamic in orientation. These mobilizations lead us to a more complex perspective on networks. Networks are not only a sine qua non for any successful mobilization; they are also a framework constraining decisions, meaning, and the extent of mobilizations.

The emergence of many human rights, women's rights, and labor rights organizations is a salient indicator that terms from the rights-based political lexicon of the North are easily adopted across the Middle East and North Africa (with the notable exception of Saudi Arabia) thanks to the accelerated global circulation of cultural concepts and the foreign funding that rewards politically correct discourse. Optimistic proponents of "world society" theory (Meyer et al. 1997) argue that this is a positive phenomenon and an aspect of the emergence of a global civil society.

But what is still uncertain is whether these organizations are "engaged in a sustained contentious interaction with powerholders" (Tarrow 1998, 31) and the extent to which they will or will not be contained by authoritarian regimes that have also learned to adopt the discourse of economic development, democracy, and change (or "new thinking," as Egypt's former first son, Gamal Mubarak, put it). While we wait to determine whether democratic transformations are emerging—and our inclination is to argue that they are not—it is important to analyze the actual political changes that are taking place, without the encumbrance of teleological assumptions about the democratic end of history.

Many elements of the repertoires of collective action examined in this book will sound familiar to Western observers and are among the contentious practices commonly considered by SMT. Other practices, while not unique to the Middle East and North Africa, are far less often considered by SMT. In all cases the contributors to this volume take social practices, especially those that are not typically prominent in the conceptual map of comparative politics or political sociology, as their point of departure to understand both broader processes of contention and the precise definition of the pertinent context for each mobilization.

Islamic activism in particular demonstrates a surprising repertoire with regard to violence and nonviolence as well as the role of women in such movements. Islamic activism has typically been analyzed with regard to its use of violence, its contribution to or obstruction of democratization, or its potential for moderation. The three contributors who discuss Islamic activism in this volume do not engage in these discussions. Rather, by examining concretely what movements and networks actually do—how they mobilize, demobilize, and transform from within—they present a much richer empirical account of Islamic activism as well as a more nuanced capacity to integrate these phenomena into the broader discourse of social science.

For secular mobilizations as well, we argue that the repertoire of contention to be considered in understanding social and political mobilizations in the Middle East and North Africa should include a broad range of practices that intentionally avoid directly contesting constituted authority. Over time indirect or limited contestations have reshaped the political field. However, they have done so largely within the framework of renewed forms of authoritarian rule rather than as elements in democratic transformations.

Because the authoritarian contexts of the Middle East and North Africa are far from being conducive to mobilizations, they allow us to challenge the idea that people mobilize in order to take advantage of opportunities, however broad a definition we might have. Frequently people mobilize in reaction to threats. In these situations repression is not the only fuel for contention. Actors may also perceive public policies and their consequences as a threat to their values, interests, and understandings of the public good. People mobilize not only because they can but also and probably even more readily when they are compelled to do so: when they feel their sense of justice or morals, their basic rights, or the possibility of offering decent living conditions to their children are being attacked.

. . .

The contributors to this book believe it is worth engaging with SMT, albeit with a critical eye, when traveling to the Middle East and North Africa. We bring back from our fieldwork firsthand material that has value, not only for Middle Eastern and North African studies but for the social sciences more broadly. We believe that reciprocal interactions between SMT—whatever version one has in mind or favors—and the Middle East and North Africa are valuable for SMT because these regions challenge some of the theory's routine questions and because the import of these questions may be differently understood when exposed to this particular comparative light. At the same time, there is a range of phenomena in these regions that we would not understand as clearly as we do if we did not deploy SMT or its derivatives as analytical tools. The aim of this conceptual travel is not simply to test tools built in the more democratic contexts of the global North and to validate their assertions while pointing to ways in which the Middle East and North Africa are exceptions. These regions are an inseparable part of global modernity, and that is why the authors of this volume regard social and political mobilization, contentious politics, and social movements from these regions as an integral part of the empirical data on which our understanding of these phenomena should be based, using the tools of SMT without embracing them uncritically. Like some of the social actors we have met during our fieldwork, we hope to modify the received wisdom of SMT when possible or bypass it when this is more fruitful.

AUTHORITARIANISMS AND OPPOSITIONS    **Part 1**

# 1 PROTESTING IN AUTHORITARIAN SITUATIONS

Egypt and Morocco in Comparative Perspective

## Frédéric Vairel

DURING THE 1990S AND ESPECIALLY SINCE 2000, the forms and means of political participation increased in Morocco and Egypt. The emergence of collective actions whose objective is not to overthrow the regime but to obtain the implementation of new policies, or changes to make the system more democratic, has transformed the streets into a major arena of reform. This chapter will analyze the contentious spaces resulting from the competition between protesting actors and regime incumbents. In these spaces, increasing public and collective indignation takes different forms, expressed in familiar collective action repertoires: demonstrations, petitions, press releases, hunger strikes, coalitions and associative networks, and sit-ins. By "contentious space" I mean a part of the social world built at the same time against and in reference to the political field and its formal institutions. Actors in contentious spaces share the idea that changing politics by mobilizations and political activism is possible. They also have common practices and skills regarding modes of action—writing a statement, organizing a sit-in, building an NGO or a group, gathering people around a cause (Mathieu 2007). People active in contentious spaces also share political comradery and friendship. Despite their diverse or even opposing political stances or their concurrences, they share a history of repression and of time served in prison.

By analyzing spaces of political competition beyond the institutional sphere and taking into account the reciprocal determinations of contentious and institutional politics, I avoid the "polity-centered bias" characterizing most of the studies of Morocco and Egypt as well as the approaches of a number of social movement theorists—although Tarrow (1990, 1993), and more precisely Goldstone (2003), have challenged the rigid distinction between the politics of movements and institutional politics or public policing. To understand the logic of these contentious spaces, one has to keep in mind that they function under coercion. The contentious arenas constitute a "new discipline" adopted by regimes against activists' organizations and mobilizations; they are part of the way authoritarianism is reinventing itself. The study of the setbacks suffered by activists' associations and groups allows us to analyze precisely how the Moroccan and Egyptian authorities constrain their activities.

In Morocco different movements have evolved around a government plan to improve women's conditions (National Plan for the Integration of Women in Development); around the repression during the "Years of Lead" and the regime's history of violence; and around Arab causes like Palestine and Iraq. In Egypt the emergence of Kifaya ("Enough!" or the Egyptian Movement for Change) in December 2004 and its mobilizations against hereditary succession and President Mubarak's authoritarian rule have attracted attention from international observers and policy makers. In April and May 2006 different groups—from leftists to the Muslim Brothers (MB)—took to the streets in defense of the independence of the judiciary. They were supporting judges who were critical of the regime and who questioned the fairness of the 2005 legislative elections. In July 2006 mobilizations against the Israeli war in Lebanon revealed both the vitality and the limits of Egyptian oppositional movements.

In Egypt and Morocco the emergence of social movements is not a result of mere window-dressing measures to satisfy key international allies like the United States or the EU. The transformation of collective action, its goals and mottoes, has rendered protests tolerable if not legitimate. Nowadays militants no longer seek to overthrow regimes as in the 1970s and 1980s. Instead they intend to transform them from within, in either a democratic or Islamic way. On the incumbents' side, democracy has become the language of power. In Egypt and Morocco incumbents are modifying the style of their domination, with an increasing tolerance for public expression of discontent. But this situation, in which regimes and oppositions share the same reference to democracy without agreeing on its content—what David I. Kertzer describes as "solidarity without consensus" (1988, 67–75)—complicates contestation.

Egypt and Morocco are two demographic and political heavyweights in Arab politics. The two countries are broadly open to the international environment. For different historical and political reasons, both have strong links with the EU and the United States. They are members of the Barcelona process and have concluded free trade agreements with the EU and the United States in the case of Morocco, and a preferential trade agreement (the QIZ agreement, see below) with Israel and the United States in the case of Egypt.[1]

During the 1990s, Morocco was often perceived as a welcoming land for transitology scholars. Their enthusiasm was based on the idea that any political changes are equivalent to democratic transformations, although Salamé (1994) expressed only measured optimism about the prospects for democracy. Economic liberalization, constitutionalism, elections, reference to the human rights lexicon, a broader range of freedom in public discourses, and the monarchical succession were thought to signal a democratic transition. A few years later, Egypt was often included in the category of "Arab springs" (International Crisis Group 2005). Here again, economic privatization,[2] constitutional reforms in 2005, the so-called pluralistic presidential election, relatively more-transparent legislative elections, and a broader range of freedom in the press encouraged many to believe that a "transition to democracy" was underway.

The two countries are involved in long-term processes of opening markets. The Morocco/EU Association Agreement entered into force in March 2000, and the Egypt/EU Agreement in June 2004. Morocco has acquired an "advanced status" with the EU, including deeper trade and political ties. For the Union, this "advanced" status is a way to avoid full Moroccan membership. In January 2000 Morocco concluded a free trade agreement with the United States. In Egypt since December 2004, over twenty qualifying industrial zones (QIZs) constitute a partial free trade agreement with the United States. Originally, goods produced in these zones enjoyed a duty-free access to US markets if they had 11.7 percent Israeli content. The required Israeli input was lowered to 10.5 percent in October 2007. Morocco and Egypt, with Tunisia and Jordan, are also part of the Agadir agreement since March 2007 and are linked together by a bilateral free trade agreement since April 1999. However, there is confusion between these indices of economic change and the more or less profound changes in the architecture of the two countries' political regimes and their exercise of power and domination.

The Arab or Muslim exceptionalism thesis has seen a renewal with the so-called third wave of democratization (Huntington 1991) and the fading of prospects for democracy in the region since the authoritarian softening of the late 1990s and early 2000s. As for electoral politics, some scholars describe what could be "an Arab more than a Muslim gap" (Stepan and Robertson 2003). But the uses of the "menu of manipulation" in electoral politics (Schedler 2002) seem rather universal. Many studies of political participation have established a binary representation of Arab political scenes. They confine political participation to elections and riots, both "hot" political moments having opposing logics and legitimacy. Arab politics is either seen through the prism of "a culture of rioting" (Badie 1986) or "a culture of deference" (Hopkins 1995;

Hammoudi 1997). Until recently, except for riots (Bennani-Chraïbi 1994) and revolutionary moments (Kurzman 1996), contentious politics raised little interest. The dynamics of the political field was the main object of study of political science; investigations were limited to institutions, political parties, and elections, all directly related to states and regimes. This trend has been reinforced by the fact that studies of social movements have been relegated to other disciplines (such as social history, urban sociology, social anthropology). These investigations have tended to minimize or obscure the very political meaning of those movements. Comparing political dynamics in Egypt and Morocco may function as a laboratory to examine research directions that can enrich more general debates about social movements. I will emphasize how the emergence of large-scale mobilizations and the long-awaited democratization are disconnected: in these situations, "civil society" is far from being the instrument of a gradual democratization so dear to democracy promoters. Rather, on the Moroccan and Egyptian political scenes "civil society" is shaped by reciprocal adaptations between reforming authoritarianisms and deradicalized activists. The huge coercion exerted against oppositional movements in Morocco and Egypt allows us to consider the broad and complex effects of repression, beyond the mere repression/radicalization binary. Finally, the multiple forms that political violence can assume also provide a way to examine the importance of threats in the process of mobilization.

## CIVIL SOCIETY AND DEMOCRATIC PASSION

Scholarship on the associational revival in the Middle East has too often fallen into the trap of considering the awakening of civil societies as a sign, a factor, and a condition for democratization (Al-Sayyid 1995; Hudson 1996). The issue at stake is not only satisfying a fashion fostered by the international expertise mechanisms—the International Monetary Fund, World Bank, and World Trade Organization—or by the UN Development Program; the democratic passion of researchers has prevailed over observable reality and has gone so far as to substitute for it. Works based on civil society have not always avoided the pitfalls of transitology, especially its teleological biases, and have linked the "awakening" of civil society with transition to democracy (Ben Nefissa et al. 2005). As noted by Schwedler (2006, 6),

> One limitation of the focus on transitions to democracy is that political change is assessed almost exclusively in terms of progress along a continuum, with

many processes characterized by stagnation (in the case of stalled transitions) or a return to autocratic practices (in aborted and failed transitions). This focus often obscures the complex ways in which political institutions and practices are restructured *even in cases where political openings do not progress very far.* That is, even limited openings may produce considerable dynamic change in the public political space—the practices and locales of political struggle—and these multidimensional restructurings demand systematic analysis. (italics in original)

In Morocco the institutionalization of a contentious space tells us a great deal about the political adjustment trajectory of authoritarianism. This institutionalization is mostly seen in the increase in the forms and means of political participation and public expressions of dissent. The tradition of demonstrating in the streets was renewed during the 1990s in large and peaceful demonstrations of solidarity with the Palestinians and the Iraqis. They were followed by the huge mobilization around the National Plan for the Integration of Women in Development and by numerous sit-ins in front of the secret jails of the Years of Lead; against inflation; or against the poor quality of privatized public services, whose prices were increasing. These movements cannot be understood only as "a survival strategy of the regimes that did not go far beyond the introduction of a mechanism for venting popular political dissent" (Schlumberger 2000, 117). On this very point I differ from Oliver Schlumberger when he adds, "The conceptual differences about civil society notwithstanding, there is hardly any evidence for societal actors independent of the state and its elites who could be said to shape the political process to any significant degree" (118).

In Egypt the outbreak of the second intifada in September 2000 (*intifadat al-aqsa*) led to the grouping together of activists of various political orientations (mostly leftists and Muslim Brothers). The Egyptian People's Committee for Solidarity with the Palestinian Intifada (EPCSPI) wrote opinion columns, organized workshops, conferences, and meetings, petitioned for the severing of diplomatic relations with Israel, and questioned the United Nations about Palestinian political prisoners' fate. On September 10, 2001, the EPCSPI demonstrated in Tahrir Square in solidarity with the Palestinian cause. This gathering attracted the authorities' attention, and many of the committee's members were arrested, sometimes (especially MB) for long periods.

Between March 29 and April 2, 2002, in Cairo (in the districts of Giza, Heliopolis, Ma'adi, Bulaq, Duqqi, and 6th of October City), and also outside the capital in Alexandria and many cities of the Delta and Upper Egypt, streets were the scene of intense political activity. Demonstrators denounced Israeli violence in the occupied territories, the Saudi peace plan, and Egyptian diplomatic relations with the Israeli occupier as well as US support for Israel. Students from the American University in Cairo, 6th of October University, and Cairo University were at the center of the movement.[3]

The Anglo-American invasion of Iraq on March 20, 2003, led to the occupation of Tahrir Square "from the very start of the bombing" as indicated in the watchword sent by text messages. The breadth and length of a movement such as this antiwar movement had been unseen since the 1972 student movement calling for "democracy" and "popular war" against Israel. For two days Cairo lived at the pace of protests and their repression, especially when al-Azhar worshippers sought to join the demonstration after the Friday prayer. Mobilizations facilitated relations between "comrades and brothers" (el-Hamalawy 2007) within the March 20th Popular Movement for Change.[4] Above all, they allowed a relocalization of targets and the stakes of the protest, which was evident later in Kifaya's 2004 "Declaration to the Nation."[5] On March 5, as the government was celebrating National Unity, 150 people demonstrated near the House of Parliament demanding an end to the state of emergency in force since 1981. In addition to US "imperialism," demonstrators denounced its "valets," an expression in vogue in the 1970s. It is not certain whether such slogans came from the most prominent leaders or rank-and-file activists. The mobilizations for "change" in Egypt seem to be linked to the forms (Anglo-American invasion of Iraq, continued support for Israel) and the terms of the renewed American hegemony in the Middle East (the Greater Middle East Initiative).

In these three moments of contention, protests shifted from foreign to domestic politics. This reminds us that it may be more fruitful to explain the launching of collective action, not from the point of view of opportunities but rather of threats perceived by the contentious actors. The occupation of Iraq, which created new conditions subordinating the Egyptian regime to its American ally and guardian, appears to have played a leading part in this situation. These demonstrations were foreshadowed by the earlier mobilizations prompted by the Israeli-Palestinian conflict. The links between leftists and MB continued with the antiwar conferences in December 2002 and December 2003 (and also subsequently up to 2008).

One of the most meaningful lessons of these movements lies in the disconnect between the development of large mobilizations and the democratization of the regime: the awakening of "civil society" was not accompanied by a transition to democracy, in contrast to what transitologists believe. This clear disconnect reveals the failure of the project of importing civil society to Egypt in its Tocquevillean, Lockean, Marxian, or Habermasian form as promoted most prominently by Saad Eddin Ibrahim, professor emeritus of sociology at the American University in Cairo and founder of the Ibn Khaldun Center for Development Studies in that city, as well as the Arab Organization for Human Rights. Though not alone in this regard, Ibrahim was more successful in promoting civil society as a slogan, referring broadly to Egyptian associational life. In Morocco and in Egypt, civil society has become a cause for some, a field to increase the value of diplomas for others, or a practical notion and landmark for international donors, journalists, diplomats, and academics. In none of the countries should these "real civil societies" be understood as a first step toward democracy (Camau 2002).[6] At the same time, although foreign funding might seem like a resource to an Arab activist, it functions as a real constraint. Foreign funds are more easily available in Morocco than in Egypt, where most contentious actors avoid any link with foreign actors for fear of being considered traitors to the nation. Accepting EU money to monitor the 2000 elections, and his report to Minority Rights Group International about the situation of Egyptian Copts, landed Saad Eddin Ibrahim in jail from 2000 to 2003.

## REPRESSION AND ITS CONSEQUENCES

Arab political scenes are profoundly marked by repression. Raising the costs of political commitment and mobilization, repression has deeply reconfigured the ways of participation.[7] Though analysis of "social control of protest" has broadened our understanding of "how non-movement actors can shape the level and form of protest" (Earl 2004, 58), the authoritarian regimes of Egypt and Morocco still rely on "violent, state-based repression rather than repression by private actors" (Earl 2009, 129). In these two countries, protest policing corresponds to the "escalated force model" elaborated by McPhail and colleagues (1998).[8] In most of the situations, these two authoritarian states resort to "state agents tightly connected to national political elites (e.g. national militaries)" (Earl 2009, 130). Egyptian security forces delegate the dirty work to plainclothes policemen, who on the ground are not easily distinguishable from hired thugs (*baltagiyya*) used to beat up protesters. Channeling is used in the control of NGOs' funding and in the various hurdles faced by political parties and NGOs when they try to register officially. Still, most of this "carrots and sticks" mix remains unobservable because of the tendency of authorities to rely on an arbitrary, informal social control of protest. In local areas intimidation, harassment, and the threat of violence as a tool to deter protest are accomplished by "state agents loosely connected to national political elites (e.g., local police)" (Earl 2009, 130). With the help of their security apparatus, Moroccan and Egyptian incumbents set the range of oppositional types, means, and stances. They decide who is allowed to play the game and how. One of their means is to assess the great political divide between "moderates" and "radicals" (Lust-Okar 2005).

The trajectory of many Islamists in Morocco demonstrates the analytical weaknesses of this binary opposition. For example, the former Islamist militant Abdellilah Benkirane has passed through al-Shabiba al-Islamiyya (The Islamic Youth), a group that was involved during the 1970s in the death of Socialist leader Omar Benjelloun. He then cofounded the group al-Islah wa'l-Tajdid (Reform and Unity), an organization that provided social services and preaching and was active in Islamic publishing with its journal *al-Raya*. During the 1990s he participated in the creation of the Justice and Development Party (PJD), which came in second in the 2007 legislative elections. Over the long run one can observe a shift in Benkirane's political career from a revolutionary, illegal stance to a reformist, legal political involvement. But if we "focus [ ... ] on [his] behaviors and tactics [ ... ] not [his] ideological orientation" (Hafez 2003, 5), we would miss a lot by classifying Benkirane's itinerary in terms of radical or moderate stances.[9]

This transformation is first the result of the severe discipline imposed by the Moroccan Ministry of Interior, which defines the "off sides" of politics and made revolutionary action a dead end. Second, Benkirane and his friends anticipated the benefits of legal activism and seized spaces opened to legitimate competition by the power elite. Subsequent doctrinal changes were produced by *'ulama'* (Muslim scholars) close to the group, to legitimize this shift.

The definition of "radical" or "moderate" positions is also linked to the state of struggles in the political field and on the Islamist scene. The so-called radicalism of Jama'at al-'Adl wa'l-Ihsan (Justice and Spirituality), the most powerful Islamist organization in Morocco, does not relate to its use of violence (the movement is pacifist). Its radicalism resides in the refusal of Justice and Spirituality leaders to enter a political game dominated by the king. It also comes from their refusal to recognize him as the Commander of the Faithful, while the PJD does. This radicalism is easily understood in relation to the struggles in the religious and political fields. Two strategies are competing. While the PJD has chosen to play within the electoral/legal politics frame set by the monarchy, al-'Adl wa'l-Ihsan pursues a popular though self-limiting strategy of mobilization. If one takes into account actors' claims and self-definitions (PJD defines its stance as "a critical though constructive opposition" while Justice and Spirituality claims to be "the sole and true opposition in Morocco"), the distinction between radicals and moderates appears to be less an analytical tool than a by-product of contests around boundaries, classifying operations, and labeling inside movements and during political confrontations with regimes (Collovald and Gaïti 2006).

The Egyptian case provides us with another good example of the analytical weakness of the radical/moderate binary. Abu al-'Ala' Madi was active in the Islamic associations at the Minya University Faculty of Engineering, then at the Engineers Syndicate and in the MB. The 1995 crackdown on MB middle cadres and the MB rejection of any attempt to create a party apart from the brotherhood itself (which does not consider itself to be a party), functioned as biographical breaks for al-Madi and his colleague 'Isam Sultan. Leaving the brotherhood in 1996 to launch a new party, Hizb al-Wasat (Center Party), they chose to "moderate their agendas not only to seize new political opportunities but also to evade new political constraints" (Wickham 2004, 213). Since 1996 the Wasat Party has been refused official registration by the Parliament Political Parties Committee four times. Since 2004 al-Madi has been one of the most prominent Islamist members of Kifaya.

We should also pay attention to the long-term effects of repression. While the radicalizing effect of repression has been well documented inside the region (Khawaga 1993; Rasler 1996) and outside (Lichbach 1987), David Cunningham's caveat remains useful: "Until recently, the most notable finding [about the relation between repression and mobilization] has been the fact that seemingly all possible relationships have been supported by empirical work in this area" (2003, 47). When it comes to the effects of violence, the repression/radicalization correlation is only positive in particular circumstances. Contrary to the hasty generalization of the relative deprivation school (Gurr 1970), the mobilizing effect of repression is only one possibility among many. It is surprising to read the "disproportionate repression leads to mobilization" argument advanced by resource mobilization theory or political process scholars. Their argument may be summarized as: "If state repression is reactive and indiscriminate it will likely induce rebellion. If, on the other hand, state repression is preemptive and selective, it will likely deter mass rebellion" (Hafez 2004, 76).

Hafez and Wiktorowicz also indicate that "violence is only one of myriad possibilities in repertoires of contention"; however, they add that it "becomes most likely when regimes attempt to crush Islamic activism through broad repressive measures that leave few alternatives" (Hafez and Wiktorowicz 2004, 62). During the 1990s the Arab world exemplified the complexity of the repression/mobilization binarism. High levels of repression have produced different outcomes, which can broadly be summarized in two directions.

The pernicious, unintended effects of the outburst of state violence against opposition forces in many parts of the Arab and Muslim world have most commonly attracted the attention of scholars and journalists. Considering domestic politics to be a deadlock and finding impossible the overthrow of their authoritarian incumbents, many Islamists like 'Abd Allah 'Azzam or Ayman al-Zawahiri chose to transnationalize their struggles (Roy 1994). The explanation of this shift in itineraries relies less on a "radical turn" nurtured by a theological or ideological hardening and more on a rational evaluation of strategic options.[10]

At the same time, high levels of repression made clear that any violent attempt to overcome power would lead to a harsh response and a bloody failure. The violence of the incumbent regimes has been the way to make implausible a forceful overthrow, whether by Socialists or Islamists, of the Moroccan monarchy or the Egyptian regimes of Sadat and Mubarak. In that sense the coercive apparatuses of both countries have been efficient, leading to trajectories of moderation of the regimes' opponents. The success of the repertoire of civil society reflects profound transformations in the activist Arab milieus. Activists' political and physical defeat by regimes and security apparatuses has led to a new understanding of their commitments: the game in town is no longer revolution but reform, be it democratic or Islamic. This new relationship between politics and activism was encouraged by the international fashion for democratization through gradual regime reform.

In Egypt the former leftists, who aimed at launching a "popular war" against Israel and overthrowing the regime during the 1970s, are now trying to reform its most authoritarian aspects. Using the "front" ( *jabha* ) as an organizational tool, their commitments are expressed now in Western-style NGOs. Their militant socialism has faded, giving way to the causes of defending human rights or protection of workers. Another piece of evidence of these changing political commitments is provided by the clear stance taken by Kifaya in every episode in the run-up to the 2005 elections (for example, the referendum on the constitutional amendment). The group requested full judicial supervision of the election process, boycotted the presidential elections, and joined the alliance of the legal opposition parties during the parliamentary elections. While Kifaya did not directly participate in the electoral competition as a political party, it had a crucial impact on the preparations for the elections and their outcome. The regime did not respond directly to the movement's demands, but Kifaya— among other movements (NGOs, judges)—set the standards for judicial super- vision, transparency, and voter mobilization on election day. Yet, these electoral practices are far from a rallying to market democracy (why would we expect a different outcome in today's Egypt?). But this is a long way from the ideologi- cal rejection of elections characteristic of the far left in the 1970s and 1980s. In the strategy of Kamal Abu Eita and Kamal Khalil, two leaders of Kifaya who ran during the fall 2005 legislative elections in their neighborhoods, the election campaign was another tool to discredit the corruption (*fasad*) and the authori- tarianism of Mubarak and the prolongation of his reign (*tamdid*), as well as the planned hereditary succession (*tawrith*), and to denounce the growing power of the military (*hukm al-'askar*) in the regime.

In Morocco actors formerly involved in far left organizations chose to in- ternationalize their struggles, but by doing so they also paid a heavy price in transforming their practices and programs from mobilization and street activ- ism to participation in public policies and cooperation with the authorities. In the late 1980s and 1990s these actors invested in converting their organizational and activist knowledge, as well as their rhetorical (most of them are bilingual) and political abilities, into the mastery of international know-how (such as set- ting up Western-style NGOs, formulating action plans framing projects, and producing reports or databases contradicting established state knowledge) in defense of human rights. These activists function as "smugglers" between the international and the Moroccan field. Entrepreneurs of the subaltern victims' mobilizations, they were at the center of establishing the Equity and Recon- ciliation Commission (IER), the Moroccan truth and reconciliation commis- sion, also called National Commission for Truth, Equity and Reconciliation, of which Driss Benzékri was among the most prominent members.[11]

In the long run, the use of violence by the regimes also had a more discreet and persistent effect, a political learning that power in numbers comes from "holding the ranks" rather than "controlling the street." Broadly, the generalized use of sit-ins—attested by media and fieldwork—testifies to the self-limitation of Egyptian and Moroccan protesters. Though protesting, they carefully avoid direct confrontation with incumbents and its possible result: a deep destabilization of the political setting that would pave the way for "radicals."

For example, during the mobilizations to demand truth and justice after the Years of Lead,[12] Moroccan activists initiated a series of sit-ins that gathered human rights activists and victims carrying candles and roses, brandishing portraits of missing people or wearing them around their necks. With these sit-ins the protesters inscribed themselves in the political space on three levels: first as contentious, since the gatherings are occasions to demand justice; then as commemorative, since they are a means to establish the truth and prevent the memory of state crimes from fading away; and last as emotional, as activists return to the place of their sufferings with candles, portraits, and roses, with the victims' children, and the reading of poems or recounting of memories.[13] These contentious gatherings are symbolical markings of space; they are ways of mapping the Moroccan dishonor of past state violence. The Moroccan Forum for Truth and Justice (FVJ) mobilizations and those of its allies and rivals, the Moroccan Association for Human Rights (AMDH) and the Moroccan Organization for Human Rights (OMDH), opened numerous and virulent debates through which the idea of a truth and reconciliation commission was imposed. In other words, their actions imposed the necessity of a settlement that would be not only a technical and financial one but one which also derives legitimacy from the way it conforms to international standards.

In 2004 the emergence of Kifaya appeared to be unique in the Middle East. Its mobilization against hereditary succession and against President Mubarak's authoritarian rule attracted attention from international observers and policy makers. By attacking the presidency directly and organizing street demonstrations in Cairo's city center, the series of public gatherings organized by Kifaya from December 2004 to September 2005 crossed the previously established red line and reached far beyond "accepted" limits of mobilization by legal opposition parties. But like their Moroccan counterparts, these activists from across the whole political spectrum strategically self-limited their mobilization, choosing carefully its extent—the most crowded sit-ins never exceeded a thousand people—and location—in downtown Cairo rather than, for example, the densely populated Imbaba working-class district. The choice of the locales for mobilization is also strongly linked to the social background of these activists and their shared representations of the social and political world. Consequently, this middle-class opposition has very few connections to more popular areas.

In summary, scholars interested in Arab mobilizations could benefit from considering the varying effects of repression: "The question should no longer be whether repression has a deterring or radicalizing effect, but which effect is to be expected under what conditions" (Opp and Roehl 1990, 523). The relationship between coercion and political protest is a function of the uses of violence by actors in power (Hoover and Kowalewski 1992). As we have seen, Arab cases provide useful examples of this point, well beyond the mere binary of radicalization/demobilization.

## PERCEPTIONS AND THREATS

Charles Tilly's remarks on how mobilizations take off under threats remind us of the importance of perceptions and anticipation. He points out that people mobilize more easily and quickly if they perceive a threat as opposed to opportunities (1978, 134–36). This is true in Egypt. In March 2006 judges Mahmud Makki and Hisham al-Bastawisi, both vice presidents of the Court of Cassation (appeals), were referred to a disciplinary court because they denounced fraudulent practices during the 2005 legislative elections and implicated some of their colleagues in the violations on the al-Jazeera and al-ʿArabiyya satellite channels. During court action against the two judges, MB and Kifaya activists mobilized, standing up for the judges in the street. The mobilization was quite strong since the independence of the judiciary is perceived as a particularly valuable collective good on the Egyptian political scene.[14] In this context activists mobilized because the disciplining of Makki and al-Bastawisi threatened a collective good. This mobilization took place in the context of a previous instance of judicial dissidence: during a meeting on May 13, 2005, judges threatened to boycott their task of supervising the balloting in the upcoming presidential elections. Such a boycott would have undermined the credibility of the elections even before they occurred. On April 26, 2006, the day before the first session of the disciplinary court to hear the charges against Makki and al-Bastawisi, Kifaya demonstrated its support for the judges and denounced the arbitrariness of the disciplinary action. A dozen people were arrested in Cairo. In Alexandria about three thousand MB followers, surrounded by as many security forces, gathered in solidarity with the judges. Six of the organizers were arrested. According to a police source, on April 27, 2006, five thousand policemen prevented access to the Judges' Club in downtown Cairo, where people mobilized to support Makki and al-Bastawisi. About a quarter of the hundred Kifaya activists who denounced the disciplining of the judges were arrested.

One week later, at the second hearing of the disciplinary court, the same scenario recurred. Downtown Cairo was cordoned off by security forces; demonstrators were arrested. On May 8, during additional protests, forty-eight people were arrested. On May 11 security forces adopted a tougher stand towards demonstrators; using violence, the police arrested 250 people, among them sixty Kifaya activists. Supporters of the judges were chased around the streets and beaten. Six journalists were forcibly arrested, particularly the al-Jazeera team. On Thursday, May 18, 210 Muslim Brothers, among them 'Isam al-'Aryan, spokesman of the organization, and Muhammad Mursi, former leader of the parliamentary group, were arrested. Kifaya activists were also assaulted by security forces. Both the persistence of the demonstrations for several weeks and the fact that al-Bastawisi was perceived to be close to the MB, which enhanced the popular appeal of this issue beyond the general concern for independence of the judiciary, were the cause of the government's progressively harsher treatment of the demonstrators. It was not only the threat perceived by demonstrators that affected the extent of mobilization; the threat perceived by the regime (and the absence of any restraint from the United States) determined the extent of the regime's repression. The victory of eighty-eight MB in the 2005 elections despite various acts of fraud—preventing voters from entering polling places and such—set off a campaign of repression that continues today and is reminiscent of the repression of the MB in the 1990s.

This contentious episode put young activists to the test and revealed the limits of their involvement. In the case of these young activists, the police beatings and the experiences of imprisonment and torture were not only a cost of contention; they also launched their careers as activists, giving them credibility that they used in the conquest of positions inside militant groups. In July 2006 these young activists became particularly visible in the organization of gatherings opposing the Israeli war against Lebanon.

During operations to maintain order, the variable intensity of violence is of particular significance: modes of maintaining order and their relative transformation are linked more to the stakes of the contentious episode than to the identities of the mobilizing groups. In April and May mobilizations backing the judges were accompanied by violence against some judges and their supporters. For the regime this was an occasion to repress the judges' dissidence and to undermine its most virulent opponents, both Kifaya and the more numerous MB. In contrast, in July 2006, mobilizations against the Israeli war triggered only a cordoning off of gatherings as a containment of contention. The repetition of protests, sit-ins, and gatherings organized almost every day in downtown Cairo, as well as the presence of the leaders of the movement, allowed demonstrators and the security forces, including conscripts of the Central Security Forces (*amn al-markazi*), to know and recognize one another. In this way, contention acquired a local dimension despite the international nature of its subject—the war against Lebanon—and its national scale in the capital city of Cairo. At the same time, a divide between demonstrators and plainclothes policemen was observable. A division of labor during the maintenance of order was clearly visible: *Amn al-markazi* conscripts smoothly cordoned off demonstrators in Tahrir Square or in front of the Foreign Ministry, while plainclothes policemen and *baltagiyya* (thugs) subjected demonstrators to physical abuse, roughing them up or beating them and finally putting them under arrest.[15]

State violence has more subtle effects than the binary deterrence/escalation. In Egypt and Morocco long-term repression led numerous 1970s and 1980s revolutionaries to embrace the civil society repertoire. Facing a deadlock, others have chosen to escape into the transnational space while they changed their targets from "impious regimes" to "Jews and Crusaders." Our inquiry demonstrates that situations were more than perceived opportunities: threats help explain how mobilizations emerge and progress.

In Morocco and Egypt governing elites are adjusting their domination to opportunities provided by globalization.[16] Using elements of democratic language and procedures, they are modifying their forms of domination. But regime architecture is very different in our two cases. In Morocco the number and strength of mobilizations go beyond what one would expect from politics under an absolute monarchy. The tradition of demonstrating in the streets was renewed during the 1990s with large and peaceful demonstrations of solidarity with the Palestinians and the Iraqis. At the same time, the sanctity of the monarchy may never be criticized, and the so-called transition prompted by the monarchical succession, far from opening opportunities for protesters, gave way to a reinvented discipline on the activist scene. In Egypt contention can literally be an obstacle course as protesters race through the streets of Cairo attempting to find an open space to gather. Protest still means opposing incumbent leaders. Authoritarianism has been consolidated around a quasi–single party system, which facilitates a harsh response from Egyptian security forces, including the sealing off of entire areas. The regime's fear of escalation remains an important factor.

Three lessons can be drawn from this comparison. First, activists do not always mobilize according to available opportunities. The cases of the Years of Lead victims in Morocco or mobilizations in support of Egyptian judges clearly demonstrate the importance of threats in protesters' calculations regarding the start of mobilizations. Second, radicalization should not be the only lens through which we observe the region. Long-term repression and modes of action encouraged by foreign funding (NGOs aiming at contributing to public policies) give birth to itineraries of deradicalization. Finally, the institutionalization of contentious spaces is linked to how actors limit their protest and the way they may use foreign resources.

# 2 EGYPTIAN LEFTIST INTELLECTUALS' ACTIVISM FROM THE MARGINS

Overcoming the Mobilization/Demobilization Dichotomy

## Marie Duboc

THE BEGINNING OF THE TWENTY-FIRST CENTURY was a period of exceptional contention and mobilization in Egyptian political life. Starting in 2001, demonstrations organized by Cairo-based intellectual elites in support of the second Palestinian intifada and against the US-led invasion of Iraq led to the formation of Kifaya, a group denouncing president Hosni Mubarak's repressive regime and his attempts to designate his son, Gamal, as successor. Workers also voiced their grievances against rising inflation and deteriorating standards of living and work. Many professionals and intellectuals, from university students to judges, also used work stoppages and sit-ins to publicly voice their concerns.

The upsurge of collective action since the early 2000s revealed a change in the political culture of protest in Egypt with overt collective action, rather than concealed actions, becoming common in the repertoire of protest. However, a wide range of dormant, quiescent daily practices that often went unnoticed continued to constitute significant components of contentious action in Egypt. I build on the seminal work of scholars who have argued that the definition of politics should not be restricted to institutions nor to the state (Singerman 1995; Scott and Kerkvliet 1986; Bayat 1997). These studies focus on the strategies of urban and rural poor, not intellectual elites, but they are relevant here because they draw attention to marginal practices. Raymond Baker (1990) argues that marginal political groups may play an important role in Egyptian history, and I embrace this approach in presenting the practices of marginalized activists—those who are not integrated into party or oppositional politics.

Political organizations in the Middle East and North Africa have faced several constraints and weaknesses that undermined their credibility and limited their ability to retain supporters, mainly due to repression and co-optation by authoritarian regimes. In the protests that toppled presidents Ben Ali in Tunisia and Mubarak in Egypt, political parties were not the center of gravity of mobilization. Rather, for several decades, oppositional intellectuals had emphasized the need for contentious action autonomous from parties and their agendas. By focusing on the experience, history, and political stances of intellectuals (writers) who took part in the activities of leftist parties and underground left-wing and communist organizations during the 1960s and 1970s, this chapter aims to shed light on this process. This entails studying their relationship to political activism in contemporary Egypt. Although these intellectuals maintained links with parties and groups such as Kifaya,[1] the Tagammu',[2] and the Nasserist and communist parties, they no longer considered these organizations to be the most appropriate channels for political participation. This did not lead them to find alternatives for achieving political transformation, but these intellectuals still considered themselves activists.

The object of study here seems marginal in Egyptian political life, not only because it does not rally a large number of individuals, but also because it focuses on "demobilization"—a phenomenon that collective action studies have mainly overlooked, apart from Olivier Filleule's (2005) seminal book on the issue.[3] Its marginal status is precisely the reason I have chosen to focus on this category with the aim of providing a heuristic device for understanding collective and individual relationships to political activism in Egypt.

To explain retreat from activism the existing literature has mainly relied on resource mobilization theory and on the mobilization/demobilization dichotomy. For example, using Social Movement Theory (SMT) and Rational Choice Theory, Florence Passy and Marco Giugni (2001) have studied "differential participation." Marjane Osa (2003) has studied dormant networks using the SMT concepts of Political Opportunity Structure (POS), resource mobilization, and framing. Charles Tilly and Sidney Tarrow argue that defection, disillusionment, repression, and institutionalization all combine to different degrees to lead to demobilization. However, their discussion remains centered on the impact of repression on demobilization, through institutionalization and escalation (Tilly and Tarrow 2007). Similarly, Verta Taylor (1979) has relied on a political opportunity framework to describe an abeyance process by which movements continue to exist and sustain mobilization despite external constraints. These studies have made a significant contribution to the study of social movements, particularly by stressing the role of networks and dormant or abeyance phases. But they rely on theoretical frameworks that do not account for internal dynamics, such as processes of social fatigue. This might be because the POS model focuses more on the origins of contention rather than on its later phases (McAdam, Tarrow, and Tilley 2001, 41). For example, according to Taylor, who analyzes abeyance structures that absorb "intensely committed" individuals, external constraints affect mobilization structures, but actors' relationship to activism remains linear and constant.

By contrast, by using the term "social fatigue," I try to express the weariness of individuals who feel alienated from their social and political environment and do not engage in debates on how to bring about an alternative to the status quo. This does not necessarily mean that social fatigue should be understood as a form of apathy; instead, I prefer to connect social fatigue to the tension between actors' longing for change and the apparent permanence of the status quo. Demobilization is not understood here as a structural problem related to organizations' deficiencies, and the focus here is not on an evaluation of movements or their failure to perform or achieve. Instead I argue that the experience of individuals and their relationships to political participation need to be studied to account for the existence of less intense or committed patterns of activism.

Thus I question the dichotomy of mobilization and demobilization. Rather than using the term "demobilization," which denotes a withdrawal from political action, I prefer to speak about a "decentered" notion of activism, meaning that the center of gravity of activist practices has been challenged and restructured. The political experience of the activists studied here—a group of leftist intellectuals—has been reshaped over several decades, from overt dissidence during the student protests in 1972–73[4] to more subtle activities in the literary field. The implication of these evolving, changing patterns of mobilization in the literary and political fields is that the boundaries between mobilization and demobilization are fluid and blurry.

This chapter draws on fieldwork conducted in Cairo in 2007 among a group of intellectuals (writers) who took part in the activities of leftist parties and underground organizations during the 1960s and 1970s. The ethnographic research involved conducting semidirected interviews and attending literary meetings organized in Cairo—at L'Atelier du Caire, the Zaytun workshop, and the short-story club and meetings held at the offices of Merit Publishing House. The interviewees were born between 1935 and 1955. They come from a lower- or middle-class background and have all graduated from a university, in humanities or engineering. Except for one writer, who enjoys less recognition in the literary field, all have worked for Egyptian cultural institutions, including the Second Program (a state radio and television channel created by Nasser), literary magazines such as *Akhbar al-Adab* (Literature news) and *Adab wa-Naqd* (Literature and criticism)—a monthly literary magazine published by the Tagammuʿ Party), and the cultural pages of Egyptian or Arab newspapers. Although they are considered members of two distinct literary and age-cohort generations, I contend that this classification is a construction that should be challenged. Thus I have chosen to study these individuals as one generational group because they share similar experiences as political activists and members of the Egyptian intelligentsia. Today they share a similar relationship to activism, one that is influenced by social fatigue and political frustration. Moreover, the declining importance of the concept of the nation in legitimizing the role of the secular intelligentsia is another factor to consider when accounting for the changing patterns of activism and feelings of frustration. Although the secular intelligentsia still identifies itself as the guardian of the nation, it has ceased to be the only producer of nationalist discourse.

## INFORMAL ACTIVISM?

As the other contributions to this volume show, informality plays an important role in the formation of social movements in the Middle East. This is also the case in other parts of the world. A large body of literature has been devoted to the relationship between informality and political participation. These studies have shown that movements take root in everyday networks of sociability and involve "non-collective" "direct action" representing "everyday forms of resistance" (Bayat 2003; Scott and Kerkvliet 1986). The notion of informality has mainly been discussed in relation to economic hardship—access to housing, water, electricity, or employment—but can be expanded to encompass symbolic struggles as well.

One way to take a broader view of informality is to use the concept of social fatigue. For former activists who remain faithful to the political vision that drew them into political action, the demise of the organizations that they belonged to, along with a lack of political change, means that they have to devise alternative means to sustain some form of political engagement. When activists are weary of forms of activism that have not produced concrete results, how do they express what is left of their desire for change?

One way to begin studying this issue is to redefine the function of informal networks. Research has mainly focused on networks in light of their mobilization function, as the root from which contentious action stems (Diani and McAdam 2003; Snow, Zurcher, and Ekland-Olson 1980). While this is an important function of networks, I contend that informality can also represent an "exit opportunity," enabling actors to keep their level of engagement minimal and thereby facilitating phasing down their activism. Thus networks do not just facilitate mobilization; they also make it possible for contention to become diffuse, uneven, and hidden. As Bayat (2003) argues, it is easy to fall into the trap of reading everyday acts and relations as necessarily conscious signs of defiance.

Moreover, these informal practices can be drawn from individuals' identifications and belongings; for the subjects of the present study, they are often institutionalized in the intellectual field. Literary production and ongoing links with the intellectual field through acquaintances and activities (such as participation in literary meetings or writing in a newspaper) constitute the continuation, in a restricted public arena, of daily resentment against the political situation. In order to make sense of these practices, it is important to understand them as part of a historical process shaping writers' self-understanding and their identification with political debates. It will therefore be necessary to outline first the relationship between the intellectual and activist fields.

## INTERDEPENDENCE OF THE INTELLECTUAL AND ACTIVIST FIELDS

I propose first to describe the Egyptian left in relation to the intellectual field, in order to map out the spaces and practices within which activism is located. Far from being autonomous, these two fields influence each other. This section links the interviewees' personal experiences to the historical development of the left in the Egyptian field of activism. I also discuss key features of the intellectual field that influence the interviewees' practices.

Egyptian writers have had a prominent role in the left, and a prominent feature of intellectual life in Egypt has been the close link between intellectual and political debates. Throughout the 1960s and 1970s Egyptian intellectuals contributed to the creation and development of Marxist groups, an experience that left its mark on their political self-representation and recognition within the literary field. Richard Jacquemond (2008) has shown that writers are expected to take part in political debates and are commonly seen as the "conscience of the nation."

Members of political groups can gain symbolic capital that grants them recognition in the political arena (Matonti and Poupeau 2004–5). In the 1960s and 1970s political activism was also an opportunity for interviewees to become integrated into a network of leftist writers and to establish their credibility in the literary field. As they became well known as writers, they could convert symbolic capital in the literary field into symbolic capital in the activist field. In other words, literary and activist capitals mutually reinforced each other. For example, as intellectuals, writers have access to the media—traditionally newspapers but now also television—that they use to express their political views.[5]

The close link between the literary and activist fields means that the politicization of writers does not simply involve being members of a political group. Literature is seen as inherently political, even when dealing with personal issues: as one interviewee put it, "even in a poem that's not political, there are politics."[6] This poet understands politics in a broad sense, as comprising every aspect of literary production. This is reflected in the writer's choice of a publishing house, or the decision to write an article for a certain newspaper (Bourdieu 1996). At the same time, writers refuse to subordinate literary production to a political cause. This is another key rule of the literary field: intellectuals claim that the activist and literary fields are autonomous. Yet the link between the two dates back to the early twentieth century and still exists: leftist groups continue to produce literary magazines and to organize literary clubs in order to attract intellectuals to their cause. For instance, one of the spin-off groups of the Kifaya movement includes writers and artists. In its founding charter, the members of Writers and Artists for Change explain that the creation of the group is motivated by the intellectual's public mission and social responsibility (Baha' al-Din Sha'ban 2006, 280). They therefore endorse a tradition dating back to the *nahda*, the Egyptian cultural renaissance of the late nineteenth and early twentieth centuries, which is regarded as a period of intellectual modernization in the region.

Writers' personal experiences show that two factors, imposed by the literary and activist fields, had a decisive influence on their involvement in activism during the 1960s and 1970s: the autonomy/politicization mission assigned to writers and the collapse of the communist movement.[7] These two decades were the first phase of activism for the interviewees.

The interviewees had been exposed to politics when they were teenagers. Those who were young adults in 1952 had a more ambivalent relationship to Nasser than those who grew up under Nasser's regime. "We weren't with him or against him," says Baha' Tahir,[8] who had been torn between supporting Nasser's foreign policies and condemning his clampdown on opposition forces. This attitude toward Nasser was widespread among left-wing groups and, depending on the group and individual, involved concessions to accept Nasser's policies (Meijer 2002).

In the 1970s Marxist groups had an appeal to university students and to those disillusioned with Nasserism following Egypt's defeat in the 1967 war, a traumatic experience for Egyptians. For some the war prompted a change in their political affiliation. As Hilmi Salim explains, "From then on, I ended my relationship with the Young Socialist Organization [the youth group of the Arab Socialist Union] and a shift of thought started to take place, a shift towards real socialism."[9] Moving away from Nasserism meant supporting Marxist organizations considered more radical. Yet personal memories and a posteriori discourse tend to overestimate the impact of the events of 1967 at the time. Sadat's policies promoting economic liberalization (*infitah*) and a greater emphasis on Islam seem to have been more decisive in the 1970s group's inclination toward communist organizations: "Political participation was forced on me, because of the context in which I lived. . . . I joined this organization because of something emotional [*'atifi*], not intellectual [*'aqli*], I felt it wasn't just my place but also my responsibility to do so."[10]

This quote highlights an important aspect of political activism during the 1960s and 1970s: political action involved being associated with a group, even if organizations were illegal and secret. Social and nationalist issues were experienced through a group, and organizational structures were seen as the best framework for resistance. An analysis of social movements that focuses on the structure of institutions can therefore be relevant to an understanding of collective action in Egypt during this period: mobilization took place within the framework of preexisting structures (McAdam, McCarthy, and Zald 1988). Yet this approach does not provide a full account of the dynamics that affect activist practices.

Activism in the 1960s and 1970s had different levels of intensity, ranging from occasional participation in a demonstration to a deep involvement encompassing every aspect of daily life. Some interviewees had refused to get married and take on responsibilities that could have jeopardized their political action. As writers, their literary production was affected by their membership in an illegal organization, since legal cultural institutions were controlled by the state.

A similar pattern took shape in the literary field. Although writing is an individual process, closely associated with its author, literary groups contributed in the 1960s and 1970s to the production of new creative models. There was a parallel between initiatives that challenged literary norms by "waging a guerrilla warfare against the cultural establishment" (Kendall 2006, 88) and modes of resistance that could be called "direct" because they both aimed at confronting the regime. I have chosen here not to differentiate between literary groups and political ones but instead to study overlapping practices that make it possible to identify political action and politicization. Under Nasser and Sadat the state had a monopoly on the production and distribution of literature. The creation of alternative cultural spaces was therefore identified as a form of opposition. "We wanted our political and artistic actions to be innovative; both were very similar because there was a change in both areas. Rebellion against the regime was accompanied by another rebellion occurring in literature. . . . We confronted the regime here and with literature."[11]

Literary groups were formed around writers who shared the same artistic views, which they expressed in magazines. *Gallery 68*, first published in 1968, was the first cultural and literary initiative to create an alternative space for production, independent from official magazines. It published poems, reviews, and literary texts. It was followed by many more publications in the 1970s, thanks to the use of new printing techniques. By means of these literary groups, interviewees promoted their literary work and expressed their rejection of established rules, which offered them a choice between working through official channels and not existing as an intellectual (Mehrez 1991, 119). These practices indicate that publishing a magazine in the 1960s or 1970s could be seen as a substitute for—or more accurately a complementary action to—joining a political organization. This was the case for Sayyid Higab, cofounder of *Gallery 68*, who after 1967 saw cultural activities as the best framework for contentious action. At the same time, he also continued to express identification with the left by participating in demonstrations.

Interviewees responded to constraints imposed on them by the state but also by the intellectual field. POS analysis fails to provide a full account of political activism in this context, since it only takes into account constraints imposed by the state. Analysis of the extent of democratic openings or repression should not be neglected. But other factors, such as internal divisions within communist organizations, the failure to articulate a political goal, and individuals' social and intellectual networks and affiliations, also shaped practices. Here I have focused on rules related to the intellectual field, particularly the avant-garde. For example, while writers were required to take a stance without subordinating their writing to a political cause, there was a wide range of ways to put this rule into practice. This resulted in different levels of integration in political groups, despite a strong inclination toward the left. Literary groups were also seen as a forum that could help intellectuals fulfill their public mission.

Memories of this period today are dominated by the collective dimension of activism then. When narrating their experience, the interviewees use "we," thus highlighting their involvement in both the literary and activist fields. This way of remembering and expressing the past raises the issue of their connection to a "generation." In the Egyptian literary field, the writers studied here are commonly seen as belonging to two generational groups: "the 1960s" and "the 1970s." This split is based on biological age and on literary grounds, on the view that every decade experiences a renewal of cultural norms and production. The division creates a sense of unity between members of each generation and justifies the reproduction of the intelligentsia, but it produces constructed boundaries between the groups. When examining intellectuals' political experiences, these boundaries are even more artificial. Alain Roussillon (1990, 250–52) argues that rather than analyzing intellectual life as an accumulation of different schools of thought, it is more fruitful to view it as a simultaneous phenomenon, highlighting the temporal overlap and interactions among those schools. Therefore I treat the 1960s and the 1970s as one generational group, regardless of differences in age and literary production. The sociological understanding of this political generation relies on common experiences, both in the intellectual and political fields (Kecskemeti 1952). Thus it seems more fruitful to focus on the contemporaneity among individuals but without falling into the trap of defining generational phenomena merely according to historical and political events. The combined factors of biological age, common experiences, and historical events offer a suitable framework to grasp the interactions and overlaps between these factors (Boumaza 2009).

The interviewees' relationship to the past is not just nostalgic. Even now, the memories of activism influence friendships or professional ties: some worked at *Al-Ahram Weekly* when it was friendly to the left and later for *al-Badil* (The alternative), a newspaper founded in 2007 by former members of the student movement of the 1970s; others have created a literary group that brings together former friends involved in leftist organizations. Memories of this distant past are documented and maintained in their writings or through commemorations of important events in the history of the student movement. Some of the interviewees have published memoirs or incorporated events from the 1970s in their novels. In the 1970s these intellectuals were highly visible in the public sphere because of their participation in student demonstrations against Sadat; similarly, they now strive to maintain their visibility by keeping the memory of those events alive. This trend does not mean that the past is idealized; on the contrary, the shortcomings and weaknesses of the communist movement of the 1970s are mentioned. Yet intellectuals (and perhaps other groups as well) who are still connected to the left continue to feel a responsibility toward this collective past. It is particularly important to protect symbolic activist capital. As Sidney Tarrow describes 1960s activists in North America and Europe who were still active in the 1980s and often embedded in networks of former activists, they try to "keep the faith by keeping in touch" (1994, 177).

Leftist intellectuals went through a traumatic time in the 1980s, the second phase of activism that changed the personal experience of the interviewees and the broader Egyptian opposition forces. The 1980s marked the organizational and ideological decline of the left, which was already weakened by internal divisions and the exile of several intellectuals, the emergence of Islamic movements as the principal alternative to the regime, and Mubarak's strategy of co-opting leftist organizations, which was embraced by the Communist Party and the Tagammuʿ.

> The government started to smile on the opposition, and the opposition stopped opposing the regime because the government offered to solve its problems. Leftist organizations and parties threw in the towel. The Egyptian Communist Workers' Party suffered from internal divisions in 1980, and by 1981 the party no longer practically existed. The Communist Party of Egypt was weakened by being submerged in the legal, but increasingly ineffective Tagammuʿ. The 8th of January Communist Party also became inactive. They all splintered on the rocks of reconciliation among the regime, the writers, the intellectuals and the politicians.[12]

The disappearance or weakening of the organizational frameworks that had prevailed in the earlier phase of political activism led to a state of confusion and to a forced withdrawal from political action. The failure of leftist ideas to be carried forward by a credible political structure led to disillusion. This phase also coincided with personal changes, such as marriage or emigration, that prompted activists to retreat from political activism. It was also a period of stronger dedication to literary production for the writers who had not written as much during their youth. The threat of prison was not a prevalent factor influencing intellectuals' relationship to activism in the 1960s and 1970s. While they experienced on a daily basis the threat of being arrested, sometimes just because they read Marxist literature, intellectuals were not discouraged from political action for that reason. The "reconciliation" between the opposition and the regime in the 1980s, which weakened the credibility of these organizations rather than opening a space in which they could operate as an opposition force, seems to have played a greater role in intellectuals' feelings of disillusion.

The collapse of organizations and parties does not mean that the ideas and ideals they represented died in the minds of their members, and the loss of the organizational framework did not lead simply to withdrawal from activism. Therefore, while the POS framework might be useful in analyzing the context, it is not sufficient to explain patterns of demobilization. Intellectuals have managed to sustain their activism in the face of the demise of political groups. Despite the existence of a "poststructuralist consensus in social movement theory," little attention is paid to social actors' subjective perceptions (Kurzman 2004, 119). In the following section, I argue that activism has been transformed and moved to different spaces. This has contributed to a redefinition of activism in which there is a degree of tension and overlap between "free spaces" (Evans and Boyte 1992) ("symbolic spaces" may be a better term) and structured organizations.

## DECENTERED ACTIVISM AND THE RISE OF "AUTONOMOUS" AND "INDEPENDENT" OPPONENTS

*The oppositional scene had been monopolized by religious currents, especially the Muslim Brothers, for too long. But Kifaya has finally carved out a different space for dissidence, and in so doing, it has paved the way for other alternatives, not all of which are necessarily overtly political—for example, Doctors for Change, and Youth for Change. Our own initiative has capitalized on this change. It [Artists and Writers for Change] will be different from other groups in various ways, for one thing we stand for change, not reform. Reform implies partial change to policy. We are rather about dramatic change. We have our political demands, but we are not a political movement. We are not in alliance with Kifaya or any other movement precisely because we are not a political entity. Yet, we do not want to isolate ourselves from the call for change now prevalent in Egypt—we share the views of these other groups. Kifaya is the founding father of the entire current, but we still insist on our independence.*

**'Adil al-Siwi [a painter and coordinator of Artists and Writers for Change] (Khallaf 2005)**

I now turn to these "alternatives" that are outside Kifaya's orbit and examine the claims for autonomy and independence. I question the enthusiasm of some commentators and actors who, like 'Adil al-Siwi, overemphasize and sometimes romanticize the militancy of secular Egyptian intellectuals. As he says, intellectuals' ongoing commitment to political change does not necessarily translate into direct political action, and we may ask whether it necessarily involves any action at all. While they continually claim to be independent of political organizations, activists cannot isolate themselves from these structures; hence the tension described by 'Adil al-Siwi regarding the relationship to Kifaya.

The 2005 presidential elections certainly opened up opportunities for overt contention. The demonstrations organized in 2001–5 challenged political taboos imposed by the regime and contributed to the creation of the Kifaya movement. However, repression alone cannot account for the gradual weakening of the movement since 2006. With some exceptions (the national strike called for April 6, 2008, by opposition groups, and the crackdown against activists who mobilized in support of the independence of the judiciary in the spring of 2006), the repression against the secular left did not increase sharply after 2005.

Therefore instead of focusing on the repression/opportunity binary, I stress internal dynamics and the challenges related to the internal weaknesses of a movement. This approach aims to avoid falling into the trap of overlooking the fluid nature of a movement whose aims, agenda, and participation never relied on clear political boundaries and commitment. Individuals took risks up to the limits they could bear. For instance, 'Abd al-Halim Qandil, the editor of the Nasserist *Karama* newspaper and a founding member of Kifaya, continued to be involved in the movement despite repeated intimidation from the security forces and even assumed the role of coordinator of the movement in 2009–10. Several factors seem to account better for the movement's decline: on the one hand, the lack of an agenda and the loss of momentum after the 2005 elections; and on the other, internal divisions resulting from the failure to reconcile differences between groups (al-Mirghani 2008, 51).

Moreover the repression/opportunity structure framework promotes a narrow view of social movements because it imposes a dichotomy between demobilization and mobilization. According to Sydney Tarrow (2011), the cycle of protest reaches a peak and then declines, leading to demobilization in two ways: either through radicalization or through institutionalization. Conflicts over strategies or the "cost" of activism divide activists and create a decline in participation. What results is the polarization of the leadership between those willing to compromise and those who want to pursue confrontation. In this framework, repression is thought to increase institutionalization and radicalization (Tilly and Tarrow 2007, 101). In addition to showing that the intensity of contentious action changes over time, Tarrow's model tries to go beyond the repression/opportunity binary by paying more attention to internal dynamics and rightly identifies exhaustion and weariness as a mechanism that contributes to the decline of movements.

However, this model does not discuss how the process of "weariness" takes place and overlooks dormant phases that do not fit in either of the categories proposed. Moreover it does not account for the sporadic character of protests in Egypt, where mobilizations flare up and die down only to reemerge on another occasion. Phases of quiescence involve changes in activists' experience and relationship to political action but are also characterized by continuity with previous phases, or at least the desire for it. Interviewees' attempts to document the past and revive the memories of their participation in leftist groups reflect their continued belief in leftist ideology and in the possibility of applying it in Egypt, despite the Islamic revival and the apparent stability of the Mubarak regime until 2011. Thus they continued to identify themselves with the left, despite the collapse of the organizations in which they previously participated, although this identification was not expressed in political action. As two interviewees said:

> I consider myself leftist. I continue to believe in Marxism, in historic and dialectical materialism, in Leninism and all the contributions of the revolutionary movement in the world. I'm still on the side of the poor, the people, but without any connection to an organization. . . .[13]

> There isn't a communist party focusing on Marxism, which does not mean that Marxism came to an end. I think it can come back but in a more advanced way.[14]

Thus the belief in a utopia is still alive; in particular, it is important for intellectuals to make political sense of their own experience, to maintain the continuity with earlier political ideals. Waiting is an important aspect of this sustained activism. In other words, intellectuals' relationship to activism has been influenced by the notion that their ideals have been postponed.

However, interviewees do not engage in debates about how to bring about an alternative. This attitude shows that activists still maintain their connection to an ideological framework linked to the left but are no longer interested in contributing to the implementation of these ideas. What seems more important is to continue to believe, but not necessarily to act. This belief does not exclude disillusionment, but in some cases disillusionment does not affect utopia, which is only postponed. The study of Egyptian leftist activists in the 1960s and 1970s shows that disillusion does not merely lead to defection. Moreover activists embedded in networks are not exempted from disillusionment. Activism is expressed through "individual opposition," enabling interviewees to reconcile disillusionment with the public role of the intellectual.

## "I'M A MEMBER . . . AND NOT A MEMBER"

I use Charles Tilly's (1978, 64) notion of inclusiveness to describe the range of intensity that characterizes the individual's relationship to activism, and I argue that there are several possible levels of interaction with an organization. Between the member and nonmember categories is an intermediate level, at which the relationship to activism seems governed by informal practices, which are clearly linked to practices borrowed from the intellectual field. The level of involvement is low and sporadic, but this is not a defection from activism. On the contrary, interviewees have devised a strategy of adjustment and adaptation to existing structures. Adaptation means that they refuse to be "active members" of an organization, but at the same time they are available to write articles, sign a press release, or demonstrate to support a movement. In this new relationship, the link between activists and organizations is not broken, as the activist is available to support the work of a group from time to time. These actions take place on an individual basis, not as a member of a group, and the mobilization of an organization's dormant network of supporters is based on personal connections and acquaintances, often within literary or journalistic circles. This is, for example, the case with Muhammad Hashim, the director of Merit Publishing House, who is also a cofounder of the Kifaya movement and who used to regularly host the meetings of the group Writers and Artists for Change. Gatherings at Merit, which usually involve heavy smoking and drinking, provide a social space for intellectuals rather than actively organizing oppositional action. Yet these personal and literary connections have facilitated the mobilization of writers when Kifaya organized demonstrations.

Starting in the 1980s, leftist activism became a much looser commitment compared to the 1960s and 1970s because of the failures of communist groups to sustain their existence. The benefit of these new interactions was that they maintained activists' involvement in the organization's work on a temporary basis. This means that critiques of activist structures became more widespread, without necessarily leading to a complete withdrawal from the organization. For leftist intellectuals, activism was "on hold," halfway between mobilization and withdrawal. Moreover the gap between organizations and activists meant that the latter's involvement became more autonomous and independent from those organizations. Writers were available to lend a hand to an organization and to contribute to maintaining its existence and visibility in the public sphere. Writers themselves used movements like Kifaya or political parties as channels to express publicly their political views. For instance, Baha' Tahir published opinion articles from time to time in al-'Arabi, the newspaper of one of the two Nasserist parties.

Interviewees were reluctant to say that they were members of these organizations, and their discourse was contradictory on this issue: "I'm a member of Kifaya and not a member,"[15] or "All my life I've been a member of the Tagammu' and not a member."[16] Their identification with a group alternates between phases of involvement and retreat. This retreat was partly forced on writers because of the limitations of the organizations they had participated in. It also reflects the existence of a new form of activism freed from the hierarchical constraints of organizations. Their relationship to political structures can be described as a marriage of convenience.

Activism is kept in abeyance and governed by practices reflecting a lack of sustained commitment. Interviewees tend to criticize the elitist agenda of existing organizations, but they have adjusted to these structures. Their links to these organizations were not broken, for two reasons. First, there are professional or practical interests: one interviewee works for the Tagammu' literary magazine, Adab wa-Naqd, while another uses the party's facilities to host a literary club. Activists are thus rewarded for their activism, and these rewards provide both literary and activist credibility as well as material resources (Gaxie 1977, 144). In this case, the Tagammu' is a channel for reaching a wider audience of intellectuals. Second, regardless of professional interests, interviewees are willing to participate in activism even if they are disillusioned about its possible outcomes. They reconcile this apparent contradiction by not directly acknowledging that they are supporting an organization. Instead they justify their involvement with Kifaya because respectable people (nas muhtaramin) take part in the movement. Criticizing an organization does not necessarily mean refusing to cooperate with it; instead, it means that there are several degrees of involvement. For instance, it is possible within the Tagammu' to find a group of like-minded activists who share the same criticisms of the shortcomings of the party; they meet, for example, through a local section or a literary group. It is therefore possible for interviewees to constitute within the Tagammu' a

subgroup enabling them to express political views that contradict the dominant practices of the organization. This also reflects their lack of motivation to
build alternatives to existing structures. This arrangement partly corresponds
to the "disillusioned" and "pragmatic" categories identified by Dina El Khawaga
(2002, 282), but I have preferred to stress here the process of accommodation
and adaptation it leads to.

The position of writers in the political field mirrors their posture in the literary field: explaining why he had suddenly decided to publish in two state-
controlled institutions, Sonallah Ibrahim, the emblem of autonomy within the
Egyptian literary field, stated that even if the publishing institutions in Egypt
colluded with the state, they still contained elements he was happy to work with
(Mehrez 2008, 36). This posture enables intellectuals to uphold the literary avant-
garde's ideal of autonomy while continuing to accept a degree of state control.

According to Patrick Haenni (2005), some members of the Muslim Brothers
also embraced this form of activist culture, rejecting the hierarchical structure
of the organization. "Independent Islamists" sought to free themselves from
the constraints imposed by the organizational framework and began to operate
independently. This new Islamic activist culture aimed confidently at implementing a political agenda, whereas on the left the insistence on independence
reflected the fading hopes for a leftist-oriented political change and the lack of
any program for bringing it about.

The interviewees did not defect from activism; instead, their activism took
place within a narrower framework. While it was important for them to continue to oppose a regime that "must change," they were no longer actively involved in an organization because their priorities and convictions were located
in a different sphere. Intellectuals created symbolic spaces for protests through
literary or journalistic writing, which provided an outlet for the personal expression of grievances. They did not simply replace activism with literary activity;
instead, they often saw literary production as an additional space enabling them
to sustain their activism as "autonomous opponents" rather than as members
of organizations. Through a combination of different practices drawn from the
literary and activist fields, they redefined their relationship to political activism.

These initiatives were diverse and included running a literary club, publishing articles in the press, and writing poetry or songs in the vernacular language.
Newspapers continued to employ writers, and the proliferation of privately
owned newspapers since 2004 offered many opportunities to publish opinion articles. Similarly, since the mid-1990s, private publishing houses such as

Dar Sharqiyyat, Dar Merit, Dar Mahrusa, and al-Dar enabled writers to publish novels or poetry outside state-controlled channels. As in the 1960s and 1970s, for some writers, choosing to publish through private publishers was a way to express their opposition to the state. The relationship between publishers and writers is fairly informal, since Egyptian writers rarely have a dedicated publisher and it is uncommon to sign contracts (except for Sonallah Ibrahim, who has published his novels with Dar al-Mustaqbal). This means that writers are free to change publishers according to personal or financial considerations. There is a parallel between these informal ties in the literary field and writers' relationship to political organizations, as if the requirement to be independent had forged a habitus affecting all the writers' interactions—with publishers, the writers' syndicate, and political organizations. Thus prevalent forms of activism are atomized in a different fashion from what Bayat describes as a "social non-movement," which he argues involves daily practices carried out by "millions who remain fragmented" (2010, 20). Considering both social fatigue and the routinization of political expression allows a fuller account of this atomization.

The ebb and flow of participation in activist structures corresponded to activists' alternation between burnout and optimism. Written expression was one outlet for a frustrated "desire for change" or the fatigue of waiting. Writing in the press, organizing a literary club, or writing songs were opportunities to maintain a symbolic identification with political opposition. The Egyptian government's policy of relaxing restrictions on freedom of expression led to the so-called newspaper democracy (*dimuqratiyyat al-suhuf*), not only offering leftist intellectuals unprecedented room to maneuver in the press (Jacquemond 2007; El Khawaga 2002, 280) but also raising questions about the political significance of writing. Baha' Tahir, who published articles in the Nasserist weekly *al-'Arabi* against, for example, the war on Iraq or Mubarak's repressive regime, felt that journalistic writing had lost its influence: "I realized that it's pointless to have freedom of expression without freedom of action. It's just an outlet. I was afraid that the importance of writing would be lost, because you write something and reality tells you just the opposite."[17]

Nevertheless literary expression offered another way to take a political stand during phases of weariness, reflecting writers' need to use available tools. In the 2000s, their relationship to activism was similar to practices that prevailed in the 1960s and 1970s; then as now, activism represented for some an opportunity to express what they believed in, as a responsibility that was forced upon them. In the 2000s, however, writers did not defend a project or a cause; they simply expressed their frustration in what seemed to be the only possible way. This in turn influenced the nature of literary projects: personal projects became more predominant, corresponding to lapses in mobilization owing to private issues, such as aging or illness, and the frustrated desire for change. Intellectuals wrote their autobiography, for example, or wrote for themselves about issues that did not have a political focus. "My background is from the middle class but at the same time I want to reach the masses and I feel strongly about them. But deep inside me I'm interested in metaphysical issues. . . . [T]hey are cut off from reality and from people's concerns, but they are part of my own personal interests."[18]

Yet rather than merely expressing their weariness toward political action, literature constituted writers' last opportunity to feel that they are still "autonomous opponents," and thus "atomized opponents." They could react to the status quo and have the sense that they were fulfilling a "pragmatic objective" (Ion 1997, 11) by doing something that had an immediate impact, even if it was in vain.

## ARE WRITERS STILL THE CONSCIENCE OF THE NATION?

In order to understand these practices in contemporary Egypt, we must also take into account intellectuals' concept of the nation. Intellectuals, and writers in particular, have had a prominent role in shaping nationalist discourse and have gained legitimacy from it. But this legitimacy declined following the collapse of the dominant nationalist discourse as a result of the 1967 war (Geer 2009). The secular intelligentsia also ceased to be the only producer of nationalist discourse, which was increasingly expressed in Islamic terms. What changed is that secular intellectuals were increasingly considered "alienated" from society. Intellectuals still appealed to nationalist beliefs when their activity as intellectuals was under threat: debates about censorship were an opportunity for intellectuals to legitimize literary production through nationalism. However, the absence of a national project capable of defending and legitimizing intellectual production in the eyes of a broad audience probably contributed to the decline of intellectuals' activism and led to a different relationship to contentious action.

While this may change after 2011, until the demise of Hosni Mubarak intellectuals still identified themselves as the consciences or guardians of the nation, but they were no longer seen that way by the general public in Egypt, and there was no longer a clear nationalist political program. This was true for a younger generation of writers (Jacquemond 2008; Mehrez 2008) such as Mansura 'Izz al-Din or Khalid Khamisi but also, and probably most dramatically, for an older generation of writers. For the latter, ideologies and organizations that had drawn them into political action lost their influence in public debates. Moreover the absence of a national project carried out by the state and intellectuals' inability to articulate an alternative agenda created a feeling of stagnation. This context fueled fatigue and weariness and influenced patterns of mobilization or their localization into narrower frameworks.

In the 2000s, the political practices of the intellectuals interviewed for this study played a role that corresponds neither to a "complete withdrawal" (Melucci 1996, 57) nor to cycles of public/private involvement (Hirschman 1982). While private life may provide "a refuge from the paroxysm and futility of public endeavors" (129), the sense of disappointment or of dissatisfaction did not necessarily lead to a full-scale retreat toward private life. This might be a tempting but painful option, "as if I was leaving my lover," in the words of one interviewee. It was a painful choice because it challenged the prevailing rules of the literary field and could mean withdrawing from the normative expectations associated with the role of the intellectual. "Frustration" and informal relations have been analyzed by one school of SMT as a catalyst for contentious action (Gurr 1970). Here I have offered a different argument by attempting to show that these factors can contribute to loosening the link to activism. In this context the mobilization/demobilization framework loses its significance; activism has moved to symbolic spaces, between institutionalized organizations and demobilization. I have tried to show that these practices are not merely informal but can be drawn from other identifications and belongings—in this case, they are often institutionalized in the intellectual field.

The construction of alternative channels of political expression, with the aim of attaining greater autonomy, is a response to the deficiencies of traditional activist structures. However, it does not replace involvement in these organizations, nor does it imply a withdrawal from political activism. Rather than merely referring to social and political crisis or apathy, one can account for the dissolution of channels of mobilization by looking at how this may benefit other frameworks. Literary or journalistic production is not simply a replacement for activism; it also provides complementary channels of political expression for disillusioned opponents who still consider themselves activists. However, this is not really political activism but a kind of misrecognition.

# 3 LEAVING ISLAMIC ACTIVISM BEHIND

Ambiguous Disengagement in Saudi Arabia

## Pascal Menoret

ON ARRIVING IN RIYADH OR JEDDAH, a researcher attempting to do fieldwork on Saudi Islamic movements soon confronts a startling fact: most of his prospective interviewees are no longer Islamic activists.[1] For one reason or another, they have left Islamic activism behind. They are therefore more open to the curiosity of researchers than are their active counterparts, who may be secretive about some of their activities and may resent fieldwork as an intrusion or even a threat. This is the reverse of the situation researchers might normally expect: to gain relatively easy access to members of political or religious groups and to experience difficulties precisely when it comes to meeting ex-members or re-pentants. The opposite is true in Saudi Arabia, in part because of the overall conditions in a country where political parties, trade unions, and demonstrations are banned, and where associations are so strictly monitored that only members of the establishment—the royal family, the merchant oligarchy, and the higher echelons of the administration—can actually create them. The situation also stems from the global war on terror and its Saudi ramifications. Saudi Islamic activists often (and not without cause) suspect foreign researchers of having dealings with Western security agencies or of taking some part in what they see as a global campaign against Islam and Muslims. Moreover, activists who later repented and became personae grata are pushed forward by Saudi authorities and presented to journalists and researchers as the witnesses of the inevitable trajectory of engagement and activism in the Saudi story. Political repentants and disengaged activists are almost invisible in democratic settings; in the authoritarian Saudi context they are a point of entry for most fieldwork. Albeit crucially important, this point is only incidentally mentioned in most works on Saudi Islamic activism: disengagement thus remains beyond the ana-lytical gaze; only the accidents of fieldwork seem to bring this notion to the center of attention. As French political scientist Olivier Fillieule (2005, 12) con-fesses, his "interest in disengagement came from a failure." During a survey on homosexual activism, the quantitative data he collected did not at all match his qualitative observations. A closer look at the context of the study revealed that he had circulated his questionnaire after a particularly spectacular feat of activism had rallied hundreds of short-lived activists, whose overwhelming but temporary presence explains the mismatch. Homosexual activism could not be understood on the basis of the different cohorts that coexisted at a given moment; a more fruitful diachronic angle would have to encompass former activists and repentants, whom Fillieule calls "the ex."

This chapter is devoted to the study of several trajectories of disengagement in contemporary Saudi Arabia, a question which is all the more interesting in that within the political contexts of authoritarian states and ubiquitous security apparatuses, defection is often understood to be closely linked to repression. The action of repressive agencies typically increases the cost of engagement and is generally described as eliciting two major developments: it may either prompt militants to radicalize and engage in an escalation of violence, or lead them to quit activism and repent altogether. Despite—or because of—its simplicity and handiness, this formula is oblivious to at least two major aspects of disengagement from Islamic activism. First, the relationship between state repression and radicalization/repentance is unstable and depends on many variables and factors: no theory can really tell whether repression, whatever its intensity, will produce a violent reaction rather than fearfulness, or an increased engagement rather than repentance. Second, the formula does not say anything about former militants who neither radicalize nor repent but instead convert their Islamic activism into other forms of social, cultural, intellectual, economic, or artistic commitment. In other words, repression may not only increase the cost of engagement; it may also steer activists toward multiple exit strategies and prompt them to recycle their skills in other domains (Cunningham 2004). While examining biographical trajectories of engagement and repentance, this chapter attempts to analyze these ambiguous forms of disengagement.

## CONTEXT AND FIELDWORK

The context of this study is the history of the Saudi Islamic movement (Al-Rasheed 2007), which many observers and actors call the "Islamic awakening" (*al-sahwa al-islamiyya*). Due to the prohibition of political activity in the country Islamic semiformal activism was born in gray areas located at the periphery of the educational system and the official religious institutions. By "semiformal" activism I mean neither formal mobilization (visible institutions or organizations with a definite membership and a published program) nor informal groups the fortuitous union of previously unconnected people, what Asef Bayat (2010, 14) calls social nonmovements or the "collective actions of non-collective actors." I rather have in mind discreet groups with no fixed boundaries, which tap into the state's resources while hiding from its gaze. These groups walk a thin line between the realm of official institutions, where they could be subjected to state surveillance or bureaucratic obstacles, and the domain of purely informal activity, as epitomized by Bayat's "nonmovements" or by clandestine networks. The Islamic awakening invested first and foremost in education: the distributive nature of a state that sits atop the largest oil reservoir of the planet explains why the activists' goal was not so much to provide basic services (as in Egypt for instance) as to educate new generations. The Islamic awakening gradually became a movement of teachers and of students who sometimes call themselves *talabat 'ilm* (students in quest of religious instruction). Saudi Islamic activism is thus best described as a politico-religious revivalist movement, that is, a proselytizing (*da'wa*) and pietistic movement fostered by charismatic leadership and growing through voluntarism (*tatawwu'*) and social networks.[2] Its pietistic nature is embodied in the study and memorization of the Qur'an in small circles (*halaqat tahfidh al-qur'an*), extracurricular activities in schools (*jama'at al-taw'iyya al-islamiyya*), the critique of all intermediaries between the believer and God, the insistence on salvation and repentance (*tawba*), and the use of innovative ways of preaching, including at different times proselytizing excursions (*khuruj*), tape-recorded and televised sermons, and the Internet. Despite its pietistic features, however, the Islamic awakening may oppose received Saudi norms and political behaviors and should not be confused with a nonconfrontational quietist movement. Its critique of all intermediaries between the believer and the sacred texts jeopardizes the official religious institution's hermeneutic monopoly (Menoret 2008, 120–23), while the Islamic activists' conspicuous display of religiosity undermines the state's control of the public sphere. Furthermore, Islamic proselytizing methods can be turned into effective weapons of political mobilization, as during the 1990 Gulf War when several Islamic networks converged in a nationwide reformist movement.

In 1993 the state began to crack down on the Islamic awakening and initiated a campaign of arrests that targeted essentially nonviolent young activists. Repression intensified after the Khobar and Riyadh bombings of 1995 and 1996, which targeted American and Saudi military and police facilities. Following a respite between 1999 and 2003, repression revived after the 2003 Riyadh bombings[3] with the state launching a new—and indiscriminate—crackdown campaign. According to a prominent Islamic activist, "There is no precedent to the repression that strikes us for thirty years." A younger activist adds, "There is no family without a relative or a member who has been arrested and put in jail." Repression targets primarily young people, who are described as easy prey for militant networks and are also easy marks for the security services. In an overall atmosphere of fear—torture is the ultimate foundation of the penal system because a guilty verdict often depends entirely on the defendant's confession, which is extorted either under torture or the threat thereof—state repression has dramatized the public sphere and ironically politicized large sectors of society. This politicization does not express itself openly, however; the same word, *iltizam*, is used to designate religious and political commitment, and the boundaries between Islamic activism and political expression are blurred since at least the 1960s and the Cold War-inspired repression of leftist and nationalist activism.

This is the context for fieldwork on politicization in the Saudi authoritarian setting, which I conducted between 2005 and 2007 in Riyadh. I focus here on three different groups: two of them belong to a federation claiming a Muslim Brothers heritage while the third is more *salafi* in orientation, which means that it calls for a stricter adherence to, and a more direct reading of, the sacred texts (Qur'an and Sunna). The Muslim Brothers began operating in Saudi Arabia in the 1950s following the Egyptian, Syrian, and Iraqi migrations to the Gulf. Saudi Salafi activism was born in the mid-1960s in the Islamic universities, around Saudi and Syrian professors. At the level of the average member, however, there are few differences between the persuasions, and whether one belongs to the Muslim Brothers or to the Salafis does not make a great difference when it comes to disengagement. I socialized with and observed members of these groups at different stages of their organizational lifespan, and could thus witness different relationships between my interviewees' personal biographies and their lives as Islamic activists.

For Islamic groups that had formed in high school, the graduation of students and their transition to college was an ordeal. Some interviewees who were trying to implant their religious activities in universities soon came under the dual fire of the administration and of more secular students. In an overall repressive context, the administration was defending its turf against any accusation of extremism among students. The secularists benefited from the general climate of suspicion towards Islamic activism and were trying to gain ground among students. This rather uncomfortable situation had an influence on my fieldwork because it enhanced the initial reluctance of Islamic activists to welcome a Western researcher.

One day, after I had attended a play at the university, both a professor and an Islamic leader asked 'Adil, my main contact in the aforementioned Salafi group, not to invite me again. 'Adil, twenty-one, was not totally legitimate in the eyes of his fellow activists, who considered him insufficiently committed to their lifestyle and goals. He himself felt that he was both inside and outside, which made him a fascinating intermediary. But this contradictory status also denied him the kind of credentials he would have needed to authorize my participation in the group's daily activities.

Easy to interview, Islamic activists were generally impossible to observe, unlike other segments of Riyadh's youth, who were far less talkative but more open to the gaze of a stranger. There is a general reason for this: ordinary youth do nothing a priori illegal and may have difficulties articulating their experience in discourse. In contrast, young Islamic activists value secrecy, realizing that they may be the target of repression; and at the same time they are eager to explain their position and to rally strangers to their cause. Ordinary youth allow you to share their activities, while Islamic activists have a high interest in protecting the secrecy of their group's deeds. With disengaged activists it was a different story: they could be both observed and interviewed, which added to the intrinsic interest of their trajectories.

## "EVERY DAY WAS MEMORIAL DAY"

How did young Islamic activists relate to their environment during the troubled period following September 11, 2001? I argue that ecological factors translated into personal malaise and, sometimes, led ultimately to disengagement. Participation in Islamic activities often produced conflicting feelings among middle and high school students. Even the harshest critics of Islamism could not but be struck by the energy and enthusiasm that emanated from religious awareness (taw'iyya) programs; yet this enthusiasm was often tinted with rage.

The experience of one of my interviewees between 1999 and 2003 is characteristic of the conflicting emotions produced by Islamic activism. The last son of a university staff member who had emigrated from a small Najdi town, Fahd, twenty-one, had joined the sahwa islamiyya as a high school youth who was looking for empowerment and guidance. When I first met Fahd, in 2002, there was a sinister look about him. Only seventeen, he was dragging an enormous body crowned by a terrible face. Constantly frowning and pouting, apparently fulminating, he had a disdainful demeanor and an air of restrained violence that impressed me and starkly contrasted with his insightful remarks and obvious intelligence. In an interview I conducted with him a few years later (Menoret 2005), he naturally elaborated on the conflicting Weltanschauungen elicited by Islamic activism:

> The Qur'ranic circle and the Islamic group teach pupils how to care about Islam, to care about [*yahtammun bi*] society. Not only our society; they want you to care about Muslim society as a whole. [ . . . ] We often had lectures on Muslims in Chechnya to discuss their horrible situation . . . The Russians thrashed them with planes and tanks; they squashed them. All these stories make you mad about what happens, and you start having doubts about everything. You start thinking that everybody is against us, against Muslims. That the other civilizations are after Islam, that everybody [ . . . ] wants to get rid of Islam and destroy it. And there is another problem: I could not trust a non-Muslim. [ . . . ] We were brought up this way. See the Muslims in Kashmir, their problem with the Hindus—not with India, with the Hindus. We started with a religious principle: the Hindus want to exterminate the Kashmiris because they are Muslims. I let you imagine the scene. I tell you what: every day was Memorial Day; we had lectures about this and that; we were constantly talking about people who went to the jihad, friends for instance. The preachers were telling all these stories. And you, you are in high school, you are seventeen; these stories get rooted in you; you become nervous and you want to do something: you want to make a difference. And you get mad about it! Everything makes you mad. Everything! You see nothing positive around you. So you are mad, all the time. I was in junior high school when the events in Palestine happened. [ . . . ] The [second] intifada. The situation was awful; everybody was upset. And the international community doesn't move a finger; no solution is proposed, and everybody repeats that whatever the international community says is pure hypocrisy, that they want to gag Muslims, that nobody will stop Israel, that America supports Israel . . . I was totally mad. Then we had September 11 and . . . I didn't know . . . I was totally mad at America but . . . I don't know . . . and I did not, not at all . . . the solution . . . violence . . . never!

For structural reasons (repression and the bureaucratic nature of the state), the energy produced by the Islamic movement could not be invested at home in the late 1990s. Caring about Muslims abroad was the solution devised by the *sahwa* activists to cope with the climate of fear perpetuated by the regime and to channel the students' enthusiasm in nonconfrontational directions. This accounts for the lengthy lectures on the Western "arc of crisis" around the Muslim world, and also the bewilderment of these middle-class students once they realized that nothing can really be done *from inside* to reform Saudi Arabia—even in a pacific guise—and that according to the Cold War policy of support for the Afghan jihad, the only possibility for action actually lies *outside* the country, in armed military action.

For institutional reasons (there being no room for activism inside the country) as well as historical reasons (Cold War rhetoric and networks) and cultural reasons (the language of jihad is on their leaders' tongues), Islamic activists were "up against the wall" in the late 1990s and pressed to either engage in violent actions abroad or champ at the bit at home. It is no wonder that Fahd became enraged and envisaged violent action, even if once in college he took his distance from his Islamic group:

> When I went to college, my way of thinking changed a bit. It changed a lot after the [2003] bombings. [ ... ] In freshman year, I was still with them [the Islamic group], but the relation was less intense. [ ... ] Now I don't see them anymore. [ ... ] I was still enraged [*ghadhib*] about the political situation, because [ ... ] I am not one of those who preach violence, even if I was, hmm ... committed [*multazim*]. But violence, definitely not! [ ... ] After I went to college, I had no activities anymore. I worked in a company for four months, and after that I quit the job to focus on my studies. And I had two car accidents, one after the other, two severe accidents that cut me from my studies. I couldn't stand it anymore; I quit college, I thought I could study other stuff ... [*long silence*] [ ... ] And, I don't deny that ... during all these years, I got busy with myself. Very busy. I mean, I was hopeless in college and ... [*sigh*] I was not interested in what was happening, in cultural or intellectual events. Then the bombings started. It was like a shock. [ ... ] And I didn't know who to be with. The problem is, you have to pick your side. With whom, against whom? With America, with bin Laden? I am not a big fan of bin Laden's methods: bombings. Because I think that ... those who died were innocent. There is no justification for this. But I was angry at America. [ ... ] I couldn't pick a side. And I was still busy with myself, but ... After the [Riyadh] bombings, I stayed at home six months, totally paralyzed, and at the same time I got busy with myself; I didn't care that much about anything. [ ... ] Inside the country, I was angry because of the economic situation. Angry, because the government's money is our money. And they [the

royal family] give priority to their own family, their entourage; they favor them over us, the people . . . and the people have lost out. I was enraged about that. [ . . . ] About six months after the bombings, I started hanging out with a new crowd; I think I wanted to meet new faces and to start anew.

Fahd repeatedly mentions his difficult psychological situation once he realized how misleading Islamic activism could be, and how hard it was to grow up in post–9/11 Saudi society. For to be "busy with oneself" signals an overall malaise, whose social and economic dimensions are at least as important as the rage produced by Islamic activism. Riddled with debts, coping with the financial consequences of his accidents (automobile insurance was not yet compulsory in the country), dropping out of college, Fahd fled reality, taking refuge in his room reading novels and browsing the Internet. In early 2004 he met new friends online, recomposed his life around new objectives, and reinvested his unused energy in an activity on which he would have frowned as an Islamic activist: the promotion of cinema in a country where for religious reasons movie theaters are banned.

## "PEOPLE DID NOT FALL FROM THE SKY"

Within a regional context infused with tensions and injustices, when activism inside the country is banned, radicalization may well be a tempting venture. Yet despite many clichés, it is quite an improbable outcome of Islamic activism. Many young activists do of course elaborate convincing arguments in favor of Islamic militancy at home or abroad. Radicalization mechanisms, however, are extremely complex, and only a tiny minority of Islamic activists actually makes the decision to join the local branch of al-Qa'ida; when they do so, they sometimes follow unexpected patterns (Menoret 2009, 2010). During an interview, 'Adil suddenly decided to open up on a topic he rarely dwelt on: radicalization.

> 'Adil: Look, it is hard to say that I'm a reformist. Why? Because you don't fix a wreck, period. You want to dive into the Atlantic and go fix the *Titanic*? It doesn't make sense [ . . . ] If you are onboard a ship that takes water, like, a little, I will cut my arms and legs to fix it; I am even ready to trade my life for twenty thousand other lives, I have no problem with that. Our problem, here, in my personal view—I mean, I am walking on eggs here, you know; I talk about this kind of stuff only once a year, maybe . . . The problem with our situation is that our ship is a wreck! There can be no reform . . . except if [ . . . ] we launch a new ship [ . . . ] Because this ship is

lost. I mean, we are a society without politics, and I feel oppressed when I think about it; we are a society without a state!

Pascal: And what will this new ship be? What is the ideal state for you?

'Adil: Well, if you ask a Muslim this question, he will answer: the state of the rightly guided caliphs [*dawlat al-khulafa' al-rashidin*]. True or not? Now, how do we come back to the state of the rightly guided caliphs? This I don't know. I only know that we urgently need a rightly guided caliph, because we are drowning. But what do we have to do in between, to prepare for this state, and can we build it with our own forces? That's what the Islamic awakening and the Muslim Brothers do, in a way: they revive the spirit, they revive society, they diffuse their call to Islam ... Or do we have to adopt other means, like the opposition in London?[4] Do we have to become terro- ... I mean, to be violent, do we have to attack and terrorize our enemy and hit him? I don't know which method to choose. [ ... ] I don't know what to do between our wreckage and the new ship we have to build in the future.

If 'Adil does not know what to do "in between," it is perhaps because after the repression of the 1990s Islamic activists grew terribly aware of their vulnerability. It would be short-sighted, however, to victimize Islamic activists and to present them as the passive subjects of state repression; in many ways the very structures of activism took an active—if unconscious—part in the crackdown process. Islamic groups are as authoritarian as the state itself, as I learned from Thamir, thirty, who was running an Islamic consciousness-raising group (*jama'at taw'iyya islamiyya*) in a high school.

Like the members of 'Adil's group, Thamir was waging a war on two fronts: against the high school principal (who did not want any activist group in his school), and against the Qur'anic circle at the local mosque (whose members accused him of corrupting the youth with too "liberal" ideas). This odd situation made my work with him both thorny and gripping. Thamir was all the more ready to look at Islamic activism with a critical eye now that he was the target of its own internal repressiveness; he was about to disengage from the Islamic awakening's dictatorial structures. According to him, activists themselves are the products of the very state they aspire to reform:

School is repressive, and so are the Islamic circles. [ ... ] Family is repressive; it is like that everywhere. Repression reigns in universities too. Wherever you go, you have to get yourself used to this. The guy above imposes himself on the guy below, by force; he tells him that he is the best one, that he is the best leader, that nobody is better than he—by force. He lets no one follow their own path, he consults nobody. That's how society works. And Islamic circles are just like that: people did not fall from the sky.

During that interview, one of Thamir's students, Hizlul, cut in and explained how the *sahwa* leaders, in order to diffuse a culture of blind obedience, literally revaluated values:

The guy who accepts their domination is [in their eyes] a remarkable individual [*al-insan al-mumayyiz*]. As for the guy who opposes their order, who feels that they harm his personal freedom or violate Islamic tenets, they say that he is a cad [*qalil adab*], a lout [*mu mutarrabi*], things like that. That's what they say to whoever resists their authority. As for the guy who puts up with the situation, who behaves just like they want or like society wants or like the guys above want, he is the best, he is a hero.

Interestingly enough, Thamir's critique of the way the Islamic groups are managed agrees with al-Qaʿida's arguments against Saudi nonviolent activism. One of al-Qaʿida's arguments against the reformist awakening circles, contrary to what might be expected, is neither that they are not Islamic enough nor that they are too "soft" and therefore do not understand the harsh necessities of combat, but that they are trapped in top-down strategies that lead them to exert too much authority on their members. According to Lewis ʿAtiyat Allah, an infamous Internet pamphleteer devoted to the cause of Osama bin Laden (Al-Rasheed 2007, 175–210), al-Qaʿida has succeeded in creating a nonhierarchical environment in which individuals compete harmoniously, thus giving their best without being constrained by rigid structures. In an imaginary dialogue with a defender of the *sahwa*, he says:

You have not allowed competences to develop freely. You never set up a comprehensive program or a clear strategy. Do you know how al-Qaʿida chooses its leaders? Unlike you, they do not select the most "obedient and disciplined" members. [ ... ] They select their leaders according to their behavior on the battlefield, for it is in the heat of the fight that individuals give their best and put aside their mundane aspirations. (ʿAtiyat Allah 2003, 197)

An organization without an organization, al-Qaʿida had already revolutionized its management practices, which the *sahwa* failed to do. Bin Laden's organization is similar, in a way, to those "*lean* firms working as *networks* with a multitude of participants, organizing work in the form of teams or *projects*." Emerging in the 1990s out of the global economic crisis, they no longer rely on a top-down structure but are rather "intent on [ . . . ] a general mobilization of workers thanks to their leaders' *vision*." As for the *sahwa*, it is more comparable to the modernist organizations of the 1950s and 1960s, characterized by "hierarchy, planning, formal authority, Taylorism, the grade of *cadre* and lifetime careers in the same firm" (Boltanski and Chiapello 2005, 73, 85). 'Atiyat Allah goes on:

> Your problem is that you judge things from your experience of activism and of organizations that are weird, rigid and bureaucratic. That's why you cannot understand how al-Qa'ida could bring about such a considerable success [9/11]. Your tortuous organizations paralyze the energies instead of integrating them, coordinating them, developing them or leading them to success. Al-Qa'ida solved this issue in two ways. First, it got rid of the worn ideas of organization and of political engagement in a monolithic structure, and embraced the idea of a university or college that trains the fighters and sends them off to the wide world to carry out a plan that everybody knows already well. [ . . . ] Second, it buried the outdated notion of partisans working in isolation from society. Al-Qa'ida's fighters are trained to blend in with the society in which they live. [ . . . ] My dear friend, your organizations walk on their heads and became a glue that paralyses your partisans. They freeze the competences and sterilize the Islamic forces at your disposal. ('Atiyat Allah 2003, 196–97)

Being a visible presence inside society, far from being an efficient vehicle of propagation, identifies the *sahwa* as a target for state repression. The distinctive clothes and demeanor of Islamic activists are deemed useless and dangerous by 'Atiyat Allah; according to him, invisibility is one of the ways al-Qa'ida evades local and global repression, because "America and its allies will never allow for the creation of an Islamic state, not even for the emergence of an Islamic force inside a given state. We all know that their politics is to crack down on any such force before it even sees the light of day" (2003, 198). The very ideas of organization and engagement are viewed as sterilizing notions, and al-Qa'ida—in 'Atiyat Allah's tract, at least—praises nothing more than the individual and his instant creativity. Albeit an obvious act of propaganda, this description highlights many elements that are crucial to the understanding of former Islamic activists' disengagement and discontent. As the example of Fawwaz will show, even able and promising activists ultimately give up and decide to leave Islamic activism behind.

### "I WAS UNDESIRABLE TO THE LEADERS, I WAS TROUBLE"

When I met Fawwaz, twenty-one, he had left a group that was itself no longer active. The group was formerly affiliated with the Muslim Brothers and was composed of high school and college students who regularly gathered around an elder student named Yahya, twenty-seven at the time of my fieldwork. Fawwaz's peculiar trajectory inside the group led him from a strong belief in his comrades' goals and means to a total disapproval of the way Yahya was asserting his authority. The group had progressively ceased to function, its members being caught between college, work, and family responsibilities. During a series of interviews, Fawwaz replayed to me his story of resistance and rebellion to the group. He went so far as to invite Yahya to a collective interview, which gradually turned into a confrontation between the young men. My fieldwork had been turned into an instrument of personal vengeance, which allowed me to closely observe the reasons a successful young Muslim Brother like Fawwaz had decided to go his own way.

According to Fawwaz, Islamic activism suffers from a crisis of authority and loses adherents every year: "They shut down Qur'anic circles every year. Because there is no administrative team, no coordinator, the number of students goes down; there are many obstacles." His own disengagement seems to provoke in him sentiments of disappointment and defiance, and this is probably why he undertakes to help me out with my fieldwork for a few weeks, investing in my project an extraordinary, yet short-lived, amount of energy. During our first meetings, I understand that I represent in his eyes this Other, who, criticized, scorned, and sometimes hated by local Najdi society, is not the sort of person Islamic activists would easily hang out with. He confessed one day, "When I first saw you, I felt like I was opening up to the Other." Helping me seemed to be part of his own rehab program and his way of assuming a new social identity.

Fawwaz broke with his Islamic group when he became a victim of power relationships. He had perceived early on that leaders or supervisors (*mushrifun*) enact hazily delineated functions: they are supervisors as well as mentors, leaders as well as educators. This murky situation allows them to play on many different levels and, ultimately, to keep the upper hand in the average member's

activities. In Fawwaz's view, this power position undermines the very brotherhood that is one of the group's most powerful slogans:

> The supervisor [al-mushrif] [ ... ] puts every member of the group [ ... ]
> under close surveillance [muraqaba]. [ ... ] For instance, the supervisor
> doesn't prepare cultural competitions himself, but he supervises them. Stu-
> dents prepare competitions and cultural activities. The supervisor only moni-
> tors these activities. He has an administrative and bureaucratic function, you
> see what I mean? Apart from that, he gives lectures. He can ... how do you
> say? You and I talked about surveillance, monitoring, supervision [ishraf],
> and we also talked about ... about leadership [qiyada], movement leadership.
> The supervisor is usually the group's leader [qa'id]; he is the guy in charge.
> [ ... ] From time to time, he acts as a teacher and tries to give you an educa-
> tion [tarbiya]. He acts in a professorial way, like: you're just a student and I
> am responsible for you. You could very rarely reach a feeling of self-fulfill-
> ment or brotherhood, you see what I mean? [ ... ] To cut it short: he acts
> with arrogance [takabbur]. I am in charge; you're only a youth. [ ... ] But
> it's a pedagogical arrogance [takabbur tarbawi]. [ ... ] Pedagogical arrogance
> means that I am higher than you and that I strive to educate you, to give you
> some culture [tathqif]. When for instance the supervisor scolds a student in
> front of everybody, and with violence, [ ... ] he [would say he] just wants to
> build up [ikhraj] the student, to educate him [tahzhib]. That's what I mean by
> arrogance, pedagogical arrogance.

Fawwaz here points to the Islamic awakening's ambivalence; in this teachers' movement, the frontier between pedagogical authority and institutional
violence is blurred, a complex situation Fawwaz brilliantly sums up as "pedagogical arrogance." According to Fawwaz, the very organization of Islamic
activism brings about injustices, because "the elders" put students in "a position of inferiority [duniyya]": "Basically, the student is always an alleged
evil doer," except "the student they like [al-talib al-mahbub], or the achiever
[al-munjiz]." Here as for Hizlul, achievement (al-injaz) is precisely measured
by one's allegiance to the group, an allegiance so overwhelming that Fawwaz
had to "take his distances from the activities for some time." In the middle of
the interview, Fawwaz mentions the reason he eventually disengaged:

> I stayed three years with them, and they never gave me any responsibility, while
> it is actually normal that students be entrusted with missions. [ ... ] They put

my brother in charge of three summer camps. As for me, I was undesirable [*ghayr maghrub fihi*] in their eyes ... And there, personal issues take more room than they should. True, I was undesirable to the leaders, I was trouble, I often criticized the activities, I criticized the group, but it is not a reason to deprive me of my right!

In Yahya's eyes, "Desirable [*maghrub fihi*] or undesirable: these terms designate your discipline [*inzhibat*], your attendance, your interaction with the activities," and Fawwaz just didn't play by the book. Asked about the benchmark he would use to grade students, Yahya answers, "You know, when you see somebody on a daily basis, you don't really need to test him." Fawwaz was right to "take his distance" "for some time": the domination of personal relationships in Islamic activism, the lack of institutions, and the absence of a culture of collective action encourage authoritarianism and poor management of human resources. Organizational issues, the lack of a political project, and absence of intellectual ambition took their toll on Fawwaz's initial enthusiasm. Yahya's influence had not been solely negative, however: through his example and despite his fits of authority, Fawwaz had actually experienced, in his own terms, "an intellectual revolution" and an "explosion" of his sentiments about the Palestinian cause and Islamic causes in general. Fawwaz's experience in this matter is quite similar to Fahd's: the energy induced by his Islamic commitment could not translate into effective action. Accused by Fawwaz of having curbed his political emotions, Yahya attempted to defend himself by referring to the overall political situation, thereby confessing the impotence of Islamic groups:

Yahya: Believe me, ninety percent of the activists don't believe in what you call politics.

Fawwaz: Of *your* activists, you mean? Of course not, they are too shallow ...

Y: You know that ninety percent of all Muslim Brothers don't know they belong to the Brotherhood?

F: I know. They are just high school kids, period [ ... ] But I mean, if we talk about the relationship between individuals and the state? Don't tell me you don't have political opinions. Everybody! Everybody! Human beings, by nature, have ...

Y: Do you really think everybody? ... No, believe me, nobody thinks about that ... [ ... ]

F: What about the relationship to the Islamic group?

Y: Well, you know how the Muslim Brothers work, right? "Hey guys, how do we organize the next cultural competition?" "Hey guys, what about the soccer tournament?" "Hey guys, when do we go to the beach?" This is what it really looks like!

## WHAT WOULD OLIVER CROMWELL DO?

How can young activists invest their organizational skills in activities more compelling than soccer tournaments, cultural competitions, and high school trips? Hanging out with Fahd gave me some elements of an answer. His new friends formed what is commonly called a clique (*shilla*), that is, a small group of ten to twenty friends who share a common goal and meet regularly in a given place, apartment, coffee shop, or private rest house (*istiraha*). These small groups bridge between public and private, professional and personal, making them one of the most important social institutions; from the teenager to the king, everybody belongs to a *shilla*, which mediates between the individual and the larger society, spreads strategic information, and allocates opportunities. After they left Islamic activism, many of my interviewees took refuge in various cliques; some of them simply came back to their high school friends, while others strove to meet new individuals and join more socially useful circles. Fahd's new *shilla* consists almost exclusively of previous Islamic activists who met through the medium of a Saudi cinema website. Originally formed by three members, the group grew in a few months to more than a dozen individuals who pledged to work together "for the sake of cinema in Saudi Arabia," having no broader program beyond their passion for watching movies and writing about them. In a country with no movie theaters, former Islamic activists were ironically advocating for the lifting of the official ban. The group stabilized after a year and met regularly in a rented rest house in the outskirts of Riyadh. Fahd was the youngest member of the group, one of the last to have joined it and one of the least qualified too. Despite this—or because of it—he was extremely active: he collected the monthly rent, organized meals and film shows, sent reminders, and recycled his activist knowhow in the management of the weekly activities of the group. The discovery of cinema was a turning point in his existence; after he dropped out of college and had two car accidents, Fahd found a couple of jobs, first with a publisher of schoolbooks then with a company selling Islamic cell phones. Joining the cinema group allowed him to cope with his situation and to envision a better future; through the group he met with young entrepreneurs in the Saudi "Islamic economy" of which he was already part. He acted in a few short movies and made good use of the aura that had impressed me during our first meeting. Cinema even introduced him to European political history, thus prompting his interest in the municipal elections organized by the state in 2005 (Menoret 2009a):

> I watched this movie about an Englishman, Oliver Cromwell. [ ... ] He was member of the House of Commons, and at the beginning, they were really fundamentalists. A few years later, he seized power and killed the king. And I think that ... [we laugh at his blunt mention of the regicide] Nooo! I didn't want to ... [laughter] I mean, [ ... ] it was something nobody could imagine at the beginning, and yet they were able to make history. I had a positive feeling, not a negative one. I understood something, all of the sudden, and it had a strong influence on me. It may even have had an influence on me for the elections. [ ... ] *Cromwell* showed me that this was the way I had to follow. The way that leads to democracy, too. As we say here: God helps those who help themselves [*Ibda' wa'l-baqi 'ala Allah*].

Other members of the group directed short movies, wrote columns in the Saudi and Arab press, and began to tour the regional film festivals. After a few years, however, an overall immobilism put an end to the group's experience. Activist skills could push forward individual successes but were soon exhausted on a collective level by the lack of a public space. Seven years after the cinema website was created, the group had become, progressively, an ordinary *shilla* that promoted nothing more than its members and fell short of putting a collective project into effect.

Members of another *shilla* similarly exhausted their activist resources. Like Fawwaz, they had left the Muslim Brothers and tried to collectively articulate a position that observers have called post-Islamism, that is, "an endeavor to fuse religiosity and rights, faith and freedom, Islam and liberty" (Bayat 2010, 243). Yahya, Fawwaz's previous chaperone, himself suffered from the Islamic group's rigidity and authoritarianism. He thus started voicing his critiques on the Internet and eventually joined other ex–Muslim Brothers who had created an intellectual club (*nadwa fikriyya*) in a middle-class neighborhood of Riyadh. Ex–Muslim Brothers and ex-Salafis aimed at responding to al-Qa'ida's intellectual and organizational challenge, and undertook to reorganize Islamic activism around small intellectual clubs, such as the one Yahya joined. The first step was to distance themselves from the Muslim Brothers. In Yahya's view, "there are no thinkers among the Muslim Brothers, and that's the problem of the Islamic movements. It repels thinkers." He went further:

> Wait, I am sorry, what is the Muslim Brothers' thinking? Today, in the Muslim world, you'll find it everywhere, from the left to the right. Salafis believe in the Brothers' thinking, communists believe in it too, which means that the Muslim Brothers do not have a definite thinking; they do not have a clear identity anymore. [ ... ] Among the Brothers, there are pacifists and warmongers, [ ... ] people who are totally liberated and have nothing to do with religion anymore, and pure rigorists [mutashaddidin]. [ ... ] I mean, when Nasir [one of Yahya's Muslim Brother friends] speaks to a nationalist, the nationalist will say, "This guy is an Islamist, one hundred percent sure." But if he speaks to a Salafi, the Salafi will say, "Wow, this guy is ultra liberal."

The trajectories of the nadwa's activists are curiously similar: according to Fawwaz, they are "people who have belonged to the Brotherhood and went over to the Salafis; people who have been Brothers and decided to leave," that is, highly mobile activists who crossed boundaries between different groups and experienced a sort of activist volatility. Disappointed with the shortcomings of Islamic movements yet conscious of the poor overall political condition in the country, they attempted to develop an intellectual niche, organized a series of lectures, and invited famous writers, historians, university professors, and journalists to speak about their experiences. At some point during my fieldwork, however, the group suddenly ceased to function, and its members, whose number had declined sharply over the last few months, left the nadwa's spacious apartment and took refuge in a private rest house in the suburbs of Riyadh. They kept coming every Thursday, but cards and soccer matches soon replaced the intellectual conversation of the last eight years. At the same time, my main contacts in the group stopped returning my calls and were obviously refusing to meet me. A few months later, when I could catch up with them again, they mentioned biographical constraints (work and family) to explain their long silence and the death of their group. Perhaps too the ubiquitous secret police (al-mabahith al-'amma) had exerted pressure on prominent members, asking them to withdraw their support for seditious activities. In any event, eight years after they had started the group, its members had exhausted the meager possibilities still open to organized action. According to one member, they had considered simply every single interesting voice within and outside the country—everything had been said, and no new voice could be heard. Since collective action was prohibited, the issue was not intellectual but rather political, and the group, despite its best intentions, could not do much about it. As for the cinema group, energies could no longer coalesce around elusive goals, and commitment itself had declined. The intellectual endeavor to reform the core tenets of Islamic activism was compelling per se, but it could not mobilize any longer what had become a "weary community" (Jahoda, Lazarsfeld, and Zeisel 1971, 36), a group for whom nothing happens, nothing can be expected, and nothing can be done.

## CONCLUSION

In a series of lectures given in 2005, Islamic activist and educator Muhammad al-Duwish summed up the many failures of the Islamic awakening: "The Muslim world is a victim of individualism. We are too individualistic, there are not enough functional institutions in this part of the world." Excessive individualism could be a result of political repression, economic transformations, or social change, but Duwish was not dwelling on the causes; rather, he was looking for a remedy. "We lack a culture of collective action [*thaqafat al-ʿamal al-jamaʿi*], even though many Islamic traditions emphasize the community and the collectivity." According to this view, individualism is not a positive development connected to the "modernization of religious practices" or the secularization of the public sphere. It has more to do with the strengthening of control over independent or at least semiformal groups. Individualism appears as a curse inflicted on any attempt at organizing collective action—the anarchical seed planted by an authoritarian and disorganized state to get rid of its competitors. Neither could individual choice do much for the young activists or ex-activists whose stories I have sketched here. While attempting to escape the poor organization and authoritarianism of Islamic groups, they fell into another evil and soon exhausted the very resources they had accumulated inside the Islamic awakening. Their example opens a wide field of investigation, and shows that questioning the way fieldwork is conducted is not merely tantamount to a methodological routine of anthropological hygiene. Indeed the focus on political repentants and former activists points to the often overlooked fact that disengagement, far from being solely imputable to repression, can also be triggered by the mismanagement and subsequent exhaustion of militant and human resources.

# 4 HIZBULLAH'S WOMEN

Internal Transformation in a Social Movement and Militia

**Anne Marie Baylouny**

HOW AND WHEN DO MOVEMENTS TRANSFORM? Change in social movements has been attributed to external, structural political opportunities and to repression, generating either moderation or radicalization, respectively. Locating all change outside the movement, however, neglects large categories of change, particularly the agency of members. Even when the influence of members is acknowledged, it is still generally limited to internal political battles for control or is viewed as reflecting changes in external political opportunities. Yet factors outside political opportunities can change members' priorities for the movement and their view of their own place in it. Economic and historical factors falling outside social movement analysis can profoundly affect extant members, while new constituencies and generations can enter the movement with different ideas. Particularly in the developing world and in authoritarian countries, much mobilizing takes place within the informal, everyday realm and within movement institutions—such as social services and the media—that are not geared to formal politics. In short, Social Movement Theory (SMT) as currently formulated omits the capacity of members, in realms outside those geared to formal politics or control of the organization, to affect the movement as a whole.

In this chapter I begin the task of melding historical, gender, and everyday perspectives with SMT to delineate the dynamics of internally driven transformation within a movement. Gathering data on internal change, as opposed to externally induced change, is difficult. Witnessing debates and deliberations within a movement can be impossible for outsiders, especially in groups labeled as terrorists. With the rise of media information technology, then, a new public view of the movement is afforded for some organizations through their own media. Media can provide insight into the battles and configurations of power within a movement. Media shows who participates, giving a view of the movement's community including its peripheral and occasional adherents beyond its core, activist constituency.

Studying the gender programming on the television station al-Manar of the Lebanese Islamist group Hizbullah facilitates analysis of intramovement transformation and the factors responsible for the specific direction of this value change. Women's programming on al-Manar demonstrates a transformed vision of women and their place in the movement and in society, along with the surpassing of religion as the predominant idiom of the movement, and the abandoning of reliance on an exclusively Shiʻa and religious constituency. The debate and variety of views in talk programs on Hizbullah's television—assumed to be a propagandistic mouthpiece—yield a different picture of a movement that accommodates and even facilitates discussion beyond its core stances. These programs promote gender equality in work and housework, a diminution of male prerogative, education and careers for women, married or not, and an end to domestic violence, broadly construed. Contrary to talk shows that promote one expert opinion, these discussions focus on the audience and their ideas. The method of communication is not dictatorial but contains significant community participation, ending in no single, authoritative solution. Pushing the bounds of ideology to include the secular, the programs do not promote secularism but do actively include other religious communities and the nonreligious. Women's programming is a window into substantive movement transformation, particularly since private life—women and the family—has been considered the last domain closed to debate in Eastern and Western societies alike. Tolerance of change and diverse lifestyles within the family is a strong indicator that change has taken place.[1]

I argue that these substantive developments in Hizbullah's media are due to the central role of women in the organization. This is clear not only from the prominence of women in the media but also in shifting norms that entail changes in male roles—a situation that departs from nationalist movements' promotion of modern women for the movements' own purposes. I begin by theorizing movement transformation and value change, and the differential power of subconstituencies. I discuss prior conceptions of women in the organization and their mobilization due to war. I then introduce the media and Hizbullah, delineating how the organization has changed over time. Women's programming demonstrates the depth of this change, as it encompasses shifting boundaries of the community, changed norms for the family and for men, and an embrace of Western and specifically American concepts of rights and civil society.[2]

## MOVEMENT TRANSFORMATION AND SUBCONSTITUENCY INFLUENCE

SMT commonly ascribes movement change to external political opportunities, such as elections, or to the denial of opportunity through repression.[3] This prime role attributed to structural factors neglects agency and change from within the movement itself (Goodwin and Jasper 2004). Understanding movement transformation necessitates moving beyond political opportunities and events outside the movement to internal dynamics.

Various internal dynamics can change a movement. Movements depend on their memberships' approval, tacit or active, of their stances. While many analyses focus on leaders, other evidence indicates that members themselves have a strong role in movement direction (Wickham 2004). Organizations are subject to internal authority contests that can determine the direction of the movement (Kurzman 1996). Schwedler's (2006) comparison of two Islamist parties concludes that internal factors such as decision-making practices and leadership structure were important variables. Where members had more of a say in the group's direction, the Islamist group could evolve over time by redefining the boundaries of legitimate behavior and practice. Clark and Schwedler (2003) demonstrate that Islamist women were able to promote their own role in their organizations, taking advantage of divisions and spaces left while Islamist men were occupied with other concerns. In Hamas, the leadership actively sought member input on the trajectory of the movement through questionnaires (Mishal and Sela 2002). Ultimately members can resign in protest; over five hundred women walked out of an Algerian Islamist party en masse, declaring that the party did not listen to them.[4] More generally the literature on framing insists that movement messages and symbols resonate with the grassroots membership. Leaders must craft their messages in line with the culture and priorities of potential supporters (Snow et al. 1986; Swidler 1986).

The influence of members is recognized by SMT but is attached to the internal political battles of the movement, or is in response to changes in the formal political realm. The notion of "the political" itself must be enlarged. Much transformation occurs through both the dynamics of everyday life and member involvement in movement institutions that are not geared to formal politics. Institutions such as social services that are not aimed at elections are recognized as having a political impact, as are informal networks (Singerman 1995; Clark 2004a). These institutions affect the movement, although the overwhelming focus of research on Islamist movements has been on how such institutions aid the leaders' stated goals; research has neglected change that arises from members in these institutions. Bottom-up change can occur from realms not focused on elections or on control of the organization.

How and why the underlying priorities and preferences of the constituencies change has been analyzed as historical fact outside of the models of social movements. SMT's bias toward the formal and overtly political neglects the politics of the everyday—encompassing history, economic conditions, informal networks, and prior activism and agency to name a few areas—and the ability of these everyday politics to ultimately alter the power dynamics within movements (Bayat 2010). I link what Bayat terms the feminism of everyday life to social movement analyses in order to understand the real-life changes within a key Hizbullah institution. I argue that female members are making changes spurred by daily life within a realm that is not overtly political, the movement's media. This power results from the position of women as a key constituency supporting the organization's military roles.

Members do not all matter equally to the movement; internal power differentials exist. The specifics of whose approval matters (and when it matters), of how desires are communicated, and of how different types of members, varying external conditions, and potential constituencies affect internal movement transformation are unclear. The membership of a movement is made up of a number of subconstituencies such as youth, women, core or original members, and new members. A subconstituency's importance to the movement can be historical and symbolic, or current and either organizational or strategic. The different roles can coincide, as when a subconstituency is a symbol of the movement's founding, is integral to the daily functioning of the organization, and represents the potential for strategic alliances with other groups deemed part of the group's strategy for success. When one subconstituency holds all three roles, that group has a wider range to maneuver within the organization and can push for new points of view. To determine which groups hold such positions, a historical analysis of the movement's founding and development, along with an assessment of its current position in the political structure and its future goals, is necessary.

Women can be an important subconstituency organizationally. The organizational needs of Islamist movements to mobilize large constituencies place a premium on organizing the general population (Abdellatif and Ottaway 2007). As in other religious movements, while men are the visible face of the movement, women perform the grassroots daily functions that have built and sustained those movements (Goodwin, Jasper, and Polletta 2001). Women in Islamist organizations have been associated with increased public participation; for example, as they reached out to peasant women in Turkey (Arat 2005). Women participate in large numbers in Jordan's Islamist party (Clark 2004; Clark and Schwedler 2003), in Hamas (Cobban 2006), and in Islamist movements generally (Nachtwey and Tessler 1999).

Women in Hizbullah represent a confluence of important roles. A core constituency of the organization, women were symbolically affirmed for generating fighters by giving up their husbands and sons, and for supporting the resistance generally. Women are integral to the current daily operations of the organization. The Women's Association of Hizbullah outfits the fighters, and women run the large and prominent social services network, which generates much prestige, legitimacy, and new members. Beyond filling internal organizational needs, women are able to bridge the gap to new constituencies for the organization. Women's prominence has increased as Hizbullah has sought to institutionalize itself within the Lebanese arena—or "Lebanize"—making itself a fully national actor. Here women are a political symbol, as they often are throughout the world. Certainly in the Muslim world, in the proclamations of both Islamists and their opponents, women and the family are a central focus. For many, the vision of a veiled woman means women's oppression, and the prospect of an Islamist group being a powerful political actor in Lebanon conjures preconceived ideas regarding an Islamist lack of regard for minority and women's rights. Women are an essential part of the modernity discussion, as they have been central concerns of the West, colonizers, socialist Arab states, monarchies, leftists, and Islamists alike (Abu-Lughod 2002; Editorial: Sexuality, Suppression and the State 2004; Brand 1998; Browers 2006; Zine 2006). Lebanon is not only a country with a significant and politically involved Christian community but also one intensely tied to the West. By allowing space for contemporary and progressive women's issues to be discussed in its media, with the participation of Christian scholars, experts, and audiences, Hizbullah communicates tolerance for diverse female and minority lifestyles.

Women or other subgroups have power in a social movement when their contribution is integral to the movement. But that power is limited by threats to the organization's survival, which take precedence. The substance of this power, what it is used for, and its duration depend on the larger employment structure of society and women's integration in the movement during the protracted political struggle Gramsci terms a "war of position." Societal context, history, and economic development matter. Educated professional women able to fill roles in the movement beyond traditional or even violent ones have a reticulating effect in the Lebanese context, reinforcing the progressive stance of the organization toward women and its need to rely on and cultivate this source of support.[5]

## THE MEDIA SPHERE OF HIZBULLAH

Media programs are windows into movement debates. Arab media and the use of information technology have exploded in recent years, as has movement use of media. According to some, the proliferation of new Arab media and establishment of hundreds of new satellite stations have altered the face of Arab civil society and created a new public sphere (Lynch 2006; Anderson 2003; Eickelman and Anderson 2003). The dominant Arab television, such as al-Jazeera, is regional because national or state media is mainly censored. But there is a third type of media that is partisan or sectarian (Cochrane 2007), joining party and media. Such stations broadcast a definite point of view and do not attempt neutral journalism. Pioneered during the Lebanese Civil War, when each militia established its own media, government and opposition factions now have their own television stations. This is a growing trend. Stations of Islamist groups, sectarian groups, and militias in Iraq and Hamas are some examples. The Internet has been an especially prolific domain for sectarian messages. Younger generations of the Egyptian Muslim Brotherhood have aired their internal and sometimes politically sensitive debates on Internet blogs (Lynch 2007).

This type of television is not new; political parties worldwide own their own media. Yet the relationship between a political party and its media has not been theorized. Anshu Chatterjee (2004) shows that such television expands beyond simple transmission of the party line in order to respond to market and global competition for an audience, as do other media. In her Indian case, both the media affiliated with the local political party and that owned by the national state competed successfully with the transnational media corporations in the marketplace of ideas by providing local-language programming that focused on a wide spectrum of local issues in order to maintain their constituencies. While it does communicate a point of view, party-owned television cannot be considered simply propaganda.

Al-Manar (the beacon, or lighthouse) is the land and satellite television station of Hizbullah, an Islamist social movement, militia, political party, and participant in government. Hizbullah began its television station in 1991, broadcasting locally in Lebanon. Beginning as a "resistance media," a station linked to the fight of Hizbullah against the Israeli occupation of southern Lebanon (Jorisch 2004), al-Manar's start was politicized and religious. In May 2000 al-Manar began transmitting by satellite. It is generally available throughout the Arab world, and in Lebanon over land, but is banned in Europe and the United States. Al-Manar has bureaus and correspondents around the world, and is most famous for its coverage of Hizbullah's military operations against the Israeli army in southern Lebanon, through reporters "embedded" with Hizbullah troops. It has also been viewed as one of the new, politically independent media (Sharabi 2003). Al-Manar operates in a media environment where political media are the norm (Dajani 2006), with channels such as Future TV, the representative of Lebanon's governing coalition.

Hizbullah and its media have changed over the years. Both have become more sophisticated, addressing themselves to a broader audience not based on religious sect (Dellios 2000). This "Lebanization" process, or becoming more Lebanese than Shi'a and changing the community references accordingly, was sped up by two major events in Hizbullah's history (Harb and Leenders 2005; Alagha 2006). The first was the decision to enter the 1992 Lebanese elections as a political party, which necessitated a decision to relinquish the goal of an Islamist state. Second was the withdrawal of the Israelis from southern Lebanon in 2000, which has been viewed as causing an identity crisis for Hizbullah, since the original justification for the organization's militia was fighting Israelis in the south. The second Palestinian intifada began soon after the withdrawal of the Israelis, possibly substituting issues for the station. But the station and Hizbullah also broadened their community of reference, attempting to reach additional audiences (Hamzeh 2004; Dallal 2001). Two recent events changed al-Manar further. The 2005 removal of the Syrian army from Lebanon left Hizbullah on its own and arguably sped up the Lebanization process. Al-Manar has become critical and open to contending points of view in its cross-fire programs in order to increase its viewership and expand its support. For the same reason, interviews began to encompass all the communities and political ideologies in Lebanon.[6] This constituency broadening was partly challenged by the effects of the July 2006 war with Israel, which promoted militarization of the party and affirmed the public relations value of al-Manar to the military.

Women-centered programs have been almost completely ignored in research on the station, despite their being aired more than any single program except the news. Research has focused almost exclusively on news and spots promoting Hizbullah. Women's programs are aired nine times a week for a total of thirteen and a half hours. One women's weekly program recently celebrated its one hundredth episode. The oversight in research reflects a bias of male and (the few) female researchers alike—an assumption that these programs are pure propaganda and need not be studied, or a belief that women in an Islamist organization would surely be portrayed negatively.[7] Indeed all media in the Arab world are generally viewed as promoting a negative, traditional, and submissive view of women (Allam 2008). Even al-Jazeera is seen as promoting a traditional view of women, contrary to its promoted self-image of challenging the Arab status quo (Dabbous-Sensenig 2006). Yet women have entered the Arab public and media spheres, changing the dialogue considerably (Moghadam and Sadiqi 2006; Skalli 2006). Sakr (2004) argues that the Middle Eastern media has become more pro-female as a result of the entrance of women.

## WOMEN AND CHANGING NORMS

The substantive ideas currently depicted on Hizbullah's media represent a significant change from the organization's stand at its founding.[8] At first, women were not much dealt with except that they should adhere to what Deeb (2006) has called "authenticated Islam," the version of Islam that rejects tradition for modern religious practices and interpretation. The emphasis was on the unity of the Shi'a community, women's duty to that community, and their role in supporting fighters and producing the next generation. Motherhood and women's public demonstration of religious practices and piety were prized (Deeb 2006; Zaatari 2003). Women and men fulfilled equal but distinct complementary roles in society, and family duties were women's first priority (Firmo-Fontan 2004). During the ongoing fight with Israel, Hizbullah utilized a discourse that emphasized male military achievements or "confrontation and triumphant masculinity" (Holt 1999). The United States along with Israel were the enemies, and relations with the Lebanese Christian community were extremely poor prior to the end of the civil war, in 1990.

The progressive ideas now aired on al-Manar appear counterintuitive. Lebanese Islamist women suffer from conditions often held to decrease women's status: they are not only involved in a revolutionary organization that has engaged in warfare (promoting male fighters), but they are also Islamists. Women's pathbreaking roles in revolutionary organizations, either as combatants or major supporters, have not been lasting. While they are almost universally used in the rhetoric promoting militarization (Bayard de Volo 2004), women in conflict situations are typically seen as victims during and after war (Al-Ali 2005; Henderson and Jeydel 2007). After the Algerian revolution (Turshen 2002) and World War II in the United States, gender boundaries were not permanently affected, as women returned to their role as homemakers. Nationalist and right wing movements have prioritized the nation over women; even when women's organizations fight to assert their status, their gains have been forsaken in the name of the nation and male employment (Henderson and Jeydel 2007). In Islamist movements images of policing women's dress and conduct in public space come to mind.

War can be a catalyst for widespread changes in women's notions of their possibilities and rights, and their vision of optimal family relations. Women may take on new, transformative roles during conflict. Rights-based struggles have often come out of other struggles. For example, the US women's movement grew in part from dissatisfaction with women's status in the civil rights movement (McAdam 1995). Although such roles can alter accepted boundaries of public versus female private spheres, men typically do not regard them as threatening, since they contribute to confronting the enemy: from carrying munitions to visiting prisoners and even taking up arms. Under conditions of repression when male political opportunities are limited, women's realm for maneuver can open (Noonan 1995). In some cases the lack of men, due to death or imprisonment, has spurred women to take their place. Women are not universally peaceful. They join militias and terrorist groups (Shehadeh 1999; Ali 2005). Such political activism can be transformative (Sharoni 2001). The bravery and risks these women assume can alter perceptions, as was the case with female journalist during the war years in Lebanon (Abu-Fadil 2007). The traditional realm of women in these circumstances extends from family to community, justifying a broad realm of activism under conditions of conflict or repression that can promote alternative views of women's correct role. In some instances the role of women caretaking and improving society may continue after war, expanding their previously private-sphere duties to the public in peacetime (Bayat 2010).

The observation that popular conflict and religious mobilization can be positive for women is qualified by their employment and educational status, their position of importance within the movement, and their external references. The dynamic of expanding women's rights and self-image in a progressive direction depends on women themselves pushing the boundaries and taking advantage of opportunities in the party. Previous experiences when women did not consolidate gains from conflict may be situational rather than perennial outcomes, contingent on the ability of women to hold important (educated) positions within the organization and on their institutional importance to the organization.

I argue that Lebanese Islamist women benefited in some ways from the civil war and from their mobilization in an Islamist group. The case of Hizbullah's women confirms the conclusions of a Carnegie study that the entrance of educated women into Islamist parties is partly responsible for those parties' increasing attention to women's issues (Abdellatif and Ottaway 2007). Broad economic changes have generated many of the issues discussed here, particularly around women working outside the home (Taraki 1995).

## WOMEN'S PROGRAMS:
## PROGRESSIVE ISSUES AND INCLUSION ON AL-MANAR

Women's programming on al-Manar demonstrates value change in several areas. The view departs from that of women solely serving religion, the family, and nation, and goes beyond the promotion of "modern" women as evidence of the organization's achievements. The programs push the boundaries of maleness along with femaleness and bring the intimate sphere of the family into open debate. The programs advance individual rights for women and children, not communal ones as Islamist groups often do, and they accept international concepts of human rights. Further the community participating in the programs is multiconfessional, incorporating, physically and rhetorically, respect for different religions and ways of life. Where the United States has been viewed as anathema, here American norms and research findings are presented as authoritative, to be admired and imitated. Lastly the programs and the range of programs on the station are multivocal, not uniform, indicating that segments of Hizbullah's constituency are promoting views that other parts oppose, and that this diversity of views is being played out partly in the media.

The multiple voices on al-Manar are a significant change from Hizbullah's roots and image in the West as a monolithic and authoritarian organization. These programs tackle core issues of family and private life presenting multiple views from experts who are often not religious and not even Muslim. One women's program, *Problem and Opinion*, was previously named *Problems and Solutions* (*Mashakil wa-hulul*), demonstrating the shift to multiple voices and offering no authoritative solution. Some programs are remarkably nonideological and devoid of Hizbullah's religious rhetoric, while others present problems from a more religious and traditional point of view.

A heterogeneous, nonideological, and nonreligious community is particularly apparent in two women's programs. I recorded data on guest dress for twenty-nine episodes of one program: 57 percent of guests were unveiled women in Western dress; 11 percent were veiled; and 33 percent were men. Often the only one veiled on stage was the hostess. Seven percent were religious leaders; they appeared particularly during programs whose content, such as adoption, men contributing to housework, societal restrictions and stereotypes of divorced women, and violence in the family, pushed the boundaries. A substantial number of the unveiled women and many men were Christian, which was apparent either from their names or language use. Some were unable to express concepts except in French, or peppered their language with French words (in one case a professor could hardly speak Arabic but kept speaking in French while the hostess translated). The audience and callers mirror this pattern. Audiences for one program were half nonveiled. (In these programs audience, callers, and participants were predominantly although not entirely female.) In *Problem and Opinion* a skit is acted out to illustrate the problem for that week, presented by a viewer. The skits demonstrate veiled and nonveiled women, depending on the week. In another example a Christian man brought a problem to the station, indicating that different religious communities participate in all capacities on al-Manar; they also turn to this Shi'a station for help.

Religious solutions and interpretations were marginalized. Hostesses would ignore (the very few) comments coming from the audience or callers that religious practices were the solution. In one case an audience member stated that memorizing the Qur'an was a solution to the day's question, which focused on raising the self-esteem and confidence of all family members (*Wujhat nazr*, 10/7/07). The hostess cut him off and did not repeat the question to the guest when the latter had failed to hear the question. "Never mind," she stated, and moved on to ask the guests another question. During the same show, a caller attempted to remind the audience of the need to confront Israel and of the needs of the nation, and the hostess cut him off. Despite the occasional presence of sheikhs on the programs and more often their call-in opinion at the end of the show, religion itself was almost completely absent as a solution, and then the interpretation was ecumenical.

Women are substantially present in al-Manar, not only in the audiences mentioned above but also in its journalistic work (Abu-Fadil 2007; Firmo-Fontan 2004). Women host thirteen out of twenty-four programs, and two more that have both male and female hosts. They are not present merely for appearance but are hard-hitting and assertive, interrupting and cutting off guests and callers, including sheikhs. A woman is the face of Hizbullah's international English language program. The two women's weekly programs demonstrate views, such as questioning marriage itself, that are sometimes an extreme, progressive departure, certainly from traditional standards but even from many in Western countries. The programs promote a more equitable distribution of responsibility and tasks among all family members. This includes more responsibility for men in sharing housework, from chores to childcare. The subject of one program was care of the house, and men's role in it (*Wujhat nazr*, 3/13/08). The assumption was that women work outside the home. The audience, mainly men, protested. One man stated that he works all day and comes home tired. The hostess responded, "OK, your wife works outside the home all day too, and then comes home and works inside the house. Do you see the problem here?" The sheikh stopped short of demanding that men help out but asserted that they should, and that this is religiously approved. Similarly where a stepmother is involved, it is the man's responsibility to be aware of what occurs between his new wife and his children. If they are oppressed, it is his duty to protect them (*Wujhat nazr*, 4/24/08). This issue also demonstrates a new spin on an old problem, placing duties on the husband in the old situation of combined families.

Outside work for women is seen not only as economically necessary but also as fulfillment for a woman, an outlet for her own separate source of self-esteem. No longer does a woman just marry and have children; now she should not marry unless she has a profession and diploma in hand. When a woman had a problem with her rebellious children, the first thing the guest experts wanted to know was whether she had her own life and her own work (*Mushkila wa-rai'*, 2/4/08). The woman could be feeling empty and unfulfilled and be placing her life expectations onto the children, and that is negative. Promotional spots show girls at the computer, and suggest that a girl's future could be as a doctor and that she should be encouraged. In the midst of news coverage commemorating the third anniversary of the historic (for Hizbullah) March 8, 2005, demonstration, which coincided with International Women's Day, the news "shed light on different examples of women." It began with a profile on a woman running her own photography studio with her husband. "They say behind every great man is a woman, but what if next to every successful woman is a successful man who encourages her as she does for him." Her husband taught her photography, and he stated that she was now better than he. Another working woman's situation was different: her husband died, but like the other woman, said the narrator, she did not give up. "I am everything to my kids. . . . Just because my husband died doesn't mean my life is over." The social and legal rules have changed regarding women's work, the narrator stated, easing women's access to work.

Domestic abuse by fathers was the subject of a segment of another program (*Mushkila wa-rai'*, 7/7/08). This demonstrated the consciousness of traditional practices being out of line with the rest of the world; the acknowledgment of the patriarchal system, but not the acceptance of it; changed economic prospects for women and the family; and information globalization as a solution. The woman, a thirty-year-old Yemeni teacher who had not married in order to help support her family, was being beaten along with her sisters by her father. The woman turned to the Internet to write and ask for help from al-Manar in Lebanon. She could not take it anymore, she wrote; even knowing that society taught her father these behaviors, she was a university-educated woman and could not tolerate the lack of respect. She could not stand a society where "the word of the father is all and a mother has no opinion."

The acceptability of women remaining unmarried is a departure from traditional and religious views of women. An episode called "Women Under the 'Microscope'" focused on the treatment of divorced women (*Mushkila wa-rai'*, 4/14/08). Divorced women are looked at disrespectfully, treated differently, and assumed to be easy or willing to marry anyone. "This woman has paid the price," the sheikh said, "and has twice been oppressed, by her husband and now her family." In another case a thirty-five-year-old woman refused all proposals for marriage and wondered what was wrong with her (*Mushkila wa-rai'*, 3/17/08). She was a professional and supported her family. The host stated that this situation is increasingly common. As men migrate and women become more educated and enter professions, women's demands of men change. No longer do fathers tell women what to do; this is no longer allowed. The advice of the guests was both essentialist and progressive. On the one hand, she was taking the role of a man, the guest stated, and there cannot be two men in the family; on the other, the guests affirmed her ability to live this life and the acceptability of her staying unmarried. The sheikh, consulted by phone, proclaimed that if she was happy, she did not need to marry. Partners in marriage need to share, each bringing some important capital—emotional, material, or intellectual—to the marriage, he stated. Girls unfortunately are raised to believe that their goal in life is marriage, and that life ends with it. Girls live without freedom, waiting for marriage, a view he argued against. This woman was mature and conscious, and could make her own life choices.

The appropriateness of diverse lifestyles is viewed as relative to the family's or the community's lifestyle. On one program guests stated that they had heard of fathers staying home and mothers going to work. How that would work would depend on the particular family. Styles of female dress, quite controversial, were judged relative to their surroundings. In a discussion of rape it was mentioned that some people attribute rape to a woman's dress style. The guest responded that this is a sensitive topic, and some people could feel she was provocative if she dressed a certain way; however, if one lives in a country where women dress that way, people should get used to it and understand that it is not provocative.

The reputed xenophobia of Hizbullah, or at least its animosity to the United States, is not evident in these programs. American scientific studies are used as proof and to demonstrate points. Western countries are lauded for their safe houses for battered women, their creativity-inspiring education, and the strong role of civil society. Hostesses discuss needing to "think outside the box"—stated in English and translated into Arabic—and the importance of "quality time." Arab education is derided and compared negatively to education in the West, which encourages free thinking. In one program discussing spanking, a caller decried the discussion of alternatives, saying that especially at this time of cultural onslaught Easterners and Lebanese should stick to their culture. He was completely ignored by the women in the audience and the hostess, who simply moved on with their discussion. The audience, veiled and nonveiled, Christian and Muslim, working and stay-at-home mothers, all agreed they should find alternatives to spanking but were frustrated as to how they could still discipline their children. This demonstrates a consensus on ideas also becoming the standard for the international Western world. And "quality time" was again discussed in the context of mixing work with family care.

In addition to domestic violence, other violent situations in daily life were presented as serious problems. Violence against children, and teachers hitting students, were portrayed as wrong. One program for youth discussed the list of human rights for children, showing UN posters of children's rights (*Taht al-'ashrin*, 4/11/08). Violence portrayed in video games was another problem, particularly since the way to win the game was to kill. This was a value the women's program did not want imparted to children (*Mushkila wa-rai'*, 7/21/08).

Embracing Western solutions and norms for numerous daily life issues does not translate into protest against Hizbullah's militia or its foreign policy. Rather, women's use of Western studies, idioms, knowledge, and experts suggests a distinction between opposition to Western foreign policy and opposition to everything Western. The two can and do coexist in numerous societies, as women eschew violence in their personal lives but partake in war, even supporting patriotic aggression. While support for progressive women's rights can coexist with support for an aggressive foreign policy, the foreign policy concerns or threats take precedence. In times of foreign crisis or during religious events, all programming is preempted, marginalizing coverage of women's issue. Threats to the movement generate a retreat and prioritization of the military, pushing all other discussion and debate to the sidelines until the crisis ends.

Furthermore not all programs within Hizbullah's media align with these views. Programs such as *To the Heart* (*Ila al-qalb*) present a religious view of family and personal life. This spectrum of views on the media is a sign of openness to multiple constituencies, while attempting to maintain the old ones. Space is afforded for diverse segments of Hizbullah supporters and potential supporters. According to Firmo-Fontan (2004), many watch al-Manar selectively for particular programs. For some segments of al-Manar's audience the difference between religious or political programs and women's programs is not a contradiction. For others, particularly nonreligious viewers or those from other religious communities, the women's programming is distinct from Hizbullah's view of the news.

The variety of voices on the station is not unlimited; it is arguably affected by self-censorship, a situation comparable to that observed in Western media. Callers using insulting language toward a person are cut off; in other cases the caller's position, if contrary to the program, is ignored. No statements crossing the line of disagreement with Hizbullah itself as an organization were witnessed. This could be because of the high degree of approval of Hizbullah in Lebanon or the nonparticipation in the television shows of those in disagreement. In the case of the 2005 elections al-Manar broadcast a series ("Word to the Nation") in which civil society leaders were asked their opinion on Hizbullah's militia. Some voiced disapproval of the militia; most did not. However, some voiced other misgivings about the organization.

## CONCLUSION

The dynamics of internal movement transformation can illuminate core changes in organizations. The views aired on Hizbullah's women's television programs are nontraditional and in some cases overtly opposed to inherited patriarchal norms. While Hizbullah's view of women generally could be characterized as more progressive than the views of many groups, states, and media in the Arab world, women are going beyond this on the television station, challenging male privilege. They deploy a rights-based discourse that is individual, not communal; that is, elevating the priorities of the individual above those of the community. Solutions to problems, when offered at all, are multicommunal and multivocal, suggesting an openness to diverse lifestyles. Violence in daily life and society is eschewed.

The concerns of the subconstituency of women have changed. Middle-class and working women's concerns are apparent in these programs. Some women in the organization, having lost a husband to military battles, are now single mothers supporting families; wage work is necessary. As a result of their increased entrance into the workforce and professions, women have encountered barriers to full inclusion and have experienced the double standard enjoyed by men, particularly in the home. They believe that Islam does not endorse this double standard, as many are believers and have fought in an Islamist organization. Women are crucial parts of the organization, both on the logistical support level in outfitting fighters, and increasingly in the performance of professional tasks in Hizbullah's media. Women have taken advantage of their importance and pushed the boundaries. Clerics have conceded their points or have at least not contradicted them on these programs.

Gender programs reveal a different side to Hizbullah regarding international affairs as well, embracing as they do global information and the use of American studies as positive examples. The progressive gender ideas and the use of the West as a role model for civil society do not translate into nonviolence in foreign policy. Domestic and societal nonviolence coexist easily with a foreign policy of fear and belligerence toward the enemy. Indeed foreign policy concerns set such movements as Hizbullah off from the usual social movement cases. The sense of external threat and the fear of attack strongly influence the direction of programming, creating tension and even halting the sphere of debate and exploration of domestic and social issues. The result is not the civil society imagined by the West, although it may hold many of the same values as the West. Hizbullah's programming is inclusive, creating alliances and expanding the community instead of limiting the community to Shi'is. While it is attractive to other communities as progressive and participatory, the framework of a religious party and militia remains.

**MOBILIZING FOR RIGHTS**

# Part 2

# 5 THREE DECADES OF HUMAN RIGHTS ACTIVISM IN THE MIDDLE EAST AND NORTH AFRICA

An Ambiguous Balance Sheet

## Joe Stork

DURING THE 1970S AND 1980S human rights, as a cause distinct from partisan political agendas, became a rallying point of opposition to dictatorships allied with the United States in Central and South America, having great effect in delegitimizing those governments as well as Washington's support for them. The principal Middle East instance was Iran's 1978–79 revolution. Human rights activism also played a substantial part in the demise of communist rule in the Soviet Union and Eastern Europe and similarly contributed to the rise of a global human rights agenda.

In the 1980s and 1990s some opposition political activists in the Middle East and North Africa concluded that their goals of far-reaching political change might best be advanced by embracing the framework of human rights. Participants and observers alike often refer to these activists and the organizations they have established as a movement. However, it is not clear to what extent the phenomenon constitutes a social movement, even where activism has been operational for years. Moreover despite the universalism claimed by the discourse of human rights, the activities, constituencies, and focus of human rights work in various countries, and even within countries, are quite differentiated.

Organizations and networks of human rights advocates nevertheless do have a social movement dimension consistent with some of the expectations of Social Movement Theory. Perhaps most saliently, they have succeeded in reframing the political discourse of both secular and religious oppositional forces, as well as incumbent regimes. Susan Waltz, writing over a decade ago, referred to the emergence of human rights "as a master frame of social protest" (1995, 160).[1] The United Nations-based human rights covenants, conventions, and mechanisms have been the primary framing resources for human rights activists in the region.[2]

In the countries discussed here—Bahrain, Egypt, Morocco, and Turkey— the leading activists have access to resources. They are professionals who have skills, financial security, and jobs, such as lawyering and teaching, that permit them to devote time and money to the cause. The organizations they lead have collaborative and sometimes contentious relationships with local political parties and trade unions as well as international rights organizations.

In many cases these activists can access funds from foreign governments and foundations. International human rights organizations like Amnesty International and Human Rights Watch have collaborated with groups in the region, and Amnesty has had local chapters in several countries.[3] In Turkey the local Helsinki Citizens Assembly has been a major player in the human rights movement.[4] While not without its problematic aspects locally, this international dimension augments the social movement claims and aspirations of Middle Eastern and North African actors (An-Naim 2000, 2001).

With the exception of Turkey and to a lesser extent Morocco, political participation in these countries is restricted and the options for organized and effective opposition political parties remain extremely limited. However, there is great diversity in state responses to human rights discourse across the region and over time. The ubiquity of this discourse leads us to ask whether human rights activism did not merely respond to "political opportunities" but actively played a role in producing political openings. And why has the frame of human rights and its associated repertoire of contention been more effective in some authoritarian states than others?

Most governments in the region have been actively hostile to human rights organizations, particularly when their activities go beyond trainings and they attempt to monitor violations and hold local authorities accountable. Egypt and Bahrain have association laws that greatly restrict the autonomy of NGOs; those that do not officially register or are not allowed to do so remain vulnerable to harassment and even closure. Morocco's law is more reasonable, requiring simple notification, but local officials often subvert it in practice by refusing to provide the receipt that proves a group has satisfied this condition. Human rights activists in Turkey, particularly those working on issues in the heavily Kurdish areas, have been the targets of official harassment and deadly assaults by shadowy vigilante elements having possible links to the state.

In Bahrain and Morocco networks of local rights activists have impacted state human rights practices and demonstrated a capacity to withstand state hostility. How well they may withstand state strategies of co-optation and marginalization is an open question. These networks share some similarities in recent political history—most obviously the scenario of a harsh and repressive regime of a ruler-father giving way to reforms by a ruler-son. More significant structurally, perhaps, is that human rights activism first took root among families and comrades of persons persecuted by the ancien régime—arbitrarily arrested, commonly tortured, forcibly exiled (Bahrain) or "disappeared" (Morocco). Organizations and sustained campaigns drew support from émigré and exile compatriots. In Bahrain a sense of widespread and institutionalized discrimination against the majority Shi'a community has given human rights activism there great resonance among that community, while many Sunnis view human rights as merely a sectarian concern. In both countries, the main organizations have relied on their leading activists for leadership staffing and core financial support and have been relatively less dependent on outside funding.

In Turkey rights activism also emerged out of campaigns by relatives and comrades of political prisoners aimed at combating widespread torture in detention. The movement there shares many structural features with those of Morocco and Bahrain. The governing Justice and Development Party (AKP), with its conservative, Islamic orientation, has been receptive to many human rights concerns. Nonetheless human rights activism appears not to have had the same impact on society and politics as in Morocco and Bahrain, perhaps because rights activism in Turkey has been complicated by the armed conflict in the mainly Kurdish-populated southeast between the state and the Partiya Karkaren-e Kurdistan (PKK).

Many activists regard that conflict as Turkey's premier human rights problem, and Kurds have been prominent in the largest organizations' leadership. Consequently, for many Turks the rights movement reflects a pro-Kurdish agenda. Yet Turkey has Mazlum-Der, one of the very few organizations in the region dedicated to promoting human rights among observant Muslims. There are also rights groups working on behalf of the sizable Alevi minority, and recently a growing movement on behalf of lesbian and gay rights. And Turkey, like Egypt, Morocco, and Bahrain, has a range of activists and groups promoting women's rights. Turkish rights groups have benefited from government liberalization regarding freedom of association as a result of pressures from the EU.

Egypt has numerous human rights organizations. But paradoxically their activities do not appear to constitute a social movement. Human rights activism in Egypt did not emerge out of prisoner solidarity networks. Instead leftist students and journalists, especially members of the Communist Workers' Party, initiated rights-based activism in response to state repression of political and labor militants, many of them still holding leading organizational positions. Neil Hicks observes "a disequilibrium between the high receptivity of international bodies to various types of advocacy, campaigning, and promotion of human rights in Egypt on the one hand, and the low capacity of domestic structures in Egypt to channel this energy into constructive pressure for human rights change on the other. As a result, too often, foreign pressure became counterproductive and was used to discredit the domestic human rights movement" (2006, 79).

Would-be social movement entrepreneurs in Egypt have been unable to build a movement despite their access to resources. The increased number of activists in human rights groups after two decades of work reflects more an entrepreneurship in response to the availability of foreign funding than the political demands and moral support of society. Despite access to resources, and a political opening in 2004–06 that continues in an attenuated form, the frame of human rights has not attracted a base of popular support in Egypt, although both the government and much of the media have adopted human rights discourse and framing.

The following discussions by country draw mainly from interviews over the past several years with key human rights activists in Bahrain, Egypt, Morocco, and Turkey.[5] They reflect on the impact of rights activism on political parties, government practices, legislative reforms, and the media; on intersections with other movements; and on the varied organizational forms that this activism has taken.

## BAHRAIN

Bahraini rights activism emerged from the crucible of struggle between the state and leftist and Islamist opposition forces. Before Bahrain's formal independence, in 1971, (illegal) parties and trade unions issued political and economic demands reflecting their communist and Arab nationalist backgrounds. Awareness of human rights as an issue developed after 1975, when the ruling Al Khalifa family shut the partially elected parliament, suspended electoral and due process provisions of the constitution, and imprisoned or drove into exile left-nationalist opponents. Repression intensified in 1981, when the authorities uncovered a plot by pro-Iranian Islamists to supplant the Al Khalifa with a theocratic state.

Extreme repression left no space for political participation. After the 1990–91 Gulf War, the limited liberalization in Kuwait's political order inspired a broadly based Bahraini "petition movement" calling for restoring the constitution and parliamentary elections. The Shi'a community also demonstrated against unemployment and social inequity. In late 1994 continual clashes erupted between security forces and street protesters in Shi'a neighborhoods. This "intifada" continued until 1999, when Shaykh Hamad succeeded his father and undertook substantial reforms that partially responded to human rights demands of the opposition (Human Rights Watch 1997).

The petition movement and the intifada deployed the language of human rights extensively, reflecting the prominence of this discourse among political exiles. One exponent was Abdulnabi Alekry, who later worked closely with the Bahrain Human Rights Society (BHRS), the first independent human rights group to acquire legal recognition (in June 2001). In the mid-1970s he was an exiled member of the Popular Front for the Liberation of Bahrain.[6] There he "was responsible for following the cases of those arrested in different parts of the Gulf—in Kuwait, Bahrain, the [United Arab] Emirates, Oman. We had only two channels: Amnesty International and the International Committee of the Red Cross. I didn't consider this my number one job, and at that time I was not aware of the potential of human rights."[7]

In the late 1970s Alekry moved to Beirut, but the 1982 Israeli invasion of Lebanon forced him to evacuate to Damascus, where the rival National Front for the Liberation of Bahrain was based. "For the first time the exiled [leftist] opposition was together in one place. We established jointly the Committee for the Defense of Human Rights in Bahrain, but it was very difficult [to operate] from Syria. One comrade had asylum in Denmark, so they applied for and received permission to operate in Copenhagen. This facilitated networking with international rights groups. By contrast, repression in Syria and other Arab countries made it difficult to communicate with like-minded activist elsewhere in the Arab world."

Alekry acknowledges that the political tradition from which he emerged "didn't have much use for human rights." In Beirut and Damascus he had access to international rights groups. "There was the need to address the problem of the detainees, more than solidarity statements from political organizations. I don't say that everybody in the front was convinced of the utility of [my human rights focus], but they said, OK, you want to work on this, go ahead."

For Alekry this work "gave a human rights dimension to the uprising. We made links with the lawyers [in Bahrain] who took the cases and made dossiers on Security Court cases. Some [lawyers] would come outside; we'd meet and collect information that we'd take to international venues." Alekry is certain that the human rights movement "contributed to the change in policy, when Shaykh Hamad took over in 1999, that enabled us to come back home [in 2001]."

Another key Bahraini human rights activist, Abdul-Hadi al-Khawaja, left Bahrain in the late 1970s to study; he could not return because of his political association with the Islamic Front for the Liberation of Bahrain. When the government arrested hundreds of Islamic Front supporters in 1981, al-Khawaja and others started the Committee to Defend Political Prisoners in Bahrain. "We took the issue of detention and torture. We had lots of details. Then we took the families who were deported because of their Persian origin. But we couldn't work independently because the Islamic Front is a political organization. We wanted to take cases of all prisoners, not only the Islamic Front. We thought having an independent organization was essential, while the Islamic Front saw the committee as part of the organization, serving its agenda. Through our work with the UN and Amnesty and other organizations, we became more familiar with human rights mechanisms and [in 1989–90] we started the Bahrain Human Rights Organization."[8] The BHRO received training in human rights monitoring standards from the Danish Center for Human Rights. "From Copenhagen the BHRO played an effective role during [Bahrain's] intifada in the 1990s, advocating for human rights on an international level."[9] After al-Khawaja returned to Bahrain in 2001, the BHRO became the Bahrain Center for Human Rights (BCHR).

For al-Khawaja the genesis of human rights activism out of work around political prisoners was not surprising. "It's the common ground between political activism and human rights. When we think, how can we defend them when we can't act locally—the only way is to use human rights mechanisms and speak about it internationally."

When al-Khawaja and others tried to register the BCHR, the authorities at first refused, claiming it would "duplicate" the work of the BHRS. Some BHRS leaders were content with this favoritism, a stance that Alekry, who worked closely with the BHRS, contested. The authorities finally did extend recognition. But in September 2004 the government closed the center and confiscated its assets after al-Khawaja publicly criticized the prime minister for corruption and human rights abuses and called on him to resign. The BCHR remains illegal, and its most active members are routinely harassed; but it continues to operate.

The proliferation of Bahraini groups adopting a rights framework reflects an organizing strategy that encourages sector-specific committees. Today there are committees of the unemployed, of families of martyrs and victims of torture, the Bahrain Youth Society for Human Rights, and so on. These committees mostly articulate the grievances of the Shi'a, especially around issues of discrimination.

In Bahrain government arrests of leading rights activists—usually for criticism of high officials or holding a demonstration without permission—have prompted sizable public demonstrations demanding their release. Bahrain may be the one country, al-Khawaja said, "where human rights is a little bit popular." This reflects the highly polarized character of Bahraini society, and the success of Shi'a activists in mobilizing their community around human rights demands.

The strategy of mobilizing using a human rights frame in the 1990s led to concrete improvements after 2001. "When we speak about real political reforms, I don't think we're there yet," al-Khawaja said. "But today the human rights situation is very different. We don't have systematic torture; there are not large numbers in exile or in jail. We as activists have some means to defend and protect ourselves. We annoy the government by pressuring them, but when they try to do something they have to think about the international reaction and the internal reaction. It wasn't the same in the old days."[10] At the same time, he said, "[regional] governments have more experience in dealing with these organizations, how to penetrate them, establish GONGOs [government-controlled NGOs]."

Al-Khawaja also observed that governments and political movements try to exploit "the differences between human rights as a culture and Islam. There are some differences, and some people try to focus on these differences with an agenda of separating people from human rights." For example, "When the family law question came up, people started finding differences. We campaigned to introduce the CEDAW [Convention for the Elimination of Discrimination Against Women] to show people, yes, there are some differences, not minor, but few. Most rights do not clash with Islam. We succeeded, especially with the women Islamists. When it comes to civil and political rights, they don't see any differences. The activists—be they Islamists or secularists or leftists—all speak about human rights."

Al-Khawaja acknowledges that the BCHR is a rare example of a human rights group emerging out of an Islamist political movement. "I don't meet many others when I attend regional conferences. As an Islamist, I do my prayers, and some of my Arab colleagues are surprised. A human rights activist doing his prayers! This is something not very familiar." This reflects, in his view, a regrettable detachment of human rights activists from society at large. "We're supposed to be working with the people, to know their problems. But how many of us are really connected with people on the ground? How can you inform people about human rights and defend them if you don't have real relations with them. [Colleagues] used to look at our Bahrain experience as special. 'Not everything you do in Bahrain can be done in our countries,' they say. I don't know. I see the mission of the human rights movement to be social change, and the dissemination of a human rights culture. It's not enough to speak about human rights in the press, or go to the United Nations. It's about changing peoples' way of thinking. Here we rely on international support and popular support. If you don't have the popular support, how can you confront the political authorities? If people don't move to defend themselves, how can you make change? I know the human rights movement isn't necessarily a popular movement, but if you are not well-connected with the people, you can't do the work, you can't make the change."

The future of human rights activism in Bahrain is far from assured, al-Khawaja feels. Hundreds of people have gone through trainings, but "we don't see people monitoring trials, or demonstrations. Not many are engaged in daily human rights work. The popular committees are . . . engaged, a few hundred—but these are not the ones with training. The people who are working on the ground need training, while the people who are trained need experience. The university is a forbidden zone for human rights as well as political activity."

Abdulnabi Alekry agreed that the popular committees distinguish Bahrain's human rights activism, and he cites the Committee for Martyrs and Victims of Torture, the Committee for the Homeless, and the Committee of the Unemployed. "They are linked together and they insist on demonstrations and protests, even though there are a lot of risks. There is strong solidarity among those people who feel they are discriminated against, marginalized, their basic rights denied. This network is there. And they see that pressure works—to get Abdul-Hadi released [from detention], for instance."

Bahrain's organizations depend very little on foreign funding. Groups with legal standing, like the BHRS, receive free office space from the state, for instance. Others, like the BCHR, depend on the time and financial resources of the most active members. Both organizations are members of the International Federation for Human Rights (FIDH).

## EGYPT

Israel's invasion of Lebanon and siege of Beirut in 1982 prompted human rights to take organizational form in Egypt. Saad Eddin Ibrahim recalled how Arab governments failed to come to the defense of besieged Palestinians. When Ibrahim and others organized a peaceful demonstration outside Cairo's al-Azhar mosque, he later wrote, "We were brutally beaten and dispersed. To compound the pain, the only public Arab demonstration allowed at the time was in [Algiers] not over the fall of Beirut, but to protest a Belgian referee's unfair ruling vis-à-vis the Algerian football team in the Mondiale [World Cup] that year. And to compound the irony, a half million Israeli demonstrators marched in the streets of Tel Aviv protesting the aggression of their own government against Lebanon" (Ibrahim 2003).[11]

Hani Shukrallah had been a student activist in the 1970s. For him the global developments of the 1970s and 1980s led to an "epistemological break with dogmatic leftist thinking. I started to see how democracy and human rights were essential for human emancipation—which was the reason I had been a Marxist in the first place."[12] Shukrallah and Ibrahim were among the founders of the Egyptian Organization for Human Rights (EOHR) in April 1985. "At that time the human rights movement was really an outsider," said Shukrallah. "The existence of the movement was put in question not just by the government but by the intellectual and political elites, including the political parties, legal and illegal." The EOHR founders were a disparate group, united in aspirations but having little concrete knowledge about how to go about the work. "The aim of course was a more humane society, but what human rights work involves—there was no grasp of these issues," said Muhammad al-Sayyid Sa'id, another EOHR founding member. "No one had any experience collecting information, checking the quality of testimony, while advocacy was very rhetorical and general."[13]

The government refused to register the EOHR as a legal entity, almost ending the effort before it began. Many on its first board, discouraged and feeling threatened by the failure to gain legal standing, urged that the organization disband. Bahey el-Din Hassan, then a journalist at *al-Gumhuriyya*, an official government daily, insisted that a human rights group worthy of the name had to stand up for its own right to exist. The board responded by appointing Hassan as secretary-general. Sa'id recalled it a bit differently: "We formed an executive group by default at that point, and were elected only later to the board."

A second moment of crisis turned into opportunity came in August 1989, when workers occupied the large state-owned Iron and Steel Company in Helwan. Security forces stormed the plant, killing one worker, injuring a hundred, and arresting hundreds more (Posusney 1997, 161). "We didn't have much staff then, so we rotated monitoring responsibilities, and the Helwan workers came up on my watch," Sa'id said. "We started getting lots of complaints that we had to check out. A number of us were arrested, including myself, and Hisham Mubarak."[14] Sa'id, Mubarak, and another EOHR board member, lawyer Amir Salim, were detained for several weeks and tortured (Rodley 2007).[15]

The Helwan strike experience also broadened human rights activism beyond the EOHR. Kamal 'Abbas was among those arrested and tortured. Several months later he became one of the founders of the Center for Trade Union and Workers Services (CTUWS), in Helwan. Aida Seif al-Dawla, who later helped to launch the Nadim Center for the Rehabilitation of Victims of Violence, recalled the iron and steel workers' strike, and the torture inflicted on Sa'id, Mubarak, and 'Abbas, as "what got me into human rights work."[16] Amnesty International had a chapter in Egypt at that time; Amnesty's "own country" rule meant that Egyptian members could not address Egyptian violations directly. But the chapter's existence contributed to the human rights "conversation" prompted by Helwan.

The activists who laid the foundations of human rights activities in Egypt had previously mostly been associated with (often illegal) parties of the left, energized by the 1970s' student movement. Bahey el-Din Hassan, Muhammad al-Sayyid Sa'id, Hisham Mubarak, and others had been active in the Communist Workers' Party, which the government smashed in the early 1980s. Some leftist parties saw the EOHR as territory to conquer. "The left underground tried to jump on whatever avenues were left open," recalled Amal 'Abd al-Hadi, an early activist with the EOHR and later director of the New Woman Center. "They jumped on the Cairo Cinema Club, for instance, issuing statements about this and that—everything except cinema! When the EOHR began confronting the government, the left saw this as a new forum to take over."[17] The EOHR board instituted a rule that prominent party leaders could not have decision-making roles in the organization.

Still, Bahey el-Din Hassan rejects the view that human rights groups were initiated only because these parties went into decline. "I don't entirely agree. The failure of the parties had been evident for a while, and those who supported human rights had left a while before. There wasn't a direct link between the decline of the parties and the move to human rights, and human rights was never a cover for political activity. Every day that goes by their political motivations count for less and less and human rights ideals are the governing factor."[18] Muhammad al-Sayyid Sa'id concurs: "To be frank, most of us were not really Nasserists or Marxists any more. We had these roots, but we no longer defined ourselves that way." But Sa'id acknowledged that human rights did engage in political activity, even if not linked to a particular party. In 1994 Sa'id and Hassan left the EOHR and started the Cairo Institute for Human Rights Studies. "The more important human rights work is to actually have an initiative to restructure society and really democratize," Sa'id said.

Politics can influence how a human rights organization shapes itself. One model involves a large and active membership that sets policies and priorities. Such organizations typically rely on members as volunteers to carry out their work. Another organizational model emphasizes a paid staff having professional skills in monitoring, advocacy, and provision of services like legal aid. In practice, given limited human and other resources, most organizations find themselves developing in one or the other direction. This structural issue precipitated and reflected major struggles inside the EOHR.

Bahey el-Din Hassan recalled that after he became EOHR secretary-general in 1988, the organization amended its bylaws to state that international standards constituted the sole reference for determining human rights violations and remedies. "We preempted all proposals to include other sources, like the Egyptian constitution," he said. But clarifying the EOHR's mission did not foreclose struggles among political factions to control the group.[19] Differences came to a head at a general assembly of the EOHR in 1994, when Nasserists within the leadership of the organization recruited other members of the party to join and ensure the election of a pro-Nasserist board.

A number of Islamists were EOHR members in the early 1990s, mainly key figures from the Muslim Brotherhood and lawyers who represented detained members of armed groups like Islamic Jihad and the Jama'a al-Islamiyya. They competed for seats on the board, but the core activists kept them at arm's length. "We didn't welcome them as board members because we witnessed their efforts to gain hegemony in several syndicates," Hassan recalls. "We would have worried about information we received from them. If we receive it as representatives of victims, we check it. But if we receive it as a rights staffer, this is something else." This concern about possible manipulation had some basis, another activist said. "Armed Islamists, when they did an operation would [immediately] send . . . a press release to the human rights groups so that the rights groups would come and do field research on the government crackdown and report on that."[20]

But Islamists were key to the growth of the movement in one important way: they were the primary victims of state abuses. "The government abuses of the Islamists were so much greater [than Islamist abuses of others], so they gained on balance from human rights reporting," Gamal Eid said. An American activist who lived in Egypt at the time recalled that the Islamists "realized they were getting a better deal using organizations [like EOHR] that weren't tainted by Islamist associations, rather than trying to build Islamist human rights organizations that the state would just crack down on anyway."[21]

Bahey el-Din Hassan said the EOHR "advocated all the time for the rights of individuals, including suspects from these [armed Islamist] groups, but condemned their acts very strongly." These were the years when Islamists assassinated secularist writer Farag Foda, and their threats forced Nawwal El Saadawi and Nasr Hamid Abu Zayd to flee the country. "I remember receiving threats from their lawyers at the same time they were asking us to defend them," said Hassan. "They rejected the [human rights] discourse but recognized it had [positive] implications for them." Muhammad al-Sayyid Sa'id said it was "never a question" of not addressing state violence against Islamists, "to the point where the police accused us of complicity with the terrorists. We defended [the Islamists], we attacked them. It looked funny but it was honest human rights work."

The EOHR was a key source of public information on the major crisis in Egypt in the 1990s: the Islamist insurgency and the government crackdown. "This was the first time that we had detailed reports about the situation in prison, torture in police stations," one journalist recalled. "Both the opposition press and the state press were discredited. There was no serious investigative journalism. EOHR was a source of reliable information that didn't exist at that time on these human rights issues."[22] President Mubarak indirectly confirmed the importance of the EOHR when he complained that "most of these [international] human rights organizations abroad get their information from a so-called human rights organization here, which is controlled by members of the former [Nasser] regime, and is stacked with people from the Muslim Brotherhood" (Weaver 2000, 166). Bahey el-Din Hassan recalled that in 1994 Osama al-Baz, a top adviser to President Mubarak, arranged a meeting with the human rights groups only to tell them that if they wanted to solve their problems with the government, they had to "stop, totally stop, our work on the 'Islamic terrorists.'"

Egyptian rights activists remain concerned about how to persuade Islamists to adopt a human rights culture. The Cairo Institute for Human Rights Studies sought to "bridge the gap between the dominant culture in the region and international [human rights] principles. Islam is the main component of this culture."[23] Muslim Brothers and other Islamists participate in most of the institute's seminars and working groups, he said. "This doesn't mean that human rights organizations have illusions about the Muslim Brotherhood's agenda or their commitment to human rights, or the added value of the so-called new Islamic discourse. I'm afraid the discourse has been the main development," said Hassan.

Ahmad Sayf, a defense lawyer who had been imprisoned and tortured on account of his leftist political activities, heads the Hisham Mubarak Law Center, which has taken up cases as wide-ranging as insurgent labor leaders, Islamists, and men charged with "depravity" for consensual sex with other men. In his view the major accomplishment of Egyptian rights activists is that human rights are now inextricably on the agendas of the state, political parties, the growing independent media, and the Islamist opposition. "There is a social consensus against torture," he said. "Ten years ago, Communists would say, secretly, it doesn't matter if Islamists are tortured, and Islamists would say, why not torture Communists. Today you don't hear this from anyone."[24] But he added that it is individuals, not political groups, who are committed to human rights. In the Muslim Brotherhood, he said, the leadership and midlevel cadres are staunchly conservative, "but among the young members we can see something happening. The Internet has played a role, promoting freedom of expression."

When the EOHR began, recalled Hani Shukrallah, Islamists regarded human rights advocacy as "the adversary." "It's not that [today] they have genuinely accepted human rights, but they deal with it without feeling the need to attack it." Muhammad al-Sayyid Sa'id recalled, "In the 1970s, women's education was a major issue for Egyptian Islamists; now not at all. Work, yes, but not education. You have to look long term, and work to entrench new values." Amal 'Abd al-Hadi sees movement also but cautions that "the human rights movement in Egypt will never be a popular movement; there are too many things working against that—women's rights, freedom of belief." Abdullahi An-Naim (2001, 721), discussing the Egyptian government's refusal for many years to grant legal recognition to many human rights groups, observed that "the ability of these organizations to operate openly in the country all this time clearly indicates a level of acceptance and credibility at the practical level."

Several activists summed up the state of human rights activism in Egypt today as a paradox. On the plus side, human rights has become an inescapable frame of reference for the media and political parties. The government also,— "[e]ven as it has taken steps to systematically eliminate an independent local human rights movement . . . has been moving forward with programs that create a formal place for international human rights norms within governmental activities" (Hicks 2006, 87).[25] The authorities recently prosecuted police officers for torture, and the number of persons arbitrarily detained under the emergency law has dropped from more than fifteen thousand to less than five thousand over the past several years, in part thanks to the work of the human rights groups. Nonetheless systemic problems remain, such as the emergency law and the stifled right of association. "Even press freedom, the most notable achievement, is relative and reversible," observed Bahey el-Din Hassan.

## MOROCCO

The human rights movement in Morocco emerged out of the activism of families of political prisoners in the late 1970s. In the view of Susan Slyomovics (2002, 216), prison experiences were formative and prison-writing "underpins current human-rights activism" in Morocco. Driss al-Yazami, a Moroccan rights activist who now sits on the official Advisory Council for Human Rights, gives particular credit to the families of the prisoners. "The prisoners themselves were mainly Marxists then, and for them human rights was a bourgeois issue," he recalls.[26] "But the mothers and sisters organized demonstrations, went to the UN office in Rabat, went to the universities, talking about the prisoners' hunger strikes—many of the prisoners then were students."

A second component of the movement was the lawyers, Moroccan and European, who came to observe trials and conduct fact-finding missions. The European lawyers who came to defend prisoners' rights were often themselves affiliated with ultraleft parties, complicating what was then a reflexive leftist dismissal of human rights.

The third component was Moroccans abroad, in France, Belgium, and the Netherlands, who were affiliated with the same political factions as their compatriots in Morocco. According to Larbi Maâninou, one of the students who formed the Association de Défense des Droits de l'Homme au Maroc (ASDHOM) in Paris in 1985, most of those who were prominent in the human rights organizations came from radical left tendencies. "We were surprised to see ourselves talking about individual rights, and all that it implies about the need for the state to establish structures and rules," he said. "This globalization of human rights was subconscious. We needed to get our people out of prison and free from torture, and we didn't have any language except sacrifice and martyrdom."[27]

Al-Yazami was also a student in France in the 1970s. Because of his activism around migrant worker issues, he was expelled in 1975. On his return to Morocco authorities arrested him and held him incommunicado for three months. His brother was active in the Ila al-Amam underground Marxist group. After his release, al-Yazami agreed to hide one of the group's leaders for a year. When his brother and others were arrested, he escaped and returned to France, in 1978, and received political asylum. His time in prison was a turning point. "I knew there was lots of repression in Morocco, but to spend these three months in an unknown place, blindfolded and shackled twenty-four hours a day, seeing people who were in there for ten years. After they're finished with you, you are two persons."

This was when mothers and sisters of the political prisoners began their activities. In France al-Yazami and others set up solidarity committees for individual prisoners in Morocco. This involved regular contact with Amnesty and other groups. "For me it was clear, at least since 1979, that human rights was a strategic matter that had to be independent from the political parties, working on concrete issues, and in the proper way," he recalled. "When you've been one year living underground in Casablanca it's easy to see we had no network in Morocco. I was helped by the French teachers in Casablanca. That was my main network."

One of the first Moroccan human rights organizations was the Association Marocain des Droits de l'Homme (AMDH), established in 1979.[28] By the mid-1980s, thanks to the synergy of Moroccan activists in Morocco and Europe and the attention of international organizations like Amnesty International, human rights had become a domestic and foreign relations problem for Hassan II. However, the political affiliations of many activists, and the competition of the leftist parties for hegemony over the organizations, meant that the visibility of the human rights issue was not matched by professional competence. Infighting between adherents of the Union Socialiste des Forces Populaires (USFP) and those to its left led to a period of paralysis in the mid-1980s. Some Socialists left the AMDH and formed the Organization Marocain des Droits de l'Homme (OMDH) in 1988.

The AMDH is membership-based, having branches in many parts of the country, while the OMDH's organizational presence is limited to major cities (Waltz 1995, 164–65).[29] As one OMDH founder, Abdelaziz Nouaydi, put it, "the AMDH believes that the fight for human rights should not be the work of the elite but has to mobilize the masses. The OMDH made another choice, to mobilize people who can give something to the movement—expertise, money, time."[30]

In May 1990 King Hassan II established the Consultative Council on Human Rights (CCDH) in order to "complete the state of law and to put an end to the critiques of the human rights situation in Morocco" (Nouaydi 2000, 5).[31]

The palace retained control of the mandate, methods, and membership of the CCDH—even of those "independents" who were not themselves state officials.[32] The king took further but similarly cautious steps to "close the books" on decades of human rights horrors by amending the preamble to the constitution in 1992 to "reaffirm" the kingdom's "attachment to human rights *as they are universally recognized*" (Slyomovics 2005, 31, emphasis added). "The king realized that the old way of ruling was no longer possible," said Sion Assidon, who was imprisoned from 1972 to 1984 for publishing leaflets and newspapers. "His objective was the survival of the monarchy, and for that he needed to make peace with his old opposition in order to confront the new opposition—the Islamists."[33] Around 1992, officials suggested that the state had razed Tazmamart, perhaps Morocco's most notorious dungeon, an unacknowledged and illegal detention site where prisoners had been "disappeared" in some cases for several decades.[34] In 1999 the CCDH issued a report that for the first time acknowledged the phenomenon of enforced "disappearances" but "in effect would reduce 40 years of authoritarianism to a list of 112 cases" (Vairel 2008, 233).

Mohamed VI succeeded his father in July 1999 and a month later set up a panel within the CCDH to determine compensation to victims (or their surviving families) who had been forcibly "disappeared" or arbitrarily detained (Human Rights Watch 2004, 9–14). In response, in November 1999 former political prisoners (some of them now human rights activists well aware of previous efforts of this sort in Chile and Argentina) established the Moroccan Forum for Truth and Equity (Vairel 2008). Slyomovics (2005, 29–32) characterizes the forum's first executive committee of ten men and three women as "a microcosm of the postcolonial history of mass political trials and forcible disappearances." In late 2002 the palace restructured the CCDH, enhancing its powers and independence and recruiting longtime former political prisoner Driss Benzekri as the secretary-general.

In 2003 the CCDH proposed establishing an Equity and Reconciliation Commission (ERC) to produce a historical record of official repression between 1959 and 1999; in January 2004 the king agreed (Vairel 2008, 212). The ERC mandate prevented it from naming perpetrators, thereby limiting its ability to address directly widespread impunity. This limitation was publicly challenged by victims and their families at several of the hearings (Vairel 2008, 238; Waltz and Benstead 2006, 181). Still, this was by far the most serious effort anywhere in the region to recognize and make amends for grave human rights violations.[35] The ERC had at least two signal achievements. First, the state formally acknowledged to the victims its responsibility for their unlawful arrest, forcible disappearance, and torture. As former prisoner Fatna el-Bouih put it, "I advocate for real truth and justice to be put in place for all. I personally am not greatly interested in trials. I can forgive if I know *la yatakarraru hadha* [never this again]" (quoted in Slyomovics 2005, 33). Second was the extensive reparations program to individual victims of repression and their families and to larger communities. Susan Slyomovics (2009, 97) documented this phenomenon and concluded,

> What might appear as top-down, state-imposed indemnification arrangements intersected with vibrant Moroccan grassroots movements that managed over time to enlarge the pool of potential claimants, earn them the label of "victim," achieve some monetary demands, and insist on larger moral considerations (e.g., improved countrywide structural developments and institutional transparency).

During this same period Morocco's Islamists entered the human rights arena organizationally, with groups like the Moroccan Center for Human Rights and Karama (Dignity), which has links to the Justice and Development Party (PJD). As with their leftist predecessors, prisoners were the catalyst. Abdellah Laamari, himself among seventy-one Islamists imprisoned in 1984 for "thought crimes" (Group 71) and subsequently a defense counsel in trials of Islamists, put it this way: "Political prisoners are like wood. When they start to burn, the machinery of human rights turns."[36]

Al-Yazami's assessment of Morocco's human rights movement is mixed. In Rabat and Casablanca there are numerous human rights organizations. "And it's more democratic than in many other countries in the region," he claimed, pointing to elections and rotating leadership. "After twenty years it's mostly the same players, but you have a real civil society in the country today, with thousands of small NGOs working in villages, working on human rights, even though they are not talking about human rights." Mustafa Soleih, who was active for years with Amnesty International's Morocco branch and now does human rights training workshops around the country, agrees: "If there is a success here today, it is in small towns. Most city meetings draw maybe a dozen, but protests in small towns get lots of people out."[37] The attraction may be the lack of alternative outlets of activity rather than the human rights cause, but it is a growing phenomenon. Sion Assidon pointed out that human rights groups like the AMDH sparked widespread organized activism around issues like the cost of living and microcredit availability.

The problem, in al-Yazami's view, is that people lack skills. "They know about the international covenants, but they can't manage a budget." The challenge, he added, is to establish coherence. He and others see women's organizations like the Association Democratique des Femmes du Maroc (ADFM) as the exception. Their organizational and political competence was reflected in the way they implemented a decision to establish a national platform comprising some seven hundred national and local NGOs linking urban areas and small rural towns to implement the revised family code issued in 2004. Adala, which works on issues relating to the independence of the judiciary and other matters relating to the administration of justice, also stands out for its professionalism.

Human rights improvements since the 1990s have been uneven and qualified: newspapers have grown bolder in criticizing government policies, but journalists are still jailed for stories judged to "disrespect" the king, and the Western Sahara remains a "red line"; the new family code has been promulgated, but its implementation and enforcement have been partial. Morocco's chief distinction in the region is that the state's efforts to "close the books" on the era of fierce repression set in train a dynamic that compelled it to acknowledge many severe violations for which it was responsible. When King Hassan II created the CCDH in 1990, he declared that its mandate was to "put an end to allegations . . . [in order] to close this dossier" (Human Rights Watch 2004, 11). Eight years later the council issued a first, tentative acknowledgment of 112 "disappearances." The king then gave the Advisory Council the impossible task of devising a plan to resolve all outstanding human rights issues within six months. The council published its report in April 1999. Human rights groups as well as families of the "disappeared" quickly derided its claim to have "closed the file" on this horrific abuse, claiming that there were at least six hundred actual cases of "disappearance," many of which they had documented themselves.

The Advisory Council proved to be only the first in a series of still-evolving steps by the authorities to address past human rights crimes. Between 1999 and July 2003 the Arbitration Panel created by King Mohamed VI paid out nearly four thousand claims. In addition, entire regions, such as the region around Tazmamart, received reparations in the form of development projects and infrastructural investments. Moroccan civil society pressed on, leading the palace to set up the Equity and Reconciliation Commission (ERC) and instruct it to make "recommendations and proposals for breaking once and for all with the practices of the past . . . and restoring and reinforcing confidence in the rule of law and respect for human rights."[38] The ERC held hearings throughout the country, many of them televised. It also established a website for receiving complaints and discussing different approaches to resolving those complaints. These efforts continued until the ERC issued its final report at the end of 2005.[39]

There were two significant shortcomings to the process as it has unfolded. First, human rights activists were not able to make the issue of torture—which was pervasive and remains a serious problem—part of an accountability agenda, although the ERC did include torture as one of a number of criteria in determining the amount of compensation. This is quite unlike the situation in Bahrain, Egypt, and Turkey, where authorities have frustrated efforts at promoting accountability but where torture has been central to the debate. In Assidon's view, one factor may be that torture affected so many thousands of Moroccans, beyond the universe of opposition political activists who suffered long-term detention and forcible "disappearance," that it represented a constituency the palace was keen to neutralize as an opposition. The king was less willing to see the door of accountability opened, since it went beyond the political actors he was most determined to co-opt. Assidon recounted that after he and other political prisoners escaped from a hospital, the authorities rounded up and tortured the nurses, who were not implicated in the escape. "For their trouble, [the authorities] got five or six different versions of how we got out, but it also gives you an idea of how many victims there are."

The other shortcoming in the process is that until now the state has refused to countenance any steps for holding accountable those individuals responsible for systematic violations and atrocities. The ERC's final report tried to push the envelope: one of its major recommendations was to adopt and implement a "national strategy to combat impunity" that is based on international standards. But to date the authorities have taken no steps to follow up on this recommendation. The Moroccan state, like others in the region, continues to pose as the authoritative voice on the state of human rights in the kingdom, most recently with the appointment of Ahmed Herzenni, a former leftist political prisoner having no particular record of human rights activism, as head of the CCDH, on the death of Driss Benzekri.

What remains unique in the region is the way Morocco's human rights community—the formal organizations, the surviving victims and the families of victims, and the fledgling human rights activists among Islamists—has leveraged the king's initial gestures into an expanding and deepening (though still incomplete) process of public reckoning, of compensation for a terrible record of abuse. Accountability, however, remains unaddressed.

Moroccan human rights activists, particularly women, have also left their mark in another area, not explored in this chapter; namely, reform of family and personal status law.

## TURKEY

The human rights movement in Turkey also emerged from efforts of families and political comrades to address mass arrests and widespread torture of prisoners following the September 1980 military coup d'état. In the subsequent four years, more than 178,000 persons were detained, of whom 64,000 were charged and 42,000 convicted. Three-quarters of those arrested were leftists, and many of the rest were "separatists"—Kurds, that is (Pope and Pope 1997, 152–53). Murat Belge, a prominent literary critic and rights activist, who did jail time in the 1970s, explained: "The prisons in the 1980s were horrid. My experience was a summer camp in comparison. Clearly the military decided they would break the dissidents, even if the cost was wasting a generation or two."[40] He and others discussed the need for an organization "above and outside" the political groups to raise these issues with the public and the authorities. After one of the radical groups, Dev-Sol, co-opted this idea and set up their own "families of victims" group, Belge recalled that he and others suggested an organization oriented to human rights generally, not just to prison conditions. The result, in 1986, was the Human Rights Association (IHD). The organization was officially registered, but authorities objected to a sentence in its statement of purpose that said the organization was established to defend human rights. "The state objected, saying the government was already defending human rights," recalled Yusuf Alataş, a defense lawyer who joined the IHD board in 1989 and later headed the organization. "They made us take that sentence out."[41]

Human rights remain highly politicized in Turkey. According to one activist, in the IHD's early years, at least, the Istanbul chapter was "serious and nonpartisan," but the Ankara branch "chose to play the more orthodox left game." The Diyarbakir branch "was basically a front for the PKK," and "there was nothing Istanbul could do about it." In 1990 the Human Rights Foundation emerged out of the IHD, focusing solely on torture issues—documentation and rehabilitation—and opening offices in several major cities. In 1991 Mazlum-Der (short for Human Rights and Solidarity with the Oppressed) emerged, bringing a devout Muslim dimension to the human rights mix. Yılmaz Ensaroğlu, president of Mazlum-Der for many years, had been arrested in 1980. At the time, he was associated with a right-wing religious organization. "After September 12 [1980], anyone with political ideas was put in jail," he said. "They focused on me because of the articles I wrote in our journal."[42]

Turkey's security services and nationalist media quickly targeted the IHD as an adversary. Particularly in Diyarbakir and other predominantly Kurdish areas, persons thought to be operating on behalf of the security services assaulted and assassinated IHD leaders with impunity. At one time or another most of its branches were forcibly closed. According to Hüsnü Öndül, a founder of the IHD who served as its president from 1999 to 2004 and again after September 2007, in recent years "we have seen a heavy legal, judicial repression rather than physical."[43] As of September 2007, he said, fourteen IHD leaders had received jail terms.

Öndül was a young lawyer "with Marxist opinions" at the time of the 1981 military coup and immediately began defending political detainees. "To be very honest, my personal objective was not purely advancing human rights when this movement began. All of us who established the movement were dissidents, leftists. Human rights was one more means of fighting the state. This is how I used to think." Eventually, he said, he developed a more "objective assessment; we realized it was not only leftists who were persecuted by the state."

Öndül sees human rights priorities in Turkey as twofold. First, "there is the issue of peace. This means the Kurdish issue." Second is the need to reform the constitutional system imposed by the military after the 1980 coup. He urged the governing Justice and Development Party (AKP) to address this. Judicial independence is a particular priority. "The judges and prosecutors who have internalized human rights can be put in key positions in critical cities." He also saw some support coming from Turkey's bourgeoisie: "It took them a while, but at the end of the day they saw the connection between democracy and selling more shirts," alluding to the EU accession process. "Turkish society is more advanced than their rulers. People's awareness about their rights has developed a lot compared to ten or twenty years ago, a result of the human rights groups and the EU process."

The armed conflict in the southeast makes Turkey one of those places—like Israel and Palestine, and Iraq—where human rights groups had also to address international humanitarian law (or laws of war) violations. According to Öndül, the IHD decided in October 1992 that it would hold the warring parties to Common Article 3 of the Geneva Conventions, which prohibits torture and summary executions, among other things, for armed groups as well as states. This was controversial in the membership. Yusuf Alataş, a defense attorney,

IHD board member, and a Kurd, said, "When the Kurdish question erupted, we realized that most leftists [in the IHD] were [Turkish] nationalists."[44] In any case, the IHD's initiative may have been one factor that prompted the PKK to claim that it abides by the Geneva principles. The state, however, wanted the IHD to label the PKK as terrorists, and interpreted the group's refusal to do so as an indication of support for the PKK.

Mazlum-Der, like the IHD, also took on issues of arbitrary detention and torture but prides itself as the one human rights organization promoting freedom of religion. The organization has been involved in the campaign against the ban on women wearing headscarves in universities and other public institutions. It also promoted legislation to protect the property rights of Armenian, Greek, and Jewish religious foundations as well as Muslim ones.

Both the IHD and Mazlum-Der are membership organizations and depend on members' volunteer labor; they have branches in cities around the country. Each struggles against dismissive public perceptions of them as Kurdish or Islamist, respectively. Some rights activists see this as reflecting a gap between the leadership and the base. In both cases, said one, "the leadership understands the problem [of public perception], but the membership is still forcing them to act on political grounds."[45] Their areas of influence are limited, outside of Istanbul and Ankara, to a few regions. The most active branches are in the (heavily Kurdish) southeast. In the west, in central Anatolia, and in the Black Sea region, the human rights groups have little if any presence.

A freedom-of-expression campaign triggered by the January 1995 indictment of prominent novelist Yaşar Kemal, after he criticized the state's policies towards Kurds, may be the most impressive display of the social movement aspect of human rights in Turkey. The campaign engaged the established groups but originated with writers and publishers, who published and republished manifestos and books that violated laws prohibiting "insults" of the state, the judiciary, the military, and so forth. By the end of 2002 the campaign had engaged nearly eighty thousand persons, according to Şanar Yurdatapan, one if its founders.[46] Another instance is the campaign featuring silent demonstrations by mothers and other relatives of persons "disappeared" by security agencies.[47]

## HUMAN RIGHTS IN THE MIDDLE EAST: A SOCIAL MOVEMENT?

This review of four countries having a significant human rights organizational presence and history indicates that there is no precise or uniform answer to the question. Morocco's human rights community has perhaps the strongest claim to being "part of a large social movement" (Slyomovics 2005, 203–4). It has had notable achievements in the key areas of state accountability and family law reform, and seems to have impact outside the main cities. In Bahrain, the case is less clear. Rights activists constitute a highly visible part of a fragmented oppositional political society. In Bahrain and in Morocco, human rights activism emerged out of political-prisoner solidarity and defense networks. These shared origins seem to have lent both movements a relatively high degree of organizational coherence. Although Turkey's human rights movement also grew out of political-prisoner solidarity activism, the impact and social movement status of human rights organizations there is less discernable.

Egyptian human rights groups enjoy less social resonance or political weight than that of groups in Bahrain or Morocco. Unclear is the extent to which this derives from more effective state suppression of civic associational life. Of these four countries only Egypt has no human rights organization with ties to communities of practicing Muslims. However, Egypt's independent print media and the pan-Arab satellite channels regularly and conspicuously use human rights framing in their reporting, reflecting a social impact that makes organizations more dispensable as framing agents.

All four states publicly proclaim to support human rights. But actual policies in Bahrain and Egypt are quite inimical to freedom of association for human rights or any civic organizations. National human rights commissions are now global phenomena, and UN experts have developed protocols (the "Paris Principles") setting out standards for their independence and effectiveness. Morocco and Egypt have such commissions; Morocco's has had far more impact. The Turkish government reportedly drafted legislation to establish an official human rights council.[48] In early 2010 Bahrain announced the establishment of an official National Human Rights Institution, but the extent to which it will function independently of the government remains to be seen.

Some activists in Egypt and in Morocco have agreed to serve on their national human rights commissions; others refuse to have anything to do with them. In Bahrain very few were asked by the government to do so. From initial appearances, Bahrain's national institution will likely resemble Egypt's, where it is an instrument for establishing state hegemony over the interpretation of its human rights record: many Egyptian rights activists have shunned it for that reason. However, to maintain any measure of credibility, the Egyptian commission's reports have had to officially confirm the prevalence of torture, for instance. The commission secretariat also takes up, and sometimes resolves satisfactorily, individual cases and grievances with the Ministry of Interior, and has also operated where there is some division in ruling circles to promote certain rights—a recent example being full citizenship rights for adherents of the Baha'i faith (Cardenas and Flibbert 2005; Stacher 2005).

Finally, as Quintan Wiktorowicz (2004, 17) observes, "[s]ocial movements . . . are embedded in a field of multiple actors that often vie for framing hegemony." Hanny Megally, an Egyptian who has worked with a number of major international rights organizations, sums up the challenge as "the perception that human rights is a foreign concept and that their activism lacks support and legitimacy in the region" (Megally 2006, 107). In the countries discussed here, the most significant framing competition is between the state and Islamic activism, broadly understood. In Bahrain, Morocco, and Turkey, some Islamists have become engaged as human rights proponents. In Egypt, the Muslim Brotherhood has adopted human rights framing for its own purposes. But no Egyptian human rights organization has emerged with a project of explicitly fusing international human rights standards and Islamic values, although the Cairo Institute for Human Rights Studies has devoted considerable resources to hosting discussions and debates that bring together prominent Islamist thinkers and Arab human rights activists from across the region and beyond.

States have consistently posed the most intractable challenge to human rights, articulating, when it suits them to do so, an "Islamic values" argument, but equally often framing human rights claims as affronts to national sovereignty—an argument that resonates in societies that perceive themselves to be under religious, cultural, and national assault (for example, Egypt on the Palestinian issue). States also use national security to dismiss human rights concerns, arguing that threats to security override concerns for human rights. One might say this is the trump card in the regional states' repertoire of framing devices.

# 6 UNEMPLOYED MOROCCAN UNIVERSITY GRADUATES AND STRATEGIES FOR "APOLITICAL" MOBILIZATION

## Montserrat Emperador Badimon

THE DYNAMICS OF COLLECTIVE ACTION represent a classic polemic in the sociology of social movements, particularly concerning the life cycle of collective action: its emergence, development, and decline. Here I focus on the practical reality of collective action in social movements. This includes the organizational structure and practices, as well as their relationship to the life-cycle stage of a social movement. My analysis of these dynamics flows from a series of questions: How does a contentious actor frame its public discourse? Which conditions inform the actor's strategies? These questions become especially critical in a repressive setting like Morocco, where the considerations informing contenders' tactical and organizational choices are crucial due to the high risk associated with involvement in social movements. In a setting where participation in a collective action can trigger violent police reactions or public defamation, considering variables that take into account relational and pragmatic dimensions is integral to understanding the shape of a given social movement.

In Morocco since the early 1990s, unemployed undergraduates, graduates, and postgraduates have been engaging in protests to demand employment in the civil service. Groups formed by holders of high school diplomas and bachelor's, master's, and doctoral degrees often seize public spaces as a form of protest. They are commonly known as *diplômés chômeurs*.[1] When collective recruitments to public sector posts are announced, these groups quickly disappear. Within these groups divisions stemming from differences in educational attainment overlap with different styles of contentious activity and uneven institutionalization trajectories. Street demonstrations have become the most common activity of unemployed graduates and take up most of their time. Since these groups do not have legal status, they are treated by law enforcement agencies as unauthorized organizations and are very often subjected to repression. During the first years of mobilization, in the early 1990s, the threat of detentions and torture was very real for activists. Nonetheless the number of contentious *diplômés chômeurs'* groups has continued to increase in Rabat.

Certain features specific to the mobilization of the Moroccan unemployed have become standard: (1) a closed-shop system classifies adherents according to their commitment, using a scoring system in nominal lists that are used during negotiations with authorities. When a recruitment agreement is achieved between the protesters and the public decision makers, jobs are distributed according to members' rankings; (2) the framing discourse focuses on the right to a job and the notion of the unemployed as a priori victims; and (3) the unemployed are detached from political markers. These features of "limited action" became even more prominent during the February 20th pro-democracy movement of 2011 organized by a coalition known as the "Freedom and Democracy Platform" and named for the date of its first national march. The unemployed graduates sought to clearly differentiate their actions from those of the February 20th movement by "going out in the street" before or after pro-democracy rallies, occupying different spaces in the town or, whenever the action implied a momentary union, distinguishing themselves by visible elements (colored jackets, exhibiting their diplomas, and so forth).

Unemployed graduates' tactical choices, infused with a normative sense of righteousness, constitute temporary criteria for positioning oneself within the space of mobilization (Mathieu 2004) in interaction with other groups and the public authorities. The final incarnation of the group depends on activists' profiles and the perceptions they hold about the feasibility of protest and the opportunities for success. During the time of my research most of the groups I monitored had reached a consensus on an "apolitical," pragmatically oriented, and self-limiting style of contention.

The choices underlying methods of protest, as well as the interactions between activists and state actors or other contentious actors, are standard topics in Social Movement Theory (SMT). Here I propose an explanatory framework based on empirically grounded variables: activist memories, their representations of politics (and therefore their definitions of collective interest and its virtuous expression), and perceptions of the coercive setting (and therefore the "rationality" and efficacy of proposals). These variables arise from my fieldwork and form a framework that allows us to understand the particular way activists execute their struggle. A relational element should also be considered; for instance, the insertion of mobilization into a multisector society (Dobry 1983), which could contribute to the modification of perceptions of actors and thus impact their calculations. Thinking in terms of a relational dimension and activist memories might allow us to grapple with the shifting nature of rules and the a priori "transgressions" of normative conventions. This reasoning also allows us to overcome the trap of perceiving only a normative resistance/collaboration binary within social movements, which can confuse our perception of the practices and interactions between contentious actors and authority figures.

My research addresses both empirical and epistemological issues arising from this framework. Why do mobilizations of the unemployed manifest themselves in these particular ways, and how do they vary? In this chapter I first elaborate on the landscape of the *diplômés chômeurs* mobilizations. Second, I address the specific features of collective action among the Moroccan unemployed. Third, I introduce an explanatory framework elaborating on the strategies and practical choices for protest among unemployed graduates. I will try to discover the relationship between my variables—the memory of the challenges and opportunities of contentious action, and the concept of mobilization in a multisector space—and "specific" features of the movement, namely, scoring systems, political detachment, and demonstrations as the most common activities.

## LABOR MARKETS UNDER NEOLIBERAL RESTRUCTURING

According to Maghraoui (2002, 25), since its independence in 1956 Morocco has had three cycles of economic restructuring. After a period of monetary stabilization (1965 to 1983), a structural adjustment program conceived by the International Monetary Fund was implemented between 1983 and 1992, followed by a program of *mise à niveau* (or upgrading) that was intended to restructure Moroccan firms to increase their capacity and competitiveness in preparation for free trade with Europe. Similar economic restructuring processes occurred in Algeria, Tunisia, Egypt, Jordan, Kuwait, Lebanon, Syria, and Yemen during the 1990s. Since the beginning of the 1980s, "most paths of autonomous national development adopted by African regimes have been undermined, the global economic crisis has deepened and mounting debts have driven governments to seek external flows of capital" (Seddon and Zeilig 2005, 16). Importantly the reasons behind these reforms may not have been exclusively economic.

Structural adjustment programs "typically involved privatisation, an end to subsidies and price controls, and the lowering of trade barriers" (Maghraoui 2002, 26). As Karen Pfeifer (1999, 25) shows for Tunisia, Morocco, Egypt, and Jordan, adjustment reforms "always exacerbate unemployment and poverty because reductions in public spending and anti-inflation efforts induce economic recessions." Morocco's labor force shrank during the most intensive period of adjustment, 1988–92. Ultimately the reforms aim to substitute the previous principal recruiter of labor—the state—with private investment, which it is claimed will provide new job opportunities. Consequently from 1982 to 1983 public sector hiring dropped from fifty thousand to five thousand recruits a year (Akesbi 2003). In the following years job creation gradually increased and stabilized, though it has never reached the levels of the 1970s. There was a secular increase in unemployment rates for university graduates (who had previously benefited the most from jobs in the public sector), from 6.5 percent in 1982 to 26 percent in 1991, 43 percent in 1997, and 40 percent in 2002.[2] The newly "unburdened" state (Hibou 1998) was charged primarily with management responsibilities, while the private sector was supposed to become the largest job provider. However, this ambition was never realized, and consequently the number of unemployed, especially graduates, increased (Mellakh 1999).

The adjustment programs sought to "remove general subsidies for commodities like basic foods, fuel and transportation" (Pfeifer 1999, 26). The effects of these policies "fell disproportionately on the popular classes" (Seddon and Zeilig 2005, 16), who protested against the social consequences of the reforms. This was the broad economic context in which the first initiatives calling for a "return" of the state as a primary employer appeared. They followed the 1983 and 1984 bread riots and the 1991 general strike. Increasing political tension permeated the country with the historical opposition led by the Union Socialiste des Forces Populaires (USFP), which represented the voice of popular discontent. The regime soon proffered the possibility of institutional change, which would later materialize in the 1998 government of Alternance—the nomination of a historic leader of the socialist opposition to the regime as prime minister, involving no power sharing between the king and his opposition.

## CLASSICAL EXPLANATIONS OF COLLECTIVE ACTION OF THE UNEMPLOYED

Classical SMT might a priori appear to be an interesting tool for analyzing unemployment as a rallying factor in sustainable collective action. In this theoretical framework the onset of mobilization is linked to a framing of issues through the prism of injustice (Snow and Benford 1988) by experienced movement entrepreneurs (McCarthy and Zald 1987). The formation and reproduction of groups is further encouraged by incipient political liberalization (McAdam 1988) and through the existence of ties linking activists together even before their employment status has changed (Oberschall 1973; Diani and McAdam 2003).

Unlike previous generations, when a diploma used to guarantee almost automatic employment (Ibaaquil 1999), during the period of structural adjustment the graduates of mass public universities were suddenly confronted with the contraction of the labor market. This exacerbated an already volatile situation triggered by the simultaneous reduction in public expenditures. In an attempt to avoid criticism of this new policy and curry favor with the middle class (Saaf 1999; Bouderbala 2003), King Hassan II created the National Council of Youth and the Future (Conseil national de la jeunesse et de l'avenir, or CNJA). The role of the institution was to quantify the problem and explore the possibilities of employment for university graduates. The public eruption of the crisis created a "window of opportunity" (Gamson and Meyer 1996) for initiatives associated with the unemployment problem. How can it be theoretically determined whether the establishment of the CNJA was an actual threat or an opportunity? Its creation could also be interpreted as limiting the problem-formulation process to a restricted space composed of public authorities and scholars. Following this logic, I interpret the first organized protests as a reaction to the hijacking of this issue by the state (Goldstone and Tilly 2001).

The pioneers of the Moroccan unemployed movement were former activists from university student unions and clandestine leftist organizations who also faced unemployment at the end of their university education. Some were former political prisoners, whose previous activism rendered them suspect for state authorities. By the end of the 1980s many questioned the viability of revolutionary ideology as a suitable form of social and political mobilization. Decades of repression, combined with the ascendance of Islamists in the academic arena, necessitated the reevaluation of activists' practices regarding new contentious issues (Vairel 2005a). The first association of unemployed diploma-holders, the National Association of Unemployed Graduates of Morocco (al-Jama'iyya al-wataniyya li'l-hamilay al-shahadat al-mu'attalin, or ANDCM [the French acronym]), was founded in 1991. Activists' expertise garnered from previous run-ins with the state facilitated the institutionalization of the group.

However, previous experiences also act as counterexamples for the organization of a new cause. Therefore this new cause prides itself on being detached from traditional politics and shies away from explicit ideological references and alliances with political groups. The framing of the "right to work" is based on a powerful notion of graduates having the right to a job in the public sector. The image of the diploma as a channel for social promotion has been solidly anchored in the collective imaginary and used to orient education-related choices

(Mellakh 1999; Vermeren 2002). However, the persistence of the issue of unemployment without a solution on the horizon renders "graduates' right to work" dubious as an acceptable symbolic frame. The recurrence of collective action has stimulated a dynamic of discrediting (by politicians, journalists, and so on), which requires actors to permanently justify their movement.[3] But despite the erosion of graduates' self-representation, the number of groups continues to increase, and they are engaging in ever-more visible protest activities.[4]

The reception of the ANDCM by the political elite can be interpreted in several ways. I argue that institutional changes emerging at the beginning of the 1990s stimulated collective action. The constitutional reforms of 1992 and 1996 offered a semblance of a political opening, sanctioned by the negotiation of the 1998 government of Alternance between the Palace and the parties of the National Movement, and by the amnesty of political prisoners. The possible change of governmental élites will likely affect the evolution of the *diplômés chômeurs* cause: opposition parties welcomed the initiative of the unemployed, seeking to renew their links with the rank and file and recruit new members in the context of increasing opportunities for parties to play a role in public affairs.

The institutionalization of the international regime of human rights (Feliu 2004) goes along with a growing tolerance vis-à-vis the development of associations (Roque 2001; Desrues and Moyano 2001). However, grassroots associations are possible only when they do not call into question authority's fundamental interests (Tozy 1994). The ANDCM will never be authorized, and the lack of official recognition "justifies" repressive and calculated measures on the part of the government—although this does not exclude the possibility of negotiations. Always illegal, demonstrations are subject to relatively unpredictable police intervention and management. Moments of tolerance by security forces are linked to activists' self-censorship. Selective incentives, in an Olsonian sense—such as a closed-shop system allocating a certain number of points for participation in each protest action, and ranking group members according to their "activist" involvement—and social sanctions, such as loss of friendship or respect, seek to alleviate uncertainty about the efficacy of personal commitment. Other factors offer better explanations of mobilization in the face of inherent risk: activist memories of constraints, experiences of previous successes, and the mutual shaping of perceptions of the feasible and the effective.

By "activist memory" I refer to the accumulation of experiences of constraints, opportunities, and general perceptions regarding the political field. Memories serve either as a repository of skills required to carry out collective action or as a transmission channel of perceptions allowing actors to calculate the pertinence of their actions. They also channel a certain representation of politics and the virtuous defense of collective interests. Activists take all of these elements into consideration as they plan their actions. Memories take on a life of their own by transformative events, which have a major effect on the construction of perceptions. Thus a wave of collective job recruitments consolidates the idea that the mobilization is an effective way to obtain a professional job. Alternatively arbitrary repression introduces uncertainty, which renders a previous notion of efficacy relative. These elements also explain why one tactical choice is prioritized over the other in an ostensibly static context.

## BUILDING A "PROFESSIONAL" MOBILIZATION

Beginning in September 2006, when I started fieldwork, unemployed groups of *chômeurs* holding master's and doctoral degrees carried out demonstrations up to four or five times per week in Rabat over a period of two years. Between five hundred and one thousand people participated in each action. In villages and small towns with ANDCM sections, protest activities tallied a higher number of participants, although public decision makers did not seem very attentive to protesters' claims. Are the *diplômés chômeurs* devoted to the cause that ties them together? A pragmatic explanation for their ties appears more suitable: activists are linked to the group by strict rules of involvement that "force" them to participate actively; failing to do that runs the risk of punishment because participation in assemblies, demonstrations, and press conferences is rewarded with points that determine eligibility for jobs during negotiations with authorities.

Reducing free riding is not the only objective of this point system. The system is also a form of standardization that aims to simplify participation because it reduces the need for creative involvement. Technical difficulties associated with group creation are minimized when it takes place within the cycle of mobilization. For example, the statutes might be copied from a previous group; or "migrant" activists (who might have been excluded from previous groups) might bring their organizational expertise to the new structure. But are these selective incentives (Olson 1971) systematically adopted?

Activists' official justification for action and mobilization is not ambiguous: the impossibility of achieving valuable professional employment through academic capital renders contention the "unique" alternative for those who do not possess "personal" connections (*piston* or *wasta*, as activists say in French or Moroccan Arabic). Graduates' "protest vocation" originates with the experience of unemployment—a very urgent experience since it implies an "injustice" vis-à-vis the "rights" the diploma supposedly confers. However, this explanation based on students' relative frustration cannot account for involvement that takes place over a longer biographical/activist trajectory (Fillieule 1997).

The organized unemployed in Morocco are almost exclusively high school and university graduates. Combining degree levels within a single group is successful only when a coherent ideological base ties the activists together. When involvement is founded on pragmatic motivations, activists avoid such combinations, pointing to the loss of cohesion, tactical power, and so on. The relative uniformity of groups according to the academic degree held distinguishes the Moroccan case from those where mobilized populations are more heterogeneous.

Thus degree level has gradually become a major factor for coherence among subcategories of activists. It partly eliminates the difficulty of defining a collective identity, which has been highlighted as a central obstacle for the collective organization of the unemployed (Fillieule 1993). But the use of the diploma criterion to give coherence to a group must also be connected to the symbols that framed the actions of the pioneers of the movement. The university unionism of the 1970s and 1980s was influenced by Marxism-Leninism, an ideology still adhered to by a remarkable proportion of unemployed activists.[5] Marxist-Leninist university student unionism defined students who came from proletarian backgrounds as the "vanguard" of the revolution, and their natural space of political intervention was the university. Within this ideological frame, the mobilization of the unemployed represents to the graduates the same thing that unions formerly represented to the students.

Thus the paradigmatic unemployed graduate activist in Morocco differs from the prototype of unemployed activists identified in Western research. The typical Western activist has less academic and political capital (fewer skills, fewer connections, no political experience, and so on) and is thus dependent on external social movement entrepreneurs (Bagguley 1991). The perception of the unemployed as a subaltern category is discussed by recent research (Maurer and Pierru 2001). In the Moroccan case the paradigmatic activist is fully skilled: educated, politicized, experienced in collective action, and so on. When competencies are lacking, the group is supposed to intervene to ensure their development.[6]

The diffusion of the scoring system is linked to the evolution of activist space and also to authorities' response to protests. The first successes of the

ANDCM at the beginning of the 1990s attracted a growing number of adherents in local sections. They soon faced an unexpected situation: more members than jobs to distribute. The scoring system solved this distribution problem. The development of sections was based on the arrival of pragmatic activists, who lacked political experience. The profile of this type of activist was different from the typical union member, for whom staying abreast and networking was a powerful motivation for involvement, perhaps even stronger than the issue of unemployment itself. The secondary import of the scoring system is that it transcended the inequalities among activists, such as differing ideological backgrounds and varying political skills.

The codification of involvement represents an effective system for successfully opening the groups to a broader array of individuals from nontraditional backgrounds without damaging the internal coherence of the group. However, the new generation of graduates did not experience the same political socialization or activist memories as the older, more traditional ANDCM activists. Thus although the codification and set of coercive rules are, from an Olsonian perspective, necessary to ensure individual involvement, they are not that "effective" in a situation where ideological or biographical commonality between activists is lacking or where the efficacy of collective action is dubious.

### WITHOUT MEMORY, NO INCENTIVE IS USEFUL

Postgraduate degree holders provide the new rank and file for the unemployed graduate field, since the ANDCM and the disability groups are numerically relatively stable. A life cycle can be identified in the twenty-year history of the movement of *diplômés chômeurs*. A new group is usually born on the initiative of graduates sharing their knowledge of previous experiences (either because they were in contact with activists in their faculties, or because they were themselves members of a former group). The new group thus inherits and selectively adopts the internal rules of a previous group. After an increase in the number of activists[7] and an implicit recognition by authorities, usually expressed through the reception of group representatives by public negotiators, the group begins street actions. Demonstrations quite frequently become a compulsory stage in the activist cycle, despite not necessarily representing an organic part of the process. Contentious actions do not work as a tangible resource (Dobry 1983). That means that their impact is determined mostly by the evolution of other sociopolitical activity: union unrest pushing for a mass recruitment of teachers; the approaching of elections; and so on. After a period, negotiations with decision makers can lead to the recruitment to the civil service of the entire group or a portion of it. The vacuum is then quickly occupied by new actors.

Does the codification of practices make the reestablishment of groups easier? The internalization of "technical" procedures allows for a quick organization of groups. However, this learning process and remobilization are possible only if they are perceived as useful. The belief in the effectiveness of participation becomes central when there is no other ideological mechanism that binds members together or constitutes a target of involvement on its own. The perception of effectiveness is built on memories of previous experiences; every success incites a new wave of groups because it informs prospective members about the reasonableness and the pertinence of involvement. Many activists would articulate sentiments similar to the remarks of one whom I interviewed in October 2008: "I used to be against these demonstrations. But then I realized that people who went out into the street were hired in the public sector. What am I going to do then? Sit down and wait at home?"

Consequently introducing uncertainty into activists' calculations is an important element of the state's management of opposition. Its impact is disheartening for mobilization. The apparently arbitrary logic of police repression confuses activists' perceptions regarding the coherence of state strategies vis-à-vis opposition. This is combined with the planting of contradictory information in group circles, which stimulates competitive relations within the group and blurs the link between protest and job recruitment that activists channel through memories.

## THE LOGICS OF INHIBITION, TRANSGRESSION, AND POLITICAL DETACHMENT

Contentious actors are not external to their environment. On the contrary, they are inserted in a social space and driven by varying strategies and interests. Still, interaction between contentious actors and their environments may be so constricted that it would be misleading to consider that structural or contextual elements necessarily exert a unilateral influence over mobilization. However, a particularity of mobilization of the unemployed is their detachment vis-à-vis traditional political markers: ideological identification, party or union membership, or participation in other contentious fields besides protesting unemployment. What are the practical implications of this detachment? What distinctions within the space of the mobilization does this allow?

The collective's detachment from political markers has implications for the forms and possibilities of collaboration with other collectives. It is either assumed by other activists to be "appropriate" or exercised only pragmatically and expediently. The collective discourse is focused on job attainment and a sense of job seekers as victims. The groups publicly claim a desire for ideological detachment. This is not unique; other mobilized groups have also claimed legitimacy by trying to remain autonomous from partisan politics (Mathieu 2002). However, the frontiers of what is feasible under this principle are extremely unstable. "Detachment" can "justify" a wide range of practical, and even transgressive, actions and be used among actors as a criterion of legitimacy. For example, during an electoral campaign, mobilized unemployed graduates may vote, boycott, or run as candidates. Whatever option is chosen will be "justified" as the most legitimate way to act, while rivals' choices will be systematically criticized.

Since its inception, the ANDCM has been located in the interstices of the political and trade union fields. The ANDCM is linked to both spheres by resources, networks, and expertise. Indeed veteran members of the association always remember this while recalling the origins of the group: "All the opposition parties and unions, along with partisan [political] newspapers, attended the constitutive assembly of the group, in 1991" (interview, May 2005). Fifteen years later the pamphlets of the association still call for the solidarity and support of all "the democratic forces." But nowadays, unlike in 1991, similar calls are answered only by specific oppositional ideological streams, which are not represented in parliament. According to the official activist discourse, participating in unemployed mobilizations constitutes an explicit rejection of corruption, nepotism, and uneven access to civil service jobs based on personal relations, as strategies of attaining employment. Unemployed graduates also call for the support of "democratic forces, political actors, unions and associations."[8] Ultimately only unions and human rights groups responded to this call. What has happened during these years? How can the call for support from political forces be combined with the principle of political neutrality?

The appearance of receptiveness toward party and union spheres has two targets. First, it reduces the risks of being accused of having ideological or organizational affiliations. Second, it preserves the possibility of receiving resources from the political arena. The positive interest shown by opposition parties in the creation of the ANDCM in 1991 can be understood in a context of institutional change. Enlargement of the rank and file and construction of an image of proximity to social problems were salient for parties that were expecting increased possibilities of participation in government. For its part the ANDCM did not want to prevent members from joining because of their party membership or ideological orientations.[9] From then on, involvement in the ANDCM (and in all groups of unemployed activists) would be based on "what unifies at the expense of what divides" (Bennani-Chraïbi 1996, 132). However, the composition of the ANDCM's central committees reveals an attempt at political balance, including representatives of all opposition forces. A secondary effect is the institutionalization of a sort of elitism within the executive organs: although the discourse emphasizes ideological "indifference," active political belonging has become a central criterion for reaching positions of responsibility. There are other explanations for the absence of independents in the leadership: independents lack resources; political partisans are better known and have more know-how and experience. Thus political detachment does not mean the democratization of the leadership bodies but rather a nonpartisan framing of action.

The belief in detachment's righteousness is also circumstantial. The evolution of parties' positioning within the political field and the recurrence of mobilizations of the unemployed modify the relations between protesters and parties. Since 1998 the ANDCM has evolved toward an overrepresentation of extraparliamentary left activists within the group. That year opposition parties entered the Alternance government headed by Abderrahmane Youssoufi, a historic socialist leader. This incorporation into state affairs encouraged the new decision makers to honor some of the promises they had extended to the unemployed graduates: members of mobilized groups who were close to governmental parties were the primary beneficiaries of the new public jobs manna. The effect on those movement members who were excluded was to reorient them toward support of extraparliamentary leftist organizations and a reanimation of contentious politics.[10]

In the evolution of unemployed graduates' mobilization, the holders of postgraduate degrees seizing the leadership of the movement has especially catalyzed change. Involvement in ANDCM has proven less conducive to realizing activists' demands than has membership in groups organized on the basis of the specific higher degree held. ANDCM adherents spend on average a much longer time in their group than do holders of higher degrees. The style of participation in ANDCM's local sections does not demand constant attendance.

Postgraduate degree holders' groups manage their membership differently. They organized independently in 1995, evoking a double refusal. One was ideological: a reaction against the ambitions of a political ANDCM effectively monopolizing the field. The second was strategic: decrees 888/99 and 965/99 of the Ministry of Civil Service stipulating that postgraduate diploma holders are exempt from entrance examinations were perceived as an asset that would make these degree holders' issue easier to resolve. Every new wave of unemployed degree holders is progressively detached from the political experiences of the leftist National Student Union of Morocco and other clandestine organizations for generational reasons or because of the presence of other social networks.

Postgraduate degree holders' groups have inherited the mainstream perception of party-style government during the Alternance: dissolution of opposition discourses, docile policies, search for private interest, and so on. Representative institutions and ideological adherence are widely discredited by citizens (Bennani-Chraïbi 1996) and perceived as mere tools for resource exchanges. Thus "apolitical" action came to be perceived as the virtuous way to act. Still, those who claim to have political experience must negotiate the framing discourse of mobilization with those from other ideological streams more visible in the university (Islamists), or with pragmatic activists. Consensus is reached on a collective framing discourse that minimizes ideological references.

The rapid development of groups makes it difficult to establish skill-transfer systems. Involvement itself is, on the contrary, quite standardized. A primary goal is neutralizing conflicts that divided activists during their university days,[11] in order to keep together adherents who display an aversion toward ideologically oriented involvements. This rationale reveals a conception of political space as being highly predatory and manipulative. Expressing an ideological orientation is perceived by some activists as dangerous, a "red line" that can render the mobilization susceptible to repression. For others politicization is associated only with partisan calculations. Both perceptions influence each other, converging in a "disciplined" attitude that makes unemployed activists more predictable, potentially useful for state operations, and less subversive (Foucault 1975). The representation of politics based on memories of repression and political manipulation has progressively created a belief about the "righteousness" (both morally legitimate and protective) of docile, nonsubversive action.

This rhetorical style acts as a valorization of activist activity as a whole; the same happens with ideological or organizational affiliations. Thus for the extreme left the diplômés chômeurs represent a renewal of militant practices: the ANDCM is considered the paradigmatic form of vanguard activism as opposed to groups organized around the degree held, which they consider easy to manipulate because of their "nonpoliticization." However, according to the groups of postgraduate degree holders, the danger of manipulation lies in the evolution of the unemployed mobilization toward a project of complete transformation of the existing social order. The difficulty in describing post-graduate groups' ideologies makes them a suspicious community with regard to partisan mobilization enterprises. In fact no party with governmental aspi-rations risks becoming too narrowly committed to the protesters. But this fact does not prevent the mobilization from being at the heart of several dynamics arising in the political arena.

## MOBILIZING IN A COMPLEX SOCIETY

There is no line of causality between forms of protest and job recruitment: the impact of contentious activity on protesters' recruitment or nonrecruitment into jobs depends on what happens in other social sectors. This mobilization is immersed in a complex context, formed by several autonomous social sectors that are linked through interdependent relations. For example, demonstrations will more easily break down public authorities' resistance during an electoral period, when public officials are interested in showing themselves to be socially concerned candidates. Or decision makers will be more responsive if actions of the unemployed are magnified by trade union or journalistic support commit-tees. Thus it is necessary to analyze the multifaceted context where the mobili-zation arises in order to understand its "results."

Mobilization arises in a complex social space; therefore, it is not external to its environment. Activists might be involved in multiple endeavors or be moti-vated by stakes of different natures (political party stakes, cultural stakes, and so on). But mobilization is also a place for the production of *politics* (where elites or framing discourses are created, for example), and it can be used as a tool in the competition among parties, unions, public decision makers, and so on. Union support committees have proven very effective in provoking a response from authorities. These committees imply a nonroutine convergence of inter-ests across groups (the unemployed and trade unionists) that alters the normal collusive transactions between the state and social groups—especially trade unions. But such committees are possible only when union members identify their interests as consistent with a resolution of the issue of unemployment.

Elections are another event that highlights the overlapping interests of unemployed activists and other actors in the political arena. An election is considered a suitable moment to inflect—in a positive or negative direction—

negotiations with authorities. Party activists play the card of proximity to voters. They are sensitive to the critical discourse that unemployed groups deploy against their electoral promises. Elections also lead to a reordering of priorities for actors engaged in multiple discourses. The ANDCM and its members have adopted different attitudes toward elections (boycotts, participation as candidates, no position at all), depending on power struggles and the attitude of their allies in the electoral field. Beyond its electoral utility, the issue of the unemployed is used in the political field by public figures trying to build up an image of proximity to voters and reasonableness. This demonstrates the extent of insertion of the unemployment issue into the political field, and the possibility of converting activist capital to a political resource when the evolution of the political arena (the need to attract disappointed voters) allows full advantage to be taken of the features of unemployed graduates.

## GOING OUT IN THE STREET OR STAYING AT HOME

If rhetoric is used as a tool of distinction, the practice of demonstrations is consensual among unemployed graduates. Demonstrations are considered the most effective way to provoke a reaction from authorities. Although they occur almost every day in Rabat, they are the result of temporary tactical choices and are just one among many types of action included in a larger repertoire, such as mailing letters to newspapers, organizing trade union support committees, hunger strikes, and participation in social forums. The choice of the form of action verifies the hypothesis contained in the notion of *repertoire* (Tilly 1978), which considers that the set of forms of action available to protesters is limited by material and cognitive possibilities and constraints, all of which are historically determined.

Demonstrations are the most valued method by the contentious collective to achieve visibility. There is a gap between the limited rhetoric and the subversive staging of the protest. Through street occupations, the function of public spaces as defined by state authorities is temporarily called into question. The form adopted by this challenge changes depending on protesters' perceptions of their limitations. There is a permanent process of tactical innovation, a fact that challenges Tilly's claim that there is a restricted repertoire of contentious action. While the notion of repertoire remains very useful, it dismisses somehow the potential for creative agency of the subalterns, who are innovating tactically within the perceived constraints.

Until 2000, demonstrations organized by the ANDCM mobilized hundreds of local section members for several days at a time in Rabat. Activists from outside Rabat used to stay in the Union Marocaine du Travail (Union of Moroccan Workers [UMT]) offices during these "days of struggle." After the dispersion of a sit-in organized by the ANDCM that lasted several days in 2001, the UMT directors banned activities in the headquarters of the union—which implied spending nights there—making it excessively difficult for unemployed people coming from distant regions to participate. The demonstration scene in Rabat was then occupied by the unemployed postgraduate degree holders. They either applied the ANDCM model (like hunger strikes, which were inherited from the repertoire of regime opponents) or engaged in unprecedented actions, like sit-ins in front of the parliament lasting for several days. Police tactics toward contention evolved: sit-ins lasting for several nights were forbidden. The shifting boundaries of constraints led to abandoning this form of action and adopting more direct ones, such as massive but short gatherings and occupations of party headquarters or public buildings. Constraints channeled by activist memory mean that the spatial deployment of activists depends on the perceived "red lines." Most of the unemployed who are detained are charged with "offense to the royal family."

What explains why a group whose organization has not significantly changed over time implements a variety of actions at different times? What kind of link can be established between the type of action implemented and a political environment where no shift in the supposed "opportunity (or constraint) structure" has occurred? No demonstration has the value of a calculable resource by itself. The state's reaction is unstable, and the severity of repression depends on what is going on in other spaces, as well as the *échange de coups* (moves and countermoves) in other fields of activity (Dobry 1990). I propose thinking about "memories" and "interactions across social sectors" to better understand these tactical choices. The ultimate choice stems from a calculation that takes into account several variables: personal dispositions of activists, security constraints, and the efficacy credited to actions that are perceived through the prism of activist memories and the positioning of the group within the complex environment. The sequence of moves between protesters and authorities constantly modifies their mutual perceptions of what is feasible. This accounts for the shifts in the types of action implemented. The eventual occurrence of "transformative events" (McAdam and Sewell 2001) such as a collective recruitment for civil service jobs or unprecedented repressive measures is a moment of seminal reconfiguration in perception among groups. These events reveal to the protesters that demonstrations can lead to recruitment or that, on the contrary, they are a risky choice.

A relationship between the profile of the group and the practice of demonstrations can be outlined. Large groups requiring a high level of commitment (like postgraduate degree holders' groups in Rabat since the second half of the 1990s) tend to prioritize intense street actions over a short period of time. These groups must optimize the compulsory presence of their adherents in the capital by doing the most in the least time possible. Street demonstration is considered the most efficient way to question authorities at a low cost. Its technical difficulty is low compared with other forms of action that demand cooperation between unemployed and other actors (unions, associations, authorities). When the small size of the group and the low level of personal involvement do not allow the organization of daily demonstrations (for example, the sections of ANDCM in the provinces), the practice of demonstrations follows a reactive scheme: they are used to deflect the perception that negotiations are taking too much time.

Associations that have other ways to ensure their contact with authorities—for instance, through personal links—may renounce demonstrations as a tactic. However, emerging from silence and engaging in demonstrations has become a common behavior, especially since the "street" has become a legitimizing resource among contenders. This pathway to action often means reacting to stagnant negotiations, or it reveals the need for transcending a state-imposed calendar.

Adopting the tactic of demonstrations implies a set of conditions: assembling a sufficient number of activists to minimize the effects of eventual repression; the perception of demonstrations as being "natural" and "legitimate"; and a certain idea about the relationship with the authorities that activists claim to establish, and an estimation of its efficacy. In order to become "natural" or "normal," the demonstration has to be tolerated. Authorities' tolerance of insurgents is linked to the latter's self-limitation tactic and mastering of the technical tricks of demonstrations. The staging of demonstrations has to take into account a set of possibilities, such as the need to protect demonstrators from the state coercive apparatuses and the need to provoke a response from the authorities. Thus demonstrations of the unemployed use shifting tactics of contention, which combine elements of submission (absence of demonstrations on national holidays; highly censored language) and subversive modalities of deployment in the public space, which question state authority or even compete with it. The discursive frame of "apoliticism" is a form of self-limitation, either unconscious or planned, which aims to consolidate a certain margin of state tolerance for demonstrations. Slogans usually restrain themselves to a presentation of the unemployed graduates as victims. In October 2008 a group (Shu'ala') started a march in Rabat with the following chant: "We are Shu'ala', the flame, the courage, the country's elite. We are against the hiring policy of the government. You want to work in Rabat or in Casablanca. But they will send you far away from home. Tell us? Where are the human rights?" (fieldwork observations). However, an important stage in a demonstration is when protesters compete with policemen for the "(dis)order" of traffic. They partially or totally block the streets, or replace policemen in their traffic-controlling function (fieldwork observations of several demonstrations, 2006–9).

The recurrence of a type of action consolidates a positive perception of its feasibility and of the state's tolerance for the activity. Standardizing the execution of such activities facilitates their geographical diffusion. However, uncertainty is always channeled by the memories of experienced repression. The demonstration is never fully "learned," nor is the image of state tolerance envisioned by activists completely reliable; the possibility of repression is always real. According to statistics compiled by the Tajammu' group, security forces were responsible for 950 wounds between November 2007 and July 2008. Most of the injuries affected the extremities (47 percent) and the back (35 percent); genitals were also frequently attacked. Two miscarriages occurred as a result of multiple concussions.

The pattern of interactions between the *diplômés chômeurs* groups and other actors also affects the calculation of what is feasible and of its efficacy. The results of a demonstration depend on the stakes within other sectors, whether they converge on the interests of the unemployed or not. When the unemployed are not closely linked to political parties, trade unions, or grassroots organizations, their actions do not reverberate strongly. But at certain moments the party, executive, and journalistic arenas, to name but a few, pay increased attention to the cause of the unemployed. Then the mobilizations of the unemployed constitute a convertible resource in other fields of activity. Thus they can influence the resolution of protests (Dobry 1995). However, much of the unemployed graduates' constituency preferred to stay on the sidelines of the February 20th movement.

Unemployment appeared in the discourse of the February 20th movement as part of its call for democracy. But the self-perception of the unemployed protestors as belonging to a larger subaltern population excluded from elite circles of privilege did not imply their automatic adoption of a discourse placing the "right to work" in the context of broader social and economic demands.

The principle of political detachment contributed to this attitude, whether it signified a formal disagreement with the February 20th vision or pragmatic, risk-avoiding behavior of the unemployed. This was especially pronounced for the postgraduate groups, which did not join the movement and stopped their protests during the first months of the February 20th mobilization.

The logic behind the periodic recognition of unemployed postgraduates' claims, undermined the evolution of a discourse demanding the "right to a job" toward a broader demand for a "right to work." However, the ANDCM was more inclined to join forces with the new movement, since its antiauthoritarian rhetoric struck a cord with its own ideological roots.

## CONCLUSION

The consolidation of what have progressively become the "rules" of Moroccan unemployed graduates' mobilizations (restriction of the contentious category to graduates, scoring systems, standardized forms of action, a collective discourse focusing on victimization) has taken place concurrently with the shifting character of these features, the uncertainty of their very often "transgressed" parameters. I have tried to provide an explanatory framework for the wide and ambiguous range of protesters' attitudes between "contestation" and a "plea to the prince," based on activist memories and the analysis of mobilization in a complex setting. Memories, historical trajectories, experiences of public action, and the coercive setting define the practices of contention. The outcome of a negotiation (whether it is self-controlling, pragmatic, or a subversive outbreak) is contingent on an unstable consensus between contenders, public decision makers, union and association activists, and so on. The plasticity of the "rules" constitutes the very nature of unemployed graduates' "way of protest," where conventions are (re)calculated at every moment.

Protest incorporates within its dynamic the stakes of competitive contentious fields. Mobilization is "used" in other fields, for example, as an evaluating criterion of activist practices, as a source of legitimacy for public policies, or as a space of political elite formation. At some point the "unemployed cause" becomes a stake within other spaces. The unemployed are aware of this possibility; thus, the opportunity to translate mobilization into a resource valuable in other social sectors affects perceptions regarding the feasibility and the efficacy of unemployed degree holders' contentious actions.

To sum up, the way in which the unemployed act contentiously depends on the horizon of feasibility of protest and the need to produce a response from the political elite. Self-control seems to be the basic principle because the unemployed shape contention on their experiences of public action. Public action has trained its opposition, and in some cases it has even "convinced" it of the righteousness of a pragmatic, apolitical mobilization. But that should not lead us to neglect the fact that tensions between different perceptions of "correct" collective action constantly arise within the activist groups themselves.

# 7 PRESENCE IN SILENCE

Feminist and Democratic Implications
of the Saturday Vigils in Turkey

## Zeynep Gülru Göker

CAN WE TALK ABOUT DEMOCRACY AND DEMOCRATIC ENGAGEMENT in a context where the institutionalization of basic rights is incomplete, where social movements risk violent repression, and where military institutions and discourses often come before efforts for democratic opening? Democratic theory rarely discusses such themes; political science in general leaves the discussion of such cases to the democratization or the transitions literature. Through a discussion of the Saturday Vigils held from 1995 to 1999 in Turkey by the relatives of the "disappeared under arrest," this chapter argues that we need to expand our understanding of the "political" to see how political subjectivities and openings are created in ways that are often overlooked in discussions of democracy and in places often neglected by Social Movement Theory (SMT). A gendered analysis of the vigils, whose participants were mostly women and called Saturday Mothers by the media, not only promises such an expanded notion of the political but also suggests the possibility of constructing gendered responses to the militarization of everyday life. What started as the actions of a small group of mostly women, often considered to do politics with a small *p*, turned into a four-year-long presence in the public sphere. The vigils not only claimed physical and symbolic space but also created an opportunity to realize the significant place of women's actions and conceptions of gender in the makeup and continuation of militarist discourses, which determine and constrain the experience of democracy and democratic citizenship in Turkey.

The literature on democratic theory often discusses democracy in the abstract, while the discussion of concrete cases where democratic institutions are vulnerable largely takes place within the area studies and transitions literature. Democracy, when defined with a set of bullet points, gets taken for granted as a quality some countries possess while others only struggle to achieve. On the basis of her study of Islamist parties in Jordan and Yemen, Schwedler (2006, 6) argues that the problem with the transitions-to-democracy literature is that it treats political change as progression on a teleological continuum and undermines the complexity and dynamism of political change. This understanding misses the very historicity of democracy and some of the ways people create opportunities in authoritarian structures or unconsolidated democracies.

Only when we think of democracy as a practice, rather than simply the name of a regime, can we capture its historicity. In contemporary democratic theory, either in deliberative accounts, which understand democracy as a process involving the public deliberation of citizens (Benhabib 1996; Bohman and Rehg 1997), or in agonistic accounts, which focus on the centrality of agonistic interaction of social groups to democracy (Connolly 1995; Mouffe 2005), attention to political practice becomes key. Although fixing a meaning to democracy or fully institutionalizing it is impossible (Mouffe 2005), the very struggle to achieve it is still important, because democracy is the productive tension between the constant struggle for the expansion of rights and freedoms, and the necessary moments of closure in defining the demos (Keenan 2003). Democracy requires the formation of democratic subjectivities (Norval 2007), and one place to look for democratic engagements is social movements. When we think about democracy as a practice—what Rancière (2006) describes as the process between man and citizen—we have to take contentious action seriously, even and especially when it takes place in authoritarian environments. Thus Wedeen notes the importance of everyday political practices, like *qat* chews in Yemen, where ordinary people as well as politicians and administrators visit while engaging in political conversations that recall Habermas's seventeenth- and eighteenth-century coffeehouse public spheres. Here democratic subjects are formed through discursive practices in the absence of a formal framework of democracy—what Wedeen (2007, 61) calls "democratic practice in the absence of a democratic regime."

Diani (2000) describes social movements as practices that usually take place outside the institutional spheres and the routine procedures of everyday life; this is also a characteristic of women's movements. Women have been integral to various social movements (Teske and Tétreault 1999), many of which have been inspired by women's everyday concerns and practices, which for a long time were considered "private" rather than "political." Using a gender lens to analyze contentious politics is useful. As Ferree and Merrill (2004, 261) suggest, "gender deeply permeates the discourses, ideologies and frames that social movement studies have offered as analytical tools." Moreover it has been an aim, and outcome, of feminist theory and women's movements to challenge the boundaries of the political. The role of women's activism in Turkey's history of social movements is especially important because at a time when "politics had ended," after the 1980 coup d'état (Tekeli 2004), women helped enliven contentious action using ad hoc, nonhierarchical, informal ways of organizing (Tekeli 2004). They have created significant political openings and challenged the gendered makeup of democratic citizenship via innovative or learned practices and international solidarities they have formed. Saturday Vigils, considered by many of their participants to be one of the first examples of civil disobedience in Turkey, created a space where people came together in their differences to create solidarities and networks in an unmediated, nonhierarchical way. This was a democratic space that promises to be a foundation for the construction of a critical stance against the militarization of everyday life.

## THE SATURDAY VIGILS

In Turkey the problem of disappearance under arrest as a systematic phenomenon began to receive public awareness in the aftermath of the 1980 military intervention, especially in the southeastern Kurdish areas, when security forces arrested thousands of people to "restore public order."[1] Violence between the security forces and Kurdish organizations escalated after 1983. The first known case of disappearance after 1980 was Hayrettin Eren, arrested in November 1980; twelve more persons were reported as disappeared by 1990, and the numbers steadily increased in the 1990s, reaching 345 people in 1994 and 1995 (Günçıkan and Ertem 1996, 15–16). Most of the reported cases were from the state of emergency (OHAL) region, the southeastern provinces of Turkey. Hasan Ocak's disappearance in 1995 in Istanbul brought his family and many others together. Frustrated by the state's lack of response, the family and supporters started hunger strikes and marches in various cities, during which Emine Ocak, Hasan's mother, who is by now the well-known face of mothers of the disappeared, served jail time. Hasan Ocak's tortured, dead body was found in a graveyard of the unidentified fifty-five days after his arrest; around the same time another disappeared, Rıdvan Karakoç, was also found dead.

The Ocak campaign came to an end, and reported cases of disappearance steadily increased. So, a group of former activists, mostly women who were already acquainted with one another from an ad hoc campaign they had initiated, started discussing what could be done.[2] Such early acquaintances created an environment of political trust and friendship (Koçali 2004). Nadire Mater, who as a journalist had closely followed the Ocak campaign, stated that she was frustrated by the conditions in which Hasan Ocak had been found, and started thinking about "new spaces where the frustration could be expressed."[3] A group of activists immediately got together to discuss what could be done. The Argentine example of the mothers and grandmothers of the Plaza de Mayo was on the table as a source of inspiration.[4] Kayılı (2004, 350), one of the few men in the initial group, states that they wanted to take an action in which anyone could participate; where continuity would be the key to creating awareness. Their claims had to be simple and clear: ethnic, religious, and cultural identities or the political leanings of the disappeared should not be the issue; what mattered was that they were disappeared (Kayılı 2004, 350). As Hüsniye Ocak, Hasan Ocak's sister, stated in a recent interview:

> All of us families are saying if our children, our brothers were guilty they should have been put in to jail. We would not have anything to say to that. At least then we would have a place to go to look for them; now people do not have anywhere to go. Of course we know that some people have reactions. We understand them, but we hope they do not experience what we experienced. Think about it, you are driven mad when your child comes home only an hour late; these people are waiting for their children to return for years. (*Milliyet*, February 16, 2009)

Kayılı (2004) states the necessity of having a simple and legitimate claim in order to prevent manipulation, and classifies the action as "naked disobedience," defined by nonviolence and noninstitutionalization. They decided not to use slogans or banners so that anyone could easily join in the publicization as an individual, having left institutional and political affiliations behind. As Nimet Tanrıkulu (2003, 279), one of the initiators of the vigils and a member of the Human Rights Association Commission Against Disappearances, states, "They used silence to have their voices heard." Kayılı (2004) also mentions the difficulties they expected to encounter, and particularly laments a general dislike of dissonance in Turkey, which causes many to approach any act of contention with distrust. He recalls a concern about leftists, who were usually unfamiliar with civil disobedience and more inclined to transform and claim the leadership of any action (351). Nevertheless, without much serious preparation, they decided to go public in the form of a weekly vigil to be held on Saturdays at noon in Galatasaray Square in the Taksim district—a visible spot in a central neighborhood.

> It had to be Saturday because everyone is on the street; 12 p.m. to 1 p.m. because then journalists can easily come and write about it. They should sleep a little,

go to Galatasaray, write about the vigil and have it published the next day. Where would it be? Galatasaray, because it's a central area; thousands pass by the square all day. So we decided to go on with it, but actually we did not know what we were going to do. Okay, we would be going there, but what would the police do? It was not a demonstration that got permission. I want to state this in another friend's words: "We wanted to sit so that everyone stands up." (personal communication with Mater, June 9, 2009)

The first vigil in Galatasaray was held on May 27, 1995. Around thirty people, mostly women, went to the meeting point and sat down holding a poster board with two pictures and a text attached, which read:

Hasan Ocak was taken under custody, hundreds disappeared and found dead. We want the murderers. Rıdvan Karakoç was arrested, disappeared like the hundreds of them and found dead. We demand the murderers (*Bianet*, February 17, 2001)

Excited, they went and sat; the police did not know what to do, because back then Galatasaray was not accustomed to hosting protests. Mater recalls that police officers, who probably had not seen the poster, came to ask what they were doing, and the activists replied nervously, "We are tired, so we sat down." The activists realized immediately that an hour would be too long, so they dispersed after half an hour and met in a teahouse to discuss what to do for the following week. They continued to go to Galatasaray for four years. At first the police did nothing. As Sebla Arcan, a member of the Human Rights Association's Commission Against Disappearances, wrote:

Our number was low and we did not make any noise so we were treated as the "Saturday Fools." But the arrests started when our actions started to take effect. (*Milliyet*, February 16, 2009)

When the police tried to disband the vigil, participants would defend themselves on the basis of the constitution[5]; from time to time famous people, activists, and artists would join in support. As Mater indicated in the interview, after half an hour of sitting they would meet up in the "cheapest teahouse" for discussion and division of labor. The immediate aim of the vigils was twofold: to stop the disappearances and to learn the whereabouts of the already disappeared. Vigil participants started to write press releases about the disappeared and had a participant read them at the end of vigils.

Only Ocak's and Karakoç's families were present at the first vigil, as it was an ad hoc action in which people informally notified one another; but in time other relatives joined, some traveling to Istanbul from their hometowns. More people had started talking about the vigils, and soon Galatasaray was filled with journalists. The name Saturday Mothers was chosen by the media, although the participants insisted on calling themselves Saturday People. In time they started to call themselves Saturday People/Mothers, which indicated the two groups—the activists and the relatives (although the latter weren't all mothers). Some had already found their relatives dead; others had no clue of their whereabouts but hoped to find them, alive or dead. The Ocak family was almost ashamed to have a grave they could visit as long as others did not know what to expect (Tanrıkulu 2003).

The relationship between the Saturday People and the Mothers was one of mutual trust and empathy. Tanrıkulu says, "Even though we had no relatives who were disappeared the relatives sensed our sincerity, and in a way we were equal with them" (*Bianet*, May 17, 2002). Mater describes the People's role as "carrying out the struggle in their name," meaning giving support and help to the relatives. Unlike the Argentinean mothers and grandmothers, who were mostly educated middle-class women and already politicized when they started their vigils,[6] the mothers in Turkey were mostly from rural, lower-class backgrounds. Most of the Kurdish women did not speak Turkish. Hence the Saturday People would take on tasks such as writing press statements and establishing connections. Yet Mater underscores the fact that the activists never intended to speak in the name of the relatives; no one would speak for another. After half an hour of sitting, mothers would start talking to the journalists themselves. Mater says, "There is no such thing as learning to talk; if a person is in such pain, she will manage to express it, and no one else can do it better than her" (personal communication with Mater, June 9, 2009). She adds that the presence of non-Kurdish activists also showed the police that the Kurdish women were not alone; the joint presence made the vigils a long-term activity. According to Mater, the vigils would otherwise have been associated with alleged illegal terrorist action and soon repressed. Thus they had to make clear that they had no political affiliations, since as Mater argues, people had doubts about all kinds of institutions, but they had none about the people who sat in Galatasaray as individuals. There were no elections, and decisions were taken together. Activists who worked the hardest and took responsibility came to be those who were listened to the most, and this was also true for the

relatives (Koçali 2004). The absence of hierarchies and the lack of organizational affiliations allowed people from different backgrounds to come together
in Galatasaray (Tanrıkulu 2003).

> We did not call this an organization—it was not an organization—but we
> cannot say it was disorganized. There was no hierarchy. Let's say there is this
> ten people: each week one would take on the task of thinking about the week
> after and call the other ten; one would prepare the press statement; one would
> let the press know that we would be in Galatasaray again next week, etc. Those
> were the kinds of things we did. We could say we were organized without an
> organization. (personal communication with Mater, June 9, 2009)

International media and human rights organizations were quick to take
notice of the vigils. In 1996 the Habitat Summit took place in Istanbul; hence
hundreds of foreigners joined the vigils. The same year Bernard Debord made
an award-winning film about the vigils, "The Mad Women of Istanbul." People
in cities such as Paris, Sidney, and London held vigils in support; and mothers came from Argentina to sit in Galatasaray. Sezen Aksu, a famous Turkish
singer, made a song about the mothers, which sold out the magazine that distributed the album. In December 1996, Saturday People/Mothers were award-
ed the Carl Von Ossietzky Human Rights Award by the International Human
Rights League. Mater says these international interactions were extremely important and helpful; thus she and another mother attended the biannual Voix
de Femmes festival in Brussels to participate in the working group on enforced
disappearances. The fact that organizations such as Amnesty International and
Human Rights Watch followed the vigils—and the violations the participants
faced—gave the issue a significant place in Turkey's human rights record. As
Mater recalls, when the prime minister traveled abroad, the first thing she was
asked to talk about would be the Saturday People/Mothers.

The attention the vigils received in such a short time not only caused the
police to become violent but also made Galatasaray popular. People who in
Kayılı's terms wanted to "revolutionize" and "politicize" (in the traditional ideological sense) the vigils came to Galatasaray (2004, 353). Galatasaray had become a space of hope at a time when Turkey was not short of human rights
violations. According to Tanrıkulu, it was mostly young people who had difficulty adapting to the form of silent protest (2003, 291). The Saturday People/
Mothers had to keep warning those who wanted to shout slogans and otherwise give the police an opportunity to repress the vigils. In our interview Mater

argued that everyone wished to claim the quick success the vigils achieved in creating awareness and stopping the disappearances.

In 1998, a critical year in which PKK leader Abdullah Öcalan was found in Italy—an event spurring ultranationalist sentiments and everyday violence in Turkey—police started to take extreme measures to prevent the Saturday People/Mothers from going to Galatasaray. The participants were beaten, dragged on the streets, and arrested every week. The legitimacy of the vigils was no longer an issue; it was already established by their persistence. The officially announced reason for repression was the allegation that the vigils were a cover for illegal terrorist organizations. The participants insisted that they had no institutional affiliations other than with the Human Rights Association (IHD), which acted only as a communication center, as Mater states. The police arrested anyone who "looked suspicious," even before they arrived at the square. Vigil participants started feeling helpless, since what had started as an action that anyone could join had turned into something that only those who could risk violence and arrest could dare to join. "The environment of terror that hundreds of police officers with masks, cops, dogs created every week had changed the face of our action beyond our will" (Koçali 2004, 358). They had to risk their jobs and health. Those with young children had other fears: what "if something happens to the rest of their children"? (358). Nevertheless they insisted on going to Galatasaray, because for them it was more than a place to protest: the square had turned into a space of commemoration; it was a graveyard where they could remember and share. When asked if she was happy to see the vigils resume in 2009, one of the relatives, Doğan, answered:

> Very much . . . my deceased mother would run to these vigils. She would forget her pain when she saw others. It was like that for me too. It happened so many times that when I saw a photograph of a disappeared person in someone's hands I dropped mine on the ground. (*Milliyet*, February 16, 2009)

On the two-hundredth week, Saturday People/Mothers collectively decided to suspend the vigils because of the sharp increase in human rights violations that had occurred over the previous thirty weeks: 431 people arrested and sometimes kept in custody as long as five days; forty put on trial. Hanım Tosun, a Saturday wife, says, "if the Galatasaray Vigils could have continued maybe there would be no new disappearances," referring to two new disappearances in 2001 (*Bianet*, February 19, 2001). Mater believes that the first set of goals—

bringing down the number of disappearances and creating awareness about the issue—was realized to a great extent. Moreover the vigils went on for four years, becoming the longest-lasting act of civil disobedience in Turkish history. She explains that success by their ability to form international solidarities, by their novel form of action, and by their resistance of institutionalization.

Ten years later, in February 2009, the Saturday People/Mothers started meeting in Galatasaray once again.[7] Today Galatasaray is much different; police always guard the square, and as Mater jokingly says, "You almost have to make reservations on Saturdays to protest in Galatasaray." Most of the initial participants still try to be present every Saturday. IHD's Commission Against Disappearances has helped organize the vigils and bring relatives together, some of whom have founded their own organizations in the meantime.

Ten years have changed the political landscape in Turkey. There have been democratic openings due to the EU candidacy process, while the Ergenekon trial investigates coup d'état plots and contra-guerilla organizing among social, political, and military elites and has brought the issue of disappearances onto the agenda again. The goal of the vigils today is still to discover the whereabouts of the disappeared but also to demand judgment of those responsible. The Saturday People/Mothers have a list of names to be brought to account, among whom are prominent political figures such as the prime minister and president who held office when most of the disappearances took place. Mater believes that activists should push for Turkey to sign the Declaration on the Protection of All Persons from Enforced Disappearance adopted by the UN General Assembly and signed by eighty-one countries since 2007. She argues that institutionalization is necessary at this point; only a legal institution, which devotes itself full-time to the cause, can handle such a task (personal communication, June 9, 2009).

## EXPANDING THE POLITICAL

Identifying any movement as a sign of the rise of civil society and uncritically associating it with democratization is misleading, since much of political practice in the Middle East takes place under the auspices of an authoritarian state (Norton 1995). Rather than treating the state as an all-powerful entity, which has clearly demarcated boundaries, following a Foucauldian notion of power as dispersed and productive, anthropologists have studied the state through its effects (Abrams 1988; Mitchell 1991). The effects of the state as they pertain to the everyday level make the study of public rituals, celebrations, and mourning necessary (Navaro-Yashin 2002) and the treatment of any contentious practice as part of an autonomous civil society misleading. We have to see the ways in which certain norms purported by the state are challenged but also embedded and reproduced in public actions.

In contrast to the ideal of transparency in liberal democracy, Taussig (1997) talks about a circle of secrecy that surrounds the state. The secrecy around the kidnapping and disappearances in Turkey, the so-called deep state, refers to the multiple levels of connections within the state among political, economic, and military elites and paramilitary groups. When the Saturday People/Mothers gathered in public space to direct attention to the disappearances, they were at once calling the state into action and opening its actions up to question. What is seen in the actions of the confused police officers, at once trying not to harass the participants, thinking that as mothers they are "deserving protection and respect," but also beating and accusing them of not being "proper mothers," reflects Brown's (1995) notion of the state becoming an object of ambivalence. An uncanny feeling surrounds the state as violence and paternalism, force and intimacy are conflated. The longing for a paternalistic state goes hand in hand with the frustration felt towards its inaction (Aretxaga 2003, 397) or meaningless action, such as the "bus of the disappeared"—an initiative of the Ministry of Interior whereby a bus would park in Galatasaray and well-dressed female officers announced that relatives should report the disappeared, even though they had already done so several times—or the Istanbul chief of police suggesting a new, significantly less central meeting point for the Saturday People/Mothers, as if all they wanted was a place to get together.

The relationship between the state and citizens is inflected by differences in class, gender, and ethnicity. At the margins of the polity in particular, encounters with the state are more intimate and closer to the skin (Aretxaga 2003, 396). The Saturday Vigils brought the everyday into confrontation with the state, hence challenging that very boundary, as women brought what is considered to be private—their emotions and bodies—into the public sphere as political tools. Arat (1998) argues that the mothers revolutionized the traditional maternal role by insisting that the state be responsible for and accountable to its citizens.

In challenging the homogeneity of Habermas's notion of the public sphere—the discursive realm of public engagement—Fraser (1992) talks about counterpublics as alternative publics from which counter-discourses emerge. While the vigils formed potential enclaves for counter-discourses, it would be a mistake to overlook the ways in which they also contained and perpetuated certain norms.

While constituting an alternative to the popular displays of statehood and citizenship, the norms and traditions that describe the proper role of women and mothers were simultaneously reproduced. Mater states that it was never their intention to present the vigils as mothers' events; the media coined the name. Yet on a pragmatic level this label helped gain wider acceptance and empathetic responses. We cannot overlook the fact that this particular presence of women in the public sphere can also be interpreted as women doing what is natural to them—mourning. Thus we should not think merely about bringing the private into the political but rather question that very dichotomy and uncover the ways in which the private and the political are constructed through relations of power and essentialist understandings of gender; and question too the very association of emotions with femininity.

Baydar and Ivegen (2006) argue that the category of motherhood, or the media's and the state's choice to focus on the maternal identity, was an effort to turn attention away from the political character of the vigils and to take emotions as central. However, drawing a distinction between the political character of the vigils and emotions is not useful since the emotions constitute the political character. We cannot think of the participants' claims as separate from the yearning, the sorrow, and the narratives they brought to the square every Saturday. This is exactly why feminists criticize the dominant public sphere theories for proposing gendered understandings of the public sphere and communication (Young 2002). Passions, desires, emotions, and narratives are political, yet they are not exclusively feminine: that is the lesson to be learned from the vigils. It is possible to take a critical stance against any essentialist understanding of gender or maternal identity while thinking of emotions as part and parcel of democratic engagement.[8] In fact fathers also publicly displayed emotions during these vigils, overriding traditional gender roles (Baydar and Ivegen 2006). Tanrıkulu (2002) argues that although people usually find it difficult to share in such intense situations, vigil participants shared and developed solidarities in friendship and love, a point that is overlooked in the press accounts but is among the most important gains of the movement.

Emotions also rarely find their place in analyses of democracy, although they have become an important element of these engagements. SMT for the most part takes emotions to be part of a framing technique. However, what we see in this case is not a coming together of leaders to figure out the best way to mobilize people (Tarrow 1998, 111–12) but a group of people reaching consensus without necessarily conducting a rational discussion about the best frame. The vigils exemplify the interaction of the personal, the political, and the emotional, and challenge the dichotomy of reason and emotion. Moreover analysis of this movement cannot simply take into consideration the decrease in the number of disappearances while overlooking the friendships and solidarities that were formed and sustained by these vigils—relationships that are critical for the formation of long-lasting bonds of political trust and friendship. Mater observes that even after the vigils were suspended, the Saturday People and the Mothers kept in touch on collective or individual levels.

The Saturday Vigils were not women-only actions, but it was mostly women who participated. It would be a mistake to overlook the participation of men, but it would also be inappropriate to characterize the vigils as mixed-gender actions. Mater explains this with women's success in pushing for "small things," while men are more occupied with "high politics":

> In this interview I answered your questions. If another friend were to be here, she would only fill in the gaps and not repeat the same things. Whereas most men, even if they have nothing new to say, always come to the fore and speak. Women are generally not like that. There are such women as well, but generally they are not; they are practical. We were practical during our meetings. We would sometimes meet in each other's houses, drink wine, and do everything together. I could explain this as the difference between "high politics" and "low politics."

Kayılı (2004, 352) explains the presence of more women than men in the vigils by what he believes to be the ability of women to relate to pain and solve conflicts:

> They were able to understand and share the mothers' pain better than anyone. Also, the soft solutions they found in all conflict situations, their intention to avoid displays of power and their rationalism had naturally put them to the fore.

We see many gendered notions at work here. Kayılı seems to adhere to a traditional association of women with emotions and pain, although we could very well explain women's presence in peace and antimilitarist activism as due to their having a greater stake in change and to their different experience of war and militarism (Cockburn 2007; Enloe 2000). Both accounts also show a difference in the perception of women's relationship to language and politics; women are associated with practical thinking and the avoidance of unnecessary displays of power. Mater explains it as the difference between what is considered "high politics" and "low politics." The irony in the turning of what is considered "low politics" into a long-lasting act of civil disobedience proves how important it is to expand our notion of the political. The simple act of a half-hour silent sitting had the potential to challenge borders of legitimacy and subjectivities beyond the expectations of the subjects themselves (Kayılı 2004, 356). We see in the vigils the formation of political subjectivities in the practice of politics, what Cockburn (2007) calls "doing politics." The expansion of the political however does not mean valorizing one form of doing politics over others. At first it was a surprising sight to see women sitting on the street, especially those whom Yurtsever (2009, 14), a member of the IHD Commission Against Disappearances, describes as traditional women coming from villages, who found themselves "in the middle of politics." But as Mater states, it would be wrong to call these women apolitical, since most of them came from the OHAL region or from an environment in which the Kurdish issue is a daily reality.

While taking into consideration the construction and transformation of political subjectivities, it is necessary to avoid discrediting life outside the public sphere—for instance, perceiving the movement as one of poor homemakers turning into heroic activists and transforming themselves; or favoring the heroic woman making a speech over the woman who is silently sitting on the ground. Such an account would not only limit our understanding of the ways in which people do politics but also run the risk of reenacting gender associations of citizenship, such as identifying publicly-acting women as becoming masculine.

The subtitle of McAdam, Tarrow, and Tilly's (2001) seminal study on social movements is *What Are They Shouting About?* The Saturday People/Mothers sat silently in Galatasaray and rejected shouting slogans, which enabled a longer presence in the public space than they could otherwise have had. Silence was part of their way of making claims, which shows how silence is a part of discourse and language rather than the antithesis of communication (Foucault 1990; Kurzweil 1981).[9]

> Silence is very important. Thinking about our initial worries, if we were to allow noises then it would be hard to perceive what would be voiced there. Silence actually shouts the action you want to make in a better way. (personal communication with Mater, June 9, 2009)

Silence can be a form of protest, a radically democratic deconstruction of hierarchies of speech (Norton 1988), a listening openness (Corradi Fiumara 1990; Ihde 2007), or a choice to avoid conflict (Bickford 1996). Saturday Vigils and the silence of the participants reflect all of these. Women in Black (WIB)—a group of women in Israel who started holding weekly vigils against the occupation after the outbreak of the first Palestinian intifada, and have since become a global peace network—have also designed their actions as silent vigils. Women in various peace and antimilitarist movements have found holding vigils to be a powerful form of action to claim public space and of doing democracy at a distance from the power structures that are usually associated with democracy (Cockburn 1998, 216). Vigils create persistence and a sense of responsibility, as silence constitutes a powerful response to militarism.

> We chose not to speak excessive words, and therefore we think that it is important to express and experience these feelings and experiences with silence. With silence like a protest here from where the war is waged, a visible silence like a cry and a warning. With silence and black we also want to speak shame and compassion. ( *WIB Belgrade*, 2002, 62)

The Saturday People/Mothers had a mutual agreement to be in Galatasaray every week, and during the rare times when they couldn't make it, they would let each other know beforehand (Koçali 2004). A long-lasting act of civil disobedience (which was not originally conceived as such—Mater only realized that their actions fit the criteria of civil disobedience after reading Thoreau) is only possible with wholehearted commitment to the issue. As Mater argues, it was not easy to go to Galatasaray every week for four years, especially for the elderly. The persistence and visibility of women from different socioeconomic, geographic, and ethnic backgrounds also created a contrast to the opacity of the state as well as to the symbolic presence of women in politics.

### GENDERED RESPONSES TO THE MILITARIZATION OF EVERYDAY LIFE

During their active presence in Galatasaray for two hundred weeks, the Saturday People/Mothers did not talk about militarism or consider themselves feminists; in fact their actions can be interpreted as both challenging and perpetuating traditional gender norms. We can still look for the unprecedented consequences of their actions since actions have consequences which, while they are available to those who narrate and judge, do not necessarily reveal themselves directly to their authors (Arendt 1958).[10] Hence I have proposed to study the vigils as they constitute gendered responses to the militarization of everyday life and promise the construction of an antimilitarist discourse. There was no antimilitarist stance taken during the vigils. In fact, as Mater argues, although most of the initial Saturday People were antimilitarists, it is harder to talk about antimilitarism in the context of the mothers, since most of them came from the state of emergency (OHAL) region, where militarism in all forms constituted a daily experience. Enforced disappearance is part of a militarist discourse and a form of everyday violence. Considering that all forms of violence, whether enforced disappearances, police violence on the street, or the violent atmosphere in the southeast, are interrelated in women's lives, considering the role of the Saturday Vigils in the construction of antimilitarist discourse becomes even more pressing.

When talking about Turkish democracy, we have to take account of the institutional presence of the military in "democratic" politics as well as the presence of military discourses in everyday public and private life. Enloe (2000, 3) defines militarization as "a gradual process where a person or a thing becomes controlled by the military and depends on militaristic ideas." This process becomes successful when it achieves normalcy and goes unquestioned. Gender relations is a front where the relationship between militarism and democracy portrays itself, marking women's relationship to the state and their citizenship as distinct from men's. Militarization acquired normalcy in Turkey in the 1930s, when the soldiering discourse required a nationalist, racist notion of Turkishness that saw all Turks as soldiers (Altınay 2004). This distinguished between the relationship of men and women to the state, as well as between some men and others, because soldiering was understood to be compulsory for healthy, heterosexual males. One of the indirect relationships through which women belong to the nation-state is motherhood, which is also a central tenet of nationalism and militarism. Najmabadi (1977) discusses soldiering as backed up by a discourse that defends itself in the name of protecting the honor of women and the eroticized (feminine) nation. A mother is perceived as one who is in dire need of protection, and soldiers must be ready to die for this cause. In fact during the same time Saturday Vigils started to occupy the attention of the public gaze, another group of mothers in Turkey was also establishing a visual presence in the public sphere. They were the mothers of the martyred—soldiers martyred during military combat in the southeast. They were portrayed by the media as "Friday Mothers," as they met in cemeteries on Fridays.

The families of the martyred and the organizations they have created retain close relationships to the army. Militarization needs the collaboration of soldier-mothers to legitimize soldiering (Enloe 2000, 237). Death for these mothers has to be acceptable death so that they do not question it. They are expected to direct their fury to those people or institutions, "the enemy," who caused the death of their sons (Sancar 2001). Ruddick (1998) talks about the mother of sorrows, *mater dolorosa*, as a potential peace figure. However, there is no single "maternal" identity. For instance, during her study of infant deaths in shantytowns of Brazil, Scheper-Hughes (1998, 229) observes another rhetoric of motherhood, one that regards death as "inevitable, acceptable, and meaningful—which shows that the conventional view of women as peacemakers is not true. This rhetoric of "letting go" is strikingly similar to military thinking and the discourse of martyrdom (Scheper-Hughes 1998). However, just as it would be an error to treat the Saturday People/Mothers as a homogenous group, it would also be a mistake to neglect alternative voices within the mothers-of-the-martyrs group. In fact they are allowed to speak only as long as they do not constitute alternative discourses to militarism; those who do speak in ways that threaten the dominant discourse are dismissed and labeled as traitors or propagandists of illegal organizations.[11]

The Saturday Mothers and the Friday Mothers were counterposed as rivals by the mainstream media. The two groups of women were presented as confrontational; martyr mothers' grief was sacralized and portrayed in ways to delegitimize the suffering and the presence of Saturday People/Mothers. Similarly "Peace Mothers Initiative," another mothers' group, consisting mostly of Kurdish women, has been portrayed as rival to the mothers of the martyred. The image of the pained mother, and the political propaganda that feeds on this image, turns the pain into a justification for militarism. In fact the confrontations have even worked to some extent to strengthen such discourses, as one type of motherhood was privileged over others and motherhood became a new source for nationalist politics (Koçali 1996).

Rather than considering women as passive, vulnerable symbols of politics and mothers as of secondary importance to militarism, a feminist analysis should build on the realization of the centrality of women's actions and gendered ideas to militarism. Only then can the real sources of the pain women are expressing be investigated to see where and how they overlap in order to construct shared spaces and struggles. The Saturday People/Mothers have proven, through their actions and in the awareness they have created, their central role in politics and their ability to bring about change without waiting for "high politics." They constituted a model of democratic engagement, as did the mothers and grandmothers of Plaza de Mayo, who created a democratic movement out of women's social needs rather than abstract political visions (Bouvard 1994); or Women in Black, who challenged gendered meanings of citizenship as they did "politics through the backdoor" (Berkowitz 2003).

Although I am stressing the need to avoid arguments such as the "moral authority of mothers" (Cockburn 2007) or the reproduction of traditional gender norms in such actions, any social movement runs that risk. This is the productive tension between the openness and closure of democracy, which is also reflected in feminism (Zerilli 2005). Thus these movements have to be studied, for they promise the construction of alternative discourses while safeguarding against essentialist, homogenous definitions of subjectivities. Neither the Saturday People/Mothers nor the Friday Mothers is a homogenous group; yet it is possible to construct a feminist discourse through their differences and bring the two groups together for a critique of militarism and the forms of violence it generates in women's lives. Men are not exempt from this struggle. The very acknowledgment that mothers have a central role to play in militarism rather than a peripheral one is the first step towards creating such an alternative discourse. Studying the vigils as social movements and vis-à-vis democratic theory to see how women actually "do democracy" and how people create significant change in ad hoc, direct actions, even in authoritarian settings, is another step. Whether the recently restarted Saturday Vigils can effect such an understanding and construct such a practice remains to be answered.

## CONCLUSION

The analysis of the Saturday Vigils shows how important it is for democratic and Social Movement Theory to take seriously political practice outside of the northern-industrialized world, not simply to enrich the set of examples studied but to rethink the theories vis-à-vis historically and politically contextualized analyses of the global South. The vigils I have analyzed here show how an action that started out as the ad hoc, silent protest of a small group of (mostly) women turned into a long-lasting social movement that brought awareness to the issue of disappearances. Becoming the longest-lasting act of civil disobedience in Turkish history, the Saturday Vigils opened up an important space in contentious practice and paved the way to constructing new political subjectivities and solidarities. Hence they offer an expanded understanding of the political, and significant insights into the role that conceptions of gender and women's actions play in contentious practice and the experience of democracy.

The Saturday People/Mothers present an example of direct, unmediated democratic action that expanded rights and freedoms and challenged gendered limits of citizenship, ideas about women's role in politics, and the militarization of everyday life. As seen in the media-produced rivalry between the

Saturday Mothers and the mothers of the martyred, militarization needs the active collaboration of women and gendered notions of citizenship. The democratic coming-together of people in their differences before a similar goal can constitute a strong response to the militarization of everyday life. Gender relations is one arena in which a strong militarist discourse constrains the practice of democracy. Therefore an analysis of the links among gender, militarism, and democracy must be undertaken in discussions of contentious action and social movements.

# 8 MOBIL!ZATIONS FOR WESTERN THRACE AND CYPRUS IN CONTEMPORARY TURKEY

## From the Far Right to the Lexicon of Human Rights

### Jeanne Hersant

THIS CHAPTER RAISES THE ISSUE of the symbolic and political role of migrants from the Balkans in the (re)definition and promotion of contemporary Turkish nationalism. My research deals mainly with the mobilization of associations representing the "Turks" from Western Thrace (Greece) who are living in Turkey. They are designated as "Batı Trakyalı" (Western Thracians) in colloquial Turkish, and I too will use this term in order to avoid any confusion between those who are Greek citizens and Turks from Western Thrace now living in Turkey who are Turkish citizens (Hersant 2008).

In the 1960s and 1970s these associations, along with ultranationalist movements, contributed to the revival of the myth of the Ottoman Empire's "lost territories" owing to a "chauvinist and aggressive" political context, which was also marked by claims on Cyprus (Tunçay 1976, 12–16). "Lost territories" refers to the National Pact adopted in 1920 by the dissident National Assembly in Ankara under the leadership of Mustafa Kemal. This assembly rejected the transfer of territories to European countries, which had been negotiated by the Ottoman government in Istanbul and confirmed by the Treaty of Sèvres. Three years later, however, the Ankara Parliament ratified the Treaty of Lausanne, which delineated the borders of contemporary Turkey and recognized Western Thrace as a Greek province. The compulsory population exchange between Greece and Turkey was organized by an addendum to the Lausanne treaty, from which the Muslim population of Western Thrace and the Orthodox population of Istanbul (and of the Turkish islands Bozcaada and Gökçeada) were exempted. They were officially defined as minorities and granted specific rights by international law for the first time.[1]

Strictly speaking, the above-mentioned National Pact did not make any claims on Western Thrace. But nowadays it is commonplace to read in Turkish newspapers that the region is "a part of our National Pact." Neither was Cyprus an issue at the end of the Ottoman Empire, whereas it is the very embodiment of contemporary nationalism based on the "Turkish world": namely, the Balkans, the Caucasus, central Asia, Iraq (Kirkuk), and Cyprus. Moreover the success of the mobilization of the Turks of Western Thrace seems to stem from their success in the 1970s in linking this issue with that of Cyprus. The EU has become an arbitrator in this issue since Batı Trakyalı, whose representatives in Greece recognize Turkey as a "kin state," became European citizens in 1981.

This chapter recounts the different stages of a mobilization that accompanied the reappropriation by official ideology, after the 1980 coup d'état, of the "Turkish world" issue, which was traditionally promoted by far rightist movements. I will first describe how organizations that represent the "Turkish world" gained the status of official interlocutor, in spite of Turkish authorities' strong distrust toward any expression of local cultural identities. Indeed the latter are considered to be a kind of "separatism," particularly in reference to Kurdish cultural demands (Hersant and Toumarkine 2005). The Western Thrace Turks Solidarity Association (Batı Trakya Türkleri Dayanışma Derneği, or BTTDD) will be presented as a case study. The aim is to recount the interactions and negotiations that are linked to the construction of a public issue in a "praetorian regime," in which, especially since the 1960s, the military, supported by the high-ranking civil bureaucracy, has exercised "independent political power, either by using force or by threatening to do so" (Hale 1994, 305)—most notably in the three coups between 1960 and 1980. In addition, "the military also intervenes in politics via its constant presence in the public sphere on the part of the highest reaches of the military hierarchy" (İnsel 2008, 3).

As a state-approved association, BTTDD has been granted financial and political support by all Turkish governments since its founding. Its leaders' rhetoric, claiming it is a "civil society organization," should not lead us to substantiate social science theories in vogue nowadays, according to which "civil society" is a factor of Europeanization and democratization challenging "official" political power (Diez, Apostolos, and Kaliber 2005). Neither is BTTDD simply a cog in the machine: the interactions between its representatives and Turkish officials are complex and consist of constant negotiations, as well as divergent opinions. On the one hand, from the 1960s onward it went beyond its stated purpose (namely, assisting the government in taking in and settling migrants) and succeeded in making the Western Thrace issue a part of the Turkish political agenda with regard to the "national struggle" (millî dava). On the other hand, in the 1970s and 1980s the association's connections with several extreme rightist organizations represented a challenge to the state's authority, as does its obvious connections today with the ruling Justice and Development Party (AKP), which is considered by the military—and a great part of the civil bureaucracy—to be a threat to Turkish secularism.[2] Associations of migrants from the Balkans and Caucasus grouped together as federations and confederations, forming a "competitive arena" of "Turks from abroad" articulated with the political one.[3] Thus it is not exact to state that the delegitimization of militant commitments after the 1980 coup d'état has confirmed the "separation between formal politics dominated by parties, and civic groups" (Kubicek 2002, 770).

This chapter will then examine the definition of an international and European strategy for promoting the Western Thrace issue in the 1990s, in consultation with state representatives. I will emphasize the de facto supervision by the Turkish state over Western Thrace Turks' mobilizations in different scenes (mainly Germany and Western Thrace), and their abandoning contentious arguments and practices for others based on lobbying for human and minority rights. The purpose of this contribution is neither to fit into one of the dominant schools in the study of social movements—the structuralist (or Political Process Theory), or the social constructionist—nor to apply the analytical tools of "civil society" and Political Opportunity Structure, the "uses and abuses" (Navaro-Yashin 1998) of which have been discussed for several years (Leca 2003; Morris 2004; Fillieule 2005). I am in sympathy with Goodwin and Jasper, who ask, "Is the political process approach still a progressive research program, or has it begun instead to constrain intellectual discovery? Where are the frontiers of theory and research in this vital area of sociology?" (2004, ix). I am inclined to believe that the approaches of classical Social Movement Theory can lead to misreading the object of study.

Unlike the conventional approach to analyzing how conflicts are "Europeanized," which contrasts institutionalized European lobbies with "ordinary Europeans" who protest outside the framework of such institutions (Tarrow 1995, 224), I stress that protest and lobbying might coexist within a single repertoire of actions and that a social movement might transform into a lobby while turning its back on grassroots mobilization. I also stress the learning and use of a European repertoire of actions (Tilly 1984, 99) by actors close to state representatives in order to promote Turkish national interests in Western Thrace. Moreover far from considering the Europeanization of conflict solely as a reaction to European-level decision making, as Tarrow does (1995, 224), I will consider the state representatives as mobilization entrepreneurs as well. Lastly "Europe" refers here not only to the EU: norms dealing with human rights standards were first defined by the Council of Europe and organizations such as the International Helsinki Federation for Human Rights before becoming a full part of the *acquis communautaire* in the 1990s. Consequently "Europe" has become part of the vocabulary framing political struggle in the Greek-Turkish rivalry. In order to address the problematic of importation of norms, I will approach highlighting the way norms and discursive categories are exploited and how they fit into local or national dynamics (Ragaru 2008). Thus I follow a methodological approach aimed at "clarifying the nature of links between protagonists, specifying what leads actors and organizations to international-ization, and studying the possible transformation of protest forms," or their renunciation (Siméant 2005).

## AGENDA SETTING IN A CONTEXT OF POLITICAL RADICALIZATION (1967–1980)

### Institutionalization of Hosting Refugees from Former Ottoman Provinces

Like the various associations of "Turks from abroad," BTTDD (until 1969 called the Western Thrace Migrants Mutual Aid Association) was created in 1946 to organize the settlement of migrants and refugees who had fled World War II and the Greek civil war. In 1954 along with other mutual aid associations for Balkan migrants, BTTDD created the Federation of Turkish Migrants and Refugees Associations, which became a state-approved organization in 1960. This federation embodied pan-Turkist nationalism vis-à-vis provinces ruled by communists and Greeks. In this respect the Turkish migratory policy regarding Western Thrace has always been ambivalent: as Western Thrace was considered a "Turkish province" since the end of the Ottoman Empire, official immigration from the region disappeared from the record books in the 1960s, though clan-destine population movements continue to take place. From the 1970s onward, the privileged relationship between BTTDD and police headquarters had been illustrated by the publication—in journals connected to the association—of precise information dealing with illegal immigrants, namely, their exact place of origin in Western Thrace, the point where they entered Turkey, and a list of persons who were granted Turkish citizenship every month.

Created in 1967, *Batı Trakya* (Western Thrace) was the first journal to pro-mote the Batı Trakyalı cause and BTTDD activities, without explicitly being the latter's organ (although its owner and chief editor, Selahattin Yıldız, led the BTTDD twice in the 1970s and then led the Federation of Turkish Migrants and Refugees Associations in the 1980s until its dissolution in 1987). The BTTDD is now a member of the Rumelian Turks Federation together with the Rumelian Turks Association and the Georgian Turks Association. In this journal, and also in the scope of protest actions, Batı Trakyalı activists appropriate themes that conform to the official historiography but that are also promoted by far right organizations such as the Association for Struggle Against Communism or the National Union of Turkish Students (see Can 2000). *Batı Trakya* reproduced their rhetoric and related their actions, which are sometimes organized in common with BTTDD members.[4] One has to keep in mind the context of the 1960 and 1970s, where political life was strongly polarized between far rightist and leftist movements, which led to a quasi civil war only ended by the 1980 coup d'état.

### Redefinition of the "National Struggle"

In the same vein as the pan-Turkist rhetorical flaying of the "enemies of the Turkish nation," *Batı Trakya*'s content was virulent toward Armenians and "Rum" (Greek-speaking Orthodox Christians) whether they were from Istanbul, Cyprus, or Greece. During the 1960s, a decade of "fragmentation and radicalisation," the Kemalist doctrine was "challenged by new ideologies and social projects" (Bozarslan 2004, 56). In 1969 the Party of Nationalist Action (Milliyetçi Hareket Partisi, or MHP) was founded by Alparslan Türkeş, who popularized the idea of a "Turco-Islamic synthesis"—a nationalist ideology considering Islam as an integral part of the Turkish identity[5]—and a Turkish nation transcending contemporary Turkey's borders. His movement clearly influenced the identity mobilization of Turks from Western Thrace, both in Turkey and Germany, in the 1980s.

In this journal there were various ways of linking the issues of Western Thrace and Cyprus. First, *Batı Trakya* reprinted official petitions signed by BTTDD leaders and addressed to the president of the republic, the prime minister, or military authorities.[6] In 1967, for instance, after the military junta came to power in Athens, the Association of Immigrants from Western Thrace (later BTTDD) petitioned President Cevdet Sunay to have "Western Thrace and Cyprus saved together."[7] After the 1974 Cyprus crisis, similar telegrams were sent to the prime minister and military officers in order to denounce Greek retaliatory measures against Turks in Western Thrace. Indeed Turkish military staff seemed to show a growing interest in the Western Thrace issue. Since the 1970s and 1980s, staff officers' interventions as experts in BTTDD journals or in conferences on the "Turkish world" have become commonplace. Appeals for military intervention then became clearer in the journal *Batı Trakya*, as illustrated by an article published in January 1975, "The Western Thrace Front in Cyprus's Peace Operation."[8] Second, narrative and semantic processes were used in order to connect events that occurred in Western Thrace and in Cyprus, such as simultaneously occurring deaths, even if no true link existed between them.[9] The national press in Turkey also tended to conflate these two situations when the junta came to power in Athens.[10]

However, a separate semantic process aimed at appropriating the expression "national struggle." It was first used in reference to Cyprus by Prime Minister Adnan Menderes in the 1950s and has since become a constant and preponderant element of the official rhetoric on that issue (Alpkaya 2002). The "national cause" or "struggle" (which can also mean "trial" in Turkish) adopted by BTTDD leaders concerning Western Thrace is omnipresent in *Batı Trakya*'s writings from the 1970s onward and also in the interviews I conducted with the association's representatives. The consequences of the 1974 conflict in Cyprus actually did, in a way, back up Batı Trakyalı militants in Turkey because the Turkish invasion of northern Cyprus had strong repercussions on Western Thrace Turks' everyday life: considered a threat, for several months they were subject to a curfew, and their hunting weapons were seized.

### Protest Action in the Wake of the Far Right

At its beginning *Batı Trakya* merely recounted the demonstrations organized by nationalist rightist groups, such as the National Union of Turkish Students (a radical pan-Turkist nationalist group that promoted the "Cyprus is Turkish" movement before joining the Islamist National Salvation Party in 1969), which advocated military intervention in Cyprus.[11] These articles' titles and content often refer to the Kemalist vulgate establishing youth as the guardian of the "Eternal Chief's" heritage. That vulgate had been appropriated by the military officers who undertook the 1960 coup and in the following decade by the different rightist and leftist factions confronting the civil government's political and economic mediocrity (Bozarslan 2004, 53–64).

According to *Batı Trakya*'s archives, a turning point occurred on April 13, 1974, when several Batı Trakyalı took part in such a demonstration for the first time. Nevertheless BTTDD was not officially involved in this demonstration, which was organized by the National Union of Turkish Students and aimed at "warning Greeks" while the situation in Cyprus was becoming worse.[12] The report's author notes that he met several acquaintances whose "national consciousness" was "finally born." Three days earlier, against the background of a breakdown in negotiations over Cyprus and adopting a mode of action that would be frequently used in the 1980s by BTTDD leaders, the National Union of Turkish Students' leader placed a funeral wreath in front of the Greek consulate in Istanbul, which bore the following inscription: "Have you forgotten September 9th?" This was a reference to the date of the capture of Izmir in 1922, the symbol of the Greek presence in Asia Minor, after Mustafa Kemal's army had defeated the Greek invasion on August 30. Afterward the crowd stood and sang the national anthem—and then scattered. In the accompanying picture one can see a group of persons wearing hoods: they were allegedly young Batı Trakyalı of Greek citizenship, who feared retaliation against themselves or their families if Greek authorities learned of their participation in this meeting.[13]

This statement could not be fully verified, but interviews conducted with Batı Trakyalı of Greek citizenship who studied in Turkey—be it in the 1970s or in the 1990s—rather suggest a desire to avoid political mobilization in order not to draw the attention of either the Greek or Turkish authorities. One of my interlocutors had to interrupt his studies in the 1970s after he was expelled from Turkey for publicly claiming his sympathy for extreme leftist movements. Until recently, studying in Turkey was for most of this population the sole path toward social mobility. Besides, political issues related to Turkey often do not make sense for people who have grown up in Greece. In any case the aforementioned demonstrations do not seem to have been designed to mobilize Batı Trakyalı students or residents. In the classic manner of collective action, they were very likely organized to show the positioning of the associations of "Turks from abroad" within extreme right movements, and to negotiate the latter's high profile in the Turkish political arena.

### Institutional Mobilization and Emergence of Specific Demands

These affirmations are reinforced by the fact that BTTDD leaders seem to have favored establishing close relationships with state representatives, to the detriment of protest actions. They would in particular send delegations to Ankara to address the prime minister or the Ministry for Foreign Affairs about the situation of "Turks" in Western Thrace. Behind the rhetorical facade designed to appeal to Turkish interests in the region, the association's purpose was to heighten government awareness of Batı Trakyalı settled in Turkey without being blamed for promoting cultural identities at the expense of national unity.

The first of these delegations, recounted in the journal *Batı Trakya*, in 1968, was dismissed by both the minister of foreign affairs and the minister of the interior.[14] This failure may illustrate the government's caution toward an association whose political commitment was obvious, whereas an important agreement providing for teacher exchange in minority schools was to be signed with Greece the same year. Yet BTTDD representatives succeeded two years later: they were received by Prime Minister Süleyman Demirel and the person in charge of the Balkans committee in the Ministry for Foreign Affairs.[15] Those visits became a kind of ritual aiming at reaffirming Batı Trakyalı's allegiance toward Turkish governments: one of them occurred on the pretext of congratulating Bülent Ecevit's government when it took office in 1974.[16] After establishing such ties, demands shifted from the situation of "Turks" in Greece to the one of Batı Trakyalı living in Turkey: securing the right to purchase property in Turkey and to have an activity in trade and business sectors and easing the procedures for gaining Turkish citizenship.[17]

A few months before the 1980 coup, even though there had been no significant Batı Trakyalı immigration to Cyprus, the Cyprus and Western Thrace Turks Solidarity Association was founded in Nicosia.[18] This was BTTDD's twin organization and led by Fikret Alasya, an ultranationalist Cypriot intellectual close to Rauf Denktaş. After the 1974 "peace operation," he became the representative in Cyprus of the Turkish Ministry of Defense.[19] Many of my interlocutors among BTTDD representatives deny that such an association existed. The legitimacy of Batı Trakyalı's political and (Turkish) identity speech is indeed based on the assurance that such an identity claim will never open the door to secessionist thought or to any Turkish territorial demand concerning Greece. It is all the more important that Turkey's presence in Cyprus is considered a military occupation from the point of view of international law. After the 1980 coup, unlike most political parties and associations, BTTDD was not banned but had to leave its activities in abeyance. In the following months, in accordance with a decision of General Kenan Evren, some six thousand Batı Trakyalı who were living in Turkey—many of them illegally—became Turkish citizens.[20] Taking advantage of the favorable context for the "Turks from outside," BTTDD claimed the creation of a "directorate general" dedicated to them and attached to the prime minister.[21] It is a fact that currently there is not only a vice prime minister but also state secretaries and state representatives at the local level who are in charge of the "Turkish world" (Özgür-Baklacıoğlu 2006).

## SINCE 1980: A STATE-SPONSORED MOBILIZATION
## TOWARD THE MUSLIM WORLD AND THE EU

### Disowning the Ultranationalist Right and the
### "Official" Demonstrations in the 1980s

Despite the fact that after the 1980 coup the movements that had been involved in the violent riots of the previous years were banned and the extreme right leader Alparslan Türkeş was imprisoned, the Turco-Islamic synthesis he had promoted became a quasi ideology of the state. At the same time, the cult of Mustafa Kemal was strengthened (Copeaux 1997, 81),[22] and "Turks from abroad" was henceforth officially recognized as a "national cause." Consequently the BTTDD's ideological line evolved during the 1980s. Allegiance rituals to Atatürk were scrupulously observed, and there was a shift in symbolic meanings: in the past BTTDD meetings were sometimes punctuated by a reading from the Koran as well as occasional expressions of homage to Atatürk; this subsequently disappeared, and the placing of a spray of flowers at the feet of a sculpture of Atatürk became part of the meeting rituals.[23]

The military returned power to civilians in 1983 after writing a new constitution allowing officers to exercise power in political life and over citizens' personal freedom, especially concerning the right to demonstrate. At that time BTTDD officially took part in street demonstrations that were obviously state-approved. On March 21, 1985, a demonstration was organized in Istanbul by several associations—including the BTTDD—representing different "Turkish nations," in support of the Turks in Bulgaria. This demonstration, reportedly gathering two hundred thousand persons, had received approval from the police headquarters, which had forwarded the application to the First Army and Martial Law Commander.[24] Considering the way Turkish authorities apply Law 2911/1983 on meetings and demonstrations—most of them are actually illegal—one may assume that the demonstrations they permit are welcomed by the government (Uysal 2005, 36). In contrast to street demonstrations in the former period, this time BTTDD leaders walked at the procession's head, and *Batı Trakya*'s editor in chief, also president of the Federation of Turkish Immigrants and Refugees Associations, led the demonstration's organizing committee.[25]

In these demonstrations the contentious dimension is often the least important one, as the following examples show. In 1989 the BTTDD organized a sit-in in front of the İpsala bridge-border between Greece and Turkey to protest the measures taken by Greek authorities to prevent Batı Trakyalı living in

Turkey from voting in general elections. This protest action remained symbolic: after a declaration from the president of the BTTDD, thirty-five persons sat down for a time before leaving.[26] To put it differently, although protest actions are organized in retaliation against Greek policy toward "Turks" in Western Thrace, they actually address Turkish authorities. Along with the laying of funeral wreaths, a protest action that was often referred to in *Batı Trakya*, some protest practices confirm the will of the Batı Trakyalı to place their struggle against the "Greek oppressor" within Turkey's republican heritage, thereby avoiding any interaction with Greek authorities. In November 1989, for instance, during Sadık Ahmet's trial in Thessaloniki,[27] the procession's target in Istanbul was not the Greek consulate, as it usually was, but rather the monument dedicated to the republic's glory in Taksim Square. This highly symbolic monument celebrates the day Allied troops left Istanbul in 1923 and can be reached only by demonstrations approved by authorities.[28]

Strikingly, the "ruder" a demonstration is, the less it addresses the authorities. When violent means are used, it is not against Greek or Turkish authorities but rather against Christian Turkish citizens, who are considered enemies of the Turkish nation by people in nationalist milieus.[29] For five days in 1991 demonstrators laid siege to the Greek Orthodox Patriarchate. The BTTDD instigated the demonstration; its aim was to protest the promulgation of a new law in Greece that canceled the provisions of Law 2345/1920 concerning the election of muftis in Western Thrace. Although not officially sanctioned, the demonstration was reportedly accepted tacitly by police headquarters. Policemen contented themselves with preventing Grey Wolves activists[30] from approaching the Patriarchate and refused to scatter demonstrators who blocked the Patriarchate's entry. The police chief of the Fatih District—where the Patriarchate is located—is said to have supported demonstrators (Aarbakke 2000, 519). The BTTDD president wanted the patriarch to denounce the Greek law; he exhorted him to cooperate and prove he could be a good citizen—in other words a loyal Turkish citizen—even though he was Christian (520).[31] My interlocutors justified the connivance with policemen, arguing that they were fighting for the "national cause," which was acknowledged by police headquarters. As a matter of fact the protest action was not motivated by the defense of Batı Trakyalı rights in Greece but was rather the reaffirmation of Turkey's far rightist credo in reaction to an attempted assault on the "Turkish" minority's status as it was defined in 1923. The quasi-official character of those demonstrations is confirmed by the banning of another demonstration planned by the BTTDD in

Istanbul, in January 1988, to protest the Davos bilateral conference that aimed at sealing friendship between Greece and Turkey.[32] This demonstration was supposed to take place to echo one organized in Western Thrace on January 29 as a protest against the court decision banning associations that bore the adjective "Turkish" in their name (Oran 1991).

Throughout the 1980s the various protest actions listed here began to be organized in reaction to precise events occurring in Western Thrace, rather than in accordance with political parties or other organizations of "Turks from abroad." During this period connections strengthened within the Batı Trakyalı network between Germany, Western Thrace, and Turkey, leading to a broader convergence of agendas and modes of action (Hersant 2007). This is related to the definition of a European strategy, to which I will return below.

### Appeal to the Islamic Conference Organization

Before turning to the EU, Western Thrace promoters appealed for support from "Muslim and sister countries." In the official lexicon this expression refers to a hierarchy and a degree of proximity with neighboring "peoples" or "countries" according to whether they adhere to Islam (in that case they are "friends") or belong to the "great Turkish family" (in which case they are "sisters"). Until 1983 and the revival of BTTDD activities, the Cyprus and Western Thrace Turks Solidarity Association was in charge of the defense of Batı Trakyalı's cause. It seems that its efforts were particularly dedicated to the strategy of internationalization[33] and at first mainly directed toward the Islamic Conference Organization (ICO).[34] That was association president Fikret Alasya's idea, in accordance with the credo of Turkey's ruling figure, General Kenan Evren.[35] Linking together Turks of Cyprus and Western Thrace—both of whom were portrayed as victims of the Greeks—was a way of making acceptable the 1983 proclamation of the Turkish Republic of Northern Cyprus (TRNC) and the island's de facto partition for the Turkish government. But the ICO is concerned only with Muslim populations, and the organization would find it out of the question to promote the "Turkish world."[36] Worse, the ICO never officially recognized the TRNC (Bertrand 2004, 239).

However, at the end of 1980s BTTDD leaders became aware of the European dimension of the Western Thrace minority issue thanks to the ties they developed with Batı Trakyalı associations in Germany. The semantic register of human rights was gradually superimposed on that of Turkish nationalism, both in official speeches and in those of the BTTDD.

### Adoption of the Language of Human Rights and Expertise
### in the EU Framework (1990s)

The European strategy was defined by Batı Trakyalı actors in Turkey at the end of the 1980s. It coincides with the launching of the BTTDD's new journal, *Batı Trakya'nın Sesi* (The voice of Western Thrace), in 1987. Considering the erratic publication of *Batı Trakya* between 1987 and 1989 before it died out, as well as the tone and content of some of the last articles published, it seems that its owner was gradually disavowed by the BTTDD leadership. This, coupled with the banning of a rival journal, *Yeni Batı Trakya* (New Western Thrace), illustrates the ambivalence of the BTTDD's political line. Created in 1983, the latter journal became the BTTDD's instrument, as the publication of official information from police headquarters—previously published in *Batı Trakya*— suggests. This journal's owner, Süleyman Sefer Ciahn, was a member of the BTTDD board from 1981 to 1984, when he was dismissed, apparently because of his sympathies with extreme rightist movements.[37]

*Batı Trakya'nın Sesi* was created in 1987 as the BTTDD's official publication after the infighting between the two former journals. It displays an intellectual ambition to break—at least formally—with the militant rightist line of *Batı Trakya* and *Yeni Batı Trakya*. After finding resources in the 1960s and 1970s thanks to radical rightist organizations' rhetoric and know-how, the BTTDD was thereafter forced to maintain a nonpolitical stand. The new journal's tone is far less virulent compared to former publications, and its articles concentrate on Western Thrace, relinquishing the Cyprus issue and denunciation of the Turkish nation's "inner enemies." With the launch of the new journal even *Batı Trakya* stopped mentioning the Cyprus and Western Thrace Turks Solidarity Association, although Fikret Alasya was one of its regular columnists throughout the 1980s. As for Rauf Denktaş, president of the TRNC between 1983 and 2005, he remains an honorary member of the BTTDD.

This turning point was illustrated by what Kemal Karpat wrote in the first issue of *Batı Trakya'nın Sesi* as a member of its academic board. The famous historian encouraged the Batı Trakyalı to publish abundantly in Greek and English, and to address their claims not only to the Turkish people. He suggested that they resort to international organizations: "One has to choose precise and influential targets: Amnesty International, European Parliament, OECD, Helsinki Committee for Human Rights . . . just as the Bulgarian Turks did."[38] Karpat also encouraged the Batı Trakyalı to invest themselves in academic conferences and research centers specializing in Southeastern Europe, which were emerging in

Europe and the United States. Throughout the 1980s the BTTDD did indeed invest heavily in creating expertise in this field, although mainly from the "Turkish world" perspective (Hersant 2007).

The underlying logic was to shift the Batı Trakyalı issue from Turkish nationalism to the framework of human and minority rights. For example, journalist Mümtaz Soysal, at a conference on the "Turkish world" organized by the BTTDD, lamented the fact that "we pay dearly for not using in due time, according to our own point of view, such a fashionable theme [as minority rights] that entered the world by our door."[39] These words allude to the suspicion engendered in Turkey by human rights, the promotion of which is closely connected to minority rights, for several reasons. First, historically, "national liberation" struggles by Christian minorities that weakened the declining Ottoman Empire were supported by European countries—especially France and Britain—that hoped to take control of strategic Ottoman provinces (Akçam 2003). Now these struggles took place in the name of political liberalism and the rights of minorities (Akçam 2002). Second, the minorities issue in Turkey became internationally oriented from 1984 onward with the establishment of the guerrilla party PKK (Kurdistan Workers' Party), which opposes the Turkish army. Furthermore, the protection of "ethnic" or "national" minorities has become one of the EU's main systems of reference, along with state law, since the collapse of the former Yugoslavia and the revival of the "Balkan powder keg." As a matter of fact, influenced by the repercussions of the 1990 Helsinki Watch report on Western Thrace (Whitman 1990), the EU has come to acknowledge Batı Trakyalı actors' claims and now advocates the recognition of a Turkish—not Muslim—minority by Greece in Western Thrace. This European injunction led to the redefinition of the political lexicon and to an evolution in the repertoire of actions used within the Batı Trakyalı identity movement.

### Abandoning the Language of Protest

At the beginning of the 1980s the political language of human rights had not yet been developed or mastered by Batı Trakyalı associations in Turkey, whereas the actions implemented by associations in Germany opened up new forms of mobilization and a new semantic register, that of the EU. In the 1980s and 1990s these associations organized several demonstrations and, in parallel, sent delegations to the European Parliament in Strasbourg. After the violent events in 1990 in Komotini, in which rightist Greek activists ransacked Turkish shops, mosques, and houses in the wake of street demonstrations, there were no more demonstrations for the rights of the "Turkish" minority in Greece. Between 1982 and 1997 six street demonstrations in Germany, one in Great Britain, and one in France (Strasbourg) occurred. They were all organized in response to events in Western Thrace, except for one in 1986 that was organized by a "Turkish organization"[40] to protest against Bulgaria's policy toward its Turkish minority. This mobilization was organized in cooperation with the identity movement in Western Thrace and soon came to be seen as a good means to promote "Turkishness" there. Moreover, since the end of 1980s Turkish authorities and the BTTDD actors have gradually become involved in associations in Germany by choosing or co-opting their leaders (Hersant 2007).

The movement away from protest actions was enunciated during the Fourth Western Thrace Turks International Conference, which took place in June 2000 in London. The goal was to put the Western Thrace Turks Federation in Europe in the forefront rather than the BTTDD, whose members are mainly Turkish citizens. The BTTDD and Turkish officials were nevertheless well represented; the symposium's proceedings were printed by the BTTDD main branch in Bursa, and the rhetoric linking Cyprus and Western Thrace was reaffirmed. The means of action recommended during this conference emphasized a lobbying strategy toward the EU. Whereas the Greek state was blamed by Turkey and the United States for offering PKK militants protection and logistical support—especially after PKK leader Abdullah Öcalan was arrested in February 1999 in the Greek embassy in Nairobi, where he had sought asylum—the strategy adopted by Batı Trakyalı actors stressed the nonviolent and sophisticated character of their own demands. The representative of the Helsinki Monitoring Committee in Greece, also a representative of the Turkish identity movement, argued that "we shall not demonstrate and shout in the streets any more; otherwise the Greek media will condemn us as a fanatic group."[41]

The abandonment of the language of protest coincided with shifting the European mobilization's center toward Western Thrace. Such an evolution is linked to the changes in the social characteristics of the identity movement's entrepreneurs in Western Thrace and their cooperation with second-generation migrants in Germany. Unlike the first-generation migrants who launched the European mobilization, these tend to be young people who have graduated from Turkey's universities and sometimes even hold master's degrees obtained in Germany or Great Britain. They speak perfect English (and Greek for youth in Western Thrace) and have skills related to the field of human rights intervention: they have considerable knowledge of international norms concerning the rights of minorities, know-how of lobbying techniques, and an understanding of the various European institutions. They are also well integrated in the forums dedicated to the promotion of the rights of minorities. In fact they are both experts and militants of their own cause.

In 2000 the Western Thrace Turks Federation in Europe was granted a consultative status in the UN Economic and Social Committee. And the Association of Graduates from the Muslim Minority in Western Thrace has conducted several projects with Minority Rights Group (MRG) in London, for example, writing an English-language "UN guide for minorities." This guide was then translated into Turkish and distributed both in Western Thrace and Turkey. This second part of the project did not involve the MRG but rather the Turkish consulate in Komotini, one of the most powerful, although there are no Turkish citizens in Western Thrace. Unlike former protest actions, the lobbying strategy that has been implemented for the last ten years systematically bypasses Greek authorities: it addresses European representatives, never members of the Hellenic Parliament or Greek members of the European Parliament.

## CONCLUSION

In this study of the politicization of the Batı Trakyalı issue—namely, its reformulation into a public issue, first in the Turkish national framework and then on a European scale—I have emphasized how the character of the Batı Trakyalı movement challenges the conventional approach to social movements, which opposes "ordinary people" to authorities or to "powerful opponents" (Tarrow 1998, 2). In this case it seems that the more access activists have to state institutions, the more aggressive their demonstrations are and the less they address Greek authorities. In a similar manner the category of "transnational social movements" fails to distinguish between contentious actions and lobbying, which can be intertwined (Siméant 2005). That is why it seems more appropriate to consider Batı Trakyalı activists as a "transnational network of militants" (Tarrow 2000, 208) or as an "advocacy coalition" (Sabatier 1998), in which NGOs or state administrations can be involved as well.

As for the appropriation of the human rights lexicon, it might at first sight appear as the illustration of the first step in the "norms socialization" process as stressed by Risse, Ropp, and Sikkink (1999, 5)—namely, "instrumental adaptation and strategic bargaining." But this model, as well as the distinction on which it is based, between "Western" and "liberal" states on the one hand and states that do not respect human rights on the other, is just not relevant.

It stresses the external pressure on states due to "domestic opposition" resorting to "international human rights NGOs/organizations" and to "Western powers" (19). Notwithstanding the fact that "NGOs" and "transnational advocacy networks"—which are supposed to bypass state authority (Keck and Sikkink 1998)—are often totally or partially state-sponsored organizations (Siméant 2005), like the BTTDD, this schema does not fit here. In their desire to "evaluate" human rights practices, these authors do not take into account the uses or bypassing of international norms, even by states that claim to uphold international law (Hersant 2008a).

More relevant is Sikkink's and Dezalay and Garth's analyses stressing the emergence of human rights between 1970 and the 1990s as a central element of US foreign policy (Sikkink 2004) and therefore as a universal reference in the "international field of practices" (Dezalay and Garth 2002). From this point of view the process of European construction involved both prescriptive and ideological aspects: it was able to prescribe a common and relatively stable perception of values such as democracy, human rights, a state of law, and citizenship. Besides, the process of Greece's European integration has often been considered to be a moment in the country's "democratic transition," following which it has reached "Western standards." This is the reason the Turkish state, although not an EU member, makes good use of European norms dealing with national minorities in order to legitimate its sovereignty over the "Turkish" minority in Western Thrace. Consequently it has succeeded in promoting its own interests concerning a European territory (Western Thrace), whereas its military occupation of northern Cyprus has been strongly opposed by the European Union.

# Part 3

# 9 BECOMING REVOLUTIONARY IN TUNISIA, 2007–2011

## Amin Allal

ANYONE SEEKING TO ANALYZE INVOLVEMENT in popular uprisings, particularly those that swept several Arab countries in 2010 and 2011, should avoid overemphasis on both unanimous revolt and mass spontaneity. Observation of "the revolutionary moment" tends to heighten the impression that the entire population joined the uprising. The revolt spread across Tunisia and reached the capital of Tunis in the second week of January 2011. With the army unwilling to repress the protesters and the Union Générale Tunisienne du Travail (Tunisian General Labor Union—UGTT), formerly the single trade union federation long controlled by the regime, hesitantly yet crucially "entering the fray," a mood of popular unanimity was hard to deny.[1] The many "street" groups that sprang up dictated the political agenda, overturning successive national governments, driving out local government representatives, police officers, and activists of the ruling *parti unique* (single party), the Rassemblement Constitutionnel Démocratique (Democratic Constitutional Rally, or RCD), and occupying and expanding a previously prohibited public space.[2] However, people became involved in the protest movement for a broad range of reasons that cannot be framed in any one particular way. Taking action at differing times and through a variety of avenues, the participants did not all have the same social background or the same relationship to authority.

Following the repression of the rally on February 25, 2011, in Tunis' Government Square, protest actions were increasingly pushed to the sidelines. This does not imply that they were on the wane; after all, they retained substantial scope. The appointment of Béji Caïd Essebsi—a former Bourguiba minister—to the position of prime minister "[put] the revolution back into the state framework" (Khiari 2012).

The second pitfall consists of assuming mass spontaneity. It is important to document and analyze the practices that emerge during events and to note the contingencies and the seemingly insignificant details that may drive social agents to rebel and take part in an uprising. But this cannot be achieved without exploring the trajectories of these agents. In Tunisia the "democratic opposition" sequence is commonly cited to explain the rise of a protest movement against the Ben Ali regime. While this explanation seems inadequate, it would be equally unfounded to claim that we are dealing with a spontaneous movement, a manifestation of an "immaculate conception" view of contention (Taylor 1989, 761, 772).

The connection between the popular uprising in the winter of 2010–11 and the dynamics of opposition to Ben Ali from political forces and the not-for-profit sector since the late 1990s is hard to establish (Khiari 2003). The protests around the 2005 UN World Summit on the Information Society in Tunis, complete with a "cyber-dissident avant-garde," marked an important step.[3] But the argument that radical political change began with the country's opposition parties and "independent civil society" does not hold much water. These elitist organizations had very little influence due to their limited audience in such a tightly controlled public space. For fifty-five years, alternatives to the hegemonic party had extremely limited scope. Opposition parties and organizations were tiny groups with only shallow roots in society. The UGTT was a docile organization dispensing patronage; its more militant members were muzzled. Drastic repression had deprived the Islamist movement of any real presence on the domestic political stage (Camau and Geisser 2003). The multisector mobilizations in the winter of 2011 were powerful precisely because they had no leader, central command, or coordinating structure (Dobry 2009). At the outset, "revolutionary" involvement was the act of day laborers, unemployed youth, whether university-educated or not, and resourceful people of the "Ben Ali generation" used to fending for themselves—people with no party affiliation, many of whom paid the ultimate price for rebelling. Middle-class urbanites who could no longer stomach what they considered the increasingly mafia-style behavior and "crass ignorance" evinced by the "cliques" in power joined them.[4]

This chapter examines the multiple pathways during the revolutionary moment by analyzing specific cases and comparing and contrasting individuals or peer groups that became "revolutionary" in the course of action. It identifies two patterns to clarify the underlying perceptions and choices of the individuals and groups engaged in this intense, rapidly unfolding movement: (1) participation in the collective protests that were gathering momentum since 2008 in the Tunisian "hinterland"; and (2) the instances of sometimes ambivalent oppositional conduct and resistance that developed among various segments of the population, which, in certain circumstances, turned into an outright challenge to the regime. This processual analysis differs from monocausal structuralist explanations of how revolutions come about because it focuses on the conditions that led to involvement—a comprehensive approach to retracing the stages in the revolutionary process rather than a concern with uncovering the initial causes of the "revolution."[5]

Starting with the large-scale protests that erupted in the Gafsa mining basin in the southwest in January 2008, and for the first time since 1984 (Lahmar and Zghal 1997; Lamloum 1999), unprecedented collective revolt became increasingly common in the impoverished regions referred to as Tunisia's "hinterland." Each of these mobilizations had its own history, reflecting specific socioeconomic conditions and local realities of political patronage, particularly the former party-state's ability to redistribute income. By probing the relationships among experiences with resistance and protest that may not have been spatially or temporally connected, we can gain insight into the revolutionary process (Bennani-Chraïbi and Fillieule 2003). Based on field work carried out since 2006 in the Gafsa region and Hammam-Lif, a working-class suburb to the south of Tunis, and the demonstrations, uprisings, and other forms of "critical" involvement in the greater Tunis area during January 2011, this chapter examines individuals' ambivalence in following these different pathways, documents the shifts, accelerations, and bifurcations along the road to protest, and weighs the role of specific locations and different historical sequences in the unfolding of revolt, and the participants' preferred forms of action. Misunderstandings, information and distortion of information, rumors and their appropriation as vehicles for denunciation rooted in specific social contexts all built up in such a way that at one brief moment, social groups with differing interests and, in some cases, conflicting socioeconomic conditions "took the plunge," entering the struggle with the common slogan, "Ben Ali, get out!"

## THE DYNAMIC OF PROTEST IN THE TUNISIAN HINTERLAND

While there is no consistent causal relationship between economic conditions and revolt, two major divides have unquestionably played a major part in the protest movement: one social and regional, the other generational. Tunisia's political and economic geography shows that the map of socioeconomic disparity coincides with the "protest map" of the years preceding 2011. Powerful protest movements broke out in impoverished areas like the Gafsa mining basin in the southwest in 2008, Ben Guerdane in the southeast in August 2010, and the Sidi Bouzid farming region and in Kasserine and Thala in the center-west of the country in December 2010. They revealed what the Tunisian "economic miracle" (Hibou 1999) had concealed from view: regional disparities, and the economic and social marginalization of large swathes of the population that were deprived of social protection because they had no access to the official employment channels.

Behind these protests were an unorganized underclass and youth with no social and political capital. The men and women at the forefront were most commonly unemployed or workers with jobs viewed as grueling and degrading: contingent workers at subcontracting companies in the phosphate industry, smugglers in Ben Guerdane eking out a living in a survival economy regularly hampered by customs officials, agricultural day laborers in the center-west of the country, university graduates forced to settle for jobs at call centers in the big cities, "boys from the hood" who spent their time hanging around in cafés and trying their luck in the informal economy.

## PROTEST IN THE GAFSA MINING BASIN

Starting on January 6, 2008, after the results of a competitive entry exam held by the public sector Compagnie des Phosphates de Gafsa (Gafsa Phosphate Company—CPG) were announced, a wave of mass protest erupted in the main villages and cities in the southwestern mining centers and lasted for six months despite severe repression. Anger over nepotistic hiring practices at CPG brought together a large number of unemployed workers (university graduates and others) and their families.

Phosphate mining is the primary activity in Gafsa, an arid region whose farming sector has been devastated by a combination of insufficient rainfall and heavy use of water at CPG washing plants. According to official statistics, the Gafsa governorate has one of the highest unemployment rates in Tunisia—nearly twice the national average; there is considerable poverty particularly in the eastern villages and the mining towns. The overhaul of CPG since the mid-1980s along neoliberal lines, supported by World Bank loans, led to a decline in local hiring. Although it is one of the world's largest phosphate producers, CPG virtually stopped recruiting and axed ten thousand jobs, two-thirds of its total workforce. In a region offering job-seekers very few other options for work, this inevitably increased unemployment, especially among youth (Allal 2010).

Initially, young men who were excluded from the world of production and struggling to find jobs made up the bulk of the 2008 protesters.[6] Their demands combined with those of both casual workers and workers with regular, higher-paying jobs at CPG. Because many of the unemployed were living under the same roof as much-envied regular employees, day laborers, or seasonal workers, their struggles had to do with improving conditions for the entire family. Women were at the forefront of the movement. Although very few of the female demonstrators were activists in political parties or voluntary organizations, demonstrations in Gafsa, Oum El Araies, M'dhila, Métlaoui, and Redeyef regularly drew wives and widows of phosphate miners and other workers, unemployed female university graduates, high school students, rank-and-file union members, and mothers and grandmothers of jailed demonstrators.

In the Gafsa area, CPG was widely perceived to be the sole alternative to poverty. Demonstrators felt that CPG owed something to the many families of workers whose had been "worn down" by the company. "They should be paying us back by giving our kids jobs," said one mother who had gone to an encampment in Oum El Araies to support her son. The slogans of 2008 also targeted the UGTT regional head. A thirty-year-old protester named Ziyad was one of the leaders of the movement where he lived—Oum El Araies, one of the four mining towns. Ziyad was one of a few dozen activists who held secret discussions starting in 2006 to set up and coordinate an Association des Diplômés Chômeurs de la Région de Gafsa (Gafsa Region Unemployed Graduates Association). In that period, he commented, "Ben Ali? I don't know who he is and I don't care about him. But this guy [the UGTT regional representative] is definitely a crook. He's the one who got us into the situation we're in today." The union leader thus embodied the sense of injustice and inevitability that the region's unemployed youth intended to fight. Indeed, as an elected representative of the RCD and the director of CPG subcontracting plants, this "big man" had a major say in who got which job at CPG. As the head of a patronage network to which these young people had no access, he epitomized the corruption they denounced and their feeling of being déclassé—a term they used in articulating their grievances—or downgraded, especially since his factories offered more precarious employment than CPG itself.

For the first two months, oppositional political groups, "independent civil society," and the UGTT played no part in organizing the movement. The revolt had already taken on considerable proportions in January 2008, with thousands of demonstrators occupying the public space in the main mining towns. In Métlaoui, barricades and burning tires made it hard for the police to regain control of the city area. In some neighboring villages, the population came out into the streets to express anger over the arrest of a "local boy." Movement leaders in Redeyef addressed extremely large outdoor crowds. During the two-month period, dissident trade unionists, high school students, "unemployed graduates," and their families all mobilized to demand that the authorities provide young people with jobs, release the hundreds of jailed demonstrators, and more. Another striking development was that the RCD party cadres did not coordinate efforts to quell the revolt in the various hotbeds, a reflection of internal struggles of the region's political and trade union elite. Some local RCD leaders initially stood on the sidelines, viewing the unrest as an effective way to oust rivals directly denounced by angry demonstrators.

In the four cities of the mining basin, heavy repression and attempts to buy off groups of protesters produced contrasting responses.[7] The movement in Redeyef, where local activists from unions of clerical employees (who disobeyed their higher-ups) played a more significant role, held out for a full six months. But in June 2008, after the main leaders had been arrested, the mobilization petered out in the entire mining area. This trend was strengthened by a tried-and-tested trick: President Ben Ali once again promised the region large-scale development projects. However, this was not enough to assuage the widespread skepticism of the population. The local worthy who was the primary focus of criticism still held on to his multiple mandates. Many protesters felt the need to continue the struggle. As soon as he was released from prison in July, Ziyad said, "This isn't the end of the movement. Now we know how much power we have, and they can't kill us all. We're going to fight until the Trabelsis and the Ben Alis of our region are out. Then we'll go after the real culprits."

Ziyad was heavily involved in the first demonstrations held in the region in December 2010. Like him, a good many veterans of the 2008 movement jumped into the fray, organizing marches, sit-ins, and other familiar forms of action. By the end of December, such efforts to coordinate the struggle were quickly outflanked by a spate of insurgent initiatives whose slogans and acts gradually came to be directed against the police, the authorities, the party, and President Ben Ali himself.

## A MOUNTING WAVE OF PROTEST

The movement of August 2010 in Ben Guerdane, on the Libyan border, represented a significant stage in the mounting wave of protest. The collective action was in response to the closing of the border when the Libyan government shut down the Ras Jdir customs post, the daily point of transit for a transnational contraband economy (Meddeb 2011). This disrupted an economy on which substantial portions of the regional population depended for their livelihood. Peaceful demonstrations demanding the reopening of the border met with harsh repression. Arrests and police brutality merely strengthened the movement, so much so that the Tunisian authorities felt compelled to negotiate with the Libyan government over reopening the border. By upsetting the inequitable yet vital balance created by an illegal, largely corrupt cross-border economy, the authorities had triggered a protest movement that took on increasing intensity in a number of locations in the Ben Guerdane area.

Four months later, Mohamed Tariq al-Bouazizi, a vegetable vendor in Sidi Bouzid, committed suicide by setting himself ablaze. This immediately publicized act came to stand for the indignation felt by a large part of the country and expressed at different times through collective action. Bouazizi became the emblematic figure of an informal economy that was being arbitrarily and violently thwarted.

While the protest movements in Tunisia's hinterland reflected specific, local modes of expression and socioeconomic conditions, they also displayed several common features. In every instance, the protesters denounced nepotism, challenged the supposed inevitability of unemployment, and engaged in collective action with little institutional backing; in any event, they were out of step with the oppositional party and trade union leadership. The dynamic of mobilization and the forms of action took on a recurrent character—marches and sit-ins came up against harsh police repression, which in turn triggered further mobilization. In response to the first arrests, demonstrators marched on police stations and other government buildings. The first casualties sparked even greater protest. Moreover, these developments revealed cracks in the edifice of party-state influence and control, as well as the authorities' difficulties in stamping out the revolt with mere repression. Yet the sources of anger changed. The key slogan in Gafsa had been "Give us jobs, and stop stealing from us." In Ben Guerdane, protesters chanted, "Open the border so we can survive!"

The sequence from 2008 to 2010, characterized by the spread of protest movements, may not have been the precondition for actions during the revolutionary moment of 2010–11, which had their own rationale. The hardships endured by the population in the hinterland regions did not generate a revolutionary "vanguard." But, they did congeal in the minds of many individuals (whether directly involved in protest or not), becoming a leitmotiv for their involvement in the revolution.

The revolutionary process marked the shift to outright protest by people previously engaged in more diffuse forms of resistance to the political status quo. The cost of overt protest in authoritarian regimes is higher than that of routine forms of resistance (Pommerolle and Vairel 2009). Understanding the popular uprising in Tunisia requires analysis of the forms of resistance and oppositional behavior that developed during the last years of Ben Ali's reign. The dichotomy between resistance and protest is less relevant here than the transition from one to the other (Bennani-Chraïbi and Fillieule 2003) because the same individuals may well engage simultaneously in activities that can be termed "resistance," "protest," and "conventional participation."

## ORDINARY RESISTANCE AND "REVOLUTIONARY" ACTION

Silence does not always imply consent. Social scientists who take their lead from Juan J. Linz (2000) have been a little too quick to equate the feeble response of dissonant voices in the institutional public arena (for example, the press, political groups, trade unions, voluntary organizations), particularly in authoritarian settings, with consent, or a lack of opinion, or the political views of the "silent majority." Although there were many critical utterances and practices in Tunisia, the public scene has often been analyzed in terms of political apathy and depoliticization due to tight control of public space by the security apparatus. In the Tunisian context, Timur Kuran's (1995) "preference falsification" seems less pronounced if "low-key" manifestations of political discontent are factored in. In many public contexts, people can voice criticism and denunciation without exposing themselves to repression because they know, even in authoritarian regimes, that others harbor similar feelings, although they may not express them in the same way. Focusing on private preferences, the ones that matter according to Kuran, therefore risks distracting attention from the constantly evolving critical perceptions that can be found in the "public" and "private" spheres alike, and that contribute to how actors redefine the options for action available to them.

Forms of resistance that had been under way for some time, and that may have looked as though they were reproducing the authoritarian status quo, began to take on a different character as political circumstances changed during the winter of 2010–11. I encountered individuals and small peer groups from various social milieus who admitted their sense of "outrage" at what they considered a mafia-style or predatory regime that they blamed for their lesser and greater misfortunes. Although they did not belong to opposition or radical groups, they did not refrain from speaking out in all circumstances; they voiced their anger in a variety of contexts. The examples presented here were chosen because looking at these particular actors and situations helps to answer the question of how the revolt in Tunisia grew, while revealing the wide range of perceptions and motives for involvement to be found among the actors.

## Yusra: The Tale of an Unlikely Dissenter Inside the Party-State

The RCD, the single party dissolved on March 9, 2011, was a protean organization encompassing a wide spectrum of statuses and functions and individuals with highly diverse characteristics and differing degrees of participation. At the July 2008 congress marking the twentieth anniversary of the adoption of the RCD name, the leadership claimed 2.2 million members in a country of ten million. There were multiple channels for joining. A large number of card-carrying members who participated in party-linked activities began to resist the status quo; these ambivalent dissenters followed bumpy roads toward open protest during the revolutionary moment.

Like Tunisia's founding president Habib Bourguiba, Yusra was born in Monastir, a city in the Sahel coastal region from which Ben Ali and many other prominent political figures hailed. "A lot of ministers and ambassadors attended my high school," she proudly told me in 2007.[8] This forty-seven-year-old woman was the daughter and niece of two activists in the national movement who had fought alongside Bourguiba. Although she never obtained her diploma, she did get a high school education. With the help of family "intervention," she landed a civil service job in Tunis and was subsequently promoted. Yusra is married and has three children: two sons, aged nineteen and fifteen, and a nine-year-old daughter. Her severely alcoholic husband had been jobless for ten years. The quarrels between them often turned violent. As the family's sole breadwinner, Yusra "needed the party," as she frequently stressed.

However, her efforts to make the most of her prestigious family background soon proved insufficient to obtain RCD favors. "Here in Hammam-Lif, I can't ask them for anything. They're just a bunch of thugs, crooks and *jbura* [country bumpkins]. In fact, I'm scared to go there on my own, with all those men ogling me in their coarse way." The petty corruption engaged in by RCD agents had been yielding fewer "extras" since the untimely deaths of her father and uncle, and she deeply resented being sidelined in this way. Yet Yusra remained a fervent Ben Ali supporter: "He isn't informed of all the shady deals those crooks are involved in, and besides, that hairdresser of his [his wife, Leila Trabelsi] has him under her spell. Her brothers and sons are all lined up to steal everything from us. I'm really worried about this country." Even so, she maintained her RCD membership and continually reaffirmed her attachment to the party, its achievements, and above all its leader. Gesturing to his portrait on her living-room wall, she said, "Make no mistake about it. Ben Ali saved us; he saved Bourguiba's legacy."

While many Tunisians were regularly subjected to similar vexations and complained about them in private, what distinguished Yusra was that she publicly vented her irritation. During her commute to and from the capital every Monday through Friday she angrily recounted the unsavory behavior of the local despots to her fellow passengers.[9] For the entire thirty-minute trip, she held forth in a train jam-packed with high school and university students, white-collar workers, workers in the Mégrine industrial park, and low-level government employees. She would denounce the "kleptocrats" and pass on the wildest rumors about the pernicious power of the Trabelsis, sometimes throwing in more accurate information about how various clans were looting public sector companies like Tunisair. What she heard from her eldest son at home in the evening provided her with extra ammunition. Thanks to his computer and Internet connection, made available at a subsidized price by local RCD cadres, he would surf the web, dodging censorship, sharing information with his Facebook friends, and fill in his mother on the latest. Some of Yusra's younger fellow train passengers considered her "suicidal." On one such trip to Tunis, a student called out with a big grin, "I think I'd better pay the supplement for traveling first class—it's too risky in here. See you later."

This woman's tendency to recriminate in public reflected both a family history of political activism and her sense of declining status, due to a "bad marriage" and loss of family support. Other experiences heightened her discontent. Her younger son's application to the high school he wanted to attend was turned down. "His grades weren't fantastic, but he still should have been given a chance to enroll. Other kids with the same grades got in. The principal was condescending to me," she said. Another episode left her with a firm opinion of the "local mafia." After her eldest son had a fight with a neighbor, Yusra requested an appointment with the local authorities, which was rejected. She then went to the local police station, where, as she put it, "I was mistreated, practically raped by those thugs. They take advantage of Ben Ali's party to rough up and hurt people, all just to lay their hands on a few extra dinars."

Ambivalent condemnation of corruption, anger over police brutality, the declining status of a low-level government employee whose working and living conditions deteriorating, resentment toward a party no longer open to some people, and gender violence were the main motives for Yusra's increasingly vocal criticisms. However, the photos her son showed her on his computer of the mutilated bodies of young men brutalized during the events in Thala and Kasserine on January 8 and 9, 2011, were what ultimately pushed her to turn to collective protest. "It's as if they'd killed my own son. . . . [Y]oung men just like him were the ones who died," she said. Subsequently going into greater detail, she stated, "A coworker of mine who's from Kasserine calls me that very evening and tells me that the kids of some colleagues from the ministry who work in the region are in prison now. Others are dead. These are ordinary people who have never made waves. So everything was jumbled in my mind. I had dreams in which my son was the one who'd died. The next day, I get this text message: 'General strike tomorrow.' That's when I decided I was going to join in to find out more."

On January 14, 2011, Yusra was on Avenue Bourguiba in downtown Tunis with her eldest son. As if to reassure herself, she told virtually everyone she encountered, "This is my very first demonstration. I've never been in a union, and when a strike is called, I usually stay home, but this time, enough is enough. They're killing kids; things just can't go on this way." Suddenly, a feeling of amused apprehension came over her as she heard people chanting a slogan that, to her way of thinking, went too far. "What? They want Ben Ali out?" For the time being, she stood quietly on the other side of the avenue with demonstrators who had left the median strip to veteran protesters. Early in the morning, the latter had gathered in front of UGTT headquarters, before setting out for the Ministry of the Interior, "the heart of a heartless regime," as a member of the Tunisian Communist Workers' Party called out. These few thousand protesters—seasoned activists, union militants, young artists and radicals, lawyers, members of legal opposition parties—succeeded in breaking through the police cordons. On Avenue Bourguiba, the rare attempts at chanting left-wing slogans were quickly met with the chant "La ilaha illa'llah" ("There is no god but Allah") by the few Islamists from the Tunisian General Students Union present. The demonstrators then struck up the national anthem to bridge this political divide, to emphasize that this was a time for unity. Meanwhile, Yusra stayed on the other side of the avenue for quite a few minutes, until the swelling crowd swept her along in the direction of the other demonstrators. Caught up in the movement, she soon found herself chanting the same slogans as the hundreds of thousands of demonstrators amassed in front of the Ministry of the Interior.

It started with the national anthem, but the enthusiasm of the crowd soon led her to join in shouting, "Ben Ali, get out!"

Yusra's profile highlights the ambivalence of the many Tunisians engaged in both "conventional" politics (through the RCD) and "unconventional" politics (sidestepping, denouncing, challenging authority), and how such people may shift from one mode to the other. This also suggests that in addition to its contradictory nature, such a protean, supposedly unified party was also the scene of internal struggles. The backdrop was a difficult fight over Ben Ali's succession, which required a revision of the constitution to allow Ben Ali to run in 2014 and which gave rise in some areas to fierce infighting between rival RCD clans (Chouikha and Geisser 2010). This was particularly apparent at the December 2010 convention of the Monastir federation (Béchir-Ayari 2013). This tendency of the party apparatus to ossify need not have resulted in a crisis of the party-state and its inaction during the uprising; it does make it easier to grasp how a number of RCD members could eventually join the rebels. However, it should be stressed that contingent events provided the opportunities for action and involvement.

Space is an important issue, a prerequisite for the kind of resistance discussed above.[10] In Yusra's experience, this meant a commuter train as the ideal place to express herself. It could also mean a specific microspace, like a café, which came to play a crucial part in the process through which young men in downtown Gafsa mobilized (or demobilized).

### A Place for Education in Dissidence: The "Freedom Aquarium" in Gafsa

This was how a group of men aged twenty to thirty-nine referred to the place where they got together on a daily basis in downtown Gafsa.[11] Their "subversive café," as they called it, actually spanned two adjacent terraces. Its perimeter was clearly marked in their minds: "If there was no room left in our area, we refrained from talking politics," explained Muhammad. Most of the twenty-something young men in the group were "wageless workers" or, as Muhammad jokingly put it, "jobless people with jobs." Their profiles included temporary warehouseman, substitute salesman, assistant in an empty photo development lab, casual waiter, and extra taxi driver on the night shift. Yet all except one of them had a baccalauréat high school diploma; some had university degrees. Most of them knew each other from growing up in the same nearby housing project. Although they hoped to get married and often talked about it, few of them were. Because they had no money, they were not in a position to do so. Most of them lived at their parents' home. Mustafa, aged thirty-eight, who worked irregularly for an intercity collective taxi service, broke down his daily expenses as follows: "Two packs of cigarettes, six capucins (cups of coffee), one hookah pipeful, and a little bit of money to shop for my mother."

These young men described a precarious existence of a kind that many Tunisians experienced, but unlike the others, they viewed themselves as "resistance fighters." Sitting around at their café, they denounced the system. Murad said loudly, "I spend my time running around left and right, like someone who's come to beg for work. They act as if they were doing you a big favor, and you have to pay them *baqshish* to get a job or be allowed to take a competitive exam." The group got together every day to discuss the depths to which politics in Tunisia had sunk. Its members made extensive use of humor with a predominantly ironic tone: "Ben 'Ali ila al-abad" ("Ben Ali forever") became their slogan in 2007. They also rendered it as "Forever BA," dubbing their group the "Forever BA Gang." They referred to their collective experience with resistance as "muqawama dud . . . al-gigna" ("resistance to boredom").

None of them belonged to opposition groups, but the source of the news they discussed was El Hiwar Ettounsi, an oppositional satellite TV channel broadcasting from abroad. Rida, in fact, emerged as an expert of sorts in installing satellite dishes for his friends and programming their favorite channel for free. The members of the group would share copies of legal opposition publications on the sly and keep each other up to date on the latest jokes about Ben Ali's in-laws. Al-Bahi, one of the few to have an Internet connection at home, sometimes brought along information copied from websites "that tell the truth" to read it to his friends.

One rather different member of the "resistance" group, Nizar, was termed a *sabbab* (fink). A former RCD activist at the University of Sousse, he landed a good position at the Ministry of Employment once he returned to Gafsa. Whenever they all met up at the café in the evening, Nizar did his best to keep the others from going overboard with their criticisms of the regime. But as Muhammad saw things, "He wouldn't dare to denounce his own friends. And anyway, I consider him a valuable resource. As long as he hangs out with us, we won't arouse suspicion."

Although the group's members came from the area around Gafsa, Sened, or El Guettar, most of them had family ties in the mining basin, in Métlaoui, and above all in Redeyef. Very few of them were interested in getting jobs at the CPG, and only two ever applied, unsuccessfully, for administrative positions at the company's head office in Gafsa. But the 2008 protest movement in the mining region became highly significant in their eyes.

The group got details about the first stage of the revolt from Muhammad's cousin, who was right in the epicenter of the struggle in Redeyef. After three weeks, Muhammad decided to visit his family there. Traveling in Mustafa's taxi, he made it through the military and police checkpoints with the excuse that he was visiting an aunt in ill health. Once they reached Redeyef, Mustafa stayed on. "My initial plan was just to drop him off and drive back, but his aunt ended up inviting us for lunch. And besides, there was such an unbelievable atmosphere there—totally insane! We were scared stiff, but we wanted to see and find out for ourselves. The movement was much larger than we'd imagined. And although we never did get to meet 'Adnan Hajji [the rank-and-file union leader who was the movement's charismatic figure], we heard and saw a great deal. There was tremendous courage; the fighting spirit of our ancestors has revived. We're standing tall again."[12]

Back at the café, the two travelers reported to the others about "the beauty of an independent mobilization," the "charisma" of 'Adnan Hajji as a speaker. Soon enough, however, after most of the movement leadership was arrested during a wave of repression in early April, their discussions took on a less romantic character, focusing essentially on what the main protesters were going through. Muhammad's cousin was arrested and tortured. To help with his defense, Muhammad informed family members living in Nantes, France, of the brutality their relative was experiencing, using coded language on the phone and in email messages. Those family members were instrumental in building support, both in Nantes and in the Belleville neighborhood of Paris, particularly at solidarity demonstrations organized by a left-wing group active in France, the Fédération des Tunisiens pour une Citoyenneté des Deux Rives (Federation of Tunisians for Citizenship on Both Shores). Meanwhile, the members of the Aquarium in Gafsa soon faced the "consequences" of their involvement in the form of direct repression. Al-Bahi's younger brother was beaten and taken to the police station after taking part in demonstrations. Al-Bahi accused Mustafa and his followers of having a bad influence on his sibling. Along with six other members of the group (including Nizar of the RCD), the two brothers withdrew from the Aquarium.

On January 14, 2011, the members of the group were not particularly active, observing the mobilizations on this last day of Ben Ali's reign as mere onlookers. One of the reasons for this was that they had distanced themselves from the violence of the previous days, which they equated with the "wild" behavior of rioters from whom they had always distinguished themselves as "resistance fighters in a sitting position." The increasingly routine quality of low-intensity protest, combined with a certain degree of boredom in the group (and the split that occurred), heightened its members' sense of alienation from the violent struggles that unfolded in rapid succession in early January. To them, January 14 seemed like just another day until the news broke that Ben Ali was on the run.

Just two days later, the entire group got back together at the café. After a week, Muhammad's cousin in Redeyef informed them that contingents of demonstrators from various regions were beginning to occupy the Kasbah's Government Square in Tunis. Mustafa immediately stepped forward as coordinator. Twelve members of the Aquarium went to the capital to camp out as well. As Mustafa emphatically put it, "The people at the Kasbah are genuine revolutionaries, people with no money who've paid a very high price for dictatorship and rebellion. We're going there to kick [the rulers] out . . . for good, to keep the revolution moving forward. We can't let them just replace a couple of ministers, because that wouldn't have the slightest impact on the constant state of siege we've been living under in Gafsa."

The Aquarium formed a "free space" (Céfaï 2007, 646ff.), much like those that have existed elsewhere, despite authoritarian and police-state rule. It was a place for expressing a sense of injustice, for speaking out against the regime, for condemning its brutality and all the ludicrous pomp and ceremony surrounding Ben Ali's autocratic power. But it was also a space for building long-term friendships grounded in mutual trust that are crucial to involvement in protest. Lastly, the café was a place for imagining and working out strategies of action.

Such forms of nonviolent resistance existed alongside other paths to political radicalization in which physical involvement was central. This was particularly true of the "young rebels" in the working-class suburbs of Tunis.

### Young Rebels in Hammam-Lif: From Avoidance to Insurrection

A group of eight young men from a poor background in a working-class district south of Tunis engaged in a mounting series of acts of rebellion.[13] These "sons of the Ben Ali generation," born after 1987 and Ben Ali's "medical" coup d'état, had no qualms about denouncing their elders and their "system," taking part in urban dissidence, getting involved with rebel artists, taking drugs, or engaging in stadium violence. They had already pushed such practices in more radical directions in 2007, before joining in the January 2011 uprising.

"On ne veut pas être des combinards, des débrouillards . . . des ringards!" (roughly: "We're fed up with scams, schemes, and has-been dreams"). Commenting on this rap stanza spray-painted in the back of his brother's store, Sami explained why he refused to live the way other people do, "during the daytime." He added, "We live by night to avoid society." Asked whether he and his friends sneak free rides, he answered by taking his metaphor further: "No, because we don't use the seats. We sit on the train roof, or on the platform between subway cars, in the shadow of society."

Sami had no intention of working, breaking his back for next to nothing, and he was willing to make do with very little money. Yet his friends nicknamed him the internship record-holder, since he had spent four years going through one training course after another, none of which ever got him anywhere. He and his friends were the children of office workers, laborers, and cleaning women, with very few prospects of upward mobility. Some of them got jobs, but invariably with long interruptions in between, never for an entire year straight. Sami added, disenchanted, "How can you be expected to explain who you are? How do you answer the question, 'What do you do for a living?' if you're forced to look for a new job every month? You're better off saying nothing, doing nothing." In the summertime, three members of the group worked as DJs at nightclubs in Hammamet, or even as far away as Sousse. This gave them the opportunity to observe the "families," with their showy lifestyles and their Hummers, semimilitary vehicles that both fascinated and disgusted them. On several occasions, they described the boorishness of the Trabelsi family.

In Echaabya, their neighborhood, belonging to the "Ben Ali generation" meant experiencing police brutality. Most of the group's members had their own stories to tell. Once, while Ahmad was praying, the police picked him up and held him for two nights in jail. "Brother, if a cop from our neighborhood hadn't stepped in, they would have bottle-raped me," he recounted. A rap artist, Ahmad sang about H'rig, his longing to escape the country, to "take off from the Hammam-Lif international airport"—the facetious nickname for a point on the Hammam-Lif shore from which boats set out for Italy. He also set himself certain moral standards: "You have to stay away from whores and depraved parties." Ahmad stressed that he was a Muslim rapper, not an Islamist rapper. He had firsthand knowledge of the Islamists. His father, an Ennahda (al-Nahda) activist from the early 1980s to the 1990s, was incarcerated several times, subjected to torture, and deprived of his civil rights. After four years in prison, he died. Ahmad's older brother was likewise involved in the Islamist movement. Although trained in engineering, he wound up selling bootleg CDs. Ahmad was highly critical of his family members, bitterly running down the list of their mistakes and their stubborn ways. Concerned with setting himself apart, he explained, "I personally don't see anything wrong with drinking or going out with decent girls, as long as you remain a Muslim and say your prayers." That, too, was made impossible by the police. "My girlfriend and I were on the beach in the summer, behind the seawall, when two policemen came over and humiliated us. They slapped me and insulted my girl." He added in conclusion, "So we aren't allowed to drink or to pray."

One particular setting where this group, like many other working-class youth, encountered police brutality was at soccer matches. As fans of the Club Sportif de Hammam-Lif and the Club Africain (one of the two major teams in the capital), they often had run-ins with the police. Hundreds of young men would leave Hammam-Lif on weekends to attend games, and on the long hike back home, it took considerable ingenuity to circumvent the security cordons and avoid getting clubbed. The participants would collectively organize ways to escape when the police charged, preparing for the upcoming battle the night before by hiding stones in the bushes along their return route.

In their neighborhood, these "rebels" would stage danger scenes, particularly at night, filming controlled skids on scooters that provoked high-speed chases with the police. These acts of urban dissidence combined with other forms of counterconduct, like cannabis use, which carries heavy penalties in Tunisia. This was regarded as a source of local pride given the city's reputation for traffic in all manner of goods. According to Ahmad, Humit al-sabun (the "soap district") derived its name from cannabis ("soap" is the term for a cake of hashish).

The political radicalization of the Hammam-Lif rebel group was triggered by an incident in the neighboring town of Sulayman in January 2007. An armed group branded "Salafi terrorists" by the government was surrounded in a private home and flushed out by the Special Forces. Sami and his brother happened to be in the area where the siege took place. Gunfire continued for several hours. Shut up in the house of friends, they filmed bits of the bloody assault. Almost as soon as they got back to Hammam-Lif, Sami was arrested and interrogated by the police for three days in Tunis. When he returned home with his face swollen, his friends gave him a hero's welcome. Many others in the neighborhood urged him to tell them all about what he had witnessed.

Starting in the spring of 2007, the group met increasingly often at night on the premises used by Sami's older brother to burn CDs and DVDs. Three computers and high-speed Internet service enabled the group to surf the web and find proxies so that they could connect up to a large number of prohibited websites. Although they spent most of their time watching movies featuring girls or fight scenes, the misdeeds of the Trabelsi clan gradually took on greater and greater importance in their eyes. It gave them ideas for political slogans they could paint on walls running alongside the train tracks during their increasingly frequent nighttime expeditions. They even considered filming the corruption engaged in by inspectors at the central police station in Hammam-Lif, making fun of how RCD bigwigs and their children used official cars for private purposes, and more.

While immersed in the world of American gangsta rap, Hollywood action movies, and video fight games, they were particularly encouraged by the Wikileaks leak, picked up in Tunisia by the dissident website *Nawaat*, about corruption at the top of the Tunisian regime. "America is dumping them," Sami concluded with great self-assurance. "They're going to send out a drone the size of a fly that's going to sting him and his hairdresser wife. It'll kill them," Ahmad confidently added. This perception of how vulnerable the people in power were emboldened them to take their revolt further.

Starting on January 10, some members of the group decided to get actively involved in the struggle. They staged nighttime raids to harass the police, while others like Sami posted videos of their confrontations on video-sharing websites. On the evening of January 13, the boys made serious preparations, braved the curfew, and set about attacking the local police station, with Sami coordinating the operation. As someone with a large network of connections, he succeeded in getting the word out to friends in one neighborhood after another. The relationships, skills, and knowledge built up by a large number of young soccer-team supporters proved especially valuable. They enjoyed and had no fear of confronting the police, and they had mastered some of the requisite skills. Along with groups from other neighborhoods, they waged the battle, hurling stones in response to gunfire. Three hours later, there were no policemen left in the central police station.

By the next morning, they had earned an entirely different reputation parallel to their new way of relating to the adults in the area—relatives, neighbors, and shopkeepers. Formerly viewed as "deadbeats" and "hoodlums," they were now hailed as "real men" and "revolutionaries" (Allal 2011). They subsequently formed neighborhood "vigilance committees," organizing trash removal and keeping watch all night to ensure the security of the population.

## CONCLUSION: "NOTHING WILL EVER BE THE SAME AGAIN"?

A radical shift in perception occurred during the month of January 2011. A large part of the population now perceived the disproportionate, increasingly unjustifiable nature of police repression, as a symptom of a regime on its last legs. The differential that people identified between events they experienced firsthand and how the strictly censored media portrayed those events crystallized discontent resulted in many Tunisians beginning to imagine the end of Ben Ali's reign. While there were a variety of patterns for getting information and making assessments, a convergent narrative emerged that pitted "them" (*al-Sulta*, that is, the regime, the police, the Trabelsi clique) against "us," the "people of Tunisia."

Disaggregating the atmosphere of unanimity characteristic of revolutionary moments, I have endeavored to highlight the fluctuating motives and modes of action apparent when different social groups become radicalized. I sought to draw attention to the multiple pathways that led individuals and groups to become involved in protest, based on their specific skills, resources, perceptions, and justifications. By emphasizing this variety of pathways, we can avoid considering the types of people I have focused on as the "losers of history" (Gaïti 1994). Once the smoke has cleared, there is a strong temptation to downplay such small-scale involvements and focus instead on "History with a capital H," the story of "great men" and victors. Yet understanding the popular uprising in Tunisia, as anywhere else, requires thorough analysis of the relations underpinning the sort of social life that may take place "underground" or be partially hidden from view.

This approach also avoids reducing everything to a question of "revolutionary mobilization" without considering the multidimensional character of the revolutionary process. The microsociological study conducted here demonstrates that socioprofessional conditions, prospects of upward mobility, neighborhood and family ties, generational issues, memories of past protests and/or experience with police repression offer far greater insights than membership in oppositional parties and other organizations into how and why people got involved in the "revolution." The multidimensionality of the revolutionary process can also be seen in the uneven weight of contextual factors like the crisis of succession for head of state against a background of rumors about the president's in-laws and the rising tide of collective protest from 2008 to 2010 in Tunisia's hinterland. Of course, it can also be seen in the series of developments that marked the "political crisis" as such, including the breakdown of command

and control in the security apparatus, the trade union federation's decision to join the movement, and the dissemination of pictures of police brutality.

"Nothing will ever be the same again," joyously chanted most of the participants in the popular uprising after Ben Ali's flight on January 14, 2011. This phrase sums up their perception that the extraordinary process they were experiencing was irreversible. Despite this apparent consensus, the diversity of life situations, social relations, and mental universes soon reasserted itself once the exhilaration of the "revolutionary moment" of January–February faded. The return to "normal" led some people to withdraw from protest and others to take their radicalism to a higher level. No longer caught up in the fast-paced revolutionary moment, each person seemed to recover his or her own pace in a rapidly shifting political situation whose full scope can only be assessed once the longer story of Tunisia's revolutionary process has become known. While Yusra has moved Ben Ali's portrait from her living room to her bedroom and swears in disgust that she will never go to another demonstration again, the young rebels of Hammam-Lif have withdrawn in their own way. They no longer occupy public space and did not take part in the October 2011 election campaign or even vote. As for Ziyad, a veteran of increasingly intense struggles in the mining basin, he claims that he will be "the next one to set himself on fire if we don't get jobs soon."

# 10 A WORKERS' SOCIAL MOVEMENT ON THE MARGIN OF THE GLOBAL NEOLIBERAL ORDER, EGYPT 2004–2012

## Joel Beinin and Marie Duboc

THE PROMINENCE OF NEW SOCIAL MOVEMENTS since the 1960s led many social theorists to imagine a postmodern political order and the demise of identities and social mobilizations based on class and nation (Inglehart 1977; Piore and Sabel 1984; Arrighi 1996; Melucci 1996). While excellent scholarship is still being done on the history and sociology of labor, workers receive far less attention than they did during the heyday of social history. A featured article in *International Labor and Working Class History* argued that labor history had lost its "élan, directionality, and intellectual purpose" (Katznelson 1994). A more recent article (Friedman 2009) in the same journal, although speaking only of the "industrialized democracies," asked even more provocatively, "Is Labor Dead?" But more than a decade of labor mobilizations in Egypt, Tunisia, Jordan, Bahrain, and Algeria demonstrate that Arab workers, at least, have not received the message that class is unfashionable and suggest that predictions of the demise of labor and class may be neoliberal wishful thinking. In Egypt from 1998 to the end of 2010 well over two million workers participated in 3,400–4,000 factory occupations, strikes, demonstrations, or other collective actions (see Tables 10.1 and 10.2 below).

The upsurge of overt workplace-based labor protests during the past decade profoundly transformed Egyptian political culture. These actions involved public and private sector factory workers, bakers, civil servants, teachers, tax collectors, medical doctors, transport workers, and garbage collectors; other public protests in this period included demonstrations against water shortages and poor housing and sit-ins staged in front of government offices. Workers most commonly presented bread-and-butter demands, sometimes literally, as in the protests over shortages of subsidized bread in the spring of 2008. They did not initiate the demonstrations that toppled President Hosni Mubarak in February 2011. But their collective actions over the course of more than a decade formed an important component of the matrix of forces propelling that mobilization.

## SOCIAL MOVEMENT THEORY AND THE EGYPTIAN WORKERS' MOVEMENT

Egyptian workers' collective actions resemble Tilly and Tarrow's (2007, 8) definition of a social movement: "a sustained campaign of claim making, using repeated performances that advertise the claim, based on organizations, networks, traditions, and solidarities that sustain these activities." But the Egyptian workers' case suggests the need to modify classical Social Movement Theory (SMT) to account for the particular combination of an authoritarian state and what Broadbent calls "other-directed" insurgents—people who do not conceive of themselves as or aspire to be fully autonomous individuals detached from the dense networks of families and friends that give meaning to their lives (2003, 222). Such cases have been undertheorized because of the historic derivation of SMT largely from evidence in the global North and pluralistic, democratic states. The Egyptian workers' movement highlights: (1) the importance of perceived threats, as opposed to opportunities, in motivating collective action; (2) possibilities for collective action and movement-building in a resource-poor, authoritarian environment; (3) local networks' capacity simultaneously to enable local mobilization while disabling mobilization on a national scale; (4) the differential effects of political change ("opportunities" in the terminology of classical SMT) on the urban intelligentsia compared to workers; (5) the continuing relevance of class; and (6) the agency of insurgent workers in expanding their repertoire of contention.

The first two points above adopt propositions advanced by McAdam, Tarrow, and Tilly in their revision of SMT (2001, 41–50). But the concept of threat used here is broader than Tarrow's (2011, 295) usage, which restricts the term "to the state's and other actors' capacity or will to control dissent." Goldstone and Tilly's (2001, 183) definition of a threat as "the costs a social group will incur from protest, or *that it expects to suffer if it does not take action*" (emphasis added) is more applicable to the Egyptian workers' movement.

The Egyptian workers' movement of the 2000s was primarily a class-based response to neoliberal economic restructuring. It is similar to protests against International Monetary Fund–imposed policies in Egypt, Tunisia, Morocco, Sudan, and Jordan from the 1970s to the 1990s (Seddon 1989; Beinin 1993). But it was more clearly based among urban workers, more protracted, and more successful. The ensemble of six points noted above explains the character of a sustained social movement that achieved substantial economic gains through a protracted series of local actions of varying and unpredictable intensity and long-lasting campaigns in several localities—but that lacked a recognized national or regional organization, program, or leadership until after the over-throw of Hosni Mubarak.

Consequently, there was not a unified "labor movement." Nonetheless, we use the term "movement" to refer to a nationwide phenomenon of collective action that relied on a common repertoire of protest to voice common grievances. Although centered on workplace issues, these grievances were a response to the ongoing restructuring of the political economy affecting workers through-out Egypt. This resulted in the "destabilization of the stable" and the "growth of precariousness . . . reach[ing] into previously stable zones of employment" (Castel 2003, 387). This destabilization, affecting workers, as well as profession-als and the impoverished lower middle classes (Kandil 2012), has redefined the meaning of "working class," which has been reconfigured by the differing status of permanent and temporary workers, especially in recently privatized firms. Labor protests have reflected this reconfiguration. Engineers and blue-collar workers have struck together to demand payment of an overdue bonus, for example, while temporary workers who are not entitled to such benefits have not participated. We understand "working class" as a structural category his-torically formed and reformed by industrial modernity, colonialism, national-ism, postcolonial anti-imperialism, and most recently global neoliberalism. It simultaneously comprises the microhistories and local cultures of social net-works in urban and suburban industrial areas.

Factories and workers' neighborhoods, such as the housing projects for public sector workers established during the era of President Gamal Abdel Nasser (1954–70), are the locus of identity and sociability. Some families have been employed in the same workplace for several generations. Jobs are often obtained through family or neighborhood connections. Families in the same apartment block or neighborhood organize mutual financial assistance. Work-mates frequent the same cafes and markets. Their children go to the same schools and commonly marry each other (Duboc 2011). These networks of so-cial relations, in which the family is the central unit, sustain the workers' move-ment and make it difficult for the government to extinguish it without using massive force. However, by their nature these highly localized working-class networks cannot easily be projected onto a national scale. In contrast to SMT approaches stressing the role of networks in connecting individuals to oppor-tunities for mobilization, Egyptian workers' local networks outside the factory have had only a limited capacity for mobilization. Their primary role is to sup-port the social fabric of the community.

Workers' protests of the 2000s and beyond commonly demanded that state authorities intervene to defend their standard of living or their rights in the face of perceived injustices committed by private entrepreneurs or public sector managers. The discourse framing these demands invokes the Arab Socialism of the 1950s and 1960s or is reminiscent of the moral economy that valorizes a nationalist populist pact (Heydemann 2007, 35). However, the concept of moral economy only partially explains the dynamics of labor protests. It focuses on the anger of those whose rights are violated and the defensive nature of mobilizations to maintain the status quo. Thus, it overlooks initiatives to challenge state-controlled unions and denounce corruption and bad management.

The empirical evidence in this chapter derives from field research conducted in Egypt between 2004 and 2012, including two years among textile workers in Mahalla al-Kubra and Shibin al-Kawm in the Nile Delta in 2008–10, in addition to unpublished and published material and interviews with nongovernmental organizations, labor journalists, and political activists. Joel Beinin's previous research on Egyptian labor (cited in the Bibliography) provides a long-term historical context.

The official trade union structure—the Egyptian Trade Union Federation (ETUF)—was an arm of the regime. After Mubarak's overthrow it remained a bastion of ancien régime loyalists. In 2012 the Muslim Brothers enticed them into collaboration to establish a condominium, whose stability is uncertain, over the organization. ETUF's legal monopoly on trade union organization was guaranteed by the Trade Union Law no. 35 of 1976.[1] Its 1,751 local union committees have usually been an impediment to achieving workers' demands. The Unified Labor Law no. 12 of 2003 legalized strikes. However, only one of the strikes referred to here was legal (and only partially) because the law permits strikes only when they have been approved by the relevant national general union and the ETUF executive committee.

The upsurge in workers' protest did not rely on "movement entrepreneurs" or "professional movement organizations" or previously existing "bases," which some social movement theorists have regarded as necessary to form a movement (McCarthy and Zald 1987, 337–92, 15–48; Tilly and Tarrow 2007, 113–14). Until 2011, none of Egypt's opposition parties, including those friendly to workers—the leftist National Progressive Unionist (Tagammu') and the Nasserist Dignity (Karama) parties—had much presence outside their Cairo headquarters. Although Hamdin Sabbahi, the Karama presidential candidate, made an unexpected breakthrough in the June 2012 elections, his party has had very limited influence in workplaces. Contrary to the Mubarak regime's accusations, labor protests were not organized by the Muslim Brothers or communists. Adherents of all parties participated, but not as leaders or initiators. For workers, the legitimacy of their protests stemmed from their independence from discredited political parties and organizations. This did not change despite the burgeoning of political parties since the fall of Mubarak (Charbel 2012). The middle-class, urban, oppositional intelligentsia had a limited relationship to the movement before 2011—mostly through several labor journalists. The movement had meager financial resources, no national organizational infrastructure, and no national-level leadership or coordination. E-mail and Internet contacts were uncommon, though a few workers blog in Arabic.[2] Irregular face-to-face meetings and mobile telephones were the main means of communication.

The workers' movement was supported by several labor-oriented NGOs and the tiny, Trotskyist Center for Socialist Studies (which split in 2010). Until the establishment of the Egyptian Center for Economic and Social Rights in 2010 the Center for Trade Union and Workers Services (CTUWS) and the Coordinating Committee for Trade Union and Workers Rights and Liberties (CCTUWRL) were the only NGOs with full-time staff in regular contact with workers, but these organizations together employed only a handful of people.[3] We know of no collective actions initiated by these institutions.

## POLITICAL MOBILIZATION OF THE MIDDLE-CLASS, URBAN INTELLIGENTSIA

There are two contexts for the emergence of this movement. The first is the political mobilization of the middle-class, urban intelligentsia, which can reasonably be explained by the Political Process Model (PPM) of SMT. In Tarrow's (1998, 19) formulation:

> People engage in contentious politics when patterns of political opportunities and constraints change and then, by strategically employing a repertoire of collective action, create new opportunities, which are used by others in widening cycles of contention.

In the fall of 2000 twenty NGOs and Nasserist and leftist intellectuals organized the Popular Committee in Solidarity with the Palestinian Intifada. In early 2001 the committee held the first legal street demonstrations not sponsored by the regime in half a century (Howeidy 2005). Subsequently Palestinian solidarity demonstrations and protests against George W. Bush's Middle

Eastern wars became regular phenomena. Popular anger over these issues compelled the regime to relax—to varying and unpredictable degrees—its control over public space and the media.

Seizing the opportunity of this limited political liberalization, the Egyptian Movement for Change was established. Its slogan and popular name—Kifaya (Enough!)—epitomized the mounting dissatisfaction with the regime. Kifaya's first public demonstration, in December 2004, featured slogans and chants opposing Hosni Mubarak's prospective run for a fifth presidential term in September 2005 and the grooming of his son, Gamal, to succeed him, and demanding reduced powers for the presidency.

Although Kifaya expressed widespread popular sentiment, in private conversations members acknowledged their weak ties with workers. Nonetheless many government spokespersons, secular opponents of the Mubarak regime, and scholars believe that Kifaya either inspired the workers' movement or created the atmosphere that allowed it to flourish.[4] Understanding the mobilization of the intelligentsia as a stimulus for the workers' movement appears attractive because it not only confirms the PPM approach but also enhances the relevance of urban, middle-class political activists, who are more accessible to Westerners. But this is based on a misreading of the history of the workers' movement—reiterated in most journalistic accounts—that wrongly dates its takeoff with the December 2006 strike at Misr Spinning and Weaving Company in Mahalla al-Kubra.

### ACCELERATED NEOLIBERAL ECONOMIC RESTRUCTURING

Historical precision about the movement's beginnings supports an alternative view: the workers' movement is a response to the threat posed by the neoliberal restructuring of the Egyptian economy and society heralded by President Anwar al-Sadat's 1974 "Open Door" economic policy and belatedly implemented by the 1991 Economic Reform and Structural Adjustment Program (ERSAP) agreements with the International Monetary Fund and World Bank. In the 1980s and 1990s protest actions typically involved public sector workers seeking to defend gains achieved in the era of Arab Socialism (Beinin 1993; El Shafei 1995; Posusney 1997; Pratt 1998). Workers' protests increased gradually after the 1991 ERSAP agreements, nearly a decade before the mobilizations of the urban middle class around foreign policy issues. Strikes and other labor actions spiked sharply in mid-2004, months before the first Kifaya demonstration, and persisted after Kifaya lost steam in late 2006.

Law 203 of 1991 implementing the ERSAP specified 314 public sector enterprises eligible for privatization. By mid-2002, 190 enterprises were fully or partially sold off (CARANA Corporation 2002). An economic slowdown slackened the pace of privatization for the next two years. Law 203 forbids mass layoffs after privatization of a firm. Therefore managers of public sector firms slated for privatization typically made them more attractive to buyers by reducing the workforce before the sale. According to a survey of sixteen firms privatized since 1995, only two increased their workforce despite all the firms having received significant new capital investment (Knight 2007).

In July 2004 Prime Minister Ahmad Nazif formed a new government, entrusting the economic portfolios in the cabinet to Western-educated PhD's or businessmen close to Gamal Mubarak. The "government of businessmen" initiated a second wave of privatizations, selling a record seventeen public enterprises in its first fiscal year in office (American Chamber of Commerce in Egypt 2005). Receipts from privatization in fiscal year 2006–7 totaled US$5.34 billion, more than the $3.12 billion in the decade before the Nazif government took office (Oxford Business Group 2008, 52). In 2007 the World Bank ranked Egypt one of the top ten economic "reformers" in the world and number one in the Middle East (World Bank 2007, 1).

Egypt's gross domestic product grew impressively as the Nazif government vigorously implemented the neoliberal program. Concurrently the gap between "emerging Egypt" and the great majority of Egyptians who have not "emerged" widened (Mitchell 2002, 272–303; Denis 2006). According to the World Bank (2007a), nearly 44 percent of Egyptians are "extremely poor," unable to meet minimum food needs; "poor," unable to meet basic food needs; or "near-poor," able to meet some basic food needs.

From 2005 to 2008 food prices rose at least 33 percent for meat and as much as 146 percent for chicken (al-Misri al-Yawm, February 28, 2008). In August 2008 the government estimated that the annual rate of inflation for foodstuffs exceeded 35 percent, while the rate of general inflation surpassed 25 percent (Radwan 2008). In the spring of 2008 shortages of subsidized bread generated a major social crisis (al-Misri al-Yawm, May 13, 17, 23, 2008).

Workers' wages were simply inadequate to cope with these conditions. Real wages were lower in 2006 than in 1988, while earnings inequality increased (Said 2009, 54–55). The monthly minimum basic wage in July 2007 was £E105.00 or about US$19.00 (Barakat 2007, 178–80).[5] Actual wages are difficult to calculate because of the many supplements to basic wages. Moreover

60 percent of employment is in the "informal sector" (Assaad 2009, xvi). In 2006–8 textile workers' monthly take-home pay ranged from £E200 to £E800 (about US$35–$145).

During the era of Arab Socialism many public sector workers came to feel a sense of ownership in their enterprises. Consequently the most common forms of worker protest were factory occupations (*i'tisam/at*) while production continued, or refusal to accept paychecks rather than strikes (*idrab/at*). In the 1970s, 1980s, and early 1990s strikes were rare, lasted a few days at most, and were normally dispersed by overwhelming force.

Strikes became more frequent after the mid-1990s and spiked sharply in 2004; they were also longer, with several lasting months (Pratt 1998, 53–55; al-Basyuni and Sa'id 2007, 13, 15, 19). In 1984–89 and the mid-1990s there were 25 to 80 collective actions a year (El Shafei 1995; Pratt 1998). From 1998 to 2003 there was an average of 118 workers' collective actions a year (see Tables 10.1 and 10.2). In 2004 there were 265 collective actions—more than double the 1998–2003 average; more than 70 percent (190) of the collective actions in 2004 occurred after the Nazif government took office in July. In 2005 there were 202 collective actions, fewer than in 2004 but still nearly double the 1998–2003 average. Workers' protests escalated slightly in 2006, reaching 222 collective actions, and in 2007 totaled an astounding 614 actions. The center of gravity of the workers' movement, as had been the case since the late 1930s, was the textile industry. But by 2007 the movement encompassed virtually every industrial sector, public services, and civil servants. In 2008 there were 609 collective actions, despite a serious setback when the regime attacked crowds demonstrating against higher prices in Mahalla al-Kubra on April 6–7, 2008 (as discussed in Tables 10.1 and 10.2).

In the 2000s the government rarely used violence to disperse workers' protests. There is no definitive evidence to explain this. During 2004–5 workers' protests became regular events reported in the private media. Consequently the regime may have feared that repression would create unfavorable publicity that might deter foreign investment. Perhaps Talcott Parsons's aphorism explains the state's response: "State coercion is like the reserves of a bank. It is not intended to be drawn on by everyone at once, and if too many people make demands, it will soon run out" (quoted in Kurzman 2004, 117). Paradoxically, then, neoliberal economic restructuring provided the threat that motivated workers' collective action and expanded the opportunities for its success.

**Table 10.1.** Number of Protesters, 2004–2011

| 2004 | Strikes | Gatherings | Sit-Ins | Demonstrations | Total |
|---|---|---|---|---|---|
| Governmental sector | 585 | 11,541 | 5,577 | 16,597 | 34,300 |
| Public business sector | 3,551 | 7,237 | 12,514 | 7,238 | 30,540 |
| Private sector | 637 | 16,465 | 303,016 | 1,388 | 321,506 |
| Subtotal | 4,773 | 35,243 | 321,107 | 25,223 | 386,346 |
| *2005* | | | | | |
| Governmental sector | 6,082 | 4,001 | 4,741 | 13,150 | 27,974 |
| Public business sector | 2,032 | 66,498 | 13,855 | 1,040 | 83,425 |
| Private sector | 11,450 | 15,692 | 1,834 | 800 | 29,776 |
| Subtotal | 19,564 | 86,191 | 20,430 | 14,990 | 141,175 |
| *2006* | | | | | |
| Governmental sector | 67,188 | 7,341 | 13.317 | 7.390 | 95,236 |
| Public business sector | 12,466 | 24,599 | 45,569 | 62 | 82,696 |
| Private sector | 5,355 | 2,289 | 12,108 | 404 | 20,156 |
| Subtotal | 85,009 | 34,229 | 70,994 | 7,856 | 198,088 |
| *2007* | | | | | |
| Governmental sector | 17,269 | 41,658 | 35,688 | 3,889 | 98,504 |
| Public business sector | 112,583 | 56,519 | 47,429 | 1,120 | 217,651 |
| Private sector | 93,178 | 18,545 | 34,340 | 12,620 | 158,683 |
| Subtotal | 223,030 | 116,722 | 117,457 | 17,629 | 474,838 |
| *2008* | | | | | |
| Governmental sector | 15,554 | 217,602 | 12,829 | 8,642 | 254,627 |
| Public business sector | 17,896 | 65,830 | 29,297 | 15,020 | 128,043 |
| Private sector | 29,341 | 80,825 | 44,348 | 4,239 | 158,753 |
| Subtotal | 62,791 | 364,257 | 86,474 | 27,901 | 541,423 |
| *2009* | | | | | |
| Governmental sector | 29,015 | 58,658 | 7,459 | 3,560 | 98,692 |
| Public business sector | 26,215 | 96,925 | 24,703 | 1,580 | 149,423 |
| Private sector | 20,708 | 27,506 | 16,881 | 5,757 | 70,852 |
| Subtotal | 75,938 | 183,089 | 49,043 | 10,897 | 318,967 |
| *2010* | | | | | |
| Governmental sector | 11,938 | 5,154 | 5,801 | 16,747 | 39,640 |
| Public business sector | 2,680 | 25,390 | 4,213 | 4,210 | 36,493 |
| Private sector | 11,362 | 6,230 | 19,872 | 32,074 | 69,538 |
| Subtotal | 25,980 | 36,774 | 29,886 | 53,031 | 145,671 |
| Total 2004–2010 | 497,085 | 856,505 | 695,391 | 157,527 | 2,206,508 |
| *2011* | | | | | |
| All Sectors | | | | | ca. 950,000 |

SOURCE: Markaz al-Ard li-Huquq al-Insan (Land Centre for Human Rights), *Silsilat al-huquq al-iqtisadiyya wa'l-ijtimaʻiyya*, no. 34 (July 2004); no. 35 (February 2005); no. 39 (August 2005); no. 42 (January 2006); no. 49 (July 2006); no. 54 (February 2007); no. 56 (July 2007); no. 58 (February 2008); no. 65 (March 2009); no. 78 (February 2010); no 84 (August 2010); no. 88 (January 2011). Available at http://www.lchr-eg.org/. As the Land Centre for Human Rights stopped publishing this data in 2011, our conservative estimate for that year is based on monthly reports of *Muʼassasat Awlad al-Ard li-Huquq al-Insan* (Sons of the Land Human Rights Association) posted on various websites. Data for 2004–8 reprinted from *The Struggle for Worker Rights in Egypt* by permission of the Solidarity Center.

**Table 10.2.** Protests, 1998–2011

| 1998 | Strikes | Other Forms of Protest[a] | Sit-Ins | Demonstrations | Total |
|---|---|---|---|---|---|
| Sector not mentioned | 40 | 42 | 18 | 14 | 114 |
| *1999* | | | | | |
| Governmental sector | 13 | 21 | 4 | 2 | 40 |
| Public business sector | 10 | 10 | 7 | 1 | 28 |
| Private sector | 15 | 4 | 4 | 1 | 24 |
| Sector not mentioned | 16 | 25 | 17 | 14 | 72 |
| Subtotal | 54 | 60 | 32 | 18 | 164 |
| *2000* | | *Gatherings*[a] | | | |
| Governmental sector | 3 | NA | 3 | 8 | 14 |
| Public business sector | 6 | NA | 10 | 10 | 26 |
| Private sector | 9 | NA | 6 | 11 | 26 |
| Sector not mentioned | 22 | NA | 29 | 18 | 69 |
| Subtotal | 40 | NA | 48 | 47 | 135 |
| *2001* | | | | | |
| Governmental sector | 6 | NA | 3 | 12 | 21 |
| Public business sector | 8 | NA | 13 | 21 | 42 |
| Private sector | 5 | NA | 16 | 31 | 52 |
| Subtotal | 19 | NA | 32 | 64 | 115 |
| *2002* | | | | | |
| Governmental sector | 8 | NA | 3 | 14 | 25 |
| Public business sector | 3 | NA | 11 | 8 | 22 |
| Private sector | 13 | NA | 12 | 24 | 49 |
| Subtotal | 24 | NA | 26 | 46 | 96 |
| *2003* | | | | | |
| Governmental sector | 6 | 13 | 5 | 2 | 26 |
| Public business sector | 3 | 6 | 3 | 3 | 15 |
| Private sector | 16 | 14 | 14 | 1 | 45 |
| Subtotal | 25 | 33 | 22 | 6 | 86 |
| *2004* | | | | | |
| Governmental sector | 24 | 37 | 45 | 20 | 126 |
| Public business sector | 10 | 26 | 22 | 14 | 72 |
| Private sector | 9 | 24 | 23 | 12 | 68 |
| Subtotal | 43 | 87 | 90 | 46 | 266 |
| *2005* | | | | | |
| Governmental sector | 21 | 31 | 21 | 7 | 80 |
| Public business sector | 13 | 25 | 29 | 5 | 72 |
| Private sector | 12 | 25 | 9 | 4 | 50 |
| Subtotal | 46 | 81 | 59 | 16 | 202 |
| *2006* | | | | | |
| Governmental sector | 17 | 26 | 24 | 13 | 80 |
| Public business sector | 13 | 27 | 33 | 6 | 79 |
| Private sector | 17 | 16 | 24 | 6 | 63 |
| Subtotal | 47 | 69 | 81 | 25 | 222 |

(*continued*)

**Table 10.2.** *(continued)*

| 2007 | Strikes | Gatherings | Sit-Ins | Demonstrations | Total |
|---|---|---|---|---|---|
| Governmental sector | 36 | 121 | 80 | 18 | 255 |
| Public business sector | 31 | 63 | 47 | 4 | 145 |
| Private sector | 43 | 80 | 70 | 21 | 214 |
| Subtotal | 110 | 264 | 197 | 43 | 614 |
| *2008* | | | | | |
| Governmental sector | 37 | 133 | 67 | 30 | 267 |
| Public business sector | 17 | 43 | 38 | 9 | 107 |
| Private sector | 68 | 77 | 69 | 21 | 235 |
| Subtotal | 122 | 253 | 174 | 60 | 609 |
| *2009* | | | | | |
| Governmental Sector | 31 | 87 | 51 | 20 | 189 |
| Public Business Sector | 12 | 28 | 21 | 6 | 67 |
| Private Sector | 41 | 65 | 54 | 16 | 176 |
| Subtotal | 84 | 180 | 126 | 42 | 432 |
| *2010* | | | | | |
| Governmental sector | 36 | 29 | 38 | 62 | 165 |
| Public business sector | 7 | 9 | 11 | 7 | 34 |
| Private sector | 33 | 23 | 61 | 55 | 172 |
| Subtotal | 76 | 61 | 110 | 124 | 371 |
| Total 1988-2010 | 570 | 889 | 779 | 385 | 2,623 |
| *2011* | | | | | |
| All Sectors | 280 | 333 | 466 | 298 | 1,377 |

ᵃ In 1998 and 1999 the LCHR used the term "Other Forms of Protest" for this rubric. In 2000 they began to call it "Gatherings."

NOTE: The Land Centre for Human Rights considers a series of actions over a dispute in a workplace (for example, a petition, a demonstration, then a strike) as one action. Counting such actions separately would result in a total of at least 3,950 collective actions for 1998–2010.

SOURCE: Markaz al-Ard li-Huquq al-Insan (Land Centre for Human Rights), *Silsilat al-huquq al-iqtisadiyya wa'l-ijtima'iyya*, no. 5 (December 1998); no. 14 (April 2000); no. 18 (May 2001); no. 22 (March 2002); no. 28 (March 2003); no. 31 (January 2004); no. 34 (July 2004); no. 35 (February 2005); no. 39 (August 2005); no. 42 (January 2006); no. 49 (July 2006); no. 54 (February 2007); no. 56 (July 2007); no. 58 (February 2008); no. 65 (March 2009); no. 78 (February 2010); no 84 (August 2010); no. 88 (January 2011). Available at http://www.lchr-eg.org/. As the Land Centre for Human Rights stopped publishing this data in 2011, our conservative estimate for that year is based on monthly reports of Mu'assasat Awlad al-Ard li-Huquq al-Insan (Sons of the Land Human Rights Association) posted on various websites. Data for 1998–2008 reprinted from *The Struggle for Worker Rights in Egypt* by permission of the Solidarity Center.

The most significant change that coincides with the upsurge in workers' collective action is the installation of the Nazif government. Intensification of neoliberal economic restructuring led to deeper economic despair and class anger. The perceived (and often quite real) threat of loss of jobs or social benefits after firms were privatized; low wages; delays or nonpayment of bonuses, incentive pay, and other allowances critical to bringing income to a level that can sustain survival animated most workers' demands since mid-2004.

The coincidence of intensified neoliberal restructuring and an upsurge in workers' collective action is not necessarily proof of causality. But it is consistent with how protest leaders framed their actions and provides a better explanation than inadequately historicized explanations privileging the activities of the intelligentsia and middle classes. We argue, therefore, that the political economy context is both the deeper structural and the proximate explanation for the eruption of the movement. Accelerated privatization of the public sector and elimination of secure jobs with social benefits exacerbated the long-term erosion of workers' economic gains during the Nasser era and the decline of public sector employment.

## PRIVATIZATION AND COLLECTIVE ACTION IN THE PRIVATE SECTOR

The strikes at ESCO Spinning Company in Qalyub, north of Cairo, exemplified the new spirit of contentious collective action that arose in response to accelerated privatization of the public sector. An Egyptian investor, Hashim al-Daghri, had leased the firm for three years in 2003 for £E2.5 million a year. A year later al-Daghri bought the enterprise for only £E4 million. ESCO workers believed that they and the public, not the state managers, were the owners of the firm. In October 2004 a workforce of about four hundred—sharply reduced in preparation for selling the firm—struck briefly to demand that their workplace not be privatized. If privatization was implemented, the ESCO workers wanted their jobs to be guaranteed; if that was not possible, they sought adequate early retirement packages. Receiving no satisfaction, they began a second strike on February 13, 2005 (Beinin 2005).

Gamal Sha'ban, a skilled worker with twenty-three years of seniority asked, "With what right was the sale conducted?" The workers owned 10 percent of the firm, but they were not consulted about the sale. "[Muhsin 'Abd al-Wahhab] al-Gilani [CEO of the Cotton and Textiles Holding Company] agreed to the sale. Was the company his property or the property of the people?" Many ESCO workers believed that they were entitled to retain their jobs rather than be replaced by new workers who would likely receive lower wages and fewer benefits (Beinin 2005).The ESCO strike was among the first of many at recently privatized public firms. Workers in such enterprises frequently complained that the new owners did not abide by their contractual commitments. The ESCO workers failed to reverse the privatization. But they achieved substantial economic gains and compelled the state to adjudicate the dispute, even though it had already sold the enterprise (Rady 2005). Workers elsewhere received the message that strikes might achieve concrete results.

One of the most intense postprivatization actions was the March 2009 strike of 4,200 workers (reduced from 11,000) at the Indorama Shibin Spinning Company, which had been privatized in late 2006 (Carr 2009, 2009a). The strike galvanized a broad spectrum of opinion against the new Indonesian owners. This compelled ETUF to authorize what labor activists believed was only the second strike in its history, in May–June 2009 at Tanta Flax and Oil Company, another newly privatized firm (with a Saudi proprietor), which had already experienced several strikes and protests. Although ETUF authorized a five-day strike, it lasted more than five months. There were also strikes at the newly privatized Omar Effendi Department Stores (also under Saudi ownership) in April and May 2009 (Carr 2009b). These strikes indicated that even if privatized firms initially offered decent wages and benefits, they could eventually be eroded by the requirements of international competition or private investors' appetite for profit.

From the 1970s through the 1990s almost all workers' collective action was among public sector workers who used their factory and neighborhood networks to organize in order to preserve their gains from the Nasser era. Workers in the new satellite cities surrounding Cairo—10th of Ramadan, Sadat, and 6th of October—did not at first have such networks; they rarely belonged to trade unions and were targeted for retaliation or dismissal if they made "trouble." However, about 40 percent of those participating in collective actions since 2004 were employed in the private sector.

One of the first protracted collective actions in the private sector was at the Egyptian-Spanish Ora-Misr Company, established in 1983 in 10th of Ramadan City. Ora-Misr manufactured building materials using asbestos for more than twenty years, despite the ban on the substance in the United States and Europe. From 1997 to 2004 eighteen employees died, forty-six contracted lung cancer, and many of the one hundred and twenty remaining on the job suffered from asbestosis. Under considerable local and international pressure (solicited by the CTUWS), in September 2004 the government ordered Ora-Misr to close and to

pay a fine and compensation to its workers. The proprietor responded by dismissing all the workers without paying compensation. In November workers
set up an encampment outside the factory and remained there for more than
nine months. In July 2005 some of them occupied the ETUF headquarters and
successfully pressured the federation to support their demands (Rady 2005a).

## STRIKES AT MISR SPINNING AND WEAVING

The largest industrial strike during 2004–10 erupted in December 2006 at the
huge Misr Spinning and Weaving Company (known as Ghazl al-Mahalla) in
Mahalla al-Kubra. The firm is a powerful political symbol. It was established
in 1927 by Tal'at Harb, widely considered a hero of Egyptian economic nationalism, and in 1960 it became one of the first industrial firms nationalized
by the Nasser regime. Nearly a quarter of all public sector textile and cloth-
ing workers (about twenty-two thousand) are employed there. Significant as
it was, this strike did not launch the workers' movement, though it increased
its momentum.

On March 3, 2006, Prime Minister Nazif decreed an increase in the annual
bonus given to all public sector workers, from £E100 to two months' salary. "December [when annual bonuses are paid] came, and everyone was anxious. We
discovered we'd been ripped off. They only offered us the same old £E100. Actually, £E89 to be more precise, since there are deductions [for taxes]," said Muhammad al-'Attar, a leader of the strike and a foreman in the garment division.[6]

On December 7 production ceased when around three thousand female garment workers left their stations. They marched over to the spinning and weaving sections, where their male colleagues had not yet stopped their machines,
and stormed in chanting, "Where are the men? Here are the women!" The men
then joined the strike.

Sayyid Habib, another of the strike leaders, said that "as night fell," the men
found it "very difficult to convince the women to go home. They wanted to stay
and sleep over. It took us hours to convince them to go home to their families,
and return the following day." Al-'Attar proudly added, "The women were more
militant than the men."[7]

On the fourth day of the mill occupation, government officials offered a
forty-five-day bonus, assurances that the company would not be privatized,
and a promise that if the company earned more than £E60 million in profit in
the current fiscal year, 10 percent of the profit would be distributed to the workers. This victory reverberated throughout the textile sector. In the subsequent

three months as many as thirty thousand workers in at least ten textile mills in the Delta and Alexandria participated in strikes, slowdowns, and threats of collective action, demanding to receive what the Ghazl al-Mahalla strikers had won. In virtually all cases the government succumbed.

The regime was caught off guard. But the sale of public assets and the high price of oil meant there was sufficient cash on hand to buy off discontent. The state apparently chose this option rather than clashes with workers that might have derailed the privatization program. However, intensifying neoliberal policies provoked more protests. As striking proved effective in achieving economic gains and entailed lower risks than before, every successful action encouraged others.

## "WORK IS POLITICS. . . . THIS IS AS DEMOCRATIC AS IT GETS"

Soon after the Ghazl al-Mahalla strike, the elected strike committee launched a campaign to impeach the official local union committee because it had not supported the workers' demands. By February 2007 nearly thirteen thousand workers had signed a petition to the General Union of Textile Workers, demanding elections for a new union committee. Otherwise they threatened to resign from ETUF.

The ETUF bureaucrats, already humiliated by the successful strike, adamantly opposed the impeachment demand. Granting it might have triggered a flurry of similar protests because the fall 2006 national trade union elections had been widely condemned as fraudulent. Several members of the Ghazl al-Mahalla strike committee had sought to run for union office, but the security forces removed them from the ballot. The CTUWS called the elections "unequivocally the worst in the history of the Egyptian trade unions" (Center for Trade Union and Workers Services 2007, 19).

Rebuffed by their national "leaders," some three thousand Ghazl al-Mahalla workers officially resigned from the General Union of Textile Workers. However, ETUF did not recognize these resignations and continued to deduct dues from their paychecks. On April 15, 2007, the strike committee organized a delegation of one hundred workers to travel to ETUF headquarters in Cairo and demand that the resignations be recognized. Police confiscated the license of the driver of the bus they had hired and then physically blocked workers from boarding a Cairo-bound train—a relatively mild form of repression.[8]

As of September 2007 promises made at the conclusion of the December 2006 strike remained unfulfilled. The Ghazl al-Mahalla workers struck for the second time in a year—and won. The second strike was even more militant than the first and belied the wishful claims of the government and its media that the strike wave had run its course.

The private Egyptian press published reports that Ghazl al-Mahalla earned between £E170 and £E217 million in fiscal year 2006–7. Consequently the workers claimed that they were due bonuses equal to 150 days' pay rather than the twenty days' they had received. After a six-day strike they won an additional seventy days' bonus pay, payable immediately. A meeting of the company's administrative general assembly after the strike was to increase this to a total of at least 130 days' pay. Much-hated CEO Mahmud al-Gibali was eventually dismissed.

The biggest victory was in the political arena: after declaring their refusal to do so, regime representatives, including ETUF president Husayn Mugawir and the minister of investment, were forced to come to Mahalla al-Kubra to negotiate with the strike committee. Thus while the workers did not formally win their demand to impeach the trade union committee, they rendered it irrelevant.

In contrast to most other workers' collective actions in the 2000s, in September 2007 some of the Ghazl al-Mahalla strike leaders explicitly framed their struggle as a political contest with national implications. Sayyid Habib told Voice of America Radio, "We are challenging the regime" (September 28, 2007). Chants and banners raised during the strike opposed the economic policies of the Nazif government. Kareem Elbehirey, a worker who writes the Egyworkers blog (in Arabic), uploaded video clips featuring workers chanting, "We will not be ruled by the World Bank! We will not be ruled by colonialism!"[9] Muhammad al-'Attar and seven other leaders were arrested for two days during the strike. On his release he told journalists, "We want a change in the structure and hierarchy of the union system in this country. . . . The way unions in this country are organized is completely wrong, from top to bottom. It is organized to make it look like our representatives have been elected, when really they are appointed by the government." Later that day al-'Attar told a pre-*iftar* (Ramadan breakfast) workers' rally: "I want the whole government to resign. . . . I want the Mubarak regime to come to an end. Politics and workers' rights are inseparable. Work is politics by itself. What we are witnessing here right now, this is as democratic as it gets" (Stack and Mazen 2007).

Ghazl al-Mahalla workers suffered a major setback following an unsuccessful campaign to increase the national minimum wage. In January 2008 workers' leaders called for a national strike on April 6 in support of a demand to raise the monthly basic minimum wage to £E1,200. On April 2 security forces occupied

Mahalla al-Kubra and the factory and exerted intense pressure on strike committee members to cancel the strike. Concurrently, the company granted several outstanding demands and agreed to implement previously promised free transportation to and from work. Succumbing to this combination of repression and co-optation, a majority of the strike committee agreed to call off the strike, but two leaders refused to back down. Few other enterprises struck on that day.

While there was no strike in Ghazl al-Mahalla, after the 3:30 p.m. shift change, a crowd of mostly young boys and women gathered in the main square and began chanting slogans denouncing the high price of unsubsidized bread.[10] Plainclothes thugs of the regime who were on hand in anticipation of "trouble" unleashed volleys of rocks to disperse the crowd while uniformed Central Security Forces fired canisters of tear gas. As the violence escalated, the crowd burned the banners of the ruling party's candidates for the municipal elections scheduled for April 8. On April 7 an even larger crowd than the day before gleefully defaced a large poster of Hosni Mubarak. Over the two days, security forces arrested 331 people, beat up hundreds, critically wounded nine, and shot dead fifteen-year-old Ahmad 'Ali Mubarak with a bullet to his head as he was standing on the balcony of his flat.

On April 8 a delegation of high-level government officials led by Prime Minister Nazif rushed to Mahalla al-Kubra to restore calm. Nazif announced a bonus of one month's pay for Ghazl al-Mahalla workers and fifteen days for all other public sector textile workers. Many of the latter promptly threatened to strike if they did not receive a thirty-day bonus. The minister of investment promised better transportation facilities, special bakeries to dispense subsidized bread, revival of the cooperative store to provide subsidized rice, oil, sugar, and flour, and new medical equipment and specialized staff for the city's general hospital (Beinin 2008).

Following the clashes of April 6–7, forty-nine protesters were tried by an Emergency State Security Court. Twenty-two were convicted and sentenced to three-to-five-year jail terms. Three workers from Ghazl al-Mahalla were arrested, tortured, and detained for two months; several of their colleagues were given disciplinary transfers, although most were ultimately reversed. This level of repression was exceptional during 2004–11. It was perhaps due to the government's sensitivity about the symbolic status of Ghazl al-Mahalla and fear that workers might successfully organize a national protest. Although the abortive strike sought to support a "nonpolitical" economic demand, the specter of a nationally coordinated workers' action was intolerable.

## TOWARD INDEPENDENT UNIONS?

The largest collective actions of the 2000s involved fifty-five thousand real estate tax collectors employed by local authorities. Demanding wage parity with tax collectors employed directly by the Ministry of Finance, they organized escalating protests during the fall of 2007, including demonstrations and refusal to collect taxes. In December about ten thousand municipal real estate tax collectors and their family members sat-in for eleven days in front of the Ministry of Finance in downtown Cairo. The strike ended when the minister of finance agreed to a bonus equal to two months' pay and raised the wages of the municipal tax collectors by 325 percent, giving them parity with those employed by the General Tax Authority (Carr 2008).

The strike committee then began to turn itself into an independent union. On December 20, 2008, after gathering endorsements of twenty-seven thousand tax collectors, the Independent General Union of Real Estate Tax Authority Workers was established at the headquarters of Cairo's Press Syndicate. Tax collectors and supporters filled the building beyond capacity, foiling the security authorities' efforts to thwart the meeting by shutting off the air conditioning. The government recognized the Independent General Union of Real Estate Tax Authority Workers in April 2009.[11]

This case is exceptional for several reasons. The tax collectors are not properly "workers" but civil servants strategically located in the state apparatus. They did forge a national network linked to NGOs and opposition political parties—especially the CTUWS and the Karama Party—and they had sufficient resources to publish a monthly newspaper.[12] Their principal leader, Kamal Abu Eita, has a history of activism and is a leading member of Karama. While these experiences enhanced his capacities to lead his own union, Abu Eita did not become a national leader of the broader movement before January 2011. Nonetheless, this mobilization inspired several other groups of civil servants; health professionals, teachers and retirees formed independent unions in 2010.

The tax collectors' success in forming an independent union was exceptional. After the strike of December 2006, the Ghazl al-Mahalla strike committee made several attempts to form an independent union and organize coordination of textile workers in the Delta and in Alexandria. But they were unable to sustain these efforts. Personality clashes and differences over whether to strike on April 6, 2008, split the leadership. By March 2009 one group had decided not to pursue establishing an independent union;[13] another faction was demoralized; a third continued to pursue a more confrontational strategy.

These developments at Ghazl al-Mahalla, where the workers' movement was best organized and nationally visible, indicate that it is not necessary to agree on values and strategies in order to constitute a movement, as Tarrow (1998, 106–22) argues. The movement developed through tactical agreements on actions to achieve specific demands and a largely implicit conception of workers' "rights," having no common political stance or explicit long-term strategy.

## WORKERS AND THE POPULAR UPRISING OF 2011

The mass protests calling for the overthrow of Hosni Mubarak that began on January 25, 2011, did not originate from factories, nor were they led by labor activists. But workers were quick to participate and seized the opportunity to assert social and economic demands along with calls for the overthrow of Mubarak. On January 30, 2011, RETA, the independent health professionals and teachers unions, the retirees' association, and groups of other workers formed the Egyptian Federation of Independent Trade Unions (EFITU). This was a revolutionary act, ending in practice (though not in law) ETUF's monopoly on union representation since 1957. It also signified labor activists' intention that regime change should include new trade union legislation ensuring pluralism and freedom of organization. The main demands put forward by the founding statement of EFITU included implementation of a minimum wage and guarantees of freedom of organization: it called on workers to organize sit-ins and strikes to achieve "the demands of the Egyptian people" (Kamal Abu 'Ayta et al. 2011).

During the first days of the uprising workers joined the protests as individuals. In contrast to collective actions that had been confined to workplaces until then, the mass demonstrations of January and February 2011 took place in the streets and public squares of Egyptian cities. Earlier sit-ins staged by workers, civil servants, and a wide range of citizens in front of the parliament and the prime minister's office in 2010 had appropriated public space to voice grievances, but the security forces had restricted their scope.

The violent outcome of the failed national strike of April 6, 2008, likely led workers to engage in the anti-Mubarak protests cautiously, as individuals rather than at the factory level, to prevent a possible repressive backlash. Moreover, in the absence of a national organized movement, workers were not in a position to take the lead. As Khalid 'Ali, the director of the Egyptian Center for Economic and Social Rights and 2012 presidential candidate, explained, "The workers did not start the January 25 movement because they have no organizing structure. . . . [But] one of the important steps of this revolution was taken when they began to protest, giving the revolution an economic and social slant besides the political demands" (Kempf 2011).

On February 7 and 8 workplaces went on strike demanding both the resolution of local grievances and the ouster of Mubarak. During February 2011, 489 labor protests took place across Egypt, involving about two hundred thousand workers, including many in strategic sectors like the subsidiary companies of the Suez Canal Authority, Ghazl al-Mahalla, the Cairo and Alexandria Public Transport Authorities, the state-owned telecommunications company, Telecom Egypt, as well as medical doctors.[14] The exact weight of these strikes in the overthrow of Mubarak is uncertain. According to the Sons of the Land Center for Human Rights, the economic paralysis created by the strikes "was one of the most important factors leading to the rapidity of Mubarak's decision to leave" (Mu'assasat Awlad al-Ard li-Huquq al-Insan 2011). Between January 28 and February 5, production in key industrial zones dropped by 60 percent because of the unrest in the country and the closure of workplaces.[15]

Strikes were not the only factor that paralyzed the economy. Government measures such as closing ATMs and imposing the curfew, which disrupted transport and the supply chain for consumer goods, also contributed. According to the American Chamber of Commerce in Egypt, few trucking companies were operating.[16] Activity at ports also declined sharply; some had to shut down from January 31. The port of Alexandria, which handles about 60 percent of Egypt's foreign trade, including vital wheat imports, was not officially closed but operated at limited capacity, putting food supplies at risk if the delay of cargo shipments lasted longer.[17]

The constraints discussed in this chapter prevented the organization of general strikes comparable to those that shut down Iran's oil industry in 1979 (Kurzman 2012). In February 2011 workers' mobilizations followed the same patterns that prevailed between 2004 and 2010: protests were centered on local workplaces and did not become a nationally organized movement. However, workers' collective actions certainly strengthened the opposition movement, and their participation in the overthrow of Mubarak enhanced workers' organizational and political capacity.

On February 11, 2011, the Supreme Council of the Armed Forces (SCAF) led by Defense Minister and Field Marshal Muhammad Hussein Tantawi removed Mubarak from office and assumed power. But labor protests did not stop. Workers continued to ask for better pay and working conditions. On February 14, EFITU staged a demonstration in front of ETUF headquarters in Cairo to demand its dissolution and the prosecution of ETUF management board. The protesters were attacked by ETUF security (Charbel 2011). At Ghazl al-Mahalla striking workers also demanded the resignation of Fu'ad 'Abd al-'Alim, CEO of the public sector Spinning and Weaving Holding Company, whose management style had been criticized by workers for years.

Workers' collective actions continued despite the SCAF's measures to criminalize labor actions. Military Decree 34 on March 24 established a fine of up to £E50,000 (about $8,333) for anyone participating in or encouraging others to join a sit-in or any other activity that "prevents, delays or disrupts the work of public institutions or public authorities." The penalty increases to £E500,000 (about $83,333) and at least a year's imprisonment in the event of violence or property damage that may lead to "destruction of means of production" or harm "national unity and public security and order." Military Decree 34 was enforced only once. On June 29, 2011, a military court sentenced five workers at Petrojet, an oil- and gas-services company operated by the Ministry of Petroleum, to a one-year suspended prison term for sitting on the pavement in front of the ministry. The severity of the sentence and its suspension reflected the uncertain balance of political legitimacy between the military and the workers' movement (Beinin 2012). During 2011 about 900,000 Egyptians participated in nearly 1,400 labor actions.[18]

There was a clear contradiction between the SCAF's antilabor policies and those of interim Minister of Manpower and Migration Ahmad Hasan al-Bura'i. In March, al-Bura'i recognized workers' right to establish unions and federations independent of ETUF. On August 4 he dissolved ETUF's board of directors and appointed an interim steering committee to manage ETUF that included eighteen independent trade unionists, leftists, and Muslim Brothers and seven ETUF stalwarts of the old regime (Basyuni 2011). This progressive momentum was reversed in November 2011, when most of the old ETUF leadership was reinstated. Several months later, Ahmad 'Abd al-Zahir, head of the General Union of Cooperatives and an associate of former ETUF president Husayn Mugawir became the head of ETUF. Law 35 of 1976 prohibiting trade union pluralism remained in force, while the SCAF blocked draft trade union legislation approved by both the Ministry of Manpower and Migration and the cabinet in August 2011 and conforming to the standards of the International Labor Organization.

The most significant gain for workers from the overthrow of Mubarak was an increase in the monthly minimum basic wage to £E700 (about $116) for public sector employees effective July 1, 2011. In October 2011 the first-ever private sector minimum wage was established at £E700 (Beinin 2012). Yet its enforcement is uncertain.

## CONCLUSION

The trajectory of the Egyptian workers' movement differs from those Tarrow (2011, 294) suggests as responses to different combinations of opportunity and threat. The intensification of collective action dating to mid-2004 was launched by relatively weak actors in midsized enterprises like Ora-Misr and ESCO, who were motivated largely by enhanced threats: deteriorating health and fears of the loss of job security and social benefits in these cases. Workers achieved significant gains by obliging ETUF and the government to exert pressure on their private sector employers. The disinclination of the government to violently repress collective action was apparent only after the Ora-Misr and ESCO workers were committed to their sit-ins; it was not perceived as an opportunity beforehand.

The strongest actors—the Ghazl al-Mahalla workers—did not join the movement until late 2006, when the pattern of greater government tolerance for workers' protest was established. Their strikes won substantial economic demands, which the government applied to the entire public sector textile industry after less intense collective actions at other workplaces. Despite their superior level of organization (until the leadership became divided in April 2008), the strategic character of their enterprise, and their historic leading role in winning economic gains, the Ghazl al-Mahalla strike committee could not establish social movement institutions or an independent union. Instead, the previously unheralded real estate tax collectors achieved the greatest economic gains of the entire movement before Mubarak's ouster and succeeded in establishing the first independent trade union in Egypt in more than half a century. Thus, contrary to McAdam, McCarthy, and Zald's assertion (1996, 13), it was not necessary and in most cases not possible to "create an enduring organizational structure to sustain collective action."

Workers' collective actions became a substantial element of a burgeoning culture of protest in the 2000s, and workers continued to assert their demands in the post-Mubarak transitional period. Of course, factors other than labor must be taken into account in understanding how mass protests were able to overthrow Mubarak: the role of the army, the highly centralized nature of state power, and global geopolitics. But several years before Mubarak's demise, a class-based social movement had successfully asserted its public presence in an authoritarian state that imposed severe limits on associational life. This phenomenon confounded the conventional wisdom of journalists, scholars, and politicians who regarded "economic reform," "democratization" (understood as electoral procedures), and the "peace process" as the most important stories in Egypt during the first decade of the twenty-first century. It deserves to be understood in its own right.

# 11 DYNAMICS OF THE YEMENI REVOLUTION

Contextualizing Mobilizations

## Laurent Bonnefoy and Marine Poirier

THE REVOLUTIONARY PROCESSES that have rocked the Arab world since 2011 underline the importance of studying political and social mobilizations in the region. Long ignored by the media and a good many experts, all too often eclipsed by the post-9/11 security agenda, this research agenda should now move to center stage. More than ever, the academic community is engaged today in discussing theories often developed in Western, democratic contexts against the experience of the Arab world. A considerable volume of literature, published inside and outside the region for over a decade has highlighted the political, economic, and social failure of authoritarian Arab regimes, along with the large number of social movements that have arisen within them (Bennani-Chraïbi and Fillieule 2003; Wiktorowicz 2004). Inquiring into the pathological causes or background conditions (for example, repression, unemployment, demographic change, cultural processes) leading up to the wave of protest and revolution in the Arab world since 2011 is therefore misplaced. A more useful approach would probe the revolutionary dynamics at work—looking at actors in their particular settings and analyzing their practices in order to grasp the motivations for taking action, the innovations involved, as well as the continuities, recurrences, and legacies attributable to the old regime (Tocqueville 1983).

From this standpoint, the Yemeni case appears well worth studying, despite the country's rather marginal status in scholarship on the Arab world. The political system of Yemen, the Arabian Peninsula's sole republic, is the product of a history marked by the division of the country into two entities: the North, home to nearly three-quarters of the population, and the South. The 1962 revolution in the North gave birth to a republican regime that endures into the present, both in its form and in its politico-cultural references, particularly to Arab nationalism. In the South, after 1967, the British colonial presence was replaced by a socialist regime beset with violence that came to be viewed as a failed state (Brehony 2011). Despite this turbulent history, North Yemen and, since 1990, unified Yemen enjoyed more than three decades of remarkably stable leadership, although there was no lack of crises. 'Ali 'Abd Allah Salih came to power in the North in July 1978 and stayed on as president of the unified country before being removed from office through a vote in February 2012. With Salih as its fulcrum, the regime achieved a political balance that long proved less repressive than elsewhere on the peninsula, allowing, in 1990, multiple political parties and free elections. Although marred by tension and violence, the phase that followed unification was one of power-sharing in the form of coalition governments. In the late 1990s, however, the growing monopoly over institutional resources exercised by the General People's Congress (GPC, founded by Salih) became increasingly apparent (Poirier 2011; Longley-Alley 2010; Phillips 2008; Wedeen 2008). In the second half of the following decade repression increased sharply, with the "global war on terror" as the primary justification (Bonnefoy 2011). Against this background new conflicts sprung up, while political alliances were reshaped.

Since June 2004, the Sa'da region, in the far north of the country along the Saudi border, has intermittently been the theater of a fierce war pitting the national army against a movement that calls for preserving the political and religious identity of the Zaydi branch of Shi'i Islam (Bonnefoy 2010; Dorlian 2011).[1] The so-called Huthi rebellion (named after its successive leaders) may be viewed as the symptom of the reactivation of the tensions underlying the civil war of the 1960s. The government has accused the Huthis of both colluding with Iran and seeking to restore the old regime of the Zaydi Imamate that ruled a large portion of Yemen for more than a thousand years. In response, the rebels claim that they are defending their religious identity and exercising their right to criticize the government's alliance with the United States. Even with the deployment of several armored divisions, the mobilization of tribal militias, and direct military assistance from Saudi Arabia to the Yemeni army, the government has been unable to defeat the Huthi rebel forces.

Meanwhile, the turmoil in the governorates of what was formerly South Yemen, experiencing an unfinished, derailed unification process that included a brief armed conflict in 1994, entered a new stage in 2007 (Mermier 2012; Day 2012). The peaceful demonstrations held by supporters of the Southern Movement (al-Hirak al-janubi) increasingly took on an overtly secessionist character, challenging both the terms of the 1990 unification and its underlying rationale. Many southerners feel that domination by the San'a' elites, who have monopolized large tracts of land previously nationalized by the socialist regime and the region's fossil fuel resources, as well as the distinct historical paths followed by North and South Yemen provide ample grounds for contesting unification, with the result that demonstrations and clashes became daily occurrences.

Armed Islamist militancy, which the government and its international partners have wrongly labeled the primary threat to stability, raises questions that cannot be treated in isolation from a broader continuum of violence, particularly in the former South Yemen. It was not until repression was stepped up in 2008 that armed Islamist movements, many of them claiming affiliation with al-Qaʻida, initiated operations targeting the state, the security forces, "foreign interests," and minorities (chief among them the Zaydis). Responding with repression, the government put an end to a policy of compromise with those movements that had regulated violence for many years (Burgat 2006).

In 2011, in the historical context of these conflicts and of various "precedents of the revolution" (Philbrick-Yadav 2011), Yemen soon followed in the footsteps of the uprisings in Tunisia and Egypt. A popular movement gradually drew in a variety of actors and parties from late January onward. Episodes of repression that came in response had the effect of nearly bringing the government down as they triggered many defections among the military and members of the ruling GPC. In the spring, however, a protracted wait-and-see phase began, marked by tensions within the revolutionary camp.[2] The supporters of ʻAli ʻAbd Allah Salih managed to reorganize and effectively exploit the security issue as a way of maintaining the tacit backing of regional and international protagonists, first and foremost Saudi Arabia and the United States. This gave them considerable control over the scale and pace of the changes under way.

The Yemeni situation poses questions about the structuration, as Giddens (1984) defines it, of a protest movement that emerges from the interactions between a specific context and the practices developed in the course of a project conceived of as revolutionary by the actors themselves. Our assumption is that the revolutionary process has a dual nature: it appears at one and the same time to be produced by those actors and constrained by a historic, social, and political structure. Awareness of this "duality of structure" makes it possible to account for the complexity and the range of the mobilizations that have marked Yemen's revolutionary process. Although widely discussed and in some cases amended on a theoretical level (Sewell 1992; Stones 2005), Giddens' approach has been insufficiently tested on Arab case studies. Its ability to go beyond the structure/agency debate seems particularly relevant to accounting for revolu-

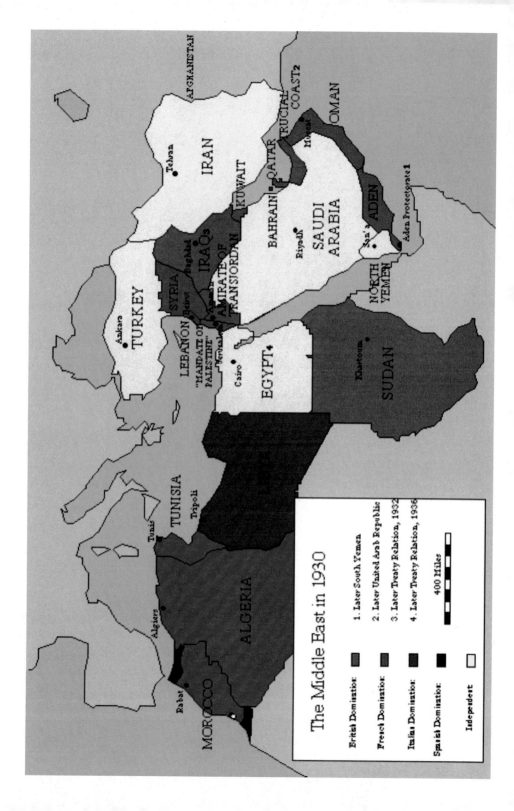

The Middle East in 1930

British Domination:
French Domination:
Italian Domination:
Spanish Domination:
Independent

1. Later South Yemen
2. Later United Arab Republic
3. Later Treaty Relation, 1932
4. Later Treaty Relation, 1936

400 Miles

MOROCCO
Rabat
ALGERIA
Algiers
TUNISIA
Tunis
Tripoli
LIBYA
TURKEY
Ankara
IRAN
Tehran
AFGHANISTAN
SYRIA
Beirut
LEBANON
"MANDATE OF PALESTINE"
Jerusalem
AMIRATE OF TRANSJORDAN
Amman
Baghdad
IRAQ 3
KUWAIT
BAHRAIN
QATAR
TRUCIAL COAST 2
Muscat
OMAN
SAUDI ARABIA
Riyadh
ADEN
Aden Protectorate 1
San'a
NORTH YEMEN
EGYPT 4
Cairo
SUDAN
Khartoum

tionary processes. Analyzing mobilizations in the context of the political crises experienced by several Arab countries, including Yemen, cannot be confined to merely describing the forms of mobilization; it must also include a dynamic, "evolutionary" (Koopmans 2005), "constructionist" (Kurzman 2004) dimension, or a concern with "tactical innovation" (McAdam 1983). Making emerging practices intelligible involves emphasizing just how extensively they interact with the multiple "structural properties of social systems" (Giddens 1984, xxi), that is, the history, the institutions, the power relations, and the mobilizations and experiences preceding them, and the part those interactions play in shaping the revolutionary process. This cannot be reduced to a simple cause-and-effect relationship (which would imply, for example, that repression leads to greater radicalism or that actors respond solely to changes in "political opportunities"); rather, the various factors feed into and condition each other. As a result of this dialectic, structure is both a medium and an outcome of actions. This is why mobilizations should be studied in their structural context, which is in turn susceptible to the mobilizations themselves (Dobry 2009, 4). Therefore interactions between revolutionary practice and its environment are the primary focus of this chapter.

In what ways have revolutionary developments in Yemen resulted from and resulted in this junction between practices based on peaceful protest, new terminology introduced by emerging actors, and the tendencies of established mobilization networks to reassert their control over the process? By analyzing new practices in relation to the "structural properties of the social system," we attempt to demonstrate that the revolutionary uprising in Yemen is part of a continuum of crises, conflicts, and social relations.[3] Consequently, the uprising became an additional variable in that context through a form of dialectical causality.

## EVOLVING SCHEMES OF MOBILIZATION

Although the protest movement in Yemen expressed strong solidarity with the revolts in Tunisia and Egypt, it was fueled by frustration and discontent rooted in the country's particular situation. During the 2000s, the regime fell back into authoritarian rule, curtailing individual and collective freedoms. At the same time, an economy already weakened by sagging oil revenues and increasingly dependent on international aid—hijacked to a large extent by the ruling elite's patronage networks—slid further downward. Thirty-five percent of Yemen's twenty-five million inhabitants live in poverty, while estimates for the unemployment rate range from 20 to 40 percent.[4] As the country has one of the world's highest population growth rates, demographics are often perceived to be a source of instability. The under-thirty age group, accounting for nearly two-thirds of the population, is particularly hard hit by Yemen's dwindling economic opportunities. These factors conducive to a wave of protest (but not sufficient in themselves to generate it) were accompanied by an attitude of widespread defiance toward "traditional" channels of political representation. More generally, there was a rejection of institutional politics, exemplified by tensions since 2006 between the ruling General People's Congress (GPC) and the Joint Meeting Parties (al-Liqa' al-mushtarak), a coalition of opposition groups including the Socialist Party, the Islamist leaning Islah (Reform) Party, representing the Muslim Brotherhood and tribal elites (Dresch and Haykel 1995), and four more marginal organizations (Browers 2007).[5]

## THE CONVERGING CALL FOR REVOLUTION

During the 2000s, the sense that there would be no comprehensive, optimal solution to the country's problems expressed itself in a variety of ways. Many people appeared indifferent to official politics and doubted the likelihood of internal reform (Philbrick-Yadav 2011). Political alienation was surely a shared characteristic of many revolutionaries long before the "Arab Spring." But it took a striking form at a rally in San'a' called by the Joint Meeting Parties on February 3, 2011. In addition to opposition activists chanting slogans and brandishing symbols of the campaign organized by the various parties, smaller contingents of demonstrators united around more subversive positions, encouraged by Ben Ali's demise in Tunisia. As seasoned activists were dispersing after the midday prayer, the latter group staged an unprecedented sit-in in front of the entrance to New San'a' University. Disregarding the conventional pleas for reform reaffirmed that very morning, the participants began chanting radical slogans, not only against President Salih and his regime ("Sit-in, sit-in, until the regime caves in!"), but also against the political parties, which they equated with the regime and accused of corruption and elitism ("No to parties from now on!"). Although roughed up by the security forces, they swore at sundown that they would not leave until Salih's regime had been overturned. This event suggested the direction the popular revolt would be heading. But it was not until February 19 that this physical space took on new political significance. From then on, it served as a continuous rallying point for a variety of actors whose common slogan called for the president to "Get out!" (*Irhal*)—and, once he had gone a year later, for an end to the regime itself and to the immunity granted to leaders guilty of crimes. This simple, yet radical slogan, and the diversity of the demonstrators were innovations in their own right. As the weeks went by, the encampment in front of the university, renamed Change Square (Sahat al-taghyir), developed into a key symbol of the Yemeni revolt.[6]

Whereas for several years political debate had been focused on state reform and negotiations over constitutional reform, demonstrators now called for "change" (*taghyir*) and the "overthrow" (*isqat*) of the regime. The break with traditional channels of political participation and mobilization (parties, NGOs, tribal structures, etc.) was expressed by the emergence of new idioms revolving around "revolution," "youth," and "peaceful change." These polysemic concepts gradually achieved recognition as terms emerging from and specific to the uprising in Yemen, with participants describing their movement as the "Peaceful Popular Youth Revolution" (al-Thawra al-shababiyya al-sha'abiyya al-silmiyya). This vocabulary was used in multiple, sometimes contradictory ways, as protesters turned to a variety of historical heritages for inspiration.

The concept of "civil state" (*dawla madaniyya*) quickly became a key reference for demonstrators. It was defined as a project for a new society centered on the rule of law, social justice, the guarantee of basic freedoms, and the need for citizens to reclaim the state and politics. In contradistinction to military or hereditary power grounded in tribal or family affiliation, the civil state advocated by protesters and self-proclaimed "revolutionary youth" (*shabab al-thawra*) promotes "civic empowerment," ability to mitigate conflicts, and the "technocratization" (or professionalization) of political leaders and officials, who were seen as owing their positions to inherited social capital rather than recognized skills they acquired.[7] The reference to a civil state, whose intellectual roots are in the Islamic reformist movement of the early twentieth century, was reappropriated, especially by self-styled "progressive," left-wing currents. Many demonstrators associated this notion with Ibrahim al-Hamdi, president of North Yemen from 1974 until his assassination in 1977, which made him a symbol of an abortive attempt to establish a modern state. Among the Islamists, in contrast, the term took on multiple meanings or was even contested. While most Islamists provide positive interpretations consistent with their conservative ideology, others such as 'Abd al-Majid al-Zindani, a spokesman for the so-called radical wing of Islah, called instead bluntly for an Islamic state. Due to its deeply polysemic character, this various political vocabulary proved particularly effective in supplying a unifying slogan that could mobilize a broad range of actors. "Civil state" has even tended to replace the dominant term "civil society," the latter extensively deployed in the 2000s by opposition groups and government supporters because it was on the international agenda (Ben Nefissa, Grabundzija, and Lambert 2008). Yemen's "armed civil society" (Burgat 2006, 10), structured to a large degree around major tribal confederations capable of counterbalancing the government's claim to a monopoly of legitimate violence, also made the concept of civil state more serviceable because it underscored the peaceful character of the revolt. Proclaiming its commitment to nonviolence, the protest movement invoked such diverse forerunners as Gandhi, Nelson Mandela, and Che Guevara. However, this rallying cry was not universal, as demonstrated by the resurgence of armed conflict at specific moments throughout the revolutionary process.

The emergence of a revolutionary idiom cannot be reduced to a mere change of vocabulary. The principles of civic empowerment and peaceful change informed new practices and patterns of sociability. They also helped transform the cognitive frameworks of many demonstrators who sensed, as they engaged in novel forms of action, that their society was in the throes of profound change.

## SHAPING A SUSTAINABLE SPACE FOR MOBILIZATION

At the encampment (*i'tisam, mukhayyam*) that formally began on February 19, 2011, in San'a', opposition to the regime took shape through unparalleled and manifold configurations of actors and practices. Spatial convergence of demonstrators on the camp simultaneously accelerated the "temporary desectorization of social space" (Dobry 2009, 126–37). As soon as opposition forces had organized a permanent space identifiable by all, what was initially a revolt waged by groups of students began attracting other participants. The publicity surrounding this unprecedented sit-in, its urban location, and the political repression meted out by the authorities drove actors with a variety of social profiles to join in. From the very first days, the encampment on Change Square brought together students, unemployed workers, tribesmen, women and children, human rights activists, and even unskilled workers, whose ideological and religious affiliations were as diverse as their geographic and social backgrounds. All claimed to identify with the revolutionary youth, many of whom were connected to previously existing intellectual and activist groups, including opposition parties. Despite this heterogeneity, the protesters organized and promoted a form of collective action previously unknown in Yemen through the continuous occupation of public space. In response to security force attacks on the first marches (initially with clubs and tear gas), arrests, and attempts at intimidation, the protesters prioritized organizing an ad-hoc space modeled on Egypt's Tahrir Square occupation. Repression contributed to developing new mobilization practices by encouraging demonstrators to adjust their strategies to confront the power structure (Combes and Fillieule 2011; Geisser, Karam, and Vairel 2006) and to hold an uninterrupted sit-in in front of New San'a' University, a place already familiar to them.

Although sit-ins were already commonplace, especially in the South, where the Southern Movement had popularized the tactic, this time, the protest was unprecedented in spatial terms.[8] To many participants, it signaled a shift— from the semiclosed, segmented space characteristic of "*qat* chews," which bring Yemenis together daily to chew this mild stimulant and which have traditionally given the government's critics an opportunity to gather—to the public space created by a sit-in.[9] Exporting *qat* gatherings to the camp made it possible to ensure the presence of a sizeable crowd and simultaneously revealed the connection between novel practices introduced by the encampment and more traditional forms of sociability. By taking possession of a public space from which they had previously felt dispossessed, demonstrators highlighted the extent to which political deadlock had pushed them to opt for street "politics" or "strategy" rather than electoral politics (Bayat 1997; Fillieule 1997a). These new practices thus led to a lasting redefinition of the symbolic and physical space in which mobilization can occur.

The first steps of the revolutionary youth in February and March 2011 were to ensure the survival of the sit-in, particularly by stopping traffic and controlling entry to the area. Composed of volunteers, the security committees played an important role in creating and sustaining the contentious space. They clearly marked off the boundaries and the points of entry, where large banners proclaimed, "Welcome to the first kilometer of dignity" and "Welcome to the land of freedom." They also made sure that participants abided by basic rules like nonviolence, which at the very least required prohibiting weapons. In reaction to clashes with security forces and pro-government armed militias (*balatija*), campaigns to set up additional tents extended the sit-in, eventually to several districts in the capital. Tents were numbered and assigned to specific locations, labeled to indicate tribal or regional affiliation, trade or profession, ideological orientation, and, in some cases, the activities they hosted. The defense and conquest of additional space for the occupation gradually led to the establishment

of "safe spaces" that allowed participants to carry out their activities independently and with a relative degree of security.[10] This process also accelerated the
inflow of sympathizers and the political education of participants while encouraging long-term commitment.

What the participants experienced as a reappropriation of public space
involved establishing a protest movement organization responsible for planning and coordinating collective action.[11] Pluralistic representation of all political currents present at the encampment was the underlying principle. But,
the leading opposition party, Islah, soon came to dominate the new structure.

"How many organizations operate on Change Square?" asked a researcher
in the summer of 2011. An opposition activist responded, "Do you mean before
or after you've asked me the question?"[12] This facetious answer highlights the
feverish hyperactivity characteristic of the camp. Although no accurate count
of the organizations that sprang up after February 2011 is available, many people questioned by the authors asserted that they numbered several hundred.[13]
Some were confined to a few friends stimulated by an atmosphere that fostered
involvement. But their activities were practically nonexistent and short-lived,
very much like the burgeoning Facebook groups engaged in what would appear to be very low intensity political work.[14] Others took on greater scope in
the vibrant daily life on Change Square, organizing talks, debates, consciousness-raising campaigns, and political education sessions. This was true of
several coalitions with unmistakable ideological leanings, or even party affiliations. For example, the Steadfastness Youth (Shabab al-sumud) espoused the
views of the Zaydi revival movement; Nasir, those of the Nasserists; the Revolutionary Youth Bloc (Takattul shabab al-thawra) those of the Socialist Party,
while the Coordination (al-Munassiqiyya), by all standards the largest coalition of revolutionaries, was deemed close to the Islah Party. These organizations revealed the links between parties and protest movements created by the
multiple positioning of activists and expressed the increasing involvement of
political parties on Change Square. Thus, the sense of political alienation favoring antiparty slogans was not shared by all. Still other organizations were
made up of individuals who stressed their independence from all parties, like
the Diversity Coalition (Tanawwu') and the Civic Coalition of Revolutionary
Youth (al-Tahaluf al-madani li'l-thawra al-shababiyya). Several coalitions, like
the Coalition on the Southern Question (al-Tahaluf li'l-qadiyya al-janubiyya),
advanced various positions on the future of the South (federalism, secession,
and other options).

## SOCIABILITY, CREATIVITY, AND TACTICAL INNOVATION

The high density of organizations and activist networks in the protest space encouraged first-time contact and cooperation between actors traditionally considered to be rivals. For example, militants and civil society cyber-activists met tribesmen (*qabili*) from the northern and central highlands, many of whom those activists had previously written off as hostile to political modernization, who came to camp in San'a' (Dresch 2000). Through their massive but peaceful involvement with such young, seemingly liberal protesters, the tribesmen helped bring about a lasting change in how tribes were perceived, underscoring their function as conflict mediators, their creative input via revolutionary poetry, and above all their oppositional role, since tribes have historically provided a counterweight to the authoritarian aims of the central state.[15] The climate of discussion and interaction facilitated by the layout of the encampment set in motion a process of assembling identities in novel ways. This dynamic facilitated convergence among opposition groups. Concurrently, it became easier to transcend primary or confessional allegiances and to outline a common political project. Emblematic of this process was the Steadfastness Youth affiliated with the Zaydi revival movement. Its members used their tent on Change Square to recruit sympathizers and extend their work to other cities in Yemen, including in areas where Zaydis were historically absent. Their strategy adopted an inclusive approach. Instead of merely espousing the Zaydi revival cause, which would have an exclusive character, the group began defending the cause of all those who suffered political discrimination at the hands of the regime. Thus, the Steadfastness Youth supported the Southern Movement's demands for autonomy and expressed its solidarity with the victims of government repression.

The camp overturned long-standing social routines (Poirier forthcoming). Participation generated powerful feelings of fraternity among camp dwellers and gave rise to unprecedented collective and individual practices, from trash collection and "cleanup" operations (like the one in December 2011 on Kentucky Roundabout, following clashes with pro-regime militias) to self-management, and promotion of shared ground rules based on mutual respect and cooperation.[16] Many campaigns were launched to raise awareness of citizens' rights and obligations followed by training in civil disobedience and strike activity. The breadth of these initiatives highlights the social and educational aspects of the encampment. A young woman from the Security Committee who went with her brothers to Change Square every day enthusiastically explained what an exciting experience this was—how the camp had made possible previously un-known forms of contact and cooperation between men and women, becoming the venue of choice for interacting and even flirting in what remained a socially conservative society.[17] Despite deteriorating living conditions (galloping infla-tion, gas shortages, power cuts, and so on) and sit-in participants devoting less time to their professional and family lives, the intensity of the newly created emotional bonds strengthened their involvement.

The sense of being part of a worthy cause and a historic event provided symbolic benefits that drove further commitment (Combes 2010). Episodes of repression were countered by consciousness-raising sessions (especially regard-ing martyrs) that kept the spirit of sacrifice alive. Camping out day after day on Change Square in San'a' or on similar sit-ins in other cities, meant "total" com-mitment with a "fast breeder effect"—the more committed you were, the more satisfaction you felt (although such feelings might be denied [Gaxie 2005]) and the harder it became to leave or move on to something else. Even as repression became more brutal as the weeks went by, the revolution remained a celebra-tion. In San'a', the camp hosted a wide range of cultural events: concerts, the-ater, political satire, workshops, and art exhibitions.[18] These activities, along with recreation areas for children, created a festive family atmosphere that at-tracted large numbers of passersby. In the evenings, groups of friends and fami-lies would amble around the square, attending concerts and drinking "Freedom Tea" (as one vendor called it), before heading home with pennants and badges displaying their support for the revolution. As armed clashes became increas-ingly common in San'a' from May 2011 onward, and some participants began to show signs of battle fatigue, the process temporarily lost momentum, with-out dying out altogether. The Change Square encampment remained a place for considerable experimentation throughout 2011 and even kept going, like camps in other Yemeni cities, after Salih officially stepped down in February 2012. Many of the actors viewed this negotiated exit as just the first stage in a long revolutionary process.

## THE DUALITY OF THE REVOLUTIONARY STRUCTURE

The movement launched in early February 2011 by the multifaceted and multi-positioned revolutionary youth gradually shifted focus over time. Although the pioneering social practices described above at no point disappeared, they were increasingly constrained. The "reassertion of control" that occurred con-currently with the extension of the San'a' encampment and that of Ta'iz, for instance, played an ambiguous role. It cannot be interpreted solely as a limitation, as new practices emerge from the interplay between revolutionary practice and contextual variables. Interaction and interdependence among all these elements to a large extent determine the dynamics of contentious mobilization and counterrevolutionary resistance.[19] It is necessary to examine both the contact or friction points and the links between contentious space and institutional politics, as well as their impact on the revolutionary process (Vairel 2005).

### Appropriation of the Revolutionary Process

The onset of the revolutionary process revealed the initial failure of Yemen's opposition parties. In the first weeks of the revolt, the Joint Meeting Parties officially stated their unwillingness to adopt an overtly revolutionary stand.[20] Their perception of the risks that such a move might entail seemed to explain this overcautious position (Goldstone and Tilly 2001). However, many of their members were already taking part in the protest movement on an individual basis. Hence, the party leaders' reservations may have been due to concern that the rise of a new political generation, including currents within Islah, might undermine some of their own status as much as fear of repression (Philbrick-Yadav 2011, 556). The balance of forces that emerged after unification in 1990 had given multiple actors a stake in the political system, including the Islamists, and offered many "opposition" figures opportunities for direct involvement with exercising power. During the 2000s, opposition parties began criticizing the government in more forceful terms. The establishment of the Joint Meeting Parties marked a significant step forward in this respect, as did the 2006 presidential election, in which the unified opposition candidate, Faysal Bin Shamlan, won 21.8 percent of the vote (Poirier 2008). However, none of this indicated a clean break with the regime. The opposition parties appeared to be going along with the political system rather than fundamentally challenging it.

For example, the Joint Meeting Parties did not decline the offer of dialog or the concessions announced by Salih on February 2, 2011, in response to the first demonstrations. This cautious approach did not disqualify them from participating in the protest movement. These well-established forces could count on the allegiance of activists operating through a powerful network of charity and educational organizations (Philbrick-Yadav 2010). Consequently, the Joint Meeting Parties elite, first and foremost its Islah component, had little trouble engaging (or reengaging) the revolutionary youth camped out on Change Square. Active solidarity networks linked to the Islamists were mobilized, especially through the Islah Association (affiliated to the party) and the University of Science and Technology, a private institution with a presence in the large cities. Its dean, Tariq Sinan Abu Luhum, happened to be secretary-general of the Islah Association (Bonnefoy and Poirier 2010). With connections to traditional tribal structures, these Islamist networks also possessed considerable media and financial firepower, thanks to backing from Hamid al-Ahmar, a wealthy businessman elected on the Islah ticket who came from the powerful Hashid tribal confederation.[21]

In San'a', Change Square was a striking place for staging a sit-in, not only because it was adjacent to New San'a' University, where young people and intellectuals gathered, but also because it was located in a neighborhood with a particularly strong Islamist social presence. Religious bookstores, Islamic charities, real estate owned by Islah figures, religious schools, and mosques represented a significant resource for revolutionaries enjoying the support of such networks. As one cadre of the ruling GPC explained, by barring access to downtown San'a', the regime had "pushed the demonstrators into the arms of the Islamists."[22] To be sure, space partially determines how protest will be defined (by shaping both social interaction and the nature and very possibility of social protest). But mobilizations may also redefine the space in which they occur by bringing about a lasting transformation of its meanings and imbuing it with a new revolutionary aura (Sewell 2001, 61, 64–65).

Starting in early March 2011, the Islah leadership, working through the Joint Meeting Parties, gradually extended its control over a movement it had not actually initiated, distorting the revolutionary process yet at the same time providing it with superior strength and organization. In doing so, Islah played both a constraining and an "empowering" role, creating both limitations and opportunities. With the introduction of a team of marshals and emergency medical service run from the field hospital set up in the mosque of the Islah charity organization, right in the middle of Change Square, and cooperating with a similar unit at the University of Science and Technology two kilometers away, contentious politics—and with it the revolutionary process—increasingly became a job for professionals.

The conspicuous presence of Islamists on Change Square, particularly those linked to the Muslim Brothers, altered the movement and its slogans, creating tension in the process. 'Abd al-Majid al-Zindani, 'Abd Allah Sa'tar, and Muhammad al-Mu'ayyad, Islah preachers described as radicals, made regular speeches from the platform, took part in talks, and delivered Friday sermons near the sit-in.[23] Conservative discourse gained ground in the encampment, as religious chants boomed out of loudspeakers and demonstrators were subjected to mounting pressure to join in prayer sessions.[24] From then on, the initial enthusiasm that fostered revolutionary innovation had to contend not only with the resistance of government supporters but also with strategic and ideological divisions among the opposition currents that made up the revolutionary youth.

On March 18, 2011, rooftop snipers near the southern entrance to Change Square opened fire on the crowd, killing fifty-two demonstrators. This event was a glaring illustration of the lengths to which certain pro-government hardliners would go; it also ushered in a new phase in which leading military figures defected, chief among them General 'Ali Muhsin al-Ahmar (not related to the al-Ahmar clan that led the Hashid tribal confederation), who commanded the army's First Armored Division. Their alignment with the radical call for regime change had an unexpected effect. Neither the more liberal-minded demonstrators nor the "Huthi" advocates reacted with much enthusiasm to the reinforcements offered by 'Ali Muhsin. Widely referred to as President Salih's foster brother, the general had been his right-hand man for a long time and in charge of operations in the Sa'da war since 2004. His past ties to armed Islamist movements and his active involvement with arms- and oil-smuggling rings gave him an unsavory reputation. Just a few days before switching sides, 'Ali Muhsin was still the butt of antiregime slogans at the sit-in, where posters included his photo in their denunciations of the president's clan. His supporters subsequently did their best to blot out his name and photo in order to get him off the "blacklist" of the revolutionary youth.

However, because they provided the movement with armed support, these military defections established a sort of "balance of terror" that allowed the protestors to reaffirm their commitment to nonviolent change. By entrusting third parties (soldiers who had joined the movement or tribal militias) with protecting them, sit-in participants could resume their efforts at peaceful innovation, albeit at the risk of being cheated out of "their revolution."

With traditional dynamics of mobilization around both the opposition parties and tribal and military leaders reactivated, the revolutionary youth found themselves controlled from the outside and pushed to the sidelines from the summer of 2011 onward. At this point, the ruling GPC and the opposition parties negotiated an agreement, brokered by the Gulf Cooperation Council, providing for a transition and the exit of Salih, while guaranteeing his immunity. After all sorts of incidents and episodes of violence, including the June 3 attack on the presidential mosque, which left Salih severely injured, an agreement was finally signed on November 23. Vice President 'Abd Rabuh Mansur Hadi, a high-ranking GPC leader, was backed by the Joint Meeting Parties in the presidential election held on February 21, 2012, as stipulated in the agreement. The vote, in which he was the sole candidate, took place in a fairly calm atmosphere, and 'Ali 'Abd Allah Salih formally relinquished power after holding it for thirty-three years.

### Commingled Dynamics

The reassertion of control by traditional political actors intersected with the tendency of the protest movement to acquire greater depth and breadth, underscoring the dialectical dynamics structuring the Yemeni revolution. This did not occur in chronological sequence, nor did the ebb of renewed external control cancel out the exciting flow of grassroots innovation. The two dynamics became commingled, feeding into each other. In addition, the negotiations and institutional transition process initiated under the agreement between the government and the Joint Meeting Parties, with the Gulf state monarchies mediating, produced further change—the removal of 'Ali 'Abd Allah Salih.

The process of exerting control by parties, Islamists, the armed forces, tribes, and international powers was met with protest, although it was not rejected on grounds of principle. A large proportion of the revolutionary youth (and the coalitions representing it) called for participating in the plebiscite vote on February 21, 2012, and greeted Salih's exit with enthusiasm. However, the immunity granted to the president and his relatives (sons and nephews in charge of various security bodies) was openly challenged. Buoyed by her Nobel Peace Prize, human rights activist Tawakkul Karman, a member of the Islah Party, advocated filing a suit against Salih with the International Criminal Court in The Hague and criticized the co-optation of the revolution by the opposition parties, while also hailing the election of 'Abd Rabuh Mansur Hadi, although he was hardly attuned to the demands voiced on Change Square.

Even as institutional politics gained traction, the popular uprising continued to take on novel forms. A prime example was the "March of Life" (*masirat al-hayat*) initiated in December 2011, with opposition to immunity for Salih and his family as rallying cry. This 250–kilometer trek from Ta'iz to San'a' succeeded in remobilizing citizens, thousands of whom joined the marchers or provided them with food and lodging, leading many journalists to compare it with Gandhi's 1930 Salt March. There was nothing random about its point of departure. After years of virtual exclusion from the power structure, Ta'iz gradually achieved recognition as the epicenter of revolt and became the symbol of Yemen's revolution (Planel 2012). On Change Square in San'a', participants from Ta'iz were noticeably overrepresented; a number of them (Tawakkul Karman, Mayzar al-Junayd, Wasim al-Qirshi, and Fakhr al-'Azab, for instance) played important roles. Ta'iz, a city historically involved with the education and modernization efforts of the state, held an intermediate status, somewhere between the northern highlands identified with tribal structures and the regime, and the south, a region still associated with the socialist government experiment that lasted until unification in 1990.

Resistance by institutional power networks had gradually brought about something like a "resectorization" of contentious politics. At this point a number of "parallel revolutions" operated as different corporate groups mobilizing to promote their own interests, an approach they felt would be more effective than the broad-based movement of early 2011 since it could not be undermined by institutional and political deals among elites. Nonetheless, their strikes, blockades, and even their campaigns denouncing staff members with ties to the regime in government administration and public sector companies like Yemenia Airways, were rooted in the style and forms of protest previously developed in Change Square. Although these parallel mobilizations focused primarily on ousting corrupt leaders, they ultimately strengthened the desectorization process characteristic of the revolutionary period. The most emblematic of these struggles was the movement of air force officers demanding the resignation of General Muhammad Salih, the half-brother of 'Ali 'Abd Allah Salih in January 2012.

The revolutionaries had no monopoly on creative approaches to political action. The strategies pursued by the authorities, particularly through networks mobilizing support for the regime, adjusted and responded to the protest movement, giving rise to a steady "exchange of moves" (Dobry 2009, 11–20). This situation of dialog and interdependence illuminates the positions taken by various actors in the confrontation. For example, Salih supporters copied the novel sit-in practices of their opponents. The Egyptian precedent likewise conferred such symbolic significance on Tahrir Square, in downtown San'a', that the government took preemptive control of the area and had its own followers camp out there, with free meals and modest handouts thrown into the bargain. With patently disproportionate resources and government patronage networks at their disposal, the ruling GPC party held its own rallies every Friday in San'a', drawing hundreds of thousands until the autumn of 2011. Although they could not match the daily spontaneous mass demonstrations staged by their opponents across the entire country, these pro-regime rallies did help convey the image of a Yemeni "people" unswervingly loyal to President Salih. The GPC also organized talks, a national dialog congress, marches, and other similar events that were combined with tight control of the city by security forces and various ploys for intimidating the insurgents, including people's committees set up by neighborhood authorities.[25]

Such initiatives can be viewed as an extension of the GPC's long-standing, tried-and-true schemes for mobilizing patronage networks, legitimating the regime, and criminalizing the opposition. At the same time, they had a novel character, entailing a new approach to managing urban space and gradually arming pro-Salih forces in neighborhoods that the opposition did not control. In that sense, they amounted to a "countermovement" defining itself by its interaction with a mobilization by an oppositional social movement (Meyer and Staggenborg 1996). The reciprocal influences between government supporters and their most determined opponents and the ways each side borrowed from the other's repertoire were arresting. Slogans, anthems, names for Friday demonstrations, catchphrases painted on demonstrators' faces, chests, and backs, sit-ins, Facebook groups—GPC activists clearly adopted the forms of expression developed by their foes. In appropriating and adapting opposition practices, the pro-Salih forces highlighted the dynamic character of collective action and the ways it is continually rearranged in highly fluid political settings.

## CONCLUSION

The Yemeni experience confirms the heuristic value of Giddens' structuration theory for an analysis of the revolutionary processes under way in the Arab world. This approach transcends the dichotomies of novelty and continuity and revolutionary practice and context, by focusing instead on the interactions between social and political phenomena and relating mobilizations to their environment. Because its temporal duration was longer than the revolutionary upsurges in Tunisia and Egypt, which have apparently waned rather quickly, the Yemeni uprising offers a good opportunity to observe actors' adjustments and their effects on practices. This study of the situation in San'a' suggests the importance of a dynamic and nonlinear approach to political mobilization, as well as the need for awareness of the complexity and diversity of its development. By emphasizing the dialectical influences at work, we can also get beyond the notion of clear-cut chronological stages, which would imply that historical and social structures determine and ultimately trump innovative practice. As we have seen, no single meaning can be assigned to institutional political actors' reassertion of control.

The San'a' sit-in initiated in February 2011, the gradual steps toward support by tribes and part of the armed forces in March, and the failed attempt on Salih's life in June should all be seen as transformative events that radically redefined the potential for revolutionary action and the accompanying cognitive frameworks, while reconnecting such action to preexisting social and cultural structures (McAdam and Sewell 2001, 101–2). The shared view of the encampment as the ideal, effective form of struggle may explain why in several Yemeni cities sit-ins were maintained well into 2012, even as the country's elites were negotiating a transition phase. Sustained mobilization, which gave the Yemeni revolution a life span without parallel in the region, underscores the need to examine both the structural processes that created the social basis and prospects for protest and the more short-term dynamics shaping the course of collective action (McAdam and Sewell 2001, 100).

Whatever may happen in the coming months and years, the revolutionary upheaval that began in 2011 cannot be considered a zero-sum game in which agency (of the revolutionaries) and structure (the counterrevolutionaries, or "control") compete and cancel each other out. The interactions generated by the mobilization process generated new practices and opportunities that profoundly transformed the expectations, strategies, and perceptions of everyone involved. On these grounds at least, although the foundational events of early 2011 are too recent to gauge their full significance, it seems warranted to describe the processes set in motion as "revolutionary."

# 12 "OH BUTHAINA, OH SHA'BAN—THE HAWRANI IS NOT HUNGRY, WE WANT FREEDOM!"

Revolutionary Framing and Mobilization
at the Onset of the Syrian Uprising

## Reinoud Leenders

AT THE END OF MARCH 2011, one week into Syria's uprising, the regime anxiously announced tax cuts and salary increases for public servants, thereby reversing a trend of fiscal prudence demanded by economic reform. Yet instead of halting the rapidly swelling protests, the measures, presented and explained by presidential advisor Buthaina Sha'ban (al-Manar TV, March 24, 2011), were met with popular contempt. Protestors in the southwestern governorate of Dar'a, evoking their origins from the Hawran (the plateau from southwestern Syria to northwestern Jordan), gathered in the streets and recited that they would not be appeased by token concessions. Picked up by the outside world via YouTube footage uploaded in Syria, protestors chanted: "Ya Buthaina, ya Sha'ban, al-Hawrani mu ju'an—bidna hu-riy-ya!" ("Oh Buthaina, Oh Sha'ban, the Hawrani is not Hungry—We Want Freedom!").[1]

This act of defiance, and the lucid way in which protestors expressed their claims, points to a number of key themes and questions that require serious scrutiny. I focus here on the acts and modes of protest, or "repertoires of contention" (Tilly 1978, 151–66), of Syria's "early risers" (Tarrow 1994, 86) in close connection with the discursive processes involved in the framing of their grievances, key demands, and the ways in which they challenged nearly fifty years of stern Ba'thist authoritarian rule. I argue that especially in a strictly authoritarian context like that of Syria, the common distinction between framing and acts of protest is inappropriate as noncompliant meaning-making already constitutes contention and a profound act of protest when collectively expressed in public. More specifically, Syria's early risers compensated for the virtual absence of a historic repertoire of contention by "revolutionary bricolage," which included drawing on the "hidden transcript" of the subordinated; copying and then amending slogans and acts of protests by their Egyptian and Tunisian counterparts; responding to the regime's utterances while appropriating and tinkering with its worn-out slogans and chants; building on common Arab and Muslim narratives and symbols of resistance and commemoration; and adapting and deploying cultural expressions and folklore to frame key demands and grievances. These, in turn, facilitated protest acts and coordination. I further contend that the values underlying cultural and religious life in Darʿa informed their way into how people interpreted and framed stiff regime repression as a cause for mobilization instead of submission. Finally, I will show how the slogans and symbols of Syria's early risers, in addition to their innovative work in developing protest tactics, set the contours of an endogenous, loose but extremely effective Syrian "master frame" and repertoire for the various instances of mass mobilization that constituted the Syrian uprising, at least so until the summer of 2011. The main sources for this chapter consist of interviews and social media material, especially YouTube footage, which despite their shortcomings and inherent biases allow us to read Syria's "stories of revolution" (Selbin 2010).

## FRAMES AND ACTS OF CONTENTION:
## WHITHER REPERTOIRES, REGIME VIOLENCE, AND DIFFUSION?

The main puzzle that this chapter addresses is threefold and can be read in conjunction with relevant theoretical debates on collective mobilization. Firstly, and given the Syrian regime's firm grip on public space and its virtual elimination of subversive, contentious politics for decades, where indeed did the breathtaking richness of the defiant protests and uncompromising claim-making by Syria's early risers come from? Mainstream Social Movement Theory (SMT) contends that "participants in public claim-making adopt scripts they have performed, or at least observed, before" (McAdam, Tarrow, and Tilly 2001, 138). Mobilizers are thought to draw and play on collective repertoires of contention. Scholars of framing processes similarly suggest mechanisms whereby mobilizers hark back to prior contentious politics, thereby embedding collective action frames in what is sensed as familiar or pretested (Benford and Snow 2000, 623, 629; Noakes and Johnston 2005, 8). Syria certainly witnessed important instances of contentious politics prior to the uprising.[2] Yet little of this resembled and none matched the collective insolence, the popular weight, and the determination exposed by the early risers of 2011. In contrast to Syria's contentious politics prior to the uprising, the new game involved a popularly driven and concerted effort to confront the regime head-on and remove it; not to negotiate a space with and next to the regime.

It has been variably argued that controlled, licensed, or even commissioned forms of contentious politics and expressions of dissent in Syria had the effect of (and were perhaps intended to) allow social actors to "let off steam" (tanaffus)—

reconfiguring but reasserting power relations in favor of the regime, reproducing conditions of obedience to the regime and its leader, "upgrading" authoritarian rule, and consolidating "recombinant authoritarianism" (Cook 2007; Wedeen 1999; Heydemann 2007a; Heydemann and Leenders 2012). Hence, the Syrian case can give us important clues to how acts and modes of effective revolutionary protest and claim-making develop without strong and consequential prior repertoires of contention due to the usurpation of public space and politics by a strictly authoritarian regime.

Secondly, how did protest repertoires and the framing of claims matter in terms of protesters overcoming formidable obstacles to collective mobilization, especially given the regime's violent response? In addressing this question, I argue that as they evoked the values of their clan-based social networks, Darʿawis' initial framing of regime violence was crucial in inducing them to rise up rather than to withdraw in submission. Accordingly, they formulated their own unequivocal answer to the question of whether and how repression dampens or furthers collective mobilization—a theme that continues to puzzle SMT scholars (Davenport, Johnston, and Mueller 2004; Koopmans 2007, 29; Earl 2011; Pierskalla 2010).

Thirdly, did the resonance of the early risers' protests and the ways in which they framed their grievances and demands play a role in the diffusion of mobilization throughout the country, and if so, how was this accomplished? Here SMT scholars' hunches of causal connections between frames' resonance and the spread of mobilization (Snow and Benford 1988) are important. But they have not been fully tested (Noakes and Johnston 2005, 16), especially in the combined contexts of strict authoritarian rule and a fragmented national space like in Syria. By analyzing the Syrian early risers' slogans and symbols, in addition to their innovative work in developing protest tactics, I will argue that they set the contours of an endogenous, loose but extremely effective "master frame" (Benford and Snow 2000, 618) for the various instances of mass mobilization that constitute the Syrian uprising. This master frame was refined, adjusted, and given endless new meanings within its broad parameters. It emboldened people before and while extreme regime violence turned a genuinely popular uprising into an armed confrontation and civil war.

## REVOLUTIONARY FRAMING AND SPEECH ACTS OF SYRIA'S EARLY RISERS

A sequence of events prompted the people of Darʿa, and subsequently early risers elsewhere in the country, to pose an unprecedented challenge to the regime. In late January 2011 two women from Darʿa, including a medical doctor named 'A'isha Abu Zayd, had been arrested, ostensibly because she had been overheard discussing on the phone Hosni Mubarak's overthrow, openly wondering whether the Syrian regime would be next in line.[3] That appears to have prompted pupils of the Arba'in school in Dar'a, including the two women's own children, to cover the walls of their school with antiregime graffiti. Security forces arrested fifteen pupils, ranging from ten to fifteen years old. Skirmishes erupted when a small number of angry protestors marched on the governor's mansion after Friday prayers on March 11, calling for the children's release. One week later, a large crowd left Dar'a's central 'Umari mosque and went into the city's streets loudly denouncing the regime.[4] Security forces opened fire, killing four men. What followed was an escalating cycle of protests to which security forces responded ruthlessly by opening fire and killing protestors, in turn prompting new protests. Regime attempts to diffuse the situation failed, as large numbers of people assembled calling for the downfall of the regime, first in Dar'a city and then soon in nearby villages. Meanwhile, demonstrations broke out elsewhere in Syria, especially from March 25 onward in places like Homs, Latakiyya, Idlib, and Deir al-Zur. Here and elsewhere thousands of protestors took to the streets, generally expressing solidarity with Dar'a and fury against the regime. As soon as security forces clamped down on mostly peaceful protestors with heavy force, mass demonstrations swelled. In early April, Dar'a remained quiet for two weeks, as the regime, overwhelmed by the sheer numbers and perseverance of the protestors, appeared to have opted for a temporary retreat. In these days Dar'a seems to have experienced a "revolutionary situation" (Tilly 1978, 189–99) as state agents no longer exercised control over the area—a scenario that was to be repeated in Deir al-Zur, Homs, and Hama in subsequent months. However, security forces, now backed by regular army units, snipers, and tanks, came back in force on April 26. What followed was a full-blown siege of the town combined with harsh repression in nearby villages. Again regime forces failed to curb protests in Dar'a and in other parts of the country. Dar'a, Homs, Idlib, and Deir al-Zur emerged as the country's heartlands of mobilization during the uprising's first few months.

Among the many things that made the early protests so remarkable was that their slogans, banners, choreography, and rich tactics developed in an extremely short period of time. Especially in Dar'a's recent and more distant past, nothing suggests that its population had been particularly versed in mobilizing for public contentious collective action from which protestors could learn. The area had a reputation of being tranquil to the degree of provincialism and of being largely loyal to the regime. It appeared disconnected from the political debates among elite activists in Damascus and the sporadic agitation in more restive parts of the country, such as in the predominantly Kurdish northeast. Indeed, the regime and opposition elites alike mistook Dar'a's tranquility for the region being largely supportive of the regime as its inhabitants were thought to have benefited from Ba'thist land reforms and from a disproportionately high number of senior appointments in the state bureaucracy, including the military and security agencies. Yet within a matter of weeks, even days, protestors eloquently and forcefully expressed their notions of justice, freedom, and dignity, and they juxtaposed them to the tyranny, cronyism, and corruption of the regime and its leaders. They organized picket lines, rallies, and night vigils, built barricades, occupied the main bridge separating the old and new parts of Dar'a, shut down their shops, listened to antiregime speeches, celebrated their fallen heroes, renamed public squares and streets, ridiculed and mocked the regime, and set up popular committees to spy on regime troops' movements, to coordinate the supply of food and medicines, and to engage in media activities—all in the face of intense regime violence and repression aimed at muzzling collective dissent and mobilization. This explosion of inventing and testing protest tactics and frames involved a process of "revolutionary bricolage" (Selbin 2010, 40–41); protestors cobbled together what to many outsiders may have looked like an amorphous challenge to the regime. Yet this effort was far from random, as it always appealed to a sense of familiarity that, to protestors and local audiences alike, made the challenge look like a persuasive and coherent endeavor.

In hindsight it appears that some of the substance of the themes, slogans, and rallying cries of the early risers had already been scripted for years, not via solid repertoires of openly contentious politics or by reenacting smaller-scale dress rehearsals in mass protest, but by what Scott (1990) calls the "hidden transcript" of the subordinated. Relatively insulated from the regime's surveillance, Dar'a's primary social networks—built around clan structures, circular labor migration, cross-border trade and population movements, and petty crime—had generated spaces for the expression of ideas and debate on a range of topics ranging from Syria's social and political ills up to the regime's foreign policies as well as regional and international politics (Leenders 2012). Protected by the built-in trust of these social networks and their relative insulation from regime surveillance, individuals jointly developed strong notions of their shared grievances and nonconforming views on Ba'thist rule. As soon as mobilization began, the framing process appeared to rely on this "hidden transcript," with protestors taking full advantage of the shock-effect created by giving a public podium to the inexpressible. The themes of government corruption, cronyism, the regime's chronic impotence in rectifying Israeli occupation of Syrian territory (the Golan), its unqualified dependency on Iran and Hizbullah in its foreign policies, and, singled out for special scorn, notorious regime officials, appeared on banners, slogans, and in speeches seemingly out of the blue. Giving extra dramatic effect to the extraordinary defiance that these public utterances of the hidden transcript signified, one of the early acts of protest included burning down the local offices of SyriaTel, the mobile-phone company owned by Rami Makhluf, Syria's foremost corrupt multimillionaire, the symbol of the regime's cronyism and a cousin of President Bashar al-Assad.[5] Leaving even less room for the imagination, statues of Hafez al-Assad were torn down across Darʿa.[6] The public airing of the hidden transcript appears to have had an almost intoxicating effect on protestors due to the awe it caused; many of them expressed profound delight in instantly recognizing their own long-standing grievances in what was now displayed and shared publicly for the very first time.[7] Apparently, this sentiment gave many Darʿawis the feeling that mobilization and protests occurred almost spontaneously, which helped foster an extraordinary level of group solidarity, camaraderie, and sense of collective purpose.

While pushing their hidden transcript into the open, activists resorted to copying and then amending slogans and acts of protests of their Egyptian and Tunisian counterparts, reinforcing the opportunity created by these Arab "revolutions" and importing their energy to their own environment. Protestors suggested parallels between the fates of the Egyptian and Tunisian dictators and what they clearly hoped would be the equally bleak future for the Syrian regime. The slogans painted on the walls of the Arbaʿin School in Darʿa were largely taken from the Egyptian and Tunisian revolutionary lexicon.[8] The fact that the slogans prompted the authorities to arrest the fifteen pupils helped to familiarize and endogenize their message, causing thousands of protestors to chant the same slogans collectively. The Egyptian protestors' practice of designating Fridays as a day of protest and naming them in reference to common themes, rallying points, and icons was adopted from the first day of mass rallying in Darʿa, on March 18, and onward, something that activists already had tried to do elsewhere, but until then with much more limited success. The rapidly developing repertoire of protest coincided with the fact that protests in Darʿa typically erupted after Friday prayers, especially at the besieged ʿUmari mosque.

Following protestors throughout the Arab world in defiantly renaming public squares (ostensibly mimicking the powerful statement of protestors occupying Cairo's Tahrir Square), Darʿawi protestors renamed the mosque's courtyard the "Courtyard of Dignity and Prestige of the Syrian people."[9] Images of Egyptian protestors in Tahrir Square embracing soldiers before the intentions of the armed forces had become clear were replicated across Darʿa, causing a small number of soldiers to defect.[10]

An even richer source of protest innovation and framing efforts involved the regime's utterances in response to the unrest and, perhaps paradoxically, its own worn-out slogans and chants. Whenever regime incumbents, including Bashar al-Assad, commented on the protests, demonstrators immediately gathered in defiance, playing on and directly countering the regime's narrative. Thus, in response to Bashar al-Assad's March 30 speech praising Darʿa for its role in resisting Israel, protestors chanted "Oh Mahir [Mahir al-Assad, the brother of Bashar al-Assad and commander of the regime's elite troops] you coward, send your army to the Golan!"[11] They directly responded to Buthaina Shaʿban's take on the protests as instigated by socioeconomic discontent by chanting the slogan cited earlier—"The Hawrani is not hungry"—alliterating in Arabic the presidential advisor's name. Demonstrators carried banners protesting the regime's depiction of the protests as instigated by Salafi "terrorists" seeking to upset the country's precarious sectarian balance, proclaiming their goal of national unity by chanting "Suriya, wahid, wahid, wahid!" ("Syria is one, one, one"),[12] and "Sunni and Alawi, hand in hand / Christian and Muslim, hand in hand / Arabs and Kurds, hand in hand."[13] Significantly, and after heralding a "Hawrani" identity, this response to the regime's dismissive narrative coincided with increasingly common displays of Syrian nationalism, such as by singing the Syrian national anthem while being shot at by security forces.[14] Protestors also countered the regime's narrative depicting the revolt as the work of low-class smugglers and criminals, by dressing in suits and holding banners indicating their middle-class professions.[15] In sum, the response to the regime's utterances quickly became routinized, perhaps because it managed to generate three powerful effects at once. It created the unprecedented and empowering effect of the people speaking back to the regime in a country where officialdom was accustomed to lecturing people without much response other than applause and staged acts of conformity.[16] It gave ample scope for ridiculing the regime (for example, by immediately mobilizing to disprove the regime's assurances about the situation "having calmed down"). It also provided the important advantage of informing actual and potential protestors, without having to coordinate much, when significant mobilization would occur (that is, whenever the regime spoke). This is likely why the regime, and especially Bashar al-Assad, soon reduced to a minimum their formal addresses to the nation.[17]

Rapid and effective protest framing was attained by appropriating and tinkering with the regime's own well-known slogans and chants. Thus, the regime's slogan "One, one, one! The people and the president are one" became "One, one, one! The Syrian people are one!" Likewise, protestors replaced the president's name by Dar'a, or any other place of protest, in the regime's motto "With our souls, with our blood, we sacrifice for you, Oh Hafez [or, Bashar]." One of the most popular protest chants, which is still in use, was "Allah, Syria, freedom, and that's it," which mimicked and mocked regime supporters' own "Allah, Syria, Bashar, and that's it."[18] Adding these slogans to protestors' repertoire was facilitated by their very resonance with the regime's dull and repetitive propaganda that few could not have memorized.

Building on common Arab and Muslim narratives and symbols of resistance and commemoration provided another important resource for protest and mobilization. Tarrow (1994) and Soule (2007), in analyzing protest repertoires, suggest the concept of "modularity"—the phenomenon whereby tactics and practices of defiance or protest, such as strikes, are relatively easily imported into various settings. Likewise, one might argue that the celebration and commemoration of martyrdom throughout the Middle East (although certainly not unique to the region or even to Islam)[19]—in Palestine, Lebanon (Hizbullah), Iraq, and, Iran—made this narrative and practice a modular and hence recognized choice for protestors in Dar'a. Moreover, as martyrs represent the ultimate sacrifice for a just cause, martyrdom resonated locally with the ways in which the regime's violence was understood as a cause for action rather than submission. Thus, immediately following Dar'a's first casualties, numerous demonstrations, speeches, and sit-ins in and outside Dar'a mourned the martyrs of the antiregime protests, prompting an iconography of martyrdom that came to dominate ensuing demonstrations and gatherings.[20] Large banners were draped on 'Umari mosque showing the portraits and names of the victims of regime violence.[21] Some streets and squares in Dar'a and surrounding villages were renamed after prominent martyrs, such as Ra'd al-Masri who joined army defectors of the 5th Brigade until he was killed in a major shootout with government forces in May 2011.[22] Martyrdom quickly became a recurrent theme in the naming of protest Fridays, as on April 1, dubbed "the Friday of the Martyrs." Perhaps in acknowledgment of the powerful mobilizing effects of commemorations of martyrs, security forces at a very early stage of the uprising began to desecrate protestors' corpses, as if their martyrdom and its mobilizing powers could be eradicated by their contempt for the dead.[23]

Cultural expressions and folklore, being familiar to all, were readily adapted and deployed to frame protestors' demands and grievances and to deliver their messages. For instance, traditional poetry recitals were used to celebrate martyrs and to call for steadfastness, often in spoken dialect rather than the more common classical Arabic as if to stress the popular quality of the uprising.[24] Traditional proverbs entered protest slogans by slightly changing them for revolutionary intent. Accordingly, the maxim "If a cold wind enters the window, close it and relax" was turned into "If the regime attacks the people with thugs, topple it and relax."[25]

Perhaps most importantly, the values underlying cultural and religious life in Dar'a inflected how people interpreted and framed repression as a cause for mobilization against the regime; at least in part, this appears to have *motivated* early mobilization. About seven major clans are key to Dar'a's social life (Leenders 2012). Religiously conservative, the clan structure maintains and guards strict Sunni Muslim values mostly associated with Sufi tendencies. Combining social conservatism with practical coping mechanisms, clans also maintain strong values and a social locus of local conflict management and dispute settlement based on notions of justice and dignity. These values were crucial in framing the regime's threats and repression as a source of action rather than a cause for submission. Accordingly, many Dar'awis viewed the initial arrest of the two women in January, combined with rumors about their heads being shaven by their captors, as a breach of their women's honor.[26] Dar'a's local security chief, 'Atif Najib, was subsequently alleged to have responded to petitions for their and the school children's release by extending an insulting invitation to send Dar'a's women to his office so "I can make them conceive some new kids" (Macleod 2011). The words attributed to Najib were crucial for Dar'awis' framing of the heavy-handed security response as a cause for standing up against regime-inflicted indignity. The clans' religious conservatism combined with their strong notions of justice, honor, and shame made their outrage a program of action. Infuriated by the regime's handling of the detainees' issue, protestors chanted *tuz!*, which roughly means "to hell with you!" as security forces opened fire.[27] Against this background, children became a common reference point in the Syrian uprising, as their ill-treatment by the regime caused widespread outrage and prompted protestors to rally around the innocence and hopes of children, as if contrasting their own cause with that of a savage regime already propelled into the past.[28]

Decades of strict authoritarianism prevented Syria's early risers from simply activating and then building on established repertoires of open contention. Yet, protest framing of Syria's early risers effectively built on preexisting shared notions and views and resonated strongly by appropriating and giving local significance to the "Arab Spring." Protestors also rapidly developed a counterframe in response to the much-rehearsed propaganda of the regime by appropriating and tinkering with well-known regime slogans and rhetoric. In sum, protestors indeed drew on their "extant stock of meanings, beliefs, ideologies, practices, values, [and] myths" (Benford and Snow 2000, 629), but engaged in revolutionary bricolage to provide the script that would frame their uprising against authoritarian rule.

Therefore, some analytical tools used in SMT help us to understand how, in their own particular ways, Syria's early risers managed to bring about intense levels of mobilization. Yet in their zeal to categorize social reality and defend their areas of specialization, some SMT scholars often stick to distinctions that, in reality, are far more blurred and amorphous than they would like to admit (McAdam, Tarrow, and Tilly 2001, 16). In Syria, this is particularly evident in the customary distinction between repertoires of contention, referring to tactics and acts of protest (strikes, petitions, rallies, and so on), and framing devices, referring to ideas and claims of a more discursive nature.[29] Yet possibly *because* Syrian protestors lacked an established repertoire of protest acts, their enthusiasm for framing and reframing the events and ideas around them was constitutive of the acts of protest they chose to engage in. By framing the regime's violence as a breach of honor, mass protests culminated in a head-on collusion with the regime; by responding to the regime's utterances, protestors managed to coordinate their mass rallies; by viewing the victims of regime repression as martyrs, funeral processions became a recurrent protest tactic and tool for mobilization. While their framing was closely linked with the "Arab Spring" in Egypt and elsewhere, protestors emulated the Egyptian example of attempting to win over regime soldiers, hoping they would defect. Indeed, in a harshly authoritarian environment like Syria's, each publicly and collectively expressed view or frame of noncompliance becomes an act of protest, or an "oppositional speech act" (Johnston 2005).

## FRAMING AND THE DIFFUSION OF MOBILIZATION:
## THE MAKING OF THE SYRIAN UPRISING

Many explanations of revolutionary mobilization, the Syrian uprising being no exception, contend that they occur when, by some objective measures, state and regime power are weakened, causing revolutionaries to see a window of opportunity (Tilly and Tarrow 2007, 57–60). According to this perspective, the Syrian regime had weakened its grip on society via its once extensive networks of patronage by embarking on a highly selective process of economic liberalization. Extreme cronyism, shrinking production, diminished employment, and high levels of inequality alienated its core constituencies (Hinnebusch 2012 is the strongest statement of this view). As Haddad (2012) put it succinctly, "Something had to give as the regime widened the gaps between itself and the majority, between the haves and the have-nots, between the city and the countryside, between manufacturing and trade. When most Syrians are disenfranchised as a few gobble up the available capital, it signals the beginning of the end." However, there is considerable evidence for an alternative view that it was not perceived weaknesses of the state or negligence of the regime's main constituencies that were primarily responsible for the Syrian uprising but a widely shared perception of the strength of the opposition.[30] Kurzman (1996, 155) argues that in the case of the 1979 Iranian revolution, a critical mass "believed the balance of forces shifted, not because of a changing state structure, but because of a changing opposition movement" that appeared potent enough to overthrow the regime. From this perspective, processes of framing gain additional significance if they are able to amplify the nationwide significance of early protests and hence may enhance perceptions of the opposition's strength. Furthermore, because of its perceived significance in forcing open the initial window of opportunity, early mobilization to a large degree defined the mass uprising by setting the broad parameters of its core objectives and establishing the claims and acts of protest that were viewed as persuasive and legitimate.

If these arguments can be upheld in the case of Syria, the example set by its early risers is all the more remarkable as, in addition to surmounting limited repertoires of protest and withstanding regime violence, protestors managed, at least temporarily, to overcome Syrian society's strong if not predominant local, regional, and transnational identities. As one political activist in Damascus, Hazim Nahar, told me prior to the uprising: "Before we even can dream of citizenship, we need to build a nation-state. Now we simply have an assembly of scattered, disconnected regions: the people of Dar'a look to Jordan, those in

Homs to Lebanon; Idlib and Aleppo are more Turkish than Syrian; and Deir al-Zur sees itself as part of al-Anbar, Iraq. That only leaves Damascus."[31] In this context, one could suspect that the regime's statements depicting early mobilization in Dar'a as merely a local and indeed marginal affair were partly genuine. Consequently, the regime quickly embarked on consultations with Dar'a's local dignitaries and later initiated assemblies throughout the country involving municipal officials to discuss local governance reform. When an MP from Dar'a, Yusuf Abu Rumiyya, on March 27, 2011, protested in parliament against the ruthless violence protestors in Dar'a had confronted, his intervention was only made possible by his singling out of security chief 'Atif Najib (letting the regime as such off the hook) but also by repeatedly evoking the "Hawrani" identity of his constituency. In contrast, he stressed, "No one in *Syria* hates Bashar al-Assad" (my emphasis).[32] Yet protestors quickly developed a simple but powerful framing tactic that countered such assumptions and that helped spread and sustain mobilization in other places in Syria, first in Latakiyya but more persistently so in Homs, Idlib, and Deir al-Zur governorates. Cross-referencing protests, mobilization, and regime violence geographically became key to framing the significance of early and arguably "localized" mobilization, first within Dar'a governorate beyond its provincial capital and then throughout the country. Thus, on March 22 residents of al-Sanamayn and on April 8 of Jasim, both in Dar'a governorate, went out onto the streets chanting, "With our souls, with our blood, we will avenge you Dar'a."[33] Villagers nearby Dar'a city organized marches in solidarity, often bringing medical and food supplies, a practice that became routinized during the siege of Dar'a in late April and early May. Elsewhere in Syria the need for and power of cross-referencing was immediately understood. Dar'a's perceived marginality and the regime's narrative of events risked reducing the protests to a local skirmish of no nationwide significance. To cite an example among many, protestors in Daraya, south of Damascus, mobilized and chanted "Oh Dar'awi, your blood is my blood. I swear by Allah, your trouble is my trouble."[34] Throughout Syria, Friday April 29 was named "the Friday of Rage and Solidarity with Dar'a." In May, during the siege of Dar'a, Syrian television actors drew up petitions supporting Dar'a and organized shipments of humanitarian aid. Protestors in Dar'a responded in kind, going into the streets expressing their solidarity with activists in scores of other places across Syria. Later, protestors nationwide named Friday, September 2, the "Friday of death rather than humiliation," adopting a slogan frequently heard in Dar'a during the early stages of the uprising.[35] With protests and repression spreading rapidly, banners and slogans reflected protestors' rediscovery of the nation's geography and now deeply felt solidarity. Typically, on April 8 protestors in Jasim chanted:

> Oh Darʿa, we are with you until death
> Oh Homs, we are with you until death
> Oh Hama, we are with you until death
> Oh Rastan, we are with you until death
> Oh Duma, we are with you until death
> Oh Hassaka, we are with you until death
> With our souls, with our blood, we will sacrifice for you, oh Darʿa![36]

Having set off this important mechanism of protest diffusion, protestors in various locations began to compete over the numbers of people mobilized, detained, or martyred in demonstrations so not to be accused of a having less courage or solidarity.[37] Protestors scornfully referred to places where people had not (yet) risen up, such as Aleppo, which was targeted with the slogan: "Even with Viagra Aleppo can't get it up."

Nationwide cross-referencing among protestors throughout the country brought about "frame amplification"—"the highlighting or accentuating of various issues, events, or beliefs from the broader interpretive sweep of the movement" (Noakes and Johnston 2005, 8). Protestors successfully framed their uprising as a national endeavor as opposed to a aggregation of disjointed local revolts. There was a growing perception that the opposition reached a critical mass, as protestors defied the regime not as Darʿawis, Homsis, Idlibis, or Deir al-Zuris, but as Syrians. Recuperated countrywide solidarity prompted and allowed protestors to formulate and accentuate a vibrant Syrian nationalism in contrast to the regime's increasingly obsolete national project. Protestors' claims of the trans- or nonsectarian nature of the uprising became common as protest Fridays were named after Alawite historical figures such as Salih al-ʿAli (June 17, 2011) or the Friday of *azadi*, Kurdish for "freedom" (May 20, 2011). Nationalist claims were emboldened as the goalkeeper of the Syrian national soccer team, ʿAbd al-Basit Sarut, led protests in Homs (Zyiad 2012). Operations of the regime's armed forces in towns and cities were routinely described as an "occupation" (*ihtilal*),[38] a term associated with the Israeli occupation, the very antithesis of Syrian or Arab nationalism. The regime was increasingly referred to as a foreign creature in its alliance with Iran, Russia, and China,[39] and protestors eventually adopted their own "revolutionary" Syrian national flag (Moubayed 2012).

Due to the prominent status gained by Syria's early mobilizers, the latter provided a tested and legitimate toolkit to be drawn upon and extended for the purposes of intense mobilization. In the course of braving regime repression they established a repertoire that both enabled and confined those who followed. Within these broad parameters protestors innovated and experimented. As in Dar'a, regime violence was received with contempt and mocked. New child victims of its repression became icons of the uprising, for example Hamza Bakkur who had his jaw blown off during the intense shelling of Homs and who was depicted in a drawing by Khalil Yunis.[40] Other protestors developed the theme of children further, setting off "freedom balloons" in crowded places.[41] Seven hundred film directors, writers, and journalists filed a petition "For the sake of our children in Dar'a" (*Akhbar as-Sharq*, May 2, 2011). Friday, June 3, 2011, was named "Friday of the Children of Freedom." Despite regime restrictions on purchasing spray cans, the graffiti of Dar'a's pupils was emulated throughout the country by activists spraying antiregime symbols and slogans on walls and buildings, even decorating garbage bins with the words "This is Bashar's house" (Zyiad 2012a). The reclaiming of public squares reached a new height in Homs where protestors, after being dispersed from its Clock Tower Square, simply built replicas of the clock tower in their own neighborhoods to defy and mock the regime's efforts to stop their protests (Zyiad 2012a). Regime slogans and rituals were appropriated and mocked as protestors in Homs staged their own choreographed movement reminiscent of the North Korea-style exercises taught at Syria's schools, and artists, organized in the revolutionary poster collective *al-Sha'b al-suri 'arif tariqha* (The Syrian people know their way), designed their answer to the regime's propaganda and glorification of its leadership.[42] The commemoration of martyrs led to streets being renamed after them at night. Stickers carrying martyrs' portraits even appeared on government buildings; public fountains suddenly poured out red-colored water, and students came to class dressed in black. Protestors refined the tactic of building on cultural expressions and folklore, as revolutionary poetry recitals proliferated and, even more importantly, traditional tunes were adapted for revolutionary use and then sung by protestors (Tahhan 2012).

In reproducing and adapting the young repertoire of contention initiated by Syria's early risers, more established activists and dissidents, such as human rights campaigners and leftist opposition elites associated with banned political parties, linked their own agendas to that of the protestors in what SMT theorists call "frame bridging"—that is, "linking two or more frames that have an affinity but were previously unconnected" (Noakes and Johnston 2005, 12). At times this was even done by individuals themselves who had no record of previous activism, as in the case of a young cartoonist in the northern village of Kafr Nabl who, inspired by the veteran Syrian cartoonist 'Ali Farzat, provided protestors with biting cartoons mocking the regime (Zyiad 2012). "Frame extension," or "extending beyond its primary interests to include issues and concerns that are presumed to be of importance to potential adherents" (Benford and Snow 2000, 625)—inevitably followed as revolutionary framing came to include a growing amalgam of claims and demands expressed before the uprising. Yet as Riyad al-Turk, Syria's veteran opposition activist and Communist Party leader, put it in his characteristic modesty: "New people, new men have entered the fray. . . . I mean they have grasped the burning core of the struggle, the core that we couldn't grasp."[43]

## CONCLUSION

By the summer of 2011 Syria was engulfed in intense and widespread mobilization, each day giving new recruits, new martyrs, and new life to a formidable challenge to the regime. By reproducing and adapting the young repertoire of contention initiated by Syria's early risers, foremost those in Dar'a, the collective call on the regime to make way had reached proportions no one could have foreseen at its onset. Two factors fundamentally changed the popular uprising, factors that have only been reconfirmed and magnified since. One was connected to the increasing success of the opposition to induce members of the armed forces to defect and join forces with the opposition. Defections failed to reach numbers that could have undermined the regime's determined reliance on increased violence and repression, adding an armed character to the uprising but without the likely prospect of defeating the regime militarily.[44] The second factor concerned foreign powers' meddling, foremost by Saudi Arabia and Qatar, who, informed by their own sectarian framing of regional politics, began to support the opposition against the regime of Bashar al-Assad in the hope of eliminating a long-standing foreign policy irritant and dealing a blow to Iran. One year later, all signs are that these two developments caused a drastic "frame transformation" (Noakes and Johnston 2005, 12) whereby sectarianism and violence has thrived and taken predominance. The regime championed both, hoping to remain in power despite numerous setbacks in its ability to fully control the country, the elite, and its population, let alone to retain any of the little legitimacy it once may have had. Astonishingly in this violent context, peaceful protests continued as demonstrators braved the very real risk of being bombed, shot, arrested, or tortured. Their revolutionary frames and repertoires, developed in a relatively short period of time, are now unlikely to determine the outcomes of Syria's current ordeal and civil war. However, if such an outcome presented itself, Syria would not be the same as it was in early 2011, when regime challengers and mobilizers invented their frames and repertoires almost from scratch. Indeed, whatever the new Syria will be like, it will have to reckon with the country's rich repertoire of contention.

**REFERENCE MATTER**

# NOTES

## Introduction

1. For the 1980–2005 period we cross-searched "Collective action," "Mobilizations," and "Social Movements" with "Middle East" or "Arab World" in two comparative politics journals (*World Politics* and *Comparative Politics*) and two sociology journals (*American Journal of Sociology* and *American Sociological Review*). Having thirteen articles, *Comparative Politics* appears to be an exception. We found two articles in *World Politics*, one in the *American Journal of Sociology*, and three in the *American Sociological Review*.

2. Though it was central in Tilly's research program up to the mid-1980s—and he later returned to it (2008)—this concept received much less attention than it deserved because most SMT scholars were more interested in the way social movements take off and are sustained. Traugott's edited volume (1995) and several passages in Tarrow (1998, 30–32, 101–4, 145–46) counter this trend.

3. Ibrahim (1982) and Denoeux (1993, 1993a) are precocious pioneers. SMT and the study of Islamic activism came together in the first decade of the twenty-first century (Wickham 2002; White 2002; Ismail 2003; Hafez 2003; Wiktorowicz 2004; Clark 2004; Schwedler 2006; Bayat 2007). Alimi (2006, 2009) is one of the few who have applied SMT to secular mobilizations (Palestinians in the Israeli-occupied territories), although he remains within the boundaries of the classical SMT concepts.

4. These can be divided into exceptionalists, such as Lewis (2004), Kramer (1996), and much more egregiously Pipes (1983), who promote an antagonistic relationship toward these actors, and those who are more empathetic and perhaps, for some, apologetic, such as Esposito (1999), Voll (1991), Eickelman and Piscatori (1996), and Burgat (2003).

5. Kurzman (2004a, 112) collects several such quotes. This structuralist understanding of opportunities was by no means specific to North Americans. Europeans (Kriesi et al. 1995; Kriesi 1995; Koopmans 1993) have contributed to it as well. While some formulations by Tarrow temper this hard version (1988), others tend to blur the difference between "structures" and "opportunities" (1998, 87).

6. We thank Michel Camau for sharing this reference.

## Chapter 1

I would like to thank Joel Beinin and Lamia Zaki for their very precise and helpful comments on earlier versions of this chapter. Nonetheless, any remaining errors are mine.

1. The US Congress refused to adopt a free trade agreement with Egypt because of its human rights violations (especially against Copts). Congress would probably not have agreed to the QIZ agreement (because of opposition from unions and the loss of American textile jobs) if it had not been linked to the (nonexistent) "peace process."

2. Contrary to what the "Washington consensus" states, economic and political reforms are disconnected, as clearly demonstrated in Kienle (2001).

3. *Al-Ahram Weekly*, April 4–10, 2002.

4. Hossam el-Hamalawy's account of the rapprochement between some of the younger MB and some of the left may be exaggerated and overly optimistic. What I saw when the two groups were together (a sit-in on August 14, 2005, in front of the Bar Association) is that the MB overwhelmingly dominated their leftist counterparts, bringing the vast majority of the participants; though slogans and mottoes were shared by Kamal Khalil, a leader of the Revolutionary Socialists, and Muhammad Habib from the MB. Joel Beinin observed the same relation of forces at the Cairo International Conferences opposing the Iraq war and the Israeli occupation of Palestine from 2005 to 2008.

5. www.harakamasria.net, "Bayan ta'sisi," August 7, 2004. Now found at www.hara kamasria.org (accessed June 20, 2010).

6. Jeffrey Alexander (1998) uses the term "real civil society" to describe civil societies as they are, as distinct from the normative dimension of the concept or a metaphysical stance ("there is or there is no civil society"), in introducing an analysis of the social and political uses of the concept.

7. I rely on Charles Tilly's early general definition of repression: "any action by another group which raises the contender's cost of collective action" (1978, 100). Davenport (2000, 6–9) provides a more detailed definition.

8. The model components are: "1. Limited concern with [human rights] of protesters and police obligation to respect and protect those rights; 2. Limited tolerance for community disruption; 3. Limited communication between police and demonstrators; 4. Extensive use of arrests as a method of managing demonstrators; and, 5. Extensive use of force in order to control demonstrators" (51).

9. The difficulty of such an inquiry is obvious in Hafez's attempt to "explain prevailing movement strategies and tactics over time, not merely to label groups as moderates or radicals" while in the same paragraph discussing the existence of "moderates" and "radicals" within a given organization" (2004, 6; see also 53).

10. For a nonidealist view on processes of moderation, see Wickham (2004, esp. 207).

11. Driss Benzékri is a former political prisoner, who spent seventeen years in jail for belonging to Ila al-Amam (Forward), a Marxist-Leninist organization. After his release in 1991, he was deeply involved in the Moroccan Organization for Human Rights

(OMDH). In 1998 he left his position as executive director of the OMDH because he thought the group was too subservient to the regime. Afterward he participated in the discussions that led to the creation, in November 1999, of the Moroccan Forum for Truth and Justice (FVJ), becoming its first president. This former leftist is well known as president of the Equity and Reconciliation Commission, which between January 2004 and November 2005 was charged with resolving the legacies of state violence. After that, Benzékri became president of the Moroccan Advisory Council on Human Rights (CCDH), an institution appointed by the king.

12. See also Slyomovics (2005).

13. Observation by the author during a sit-in in front of El Korbès, a secret detention center, Casablanca, May 27, 2001. In front of this hangar of the former Anfa military airport, transformed into a secret jail during the 1970s, human rights activists were chanting, "Today or tomorrow, you'll have to tell the truth!" and "Where are they? Where are the people's abducted children?"

14. On situations where people mobilize more intensely when a valued good is threatened, see Chazel (2003, 127).

15. Observation by the author, Cairo, July 26, 28, and 30, 2006.

16. I provide a more detailed version of this argument on the Moroccan case in my doctoral thesis (Vairel 2005); for other cases confirming this argument, see Guazzone and Pioppi (2009).

## Chapter 2

I thank Joel Beinin, Hamit Bozarslan, Benjamin Geer, and Frédéric Vairel for their comments on earlier drafts.

1. On Kifaya, see Chapter 1 of this volume.

2. Founded in 1976, the Tagammu' was originally the left-wing of the Arab Socialist Union and comprises Marxists, Nasserists, communists, and socialists. Its leader is Rif'at al-Sa'id; it was the only legal leftist party in Egypt in the Sadat-Mubarak era. The party once had up to 150,000 members, but membership declined sharply. In the late 1980s, the Tagammu' allied with the Mubarak regime against the Muslim Brothers. In the 2005 parliamentary elections it won two seats.

3. Fillieule argues that collective action needs to be understood as a long-term process, one that does not rely solely on rational commitments but also involves benefits and emotions. Mounia Bennani-Chraïbi and Fillieule (2003) discuss demobilization by describing the different paths that activism follows: co-optation by the regime; ongoing political involvement; demobilization with withdrawal from contentious activities; and transfer to other arenas (such as cultural activities). Ion (1997) discusses demobilization in a European context. Disengagement has also been studied in the context of other social roles, not specifically social movements—religion, marriage, and professional career (Ebaugh 1988).

4. For details on the student movement in the 1970s, see Abdallah (1985).

5. However, literary production is not considered a legitimate way for writers to voice their political views; rather, media or literary events are an opportunity to do so. The state has taken this logic into account: the Nasser regime did not arrest intellectuals because of the content of their literary production; repression was the response to their participation in political groups or to press articles (Stagh 1993, 67).

6. Interview with Hilmi Salim, Cairo, April 1, 2007. Born in 1951, Hilmi Salim started publishing poems in the early 1970s and participated in Marxist groups. He is one of the founding members of Ibda' 77, an avant-garde poetry group. He is the managing editor of *Adab wa-naqd*, the literary magazine published by the Tagammu' Party and founded in 1984. He is a former member of the Communist Party of Egypt. An attempt was made to censor one of his poems, published by Dar Mahrusa in 2007, for allegedly "insulting the Divine Being," after it was quoted in the literary magazine of the Egyptian General Book Organization, the official state publishing house. Salim was a member of Kifaya.

7. For a history of the communist movement in Egypt, see Schrand (2004); Mahfouz (1972); al-Sa'id (1988); Ismael and Sa'id (1990); Ismael (2005); Botman (1988); and Ginat (2011).

8. Interview with Baha' Tahir, Cairo, May 7, 2007. Born in 1935, Baha' Tahir has worked for the Second Program. Under Sadat he was prohibited from working in broadcasting and his books were banned because of his connections with leftist and opposition literary groups. He worked for the United Nations as a translator and returned to Egypt on his retirement in 1995. He is a Nasserist and was a founding member of Kifaya.

9. Interview with Hilmi Salim, Cairo, April 1, 2007.

10. Interview with Mahmud al-Wardani, Cairo, April 11, 2007. Born in 1950, Mahmud al-Wardani was employed as a social worker until the late 1980s and was an active member of the Egyptian Communist Workers' Party. He then began writing for the state newspaper *al-Akhbar* and its literary magazine, *Akhbar al-Adab*. Following a conflict with the editor (novelist Gamal al-Ghitani), al-Wardani left the magazine in 2007. He worked from then until 2009 for the independent daily *al-Badil*.

11. Ibid.

12. Interview with Sha'ban Yusif, Cairo, April 18, 2007. Born in 1955, Sha'ban Yusif was an active member of the Egyptian Communist Workers' Party in the 1970s. He works as a journalist and literary critic for newspapers in Egypt and in the Gulf. He was a member of Kifaya and coordinates a literary group, the Zaytun workshop, on the premises of the Tagammu' Party.

13. Interview with Sayyid Higab, Cairo, April 22, 2007. Sayyid Higab was born in 1940 in the Delta. His poems in Egyptian dialect were first published by Salah Jahin. He was a founding member of *Gallery 68*, an independent cultural magazine created in 1968. He was close to Marxist groups and has coordinated a writers' committee for the

Tagammu' Party. Higab was a member of Kifaya. He has had a successful career in the film and music industries.

14. Interview with Sha'ban Yusif, Cairo, April 18, 2007.

15. Ibid.

16. Interview with Fathi Imbabi, Cairo, April 24, 2007. Born in 1952, Fathi Imbabi is a novelist and works as an engineer. After his studies, he worked in the Persian Gulf and in Europe until 1979. He participated in the student-movement protests in 1972 and is a member of the Tagammu' Party and Kifaya.

17. Interview with Baha' Tahir, Cairo, May 7, 2007.

18. Interview with Sayyid Higab, Cairo, April 22, 2007.

## Chapter 3

1. In order to stick to the Arabic *al-harakat al-islamiyya* and not to hastily politicize movements whose political engagement is far from being obvious, especially in the Saudi context, I prefer to use "Islamic" instead of "Islamist."

2. On religious revival in North America, see McClymond (2004, 1–46). For a comparison with Islamic revivalism, see Utvik (2006).

3. In May and November 2003, al-Qa'ida in the Arabian Peninsula struck two gated communities in Riyadh. In addition to Westerners, the attacks killed many Saudis and Arabs, creating a rift between al-Qa'ida and what was until then a supportive or neutral general public.

4. Several activists fled repression in the 1990s and criticized the Saudi diplomatic and economic policies from abroad. In 1994 Muhammad al-Mas'ari transferred the Committee for the Defense of Legitimate Rights (CDLR) to London. Sa'd al-Faqih seceded from the CDLR in 1996 and created the Movement for Islamic Reform in Arabia (Fandy 1999, 115–75).

## Chapter 4

1. This chapter is part of an ongoing research project. Whether the programs reflect the precise line the organization desires to project or the influence of women against the organization does not matter for the primary thesis of this chapter. Even if these programs reflected the strict line of Hizbullah, that line demonstrates transformation and the incorporation of various lifestyles, tolerance, and Western norms. If by contrast they reveal women pushing a line against the organization, this demonstrates the organization's tolerance in allowing women space and freedom to forward different ideas and also the organizing power of this subconstituency.

2. Research for this chapter was conducted primarily by watching al-Manar during the periods November–December 2004, May–June 2005, October–November 2007, and from January 2008 to mid-2010. The 2004 research was completed with the aid of a research assistant; the rest, on my own. Programs in 2007–8 were viewed streaming over

the Internet. The data set for 2008 includes forty-four weekly women's programs and thirty-three morning programs, in addition to other programs geared to women and family. A few of the broadcast dates are of rebroadcasts.

3. An important exception is Kurzman (1996).

4. *Arab Reform Bulletin*, "Algeria: Women Leave Islamist Party," May 2009, http://www.carnegieendowment.org/arb/?fa=show&article=23069 (accessed June 14, 2010).

5. By tradition I mean both past and current practices that are inherited and neither questioned nor scrutinized, as they are considered common sense (for example, ideas against higher education for women, or promoting a subordinate role for them). Some political Islamists, and Hizbullah in particular, pride themselves on subjecting knowledge to questioning and reason in light of science. See Deeb (2006).

6. Interview with Lebanese Ministry of Information official, June 24, 2005; interview with Shameem Rassam, Arab media analyst and senior analyst at the International Research Center, November 19, 2008, Monterey, California.

7. This could also be an effect of the time frame of their studies: there has been a recent notable increase in women's programming and the progressive nature of women's issues covered, whereas female researchers conducted their studies of the station several years ago. Arguably the progressive nature of the programs was not then apparent.

8. It could be argued that the Hizbullah-Shi'a view of women has been more progressive than that of Sunni revivalists. However, the view presented in Hizbullah's media stretches beyond a progressive religious view to a multicommunal one.

## Chapter 5

1. Waltz's (1995, 156–66) discussion of human rights as a social movement emphasizes the Tunisian experience and how it differed from those of Algeria and Morocco.

2. For an overview of the international dimension, see Donnelly (1993). On the role of the United Nations, see Normand and Zaidi (2008). On the impact of international human rights instruments, see Risse, Ropp, and Sikkink (1999). For a critical evaluation of the approach of Risse, Ropp, and Sikkink to the case of Egypt, see Hicks (2006).

3. Amnesty members work on countries other than their own, but that work provides exposure to human rights standards as well as regional and international rights mechanisms. Today there are active Amnesty sections in Algeria, Tunisia, Morocco, and Israel; more or less active groups in Bahrain, Jordan, Lebanon, and Yemen; and "international members" in other countries, including Saudi Arabia and a number of Persian Gulf countries.

4. The Helsinki Citizens Assembly (HCA) was formed in Prague in 1990 as an organization of national chapters. The website of the Turkey HCA is http://www.hyd.org.tr (accessed June 20, 2010).

5. For an earlier interview-based discussion of human rights in Egypt, Tunisia, and Morocco, see Dwyer (1991).

6. Bahrain's Popular Front organization began as the Bahraini component of the Popular Front for the Liberation of Oman and the Occupied Arab Gulf (PFLOAG) and emerged as a distinct organization in 1974. For more details, see Halliday (1974). In the early 1970s Alekry worked with the PFLOAG information bureau in Aden.

7. Interview with Abdulnabi Alekry, Manama, June 22, 2007. Alekry is also a spokesman for the Committee for the Rights of the Returned [from exile], which demands pensions, housing, and other benefits for persons the state forced to live abroad for decades; in 2009 he became chair of the local Transparency International chapter.

8. Interview with Abdul-Hadi al-Khawaja, Manama, June 22, 2007. Al-Khawaja is now the Middle East field representative for Frontline, a Dublin-based international rights group that specializes in defending local human rights activists worldwide.

9. E-mail communication from Abdul-Hadi al-Khawaja, August 30, 2009.

10. Interview, June 22, 2007. Beginning in December 2007, arbitrary arrests and allegations of torture in detention increased in Bahrain (Human Rights Watch 2010).

11. Now professor emeritus of sociology at the American University in Cairo, Ibrahim founded and directed the Ibn Khaldun Center and is presently chair of its board of directors. He was also a founder of the Arab Organization for Human Rights and the EOHR. In 2000 Ibrahim was arrested for allegedly defaming Egypt's image abroad and sentenced to seven years in prison; in 2003 Egypt's highest civil court cleared him of all charges. In August 2008 another court sentenced him to two years in prison for "defaming Egypt." This sentence too was quashed on appeal. Ibrahim lived abroad from 2007 to 2010 to avoid arrest and threats of harm.

12. Interview, Cairo, February 28, 2007. Shukrallah was a founding member of the Egyptian Organization for Human Rights and for many years was chief editor of the *Al-Ahram Weekly.*

13. Interview, Cairo, February 28, 2007. Unless otherwise indicated, all quotes of Muhammad al-Sayyid Sa'id are from this interview. Sa'id, who died in early October 2009, was also a founding member of the Cairo Institute for Human Rights Studies, deputy director of the Al-Ahram Center for Political and Strategic Studies Center, and founding editor of the daily *al-Badil.*

14. Mubarak eventually left the EOHR and established the Center for Human Rights and Legal Aid in 1994.

15. Rodley (1997) reported that the three were arrested for their alleged membership in the Communist Workers' Party and taken to Abu Za'bal prison, where they claimed they had been tortured (para. 223). In prison Mubarak established relationships with Islamist prisoners, which enabled him to write some of the most insightful work on Egypt's radical Islamists before his death of a heart attack at the age of thirty-five in January 1998. His *Al-Irhabiyun qadimun: dirasa muqarana bayna mawqif "al-ikhwan al-muslimin" wa-jama'at al-jihad min qadiyat al-'unf (1928–1994)* (The terrorists are coming: A comparative study of the position of the Muslim Brothers and the jihadist groups regarding

violence) (1995) has not appeared in English. *Cairo Times* published two of Mubarak's articles (1998, 1998a) on relations between radical Islamists and the government. See also his interview with Jama'a al-Islamiyya leader Tal'at Fu'ad Qasim (1996).

16. Interview, Cairo, February 22, 2007. Seif al-Dawla is a longtime human rights and women's rights activist. She teaches psychiatry at 'Ayn Shams University and is a founder of the Nadim Center for the Rehabilitation of Victims of Torture.

17. Interview, Cairo, February 2007.

18. Interview, Cairo, February 11, 2007. Two other human rights activists from that period, Negad al-Borai and Amir Salem, put greater emphasis on links between political ideology, the failure of political parties, and their human rights activism. See Hicks, "Transnational Human Rights Networks and Human Rights in Egypt" (2006, 74).

19. In Hassan's view, one formative debate in the EOHR had to do with the position the organization should take toward violent Islamist groups. See Hassan (2006, 37–48).

20. Interview with Gamal Eid, Cairo, February 12, 2007. Eid is a defense lawyer and founder and director of the Cairo-based Arab Network for Human Rights Information (ANHRI), which promotes freedom of expression on the Internet and publishes a daily digest of information from more than one hundred Arab human rights organizations.

21. Interview with Clarisa Bencomo, Cairo, February 12, 2007.

22. Interview with Karim al-Gawhary, Cairo, February 26, 2007.

23. Interview with Bahey el-Din Hassan, Cairo, February 11, 2007.

24. Interview, Cairo, February 12, 2007.

25. Hicks continues, "State sponsorship of the domestic human rights debate, while not ideal, may well be better than a conscious policy of state obstruction and official defamation of human rights ideas" (88).

26. Interview with Driss al-Yazami, Paris, April 11, 2007. Al-Yazami is secretary-general of the International Federation of Human Rights (FIDH) in Paris and currently serves as a member of Morocco's official Consultative Council for Human Rights (CCDH).

27. Interview with Larbi Maâninou, Paris, April 13, 2007.

28. A Moroccan League for Human Rights was established in 1972 under the aegis of the center-right Istiqlal Party; it was never very active, though it still exists. On the formative years of Morocco's main human rights organizations, see Waltz (1995, 144–49) and Rollinde (2002, 201ff.).

29. According to Waltz, the AMDH and OMDH emerged from the USFP. But the OMDH relied heavily on its links to the party, while the AMDH, despite its formal USFP affiliation, operated more independently.

30. Interview with Abdelaziz Nouaydi, Amman, June 28, 2007. Nouaydi teaches constitutional law at Mohamed V University in Rabat; he was active in the OMDH and is a founder of Adala, a human rights organization that deals with administration of justice issues. According to Waltz, "By the time the OMDH was shaped, the discourse of human

rights had gained respect internationally and across the Maghrib, and in consequence, of all the Maghribi groups, the OMDH at its creation projected the clearest purpose of promoting and defending human rights" (1995, 157). According to Nouaydi, the AMDH currently has eighty-eight sections and nearly ten thousand members.

31. In January 1990 Amnesty International released a report on torture during *garde à vue* (police custody) detention, which Nouaydi believes "accelerated the process of the creation of the ACHR [CCDH]."

32. For example: "Four individuals have been chosen under the pretext that they represent university teachers, without any reference to the sole and independent union of university teachers. Among the teachers selected at least two are known to be close friends of the Minister of Interior" (Nouaydi 2000, 7).

33. Interview with Sion Assidon, Washington, DC, August 22, 2009. Assidon was convicted of "endangering the security of the state." He escaped from a prison hospital in 1979 but was rearrested and sentenced to an additional term. He was released in 1984 but was denied the right to travel until 1992.

34. Tazmamart was a secret military prison whose existence was publicized by Amnesty International and Human Rights Watch as well as Moroccan exiles in Europe; in Morocco the OMDH was the first to mention it publicly. "The Palace continued to deny even the existence of a prison at Tazmamart" (Waltz 1995, 211). Then, prior to a visit by the king to Washington, scheduled for September 1991, Moroccan authorities released some forty Tazmamart prisoners. "Almost simultaneously, a highly placed Moroccan official leaked news to Reuters that Tazmamart had been emptied and razed" (211). In fact the prison dungeons remain. In October 2000 the Forum for Truth and Justice organized a "pilgrimage" of more than a thousand persons to the site of the former prison. "On the level plain facing the entrance to the prison, pilgrims held photographs of the disappeared, lit candles, and scattered rose petals on the land" (Slyomovics 2005, 65). The visitors were not permitted to enter the barracks. According to Slyomovics, former prisoner Fatna el-Bouih recalled that a lone guard, peering over the wall, told the crowd, "I swear there is no longer anyone inside." In fact no one claims that prisoners are still held in Tazmamart.

35. For an evaluation of its accomplishments and shortcomings, see Human Rights Watch (2005).

36. Quoted in Slyomovics (2005, 191). On Group 71 and human rights activism among Moroccan Islamists, see 182–94.

37. Interview, Casablanca, June 25, 2008.

38. Kingdom of Morocco, Advisory Council for Human Rights, "Recommendations for the Setting Up of a 'Justice and Reconciliation Commission'" (quoted in Human Rights Watch 2004, 155). The commission had no authority, however, to name the perpetrators of the abuses it documented, and it was not authorized to investigate serious abuses such as torture.

39. An English summary of the ERC's final report is available at http://www.ictj.org/static/MENA/Morocco/IERreport.findingssummary.eng.pdf (accessed August 28, 2009).

40. Interview, Utrecht, March 31, 2007.

41. Interview, Ankara, September 8, 2007.

42. Interview, Ankara, September 7, 2007. Ensaroğlu here refers to a journal he worked with before the establishment of Mazlum-Der.

43. Interview, Ankara, September 8, 2007.

44. Ibid.

45. Interview, Ankara, September 7, 2007.

46. Yurdatapan, a prominent secularist, discusses the campaign in a collection featuring his essays along with those of Islamist thinker Abdurrahman Dilipak (Yurdatapan and Dilipak 2003). Turks supporting freedom of expression also rallied in 2005 when authorities charged novelist Orhan Pamuk with violating the law prohibiting "insulting the Turkish Republic." In an interview in a Swedish magazine, Pamuk had criticized Turkish silence regarding mass killings of Kurds and Armenians.

47. See Zeynep Gülru Göker's contribution to this volume, Chapter 7.

48. On May 21, 2009, a coalition of Turkish human rights groups including the IHD, Mazlum-Der, Helsinki Citizens' Assembly, the Human Rights Foundation of Turkey, and the Turkish section of Amnesty International issued a joint statement criticizing the draft law.

## Chapter 6

I would like to thank Bozena Welborne for enormous help with editing in the early stages of preparing this chapter.

1. *Diplômé chômeur* is the French translation of "unemployed graduate." In Moroccan Arabic (*darija*) this category is simply called *al-mu'attalin* (the unemployed). In conversations in *darija*, the unemployed graduates are usually referred to as *les Diplômés chômeurs*. Some of these protesters are also physically disabled, especially blind.

2. The same trend is apparent among high school certificate holders, whose situation is better than university graduates. For them the unemployment rate was 14.6 percent in 1984, 38.8 percent in 1991, 35 percent in 1997, and 34 percent in 2002 (Haut Comissariat au Plan, *Activité, Emploi et Chômage*, several years). The general unemployment rate was 18.4 percent in 1984, 16 percent in 1992, 16.9 percent in 1996, 11.9 percent in 2002, and 9.7 percent in 2006. The number of university graduates has increased more than fifteen-fold between 1985–86 (4,348 graduated students) and 2005–6 (62,041 graduated students) (Ministère de l'Enseignement supérieur, de la formation de cadres et de la récherche scientifique, www.enssup.gov.ma).

3. Unemployed graduates are treated by the press as a "new socio-professional category." Their collective action is sometimes described as being on the edge of psychopathological or sectarian behavior (*Tel Quel* 216, March 11–17, 2006).

4. In 2005 four groups organized almost daily demonstrations in Rabat: Ittihad -al-utur al-'uliya (Unemployed High Graduates Union); Amal (Hope); Khams (Five); and Nasr (Victory). The adherents of these groups were recruited to the civil service in September 2006. Since March 2006 four other groups occupied public space: Mubadara (Initiative); Hiwar (Dialogue); Istihqaq (Merit); and al-Majmu'a al-wataniyya li'l-dakatira al-mu'attalin (Unemployed PhD Holders National Group); as well as some remainders of Nasr. They turned into five groups in September 2008 after a series of alliances and fusions: Majmu'at al-arba' al-utur al-'ulya al-mu'attalin (the Four Groups of Unemployed Higher Degree Holders); Tansiqiyya-Dakatira (Coordination-PhD Holders); Tajammu' (Gathering); Fatiya (Youth); and Shu'ala (Torch).

5. ANDCM is the result of the coordination of experienced activists. Most of them come from the National Student Union of Morocco (UNEM), which in the 1970s and 1980s was influenced by Marxism-Leninism. The cost of the repression suffered during the "Years of Lead" by clandestine left organizations oriented the reinvolvement of activists towards alternative issues: human rights, employment rights, and so on.

6. My fieldwork observations revealed that the weekly general assemblies, or the work division within several committees, constitute moments of ideological and practical-experience transmission from "politicized" activists to less experienced ones.

7. The numerical barrier has been influenced by the recurrence of mobilization. The first group of postgraduates (including 193 members) organized sit-ins lasting several days in front of parliament. Today, after fourteen years of waves of protest and the constant adaptation of authorities (McAdam 1983), activists consider it impossible to carry out these types of activities with a reduced number of members, or even to carry them out at all.

8. Pamphlets from al-Ittihad al-watani li'l-utur al-'ulya al-mu'attalin, al-Tansiqiya al-wataniyya li'l-utur al-'ulya al-mu'attalin wa'l- dakatira al-mu'attalin, al-Nasr.

9. The UNEM included different tendencies: some were close to parliamentary and governmental left parties, and the so-called qa'idiyyun ("those closest to the base") followed a more radical Marxist-Leninist orientation. Some activists regard the internal quarrels as responsible for the failure of the union, especially the lack of openness towards the Islamists, whose influence was growing in the university.

10. Groups such as al-Barnamij al-Marhali, al-Nahj al-Dimuqrati, al-Yasar al-Dimuqrati, Trotskyist groups, and parties taking part in the elections as Parti Socialiste Unifié (PSU) (al-Hizb al-Ishtiraki al-Muwahhad) and Parti de l'Avantgarde Démocratique et Sociale (PADS) (Hizb al-Tali'a al-Dimuqratiyya wal-Ishtirakiyya) had always been present in the ANDCM. Since 1998 their presence in the executive organs has become more visible.

11. Most of the ANDCM activists studied in the university during the 1980s and the 1990s. Most of them did not join the ranks of the ANDCM at the end of their university studies but rather after several years of working as professionals. But Marxist-Leninist

(*qaʿidiyyun*) involvement is frequently evoked as a legitimate background, especially valued in the association. The members of the postgraduate groups attended university in the 1990s and 2000s when leftist streams were less visible than the Islamists, who have assumed the direction of the UNEM.

## Chapter 7

1. Article 2 of the International Convention for the Protection of All Persons from Enforced Disappearance adopted by the UN General Assembly defines enforced disappearance as "the arrest, detention, abduction or any other form of deprivation of liberty by agents of the State or by persons or groups of persons acting with the authorization, support or acquiescence of the State, followed by a refusal to acknowledge the deprivation of liberty or by concealment of the fate or whereabouts of the disappeared person, which place such a person outside the protection of the law." See http://www2.ohchr .org/english/law/disappearance-convention.htm.

2. "Do Not Touch My Friend" was a campaign built to raise awareness about the oppression of and discrimination against people—whether Jewish, Kurdish, or Armenian. Participants used to distribute pins that read "Do Not Touch My Friend," and they went to public spaces such as theaters to distribute flyers (Nadire Mater, personal communication, June 9, 2009).

3. Interview, June 9, 2009. Mater is a well-known journalist and human rights activist. She has served as the representative of Interpress Service in Turkey and has been active in numerous human rights movements including the Saturday Vigils. Mater still works as the editor of BİA, Independent Communication Network.

4. Since 1977 Argentinean mothers and grandmothers of the disappeared have held vigils in Plaza de Mayo in Buenos Aires every Thursday at 3:30 t to demand information about the whereabouts of their children who disappeared under the military junta that ruled the country from 1976 to 1983.

5. Turkish law on meetings and public demonstrations, clause 2911, ratified October 6, 1983 (*Resmi Gazete*, no. 18185, October 8, 1983), includes the right to peaceful protest in certain situations. However, the original article also contained a statement that actions which threaten the indivisible unity of the nation can be banned (Baydar and Ivegen 2006).

6. Unlike its counterpart in Turkey, the movement in Argentina transformed into a movement that attended to other human rights violations and political issues.

7. What kind of contentious action the new vigils will constitute remains to be seen. In this article I am referring to the vigils that took place between 1995 and 1999.

8. Dietz (2002) criticizes maternalists such as Ruddick (1989) and Elshtain (1981) for suggesting an exclusive, nongeneralizable identity, such as motherhood, as the basis of democratic citizenship. We need to dissociate democratic citizenship from gendered associations, such as that between emotions and femininity/privacy, or between reason and masculinity/publicness.

NOTES TO CHAPTERS 7 AND 8    277

9. From Aristotle to contemporary democratic theory, political actors have been conceived as speaking actors. Aristotle's (1998) political animals are speaking animals; Arendt's (1958) public sphere is marked by words, similar to Habermas's (1996) concept of the public sphere as a discursive space, which inspired deliberative democracy (Benhabib 1996). Silence has found its place in political theory largely within studies of civil disobedience or in feminist and postcolonial literature, where gendered hierarchies embedded in communication are analyzed (Sanders 1997; Young 2002), or the hegemonic, articulate white heterosexual female is criticized (Anzaldúa 1990). Yet while speaking freely and openly has been a central organizing principle for many social movements, the privileging of speech as a way of revealing what is private or as an exercise of freedom has not been adequately challenged.

10. Feminist interpreters of Arendt's work conceptualize political subjectivity as produced through action (Honig 1995) and argue that it is possible to envision a performative feminist politics aligned with democracy (Zerilli 2005) while challenging its gendered and essentialist base.

11. For example, in 2006 when some parents of the martyred soldiers said they did not want to say, "Long live the country," that they would have preferred to have their sons live, conspiracy theories proliferated treating these cases as a new terrorist tactic (Temelkuran 2006, 2006a). In 2008 when Bülent Ersoy, a famous transsexual singer, said on television that if she had a son, she would not want to send him to war, she was sent to court for "insulting the Turkish military and discouraging men from soldiering" (Zengin 2008). Immediately thereafter a number of famous women competed to show how patriotic they were by dismissing Ersoy's statements. Because Ersoy cannot biologically conceive, this also opens up an important discussion of gender and sexuality about who can be considered a "proper" mother. The fact that her comments spurred such a heated public debate sheds light on the extent to which soldiering rests on women's collaboration.

## Chapter 8

I would like to thank Mounia Bennani-Chraïbi, Joel Beinin, and Frédéric Vairel for their helpful comments on the first drafts of this chapter.

1. Actes signés à Lausanne le 30 janvier et le 24 juillet 1923 et actes signés à Sèvres le 10 août 1920, Paris: Imprimerie nationale, 1923.

2. The Muslim conservative party, AKP (in power since 2002), is considered by the military and a great part of the civil bureaucracy as a threat to Turkish secularism. In April 2007 the military threatened to use force to prevent AKP nominee Abdullah Gül from being elected president of the Turkish Republic. Moreover state-approved associations must remain apolitical.

3. In 2004, for instance, among the thirty BTTDD representatives to the Rumelian Turks Federation were listed Mustafa Dündar, a member of parliament, and Mehmet Müezzinoğlu, president of the Istanbul local assembly, both AKP members. Since 2000

there have been several studies of the associations of "Turks from abroad" and the way they interact with both the political field and the definition of the Turkish foreign policy (Hersant 2008; Danış and Parla 2009), but mainly from a civil society paradigm perspective (Toumarkine 2000; Kaya 2001; Özgür-Baklacıoğlu 2006).

4. See, for instance (in Turkish), "Statement of the Association for Struggle Against Communism," *Batı Trakya*, no. 4, August 1967; "Prayers in Memory of the Martyrs of the War of Independence," *Batı Trakya*, no. 5, September 1967.

5. The MHP is the third-largest political force in Turkey.

6. "Telegrams," *Batı Trakya*, no. 90, October 1974 (in Turkish). See also Altınay and Bora (2002).

7. "Telegrams from the Western Thrace Immigrants Mutual Aid Association," *Batı Trakya*, no. 8, December 1967 (in Turkish). Cevdet Sunay was himself a former staff officer, and he approved the 1971 military coup d'état; see Bozarslan (2004, 59).

8. "Western Thrace Front in Cyprus's Peace Operation," *Batı Trakya*, no. 93, January 1975 (in Turkish). "Peace operation" is the official expression used to name what is considered by international law as the military invasion of northern Cyprus by the Turkish army in 1974, after the failure of the coup d'état planned by Makarios and the Greek junta.

9. "Two Turks Were Killed in Cyprus and Western Thrace," *Batı Trakya*, no. 3, July 1967 (in Turkish).

10. "Turks in Western Thrace and Cyprus," *Batı Trakya*, no. 4, August 1967 (in Turkish); based on an article published in *Sabah* daily newspaper.

11. "Turkish Youth Has Had Its Voice Heard in Meetings Organized in Istanbul and Ankara," *Batı Trakya*, no. 7, November 1967 (in Turkish).

12. "Beyazıt Square in Istanbul Experienced a Historical Day," *Batı Trakya*, no. 84, April 1974 (in Turkish). One of the Western Thrace movement's leaders, Ahmet Aydınlı made a speech "on behalf of the Batı Trakyalı." In 1971 he published a satire entitled *Western Thrace's Disaster*, which made him known as an intellectual of the Western Thrace cause. He was also president of BTTDD between 1981 and 1984.

13. "Wreath Deposit at Consulate's Door and Meeting Illustrate Demonstrators' Maturity," *Batı Trakya*, no. 84, April 1974 (in Turkish).

14. "Contacts of the Board of the Association of Immigrants from Western Thrace in Ankara," *Batı Trakya*, no. 14, June 1968 (in Turkish).

15. "The Association's Board Was Received by Our Prime Minister, Mr. Demirel," *Batı Trakya*, no. 37, May 1970 (in Turkish).

16. "Contacts of the Association's Leaders in Ankara," *Batı Trakya*, no. 83, March 1974 (in Turkish).

17. "The Claims of Western Thrace Turks Living in Turkey but Who Still Have Greek Citizenship," *Batı Trakya*, no. 85, May 1974 (in Turkish).

18. "The Anniversary of the Association of Western Thrace and Cyprus Turks Association Was Celebrated," *Batı Trakya*, no. 169, May 1981 (in Turkish).

19. "Turks from Cyprus and Western Thrace," *Batı Trakya*, no. 209, September 1984 (in Turkish).

20. "6000 Batı Trakyalı Fellow Countrymen Are Granted Turkish Citizenship," *Batı Trakya*, no. 167, March 1981 (in Turkish).

21. "A Directorate General for the Turks from Abroad Depending on Prime Minister Should Be Created," *Batı Trakya*, no. 168, April 1981 (in Turkish).

22. Until the 1980 coup, textbooks' covers did not even bear the effigy of Atatürk (Copeaux 1997).

23. "Our Ordinary Assembly Gathered in an Atmosphere of Great Maturity," *Batı Trakya*, no. 158, June 1980 (in Turkish).

24. "Protest Meeting Against Bulgaria Will Take Place on March 21st," *Batı Trakya*, no. 215, March 1985 (in Turkish).

25. "A Huge Protest Meeting Against Bulgaria," *Batı Trakya*, no. 216, April 1985 (in Turkish).

26. "Protest Against Greece at Border," *Batı Trakya*, no. 257, October–December 1989 (in Turkish). Between 1989 and 1993, because of the emergence of independent "Turkish" members of parliament in Western Thrace, Greek authorities would prevent buses coming from Turkey from crossing the border just before elections.

27. Ahmet (1947–95), a leading figure in the Turkish identity movement in Western Thrace, was the first Batı Trakyalı to be elected a member of parliament without being affiliated with a Greek political party. He was tried for "Turkish propaganda" during his electoral campaigns. He is also known for his connections with extreme right-wing movements in Turkey.

28. For example, after the bloody repression of demonstrations in 1977, May First trade union demonstrations were not allowed to reach this monument until 2009. "A Sensible End: A Consequence of Strong Bargaining, Certainly, but May 1st Was Celebrated at Taksim Square for the First Time Since 1978," *Radikal*, May 5, 2009 (in Turkish).

29. Examples of the climax of this hate include the events of September 6–7, 1955; the murder of journalist Hrant Dink in 2007; and the fact that several priests have been murdered in Turkey in the last few years.

30. A branch of the Nationalist Action Party (MHP). Interview with the former president of a BTTDD local branch who took part in the blockade (interviewed February 2004). Another former BTTDD leader recounted this demonstration and was very proud of what happened (interviewed July 2003).

31. Aarbakke relies on an edition of the extreme rightist daily newspaper *Türkiye*, August 27, 1991, for this information.

32. "Protest Meeting Against Greece Was Canceled," *Batı Trakya*, no. 250, February 1988 (in Turkish).

33. "The Anniversary of the Foundation of the Cyprus and Western Thrace Turks Solidarity Association Was Celebrated," *Batı Trakya*, no. 169, May 1981 (in Turkish); "A

New Directorship Was Elected During Our Annual General Meeting," *Batı Trakya*, no. 169, May 1981 (in Turkish).

34. See, in Turkish: "A Diplomatic Note Sent to the Islamic Conference," *Batı Trakya*, no. 145, May 1979; "Western Thrace Turks Attend the Meeting of Foreign Affairs Ministers at the Islamic Conference," *Batı Trakya'nın Sesi*, no. 9, March–April 1989; "Western Thrace Turks Attend Islamic Conference," *Batı Trakya'nın Sesi*, nos. 18–20, 1990; "Islamic Conference Organization Stands Up for Western Thrace Turks," *Batı Trakya'nın Sesi*, no. 37, December 1991.

35. "Cyprus and Western Thrace Turks," *Batı Trakya*, no. 209, September 1984 (in Turkish).

36. This is valid a fortiori for "Turks" in Iraq, to Pan-Turkish militants' great displeasure: "Mufti of Xanthi Was Invited to Iraq," *Batı Trakya*, no. 160, August 1980 (in Turkish).

37. He is now a sympathizer of the *İşçi Partisi* (Workers' Party), an ultranationalist organization mobilized in particular for the Cyprus issue. The president of *Yeni Batı Trakya*'s editorial board since 2003 is retired general Veli Küçük, who was in 2008 one of the main defendants in the trial of the substate organization Ergenekon. Gathering officers, politicians, and journalists, this ultranationalist organization was suspected of journalist Hrant Dink's assassination and of planning a coup d'état. See, for instance, "'Deep State Plot' Grips Turkey," *BBC News*, February 4, 2008, http://news.bbc.co.uk/2/hi/europe/7225889.stm.

38. "About Western Thrace, with Professor Kemal Karpat," *Batı Trakya'nın Sesi*, no. 1, November–December 1987. Helsinki Watch also published a famous report in 1991 that contributed to publicizing the Western Thrace Turks' issue. According to one Helsinki Federation representative (interviewed in November 2000), Turkish officials suggested writing this report as a precondition to issuing a report on the situation of Kurds in Turkey.

39. Mümtaz Soysal, quoted in "A Panel of Experts on Greek-Turkish Relations, Lausanne Treaty and Western Thrace Turks," *Batı Trakya'nın Sesi*, no. 1, November–December 1987 (in Turkish).

40. "Protest March Against Bulgaria in Düsseldorf," *Yeni Batı Trakya*, no. 34, 1986. The march (which is said to have gathered five thousand persons) is recounted by one of the participants, who does not name the "Turkish organization."

41. "Speeches, Commission Reports, Conclusions," Fourth International Western Thrace Turks Conference, June 16–18, 2000, London and Bursa: BTTDD (in Turkish).

## Chapter 9

1. The UGTT called a general strike, initially limited to the Sfax area on January 12, which became national on January 14, 2011. In so doing, the organization contributed to the mass movement on the last day before Ben Ali fled (Allal and Geisser 2011).

2. The president's party had enjoyed uninterrupted hegemony since 1959. The *parti unique*, renamed the RCD under Ben Ali in 1988, brooked no competition, despite the introduction, for appearances' sake, of a multiparty system in 1981. In all legislative, city, and presidential elections, the RCD garnered a hegemonic share of the votes. Thus, the party became a de facto administration, with its local cadres serving as middlemen for provision of all kinds of "public services."

3. For an analysis of the "Collective of October 18, 2005," its beginnings and its failure, see Geisser and Gobe (2007); Geisser and Gobe (2009).

4. The tendency to break out of sectoral boundaries only went so far, given that the major employers at no time denounced the regime. In any case, they had always managed to work things out with the Ben Ali family (Hibou 2008).

5. The adjective "revolutionary" (*thawri*) has become commonplace in Tunisia. I employ it here without entering into a normative discussion on whether the events qualify as revolutionary or presuming to predict the outcome of the political developments under way. This does not obviate the need to examine this new commonsense notion and the many controversies over the meanings and classifications underlying the "revolution" label, as Kmar Bendana (2012) has done.

6. Quotes are drawn from observation and interviews conducted in Redeyef, Métlaoui, Oum El Araies, and M'dhila, January through June 2008.

7. Talks were held with small groups of protesters like the "Widows of Oum El Araïes," a group of wives of CPG workers who had died due to workplace accidents. The widows, who had set up tents and demanded that their children be hired, cleared their encampment in February after the authorities promised to meet their demand.

8. All quotes from Yusra are from five interviews held between March 2007 and February 2011.

9. Observations starting in March 2007 on the Hammam-Lif-Tunis commuter train.

10. As a variety of specialists have pointed out, space is an important aspect of collective protest (Auyero 2005; Martin and Miller 2003; Sewell 2001; Tilly 2003). However, very little research has used ethnographic analysis to study the usage and appropriation of spaces on the dynamics of contention. Bayat (1997) and Hmed (2008) have begun to address this issue.

11. I met them during a field trip in spring 2006 and subsequently interviewed and observed them many times through March 2011. All quotes are from those encounters.

12. The reference is to a shared memory of struggle. The region provided a large share of the country's independence fighters and figures active in the union struggles and revolts of the late 1970s and early 1980s (Allal 2010, 119).

13. These were neighbors of my family, three of whom I first met as friends of a cousin. The "sociological" curiosity aroused in this way led to a large number of encounters and interviews between June 2006 and November 2011 from which the quotes are taken.

## Chapter 10

More detailed accounts of some events mentioned here appear in Beinin (2005, 2007, 2008, 2008a) and Beinin and el-Hamalawy (2007, 2007a). Some of the research on which this chapter is based was undertaken in conjunction with the preparation of a report for the Solidarity Center, AFL-CIO, *The Struggle for Worker Rights in Egypt* (Beinin 2010a) supervised by Heba El-Shazli, then regional program director for the Middle East and North Africa. Marie Duboc was a research assistant on that project.

1. ETUF is composed of twenty-three national general unions organized by industrial sectors. All local union committees must belong to one of them. The literal translation of al-Ittihad al-ʿAmm li-Niqabat ʿUmmal Misr is the General Federation of Egyptian Trade Unions.

2. The best known is Kareem el-Behirey, http://egyworkers.blogspot.com.

3. The Egyptian Center for Economic and Social Rights, established in 2010 was active among workers since its inception, especially on the issue of a national minimum wage.

4. For example, Nadia Oweidat and colleagues (2008, 25). Kifaya general coordinator George Ishaq and some fifty members were arrested following the abortive April 6, 2008, strike in Mahalla, apparently because the government incorrectly thought they had something to do with the strike call.

5. Figures are based on Law 53 of 1984.

6. Quotes and the narrative of the strike are based on interviews with Muhammad al-ʿAttar and Sayyid Habib, in al-Mahalla al-Kubra, March 9, 2007. See Beinin and el-Hamalawy (2007).

7. The prominence and militancy of women at Mahalla was not exceptional but part of a broader phenomenon in this period. On the role of gender dynamics in labor strikes, see Duboc 2013.

8. Telephone interview with Muhammad al-ʿAttar, April 15, 2007.

9. http://arabist.net/arabawy/2007/09/24/videos_mahalla/ (accessed June 1, 2009).

10. "Ya basha, ya bey, rghif al-ʿaysh bi-rubʿ gneyh" ("Oh pasha, oh bey, a loaf of [subsidized] bread costs a quarter of a pound"). Joel Beinin witnessed these events.

11. "Appeal for Solidarity: The Employees of the Real Estate Taxes Authority Establish the Independent General Union of RETA Workers," http://ctuws.jeeran.com/archive/2008/12/750177.html (accessed December 10, 2008); CTUWS, press release, April 24, 2009, http://ctuws.jeeran.com/archive/2009/4/ 861473.html (accessed May 24, 2009).

12. The first issue of *Nubat suhyan: sawt daraʾib al-ʿaqariyya al-hurr* appeared in October 2008. It was published monthly for the remainder of the year and perhaps beyond.

13. Interview with Sayyid Habib, Faysal Laqusha, and Gamal Abuʾl-ʿAla Hasanayn, in al-Mahalla al-Kubra, March 20, 2009.

14. Muʾassasat Awlad al-Ard li-Huquq al-Insan, monthly reports.

15. American Chamber of Commerce in Egypt, *Business Monthly*, March 2011.

16. Ibid.

17. Port Technology International, "Egyptian Ports and Terminals Closed; Suez Canal Unaffected," February 1, 2011, http://www.porttechnology.org/news/port_termi nals_and_operations_close_in_crisis_hit_egypt/; "Egyptian Ports Still Running on a Limited Basis," February 3, 2011, http://www.porttechnology.org/news/egyptian_ports _still_running_on_a_limited_basis/; and "Egyptian Ports Facing Backlogs as Crisis Continues," http://www.porttechnology.org/news/egyptian_ports_facing_backlogs_as _crisis _continues (accessed September 10, 2012).

18. Mu'assasat Awlad al-Ard li-Huquq al-Insan monthly reports.

## Chapter 11

This chapter is a revised and updated version of "La structuration de la révolution yéménite: essai d'analyse d'un processus en marche," *Revue française de science politique* (2012). The authors thank Mounia Bennani-Chraïbi and Olivier Fillieule for their useful comments on earlier versions.

1. Founded in 897 in Sa'da and overturned by the revolution of September 26, 1962, the Zaydi imamate was a strongly isolationist, highly conservative regime dominated by a religious and social elite. Zaydism is a branch of Shi'a Islam that stands apart from the Twelver Shi'ism predominant in Iran, Iraq, and Lebanon. Roughly one-third of all Yemenis nominally belong to this current, with Sunnis of the Shafi'i school forming the majority of the population. But the political and social component of Zaydi identity has grown weaker over the last few decades. Only a minority advocating revitalization of Zaydism has asserted this identity in connection with opposition to discrimination against Zaydis.

2. The use of the terms *revolution* and *revolutionary* to describe the popular revolt initiated in January should not be taken as a statement about the outcome of the political and social process still under way. Rather, we use the categories employed by the participants to underscore the extent to which this process has led to the perception of a radical change and a major break with the past.

3. Although we observed similar dynamics at work in other Yemeni cities, particularly Ta'iz, a major hotbed of protest, this chapter covers only events in the capital, San'a'.

4. According to World Bank and United Nations Development Program statistics (2009, 2011).

5. "Institutional politics" refers to the full range of actors, institutions, and practices that make up the "legitimate" political realm. Although this is a reductionist category that tends to lump too much together, it does help to grasp how various actors perceive the political scene. For a discussion, see Bennani-Chraïbi 2011.

6. As a counterweight to Tahrir Square, which was preemptively occupied by President Salih's supporters.

7. These concepts are central to a short book edited by several leaders of the "revo-

lutionary youth": Mahmud Ghalib al-Bukari, Munir 'Abd al-Raqib Muhammad, Murad al-Ghariti, *Dalil al-muwatin ila al-dawla al-madaniyya* (San'a': Tamkeen Development Foundation, 2011).

8. Interview with a Socialist Party member who participated in the sit-in to defend the *al-Ayyam* newspaper, Aden, March 6, 2008.

9. "*Qat* chews" provide occasions for socialization, interaction, and political discussion, and they may even function as a public sphere (Wedeen 2008, 120–47).

10. According to Evans and Boyte (1986, 17), safe spaces are "public places in the community . . . the environments in which people are able to learn a new self-respect, a deeper and more assertive group identity, public skills, and values of cooperation and civil virtue."

11. Interview with an opposition activist, San'a', March 25, 2011.

12. Ethnographic notes shared by Maggy Grabundzija, a researcher and consultant in Yemen, summer 2011.

13. Phone interviews with revolutionary youth activists, fall 2011.

14. For example, the Union of Leftist Youth (Ittihad shabab al-yasar), the Liberal Youth Current (al-Tayar al-shababi al-hurr), or the Organization of Independent Civil Youth (Munazzamat al-shabab al-mustaqillin al-madaniyyin).

15. Interview with a shaykh from the Bakil confederation, San'a', February 21, 2011.

16. Photo essay, "Life on Change Square in Sanaa," *Mareb Press*, February 22, 2011.

17. Interview with a female Security Committee member, San'a', March 10, 2011.

18. Atiaf, Alwazir, "Art for Change," *La Voix du Yémen*, May 7, 2011.

19. "The various actors are connected to each other through a series of interdependent relations, with the result that their decisions, anticipations, and possible calculations are informed by the decisions, anticipations, and calculations of both their partners and their opponents" (Combes and Fillieule 2011, 1065).

20. Speech by Muhammad al-Sa'di, deputy secretary-general of al-Islah, Markaz Ab'ad, San'a', January 22, 2011.

21. For a critical analysis of the role played by Hamid al-Ahmar in the revolutionary process, see Nabil Subay', "Cynicism is a treasure that never wears out," *News Yemen*, September 8 and 11, 2011.

22. Interview with a GPC cadre, San'a', March 17, 2011. While accurate, this comment is part of a concerted effort to condemn the revolutionary process, an operation orchestrated by the Muslim Brothers according to the official media.

23. Other preachers and religious figures were exploited by the government, which encouraged them to set up different structures to bring together '*ulama*', especially those close to the Salafis, and to call for recognition of President Salih's legitimacy in opposing the revolutionaries (Bonnefoy 2012).

24. Interview with a revolutionary youth activist, San'a', March 4, 2011.

25. Nabil Subay', "The last secret meeting of the 'ruling' party," *al-Taghyir*, April 17, 2011.

## Chapter 12

The author thanks the Dutch NGO Hivos, which made the research for this chapter possible in the framework of its program on Civil Society in West Asia, and Abeer El-Sayed, who provided research assistance.

1. http://www.onsyria.com/?clip=13023&cat=5&parent=1&page=274&sort_order=timestamp (accessed October 31, 2012).

2. These included Syria's timid steps toward allowing more leeway for "civil society," social development, and charity organizations prior to the uprising (De Elvira 2010), Muslim clerics' wrangling with the state (Pierret 2012; Donker 2012), human rights activists calling for the rule of law, and dissident writers and filmmakers (Weiss 2012; Cooke 2007).

3. Interview with activist from Dar'a, September 19, 2011; Yasir Abu Hilala in *al-Hayat*, August 16, 2011. The second woman, also from Dar'a, was Diana al-Jawabra, who was arrested after taking part in a small demonstration in Damascus (Reuters, March 20, 2011).

4. http://www.youtube.com/watch?v=IetDsvlmTtk&feature=player_embedded (accessed October 31, 2012).

5. http://www.onsyria.com/?clip=5303&cat=5&parent=1&page=274&sort_order=timestamp (accessed October 31, 2012).

6. http://www.youtube.com/watch?v=4kR9CpTFLDo (accessed on December 2, 2011); http://www.youtube.com/watch?v=H9_BOjkD2wY&feature=player_embedded (accessed October 31, 2012); http://www.onsyria.com/?clip=4209&cat=5&parent=1&page=274&sort_order=timestamp (accessed October 31, 2012); http://www.onsyria.com/?clip=4207&cat=5&parent=1&page=274&sort_order=timestamp (accessed October 31, 2012).

7. Interviews with Syrian activists and with Dar'a residents, September–November 2011.

8. BBC's Panorama documentary on the uprising in Dar'a (September 26, 2011) showed the graffiti on the school's walls.

9. http://www.onsyria.com/?clip=13040&cat=5&parent=1&page=274&sort_order=timestamp (accessed October 31, 2012).

10. http://www.aljazeera.com/indepth/opinion/2011/04/2011426115117817489.html and http://www.onsyria.com/?clip=4093&cat=5&parent=1&page=274&sort_order=timestamp (accessed October 31, 2012).

11. http://www.onsyria.com/?clip=13040&cat=5&parent=1&page=274&sort_order=timestamp; http://www.onsyria.com/?clip=12999&cat=5&parent=1&page=279&sort_order=timestamp; and http://www.onsyria.com/?clip=4198&cat=5&parent=1&page=279&sort_order=timestamp (accessed October 31, 2012).

12. Refuting regime claims about Salafists leading the uprising, the minaret of Dar'a's Umari mosque repeatedly broadcast the protest song, "Ya hayf" (Oh, shame). Strict Salafists would have considered that to be impermissable (Tahhan 2012a).

13. http://www.onsyria.com/?clip=5339&cat=5&parent=1&page=314&sort_order =timestamp (accessed October 31, 2012).

14. http://www.youtube.com/watch?v=L-46NfCv6do&feature=player_embedded (accessed October 31, 2012).

15. http://www.onsyria.com/?clip=25522&cat=5&parent=1&page=314&sort_order =timestamp and http://www.onsyria.com/?clip=5148&cat=5&parent=1&page=308&sort _order=timestamp (accessed October 31, 2012).

16. Expressing this sense of empowerment, a virtual puppet theater group from Damascus later repeatedly satirically referred to "Bashu" (Bashar al-Assad) being perplexed and at a loss when ordinary people and protestors dared to counter him. http://www .youtube.com/MasasitMati (accessed October 31, 2012).

17. Not talking, however, prompted rumors about Bashar al-Assad not being in control or underscored views about him having lost touch with popular sentiments. Naturally, activists keenly magnified and capitalized on such impressions. This paradox can perhaps be added to the "dictator's dilemma" described by Francisco (2005).

18. See, for instance, http://www.youtube.com/watch?v=VC6G8kc9VmU (accessed October 31, 2012).

19. Laba (1990) describes how the Solidarity movement in Poland borrowed from Catholic symbolism for the veneration of its martyrs.

20. http://www.onsyria.com/?clip=12924&cat=5&parent=1&page=314&sort_order =timestamp; http://www.onsyria. com/?clip=4029&cat=5&parent=1&page=314&sort _order=timestamp;http://www.onsyria.com/?clip=4028&cat=5&parent=1&page=314& sort_order=timestamp; http://www.onsyria.com/?clip=4161&cat=5&parent=1&page =314&sort_order=timestamp (accessed October 31, 2012).

21. http://www.onsyria.com/?clip=5408&cat=5&parent=1&page=310&sort_order =timestamp (accessed October 31, 2012).

22. Interview with activist from Dar'a, September 19, 2011.

23. See, for example, (very graphic) https://www.accessnow.org/video/country/22/ P5/ (accessed December 2, 2011).

24. http://www.onsyria.com/?clip=5422&cat=5&parent=1&page=311&sort_order =timestamp;http://www.onsyria.com/?clip=5585&cat=5&parent=1&page=307&sort_order =timestamp (accessed October 31, 2012).

25. Reuters, February 10, 2012.

26. Interview with Dar'a emigrant, October 19, 2011.

27. http://onsyria.com?clip=4136&cat=5&parent=1 (accessed on October 31, 2012).

28. In February, following the torture of Dar'a's fifteen schoolchildren, and in May with the death and mutilation of Hamza al-Khatib, also in Dar'a. See (very graphic): https:// www.youtube.com/verify_age?next_url=/watch%3Fv%3DaNee6jHKmTE; and http:// www.onsyria.com/?clip=4198&cat=5&parent=1&page=279&sort_order=timestamp (accessed October 31, 2012).

29. For a different view, see Swidler (1986, 273).

30. Naturally, the argument requires a more in-depth examination. I do not claim that cronyism and growing socioeconomic inequalities played no role in the Syrian uprising whatsoever, if only because these themes recurred in protest framing.

31. Interview, March 2010.

32. http://www.youtube.com/watch?v=O7VPxcgR_zE (accessed on October 31, 2012).

33. http://www.onsyria.com/?clip=4104&cat=5&parent=1&page=274&sort _order=timestamp; and http://www.onsyria.com/?clip=13365&cat=5&parent=1&page = 312&sort_order=timestamp (accessed on October 31, 2012).

34. http://www.onsyria.com/?clip=3955&cat=6&parent=1&page=440&sort_order =timestamp (accessed October 31, 2012).

35. BBC Arabic, September 2, 2011.

36. http://www.youtube.com/watch?v=hwoLgOQphfI (accessed October 31, 2012).

37. Interview with Syrian activist, October 2011.

38. http://www.youtube.com/watch?v=uGPy-kBofnk (accessed October 31, 2012).

39. http://www.youtube.com/watch?v=72lZOw9nspc (accessed October 31, 2012).

40. http://monde-arabe.arte.tv/wp-content/uploads/hamza.jpg (accessed October 31, 2012).

41. http://www.youtube.com/watch?v=Qqn65bZiUZY (accessed October 31, 2012).

42. http://www.facebook.com/Syrian.Intifada (accessed October 31, 2012).

43. Documentary film *Ibn al-'Amm*, by 'Ali 'Atassi, at http://www.youtube.com/watch ?v=BFOdOdCVKiE (accessed October 31, 2012).

44. Strikingly, the normative literature on nonviolent revolutions highlights peaceful tactics in promoting defections of regimes' security or armed forces but provides no answers to the violent consequences of partial success (Nepstad 2011, 14–16; Stephan and Chenoweth 2008). Neither, of course, did Western leaders who called for mass defections in Syria.

# BIBLIOGRAPHY

Aarbakke, Vemund. 2000. "The Muslim Minority of Greek Thrace." PhD dissertation, Bergen University.

Abdallah, Ahmed. 1985. *The Student Movement and National Politics in Egypt, 1923–1973.* London: Al Saqi Books.

Abdellatif, Omayma, and Marina Ottaway. 2007. "Women in Islamist Movements: Toward an Islamist Model of Women's Activism." *Carnegie Papers*, no. 2. Washington, DC: Carnegie Endowment for International Peace.

Abrams, Philip. 1988. "Notes on the Difficulty of Studying the State." *Journal of Historical Sociology* 1: 58–89.

Abu Eita, Kamal, et al. 2011. "Matalib al-'ummal fi al-thawra," February 19. http://www.e-socialists.net/node/6509 (accessed June 5, 2012).

Abu-Fadil, Magda. 2007. "Lebanese Women Journalists Brave War Odds." *Arab Media and Society*, no. 1. http://www.arabmediasociety.com/?article=22 (accessed July 15, 2009).

Abu-Lughod, Janet L. 2002. "Do Muslim Women Really Need Saving? Anthropological Reflections on Cultural Relativism and Its Others." *American Anthropologist* 104: 783–90.

Akçam, Taner. 2002. "Türk Ulusal Kimliği Üzerine Bazı Tezler." In *Modern Türkiye'de Siyasî Düşünce: Milliyetçilik*, vol. 4, ed. Tanıl Bora, 53–62. Istanbul: İletişim.

———. 2003. "Another History on Sèvres and Lausanne." In *The Armenian Genocide and the Shoah*, 2d ed., ed. Hans-Lukas Kieser and Dominik J. Schaller, 281–99. Zürich: Chronos Verlag.

Akesbi, Azzedine. 2003. "Ajustement structurel et segmentation du marché du travail." *Annales marocaines d'économie* 7: 3–12.

Alagha, Joseph Elie. 2006. *The Shifts in Hizbullah's Ideology: Religious Ideology, Political Ideology, and Political Program.* Leiden: ISIM; Amsterdam: Amsterdam University Press.

Alexander, Jeffrey C. 1998. *Real Civil Societies: Dilemmas of Institutionalization.* London: Sage.

Ali, Farhana. 2005. "Muslim Female Fighters: An Emerging Trend." *Terrorism Monitor* 3 (21): 9–11.

Al-Ali, Najde. 2005. "Reconstructing Gender: Iraqi Women Between Dictatorship, War, Sanctions and Occupation." *Third World Quarterly* 26: 739–58.

Alimi, Eitan. 2006. "Contextualizing Political Terrorism: A Collective Action Perspective for Understanding the Tanzim." *Studies in Conflict and Terrorism* 29: 263–83.

———. 2007. *Israeli Politics and the First Palestinian Intifada: Political Opportunities, Framing Processes and Contentious Politics.* London: Routledge.

———. 2009. "Mobilizing Under the Gun: Theorizing Political Opportunity Structure in a Highly Repressive Setting." *Mobilization* 14: 219–37.

Allal, Amin. 2010. "Réformes néolibérales, clientélismes et protestations en situation autoritaire. Les mouvements contestataires dans le bassin minier de Gafsa en Tunisie (2008)." *Politique africaine* 117: 107–25.

———. 2011. "'Avant on tenait le mur, maintenant on tient le quartier!' Germes d'un passage au politique de jeunes hommes de quartiers populaires lors du moment révolutionnaire à Tunis." *Politique Africaine* 121: 53–68.

Allal, Amin, and Vincent Geisser. 2011. "Tunisie: 'Révolution de jasmin' ou Intifada?" *Mouvements* 66: 62–68.

Allam, Rasha. 2008. "Countering the Negative Image of Arab Women in the Arab Media: Toward a 'Pan Arab Eye' Media Watch Project." *Middle East Institute Policy Brief*, no. 15.

Alpkaya, Gökçen. 2002. "Türk Dış Politikası'nda Milliyetçilik." In *Modern Türkiye'de Siyasî Düşünce: Milliyetçilik*, vol. 4, ed. Tanıl Bora, 155–67. Istanbul: İletişim.

Altınay, Ayşe Gül. 2004. *The Myth of the Military-Nation: Militarism, Gender, and Education in Turkey.* New York: Palgrave Macmillan.

Altınay, Ayşe Gül, and Tanıl Bora. 2002. "Ordu, Militarizm ve Milliyetçilik." In *Modern Türkiye'de Siyasî Düşünce: Milliyetçilik*, vol. 4, ed. Tanıl Bora, 140–54. Istanbul: İletişim.

American Chamber of Commerce in Egypt. 2005. *Egypt Watch Bulletin*, September 15. http://www.amcham.org.eg/BSAC/WatchBulletin/view_article.asp#v (accessed October 1, 2008).

Aminzade, Ronald, et al. 2001. *Silence and Voice in the Study of Contentious Politics.* Cambridge: Cambridge University Press.

Anderson, Jon W. 2003. "New Media, New Publics: Reconfiguring the Public Sphere of Islam." *Social Research* 70: 887–906.

An-Naim, Abdullahi. 2000. "Problems of Dependency: Human Rights Organizations in the Arab World" [interview]. *Middle East Report*, no. 214: 20–23, 46–47.

———. 2001. "Human Rights in the Arab World: A Regional Perspective." *Human Rights Quarterly* 23: 701–32.

Anzaldúa, Gloria, ed. 1990. *Making Face, Making Soul = Haciendo Caras: Creative and Critical Perspectives by Women of Color.* San Francisco: Aunt Lute Foundation Books.

Arat, Yeşim. 1998. "Feminists, Islamists and Political Change in Turkey." *Political Psychology* 19: 117–31.

————. 2005. *Rethinking Islam and Liberal Democracy: Islamist Women in Turkish Politics.* Albany: State University of New York Press.

Arendt, Hannah. 1958. *The Human Condition.* Chicago: University of Chicago Press.

Aretxaga, Begona. 2003. "Maddening States." *Annual Review of Anthropology* 32: 393–410.

Aristotle. 1998. *Politics.* Indianapolis, IN: Hackett.

Aristotle, Ernest Barker, and R. F. Stalley. 1998. *Politics.* Oxford, UK: Oxford University Press.

Arrighi, Giovanni. 1996. "Workers of the World at the Century's End." *Review* 19: 335–51.

Assaad, Ragui. 2009. "Preface." In *The Egyptian Labor Market Revisited,* ed. Ragui Assaad, xv–xvii. Cairo: American University in Cairo Press.

'Atiyat Allah, Lewis. 2003. *Min burayda ila manhattan: hiwar suʿudi salafi hawla al-qaʿida wa-tafjirat Nyu Yurk.* London: Dar al-Riyadh.

Auyero, Javier. 2005. "L'espace des luttes. Topographie des mobilisations collectives." *Actes de la recherche en sciences sociales* 160: 122–32.

Badie, Bertrand. 1986. *Les deux États: pouvoir et société en Occident et en terre d'Islam.* Paris: Fayard.

Badr, Intisar, principal investigator. 2007. *Nisaʾ fi suq al-ʿamal: al-ʿamilat wa-siyyasat al-khaskhasa.* Cairo: New Woman Foundation.

Bagguley, Peter. 1991. *From Protest to Acquiescence: Political Movements of the Unemployed.* London: Macmillan.

Baha' al-Din Shaʿban, Ahmad. 2006. *Raffat al-farasha: kifaya, al-madi w'al-mustaqbal.* Cairo: Matbuʿat Kifaya.

Baker, Raymond. 1990. *Sadat and After: Struggles for Egypt's Political Soul.* London: IB Tauris.

Balme, Richard, Didier Chabanet, and Vincent Wright, eds. 2002. *L'action collective en Europe.* Paris: Presses de Sciences Po.

Barakat, Sabr. 2007. *al-Haqq fi al-ʿamal wa-huquq al-ʿummal.* Cairo: Markaz Hisham Mubarak li'l-Qanun.

al-Basyuni, Mustafa. 2011. "al-Haraka al-niqabiyya baʿd al-thawra al-misriyya." *al-Akhbar,* September 26. http://www.al-akhbar.com/node/22072 (accessed August 31, 2012).

al-Basyuni, Mustafa, and 'Umar Saʿid. 2007. *Rayat al-idrab fi samaʾ misr: 2007, haraka ʿummaliyya jadida.* Cairo: Markaz al-Dirasat al-Ishtirakiyya.

Bayard de Volo, Lorraine. 2004. "Mobilizing Mothers for War: Cross-National Framing Strategies in Nicaragua's Contra War." *Gender and Society* 18: 715–34.

Bayat, Asef. 1997. *Street Politics, Poor People's Movements in Iran.* New York: Columbia University Press.

————. 2003. "Globalization and the Politics of the Informals in the Global South." In *Urban Informality: Transnational Perspectives from the Middle East, Latin America, and South Asia,* ed. Ananya Roy and Nezar AlSayyad, 79–102. Lanham, MD: Lexington Books.

———. 2007. *Making Islam Democratic: Social Movements and the Post-Islamist Turn.* Stanford, CA: Stanford University Press.

———. 2010. *Life as Politics: How Ordinary People Change the Middle East.* Stanford, CA: Stanford University Press.

Baydar, Gülsüm, and Berfin Ivegen. 2006. "Territories, Identities, and Thresholds: The Saturday Mothers Phenomenon in Istanbul." *Signs* 31: 689–715.

Béchir-Ayari, Michael. 2013. "La 'Révolution tunisienne,' une émeute politique qui a réussi?" In *Devenir révolutionnaires. Au cœur des révoltes arabes,* ed. Amin Allal and Thomas Pierret. Paris: Armand Colin/Recherches.

Béchir-Ayari, Michael, and Éric Gobe. 2007. "Les avocats dans la Tunisie de Ben Ali: une profession politisée." *L'Année du Maghreb* III: 105–32.

Beinin, Joel. 1993. "Will the Real Egyptian Working Class Please Stand Up?" In *Workers and Working Classes in the Middle East: Struggles Histories, Historiographies,* ed. Zachary Lockman, 247–70. Albany: State University of New York Press.

———. 2005. "Popular Social Movements and the Future of Egyptian Politics." *Middle East Report Online,* March 10. http://www.merip.org/mero/mero031005.html (accessed November 10, 2010).

———. 2008. "L'Égypte des ventres vides." *Le Monde Diplomatique,* May.

———. 2008a. "The Egyptian Workers Movement in 2007." In *Chroniques égyptiennes/Egyptian Chronicles 2007,* ed. Hadjar Aouardji and Hélène Legeay, 219–40. Cairo: CEDEJ.

———. 2009. "Neoliberal Structural Adjustment, Political Demobilization, and Neoauthoritarianism in Egypt." In *The Arab State and Neoliberal Globalization: The Restructuring of State Power in the Middle East,* ed. Laura Guazzone and Daniela Pioppi, 19–46. Reading, UK: Ithaca Press.

———. 2010. "Egyptian Textile Workers: From Craft Artisans Facing European Competition to Proletarians Contending with the State." In *The Ashgate Companion to the History of Textile Workers, 1650–2000,* ed. Lex Heerma van Voss, Els Hiemstra-Kuperus, and Elise van Nederveen Meerkerk, 172–97. Surrey, UK: Ashgate Press.

———. 2010a. *The Struggle for Worker Rights in Egypt.* Washington, DC: Solidarity Center.

———. 2012. "The Rise of Egypt's Workers." *Carnegie Papers.* Carnegie Endowment for International Peace, June.

Beinin, Joel, and Hossam el-Hamalawy. 2007. "Egyptian Textile Workers Confront the New Economic Order." *Middle East Report Online,* March 25. http://www.merip.org/mero /mero032507.html (accessed November 10, 2010).

———. 2007a. "Strikes in Egypt Spread from Center of Gravity." *Middle East Report Online,* May 9. http://www.merip.org/mero/mero050907.html (accessed November 10, 2010).

Beinin, Joel, and Zachary Lockman. 1987. *Workers on the Nile: Nationalism, Commu-*

*nism, Islam and the Egyptian Working Class, 1882–1954.* Princeton, NJ: Princeton University Press.

Beissinger, Mark. 2007. "Structure and Example in Modular Political Phenomena: The Diffusion of Bulldozer/Rose/Orange/Tulip Revolutions." *Perspectives on Politics* 2: 259–79.

———. 2011. "Mechanisms of Maidan: The Structure of Contingency in the Making of the Orange Revolution." *Mobilization: An International Journal* 1: 25–43.

Bendana, Kmar. 2012. "Vous avez dit Révolution?" Communication at the ISHM Tunis, January 14.

Benford, Robert D., and David A. Snow. 2000. "Framing Processes and Social Movements: An Overview and Assessment." *Annual Review of Sociology* 26: 611–39.

Ben Nefissa, Sara, Maggy Grabundzija, and Jean Lambert, eds. 2008. *Société civile, associations et pouvoir local au Yémen.* Sanaa: CEFAS/FES.

Ben Nefissa, Sara, et al. 2005. *NGOs and Governance in the Arab World.* Cairo: American University in Cairo Press.

Benhabib, Seyla. 1996. *Democracy and Difference: Contesting the Boundaries of the Political.* Princeton, NJ: Princeton University Press.

Bennani-Chraïbi, Mounia. 1994. *Soumis et rebelles: les jeunes au Maroc.* Paris: CNRS Éditions.

———. 1996. *Soumis et rebelles: les jeunes au Maroc.* Casablanca: Le Fennec.

———. 2011. "Jeux de miroir de la 'politisation': les acteurs associatifs de quartier a? Casablanca." *Critique internationale* 50: 55–71.

Bennani-Chraïbi, Mounia, and Olivier Fillieule. 2003. "Exit, voice, loyalty et bien d'autres choses encore. . . ." In *Résistances et protestations dans les sociétés musulmanes,* ed. Mounia Bennani-Chraïbi and Olivier Fillieule, 43–126. Paris: Presses de Sciences Po.

———, eds. 2003. *Résistances et protestations dans le monde arabe et musulman.* Paris: Presses de Sciences Po.

Berkowitz, Sandra J. 2003. "Can We Stand with You?: Lessons from Women in Black for Global Feminist Activism." *Women and Language* 26: 94–100.

Berlin, Isaiah. 1996. "On Political Judgment." *New York Review of Books,* October 3.

Bertrand, Gilles. 2004. *Le conflit helléno-turc: la confrontation des deux nationalismes à l'aube du 21ème siècle.* Paris: Maisonneuve & Larose.

Bickford, Susan. 1996. *The Dissonance of Democracy: Listening, Conflict, and Citizenship.* Ithaca, NY: Cornell University Press.

Bohman, James, and William Rehg. 1997. *Deliberative Democracy: Essays on Reason and Politics.* Cambridge, MA: MIT Press.

Boltanski, Luc, and Eve Chiapello. 2005. *The New Spirit of Capitalism.* New York: Verso.

Boltanski, Luc, and Laurent Thévenot. 2006. *On Justification: Economies of Worth.* Princeton, NJ: Princeton University Press.

Bonnefoy, Laurent. 2010. "La guerre de Sa'da: des singularités yéménites à l'agenda international." *Critique internationale* 48: 137–59.

———. 2011. "Violence in Contemporary Yemen: State, Society and Salafis." *The Muslim World* 101: 324–46.

———. 2012. *Salafism in Yemen: Transnationalism and Religious Identity.* New York: Columbia University Press.

Bonnefoy, Laurent, and Marine Poirier. 2010. "The Yemeni Congregation for Reform (al-Islâh): The Difficult Process of Building a Project for Change." In *Returning to Political Parties? Partisan Logic and Political Transformations in the Arab World,* ed. Myriam Catusse and Karam Karam, 61–99. Beirut: Lebanese Center for Policy Studies.

Botman, Selma. 1988. *The Rise of Egyptian Communism, 1939–1970.* Syracuse, NY: Syracuse University Press.

Bouderbala, Najib. 2003. "La trajectoire du Maroc indépendant: une panne dans l'ascenseur social." *Critique économique* 10: 5–30.

Boumaza, Magali. 2009. "Les générations politiques au prisme de la comparaison: quelques propositions théoriques et méthodologiques." *Revue internationale de politique comparée* 16: 189–203.

Bourdieu, Pierre. 1996. *The Rules of Art: Genesis and Structure of the Literary Field.* Stanford, CA: Stanford University Press.

Bouvard, Marguerite Guzman. 1994. *Revolutionizing Motherhood: The Mothers of the Plaza de Mayo.* Wilmington, DE: Scholarly Resources.

Bozarslan, Hamit. 2004. *Histoire de la Turquie contemporaine.* Paris: La Découverte.

Brand, Laurie. 1998. *Women, the State, and Political Liberalization: Middle Eastern and North African Experiences.* New York: Columbia University Press.

Brehony, Noel. 2011. *Yemen Divided: The Story of a Failed State in South Arabia.* London: IB Tauris.

Broadbent, Jeffrey. 2003. "Movement in Context: Thick Networks and Japanese Environmental Protest." In *Social Movements and Networks: Relational Approaches to Collective Action,* ed. Mario Diani and Doug McAdam, 204–29. Oxford: Oxford University Press.

Browers, Michaelle L. 2006. *Democracy and Civil Society in Arab Political Thought.* Syracuse, NY: Syracuse University Press.

———. 2006a. "The Centrality and Marginalization of Women in the Political Discourse of Arab Nationalists and Islamists." *Journal of Middle East Women's Studies* 2 (2): 8–34.

———. 2007. "Origins and Architects of Yemen's Joint Meeting Parties." *International Journal of Middle Eastern Studies* 39: 565–86.

Brown, Wendy. 1995. *States of Injury: Power and Freedom in Late Modernity.* Princeton, NJ: Princeton University Press.

Brownlee, Jason. 2002. "The Decline of Pluralism in Mubarak's Egypt." *Journal of Democracy* 13: 6–14.

———. 2007. *Authoritarianism in an Age of Democratization.* Cambridge: Cambridge University Press.

Buechler, Steven M. 1990. *Women's Movements in the United States: Woman Suffrage, Equal Rights, and Beyond.* New Brunswick, NJ: Rutgers University Press.

Burgat, François. 2003. *Face to Face with Political Islam.* London: I. B. Tauris.

———. 2006. "Le Yémen après le 11 septembre 2001: entre construction de l'Etat et rétrécissement du champ politique." *Critique internationale* 32: 11–21.

Camau, Michel. 2002. "Sociétés civiles 'réelles' et téléologie de la démocratisation." *Revue internationale de politique comparée* 9: 213–32.

Camau, Michel, and Vincent Geisser. 2003. *Le syndrome autoritaire. Politique en Tunisie de Bourguiba à Ben Ali.* Paris: Presses de Sciences Po.

Can, Kemal. 2000. "Youth, Turkism and the Extreme Right: The 'Idealist Hearths.'" In *Civil Society in the Grip of Nationalism,* ed. Stefanos Yerasimos, Guenter Seufert, and Karin Vorhoff, 335–73. Istanbul: Orient-Institut /IFEA.

CARANA Corporation. 2002. *Privatization in Egypt Quarterly Review,* April–June. Cairo: CARANA for USAID.

Cardenas, Sonia, and Andrew Flibbert. 2005. "National Human Rights Institutions in the Middle East." *Middle East Journal* 59: 411–36.

Carr, Sarah. 2008. "Increase Minimum Wages to Match Price Increase." *Daily News Egypt,* February 29.

———. 2009. "Factory Workers Strike in Menufiya, Demand Bonuses." *Daily News Egypt,* March 11.

———. 2009a. "Indorama Workers Transferred 'To Teach Them a Lesson,' Says Manager." *Daily News Egypt,* May 7.

———. 2009b. "Omar Effendi Workers Resume Strike Against Wage Discrimination." *Daily News Egypt,* May 7.

Castel, Robert. 2003. *From Manual Workers to Wage Laborers: Transformation of the Social Question.* New Brunswick, NJ: Transaction Publishers.

Catusse, Myriam. 2002. "Le charme discret de la société civile: Ressorts politiques de la formation d'un groupe dans le Maroc 'ajusté.'" *Revue internationale de politique comparée* 9: 297–318.

Céfaï, Daniel. 2007. *Pourquoi se mobilise-t-on? Les théories de l'action collective.* Paris: La Découverte.

Center for Trade Union and Workers Services. 2007. *Facts About the Trade Union Elections for the Term, 2006–2011.* Cairo: Center for Trade Union and Workers Services.

Central Agency for Public Mobilization and Statistics (Egypt). 2006. Labor Force Sample Survey.

Charbel, Jano. 2011. "Workers Demand Dissolution of State-run Trade Union Federation." *Egypt Independent,* February 14. http://www.egyptindependent.com/news/workers-demand-dissolution-state-run-trade-union-federation (accessed September 10, 2012).

———. 2012. "Mahalla Resurgent: Workers Assert Political Independence." *Egypt In-*

*dependent*, July 19. http://www.egyptindependent.com/news/mahalla-resurgent -workers-assert-political-independence (accessed September 10, 2012).

Chatterjee, Anshu. 2004. "Globalization, Identity and Television Networks." In *The Network Society: A Cross-cultural Perspective*, ed. Manuel Castells, 402–19. Cheltenham, UK: Edward Elgar.

Chatterjee, Partha. 2004. *The Politics of the Governed: Reflections on Popular Politics in Most of the World*. New York: Columbia University Press.

Chazel, François. 1985. "Les ruptures révolutionnaires." In *Traité de science politique*, ed. Jean Leca and Madeleine Grawitz, 635–86. Paris: Presses Universitaires de France.

———. 1989. "Idéologie et processus révolutionnaires." *Revue française de sociologie* 30: 431–54.

———. 2003. *Du pouvoir à la contestation*. Série sociologie, no. 36. Paris: LGDJ.

———. 2003a. "De la question de l'imprévisibilité des révolutions et des bonnes (et moins bonnes) manières d'y répondre." *Revue européenne des sciences sociales* 126: 125–36.

Chouikha, Larbi, and Vincent Geisser. 2010. "La fin d'un tabou: enjeux autour de la succession du président et dégradation du climat social." *L'Année du Maghreb* VI: 375–426.

Clark, Janine A. 2004. "Women in Islamist Parties: The Case of Jordan's Islamic Action Front." *Arab Reform Bulletin* 2 (7). http://carnegieeurope.eu/publications/?fa=21230 (accessed June 14, 2010).

———. 2004a. *Islam, Charity, and Activism: Middle-class Networks and Social Welfare in Egypt, Jordan, and Yemen*. Bloomington: Indiana University Press.

Clark, Janine A., and Jillian Schwedler. 2003. "Who Opened the Window? Women's Activism in Islamist Parties." *Comparative Politics* 35: 293–312.

Cobban, Helena. 2006. "Sisterhood of Hamas." Salon.com, March 14. http://www.salon .com/news/feature/2006/03/14/hamaswomen/print.html (accessed July 10, 2009).

Cochrane, Paul. 2007. "Are Lebanon's Media Fanning the Flames of Sectarianism?" *Arab Media and Society*, no. 2. http://www.arabmediasociety.com/?article=206 (accessed July 15, 2009).

Cockburn, Cynthia. 1998. *The Space Between Us: Negotiating Gender and National Identities in Conflict*. London: Zed Books.

———. 2007. *From Where We Stand: War, Women's Activism, and Feminist Analysis*. London: Zed Books.

Collovald, Annie, and Brigitte Gaïti. 2006. *La démocratie aux extrêmes*. Paris: La dispute.

Combes, Hélène. 2010. "Camper au cœur du pouvoir. Le planton post-électoral de 2006 à Mexico." *Revue internationale de politique comparée* 17: 53–70.

Combes, Hélène, and Olivier Fillieule. 2011. "De la répression considérée dans ses rapports à l'activité protestataire. Modèles structuraux et interactions stratégiques." *Revue française de science politique* 61: 1047–72.

Connolly, William E. 1995. *The Ethos of Pluralization*. Minneapolis: University of Minnesota Press.

Cook, Miriam. 2007. *Dissident Syria: Making Oppositional Arts Official*. Durham, NC: Duke University Press.

Copeaux, Etienne. 1997. *Espaces et temps de la nation turque*. Paris: Editions du Centre National de la Recherche Scientifique.

Corradi Fiumara, Gemma. 1990. *The Other Side of Language: A Philosophy of Listening*. London: Routledge.

Cummings, Bruce. 2002. *Parallax Visions: Making Sense of American-East Asian Relations*. Durham, NC: Duke University Press.

Cunningham, David. 2003. "State Versus Social Movement: FBI Counterintelligence Against the New Left." In *States, Parties, and Social Movements*, ed. Jack A. Goldstone, 45–77. Cambridge: Cambridge University Press.

———. 2004. *There's Something Happening Here: The New Left, the Klan, and FBI Counterintelligence*. Berkeley: University of California Press.

Dabbous-Sensenig, Dima. 2006. "To Veil or Not to Veil: Gender and Religion on Al-Jazeera's 'Islamic Law and Life.'" *Westminster Papers in Communication and Culture* 3: 60–85.

Dajani, Nabil. 2006. "The Re-feudalization of the Public Sphere: Lebanese Television News Coverage and the Lebanese Political Process." *Transnational Broadcasting Studies*, no. 16, www.tbsjournal.com/Dajani.html (accessed June 14, 2010).

Dallal, Jenine Abboushi. 2001. "Hizbullah's Virtual Civil Society." *Television and New Media* 2: 367–72.

Danış, Didem, and Ayşe Parla. 2009. "Nafile Soydaşlık: Irak ve Bulgaristan Örneğinde Göçmen, Dernek ve Devlet." *Toplum ve Bilim* 114: 131–58.

Davenport, Christian. 2000. *Paths to State Repression: Human Rights Violations and Contentious Politics*. Boulder, CO, and New York: Rowman & Littlefield.

Davenport, Christian, Hank Johnston, and Carol Mueller, eds. 2004. *Repression and Mobilization*. Minneapolis and London: University of Minnesota Press.

Day, Stephen. 2012. *Regionalism and Rebellion in Yemen: A Troubled National Union*. Cambridge: Cambridge University Press.

Deeb, Lara. 2006. *An Enchanted Modern: Gender and Public Piety in Shi'i Lebanon*. Princeton, NJ: Princeton University Press.

Dellios, Hugh. 2000. "With an Eye Toward Politics, Hezbollah Recasting Its Image: Savvy TV Campaign Credited in Group's Battle with Israel." *Chicago Tribune*, April 13.

Denis, Eric. 2006. "Cairo as Neoliberal Capital? From Walled City to Gated Communities." In *Cairo Cosmopolitan: Politics, Culture, and Urban Space in the Globalized Middle East*, ed. Diane Singerman and Paul Amar, 47–71. Cairo: American University in Cairo Press.

Denoeux, Guilain. 1993. "Religious Networks and Urban Unrest: Lessons from Iranian and Egyptian Experiences." In *The Violence Within: Cultural and Political Opposition in Divided Nations*, ed. Kay B. Warren, 123–55. Boulder, CO: Westview Press.

————. 1993a. *Urban Unrest in the Middle East: A Comparative Study of Informal Networks in Egypt, Iran, and Lebanon*. Albany: State University of New York Press.

Desrues, Thierry, and Eduardo Moyano. 2001. "Social Change and Political Transition in Morocco." *Mediterranean Politics* 6: 21–47.

Dezalay, Yves, and Bryant Garth. 2002. *The Internationalization of Palace Wars: Lawyers, Economists and the Contest to Transform Latin American States*. Chicago: University of Chicago Press.

Diani, Mario. 2000. "The Concept of Social Movement." In *Readings in Contemporary Sociology*, ed. Kate Nash, 155–76. Malden, MA: Blackwell.

Diani, Mario, and Doug McAdam. 2003. *Social Movements and Networks: Relational Approaches to Collective Action*. Oxford: Oxford University Press.

Dietz, Mary G. 2002. *Turning Operations: Feminism, Arendt, and Politics*. New York: Routledge.

Diez, Thomas, Agnantopoulos Apostolos, and Alper Kaliber. 2005. "Turkey, Europeanization and Civil Society: Introduction." *South European Society and Politics* 10: 1–15.

Dobry, Michel. 1983. "Mobilisations multisectorielles et dynamique des crises politiques: un point de vue heuristique." *Revue française de sociologie* 24: 395–419.

————. 1986. *Sociologie des crises politiques. La dynamiques des mobilisations multisectorielles*. Paris: Presses de la Fondation Nationale des Sciences Politiques.

————. 1990. "Calcul, concurrence et gestion du sens: Quelques réflexions à propos des manifestations étudiantes de novembre-décembre 1986." In *La manifestation*, ed. Pierre Favre, 357–86. Paris: Fondation Nationale des Sciences Politiques.

————. 1995. "Les causalités de l'improbable et du probable: notes à propos des manifestations de 1989 en Europe centrale et orientale." *Cultures et conflits* 17: 1–19.

————. 2009. *Sociologie des crises politiques, La dynamique des mobilisations multisectorielles*. Paris: Presses de Sciences Po.

Donnelly, Jack. 1993. *International Human Rights*. Boulder, CO: Westview Press.

Dorlian, Samy. 2011. "The Sa'da War in Yemen: Between Politics and Sectarianism." *The Muslim World* 101: 182–201.

Dresch, Paul. 2000. *A History of Modern Yemen*. Cambridge: Cambridge University Press.

Dresch, Paul, and Bernard Haykel. 1995. "Stereotypes and Political Styles: Islamists and Tribesfolks in Yemen." *International Journal of Middle East Studies* 27: 405–31.

Duboc, Marie. 2013. "Where Are the Men? Here Are the Men and the Women! Gender, Surveillance and Strikes in Egyptian Textile Factories." *Journal of Middle East Women's Studies* 9 (3).

————. 2011. "La contestation sociale en Egypte depuis 2004: Entre précarité et mobilisation locale." *Revue Tiers-Monde* 106, no. hors série: *Protestations sociales, révolutions civiles: Transformations du politique dans la Méditerranée arabe*, April.

al-Duwish, Muhammad. 2005. "Mu'assasat al-mujtama' wa'l-shabab," April 15. Typescript.

Dwyer, Kevin. 1991. *The Human Rights Debate in the Middle East*. Berkeley: University of California Press.

Earl, Jennifer. 2004. "Controlling Protest: New Directions for Research on the Social Control of Protest." *Research in Social Movements, Conflicts and Change* 25: 55–83.

———. 2009. "Introduction: Repression and the Social Control of Protest." *Mobilization* 11: 129–43.

———. 2011. "Political Repression: Iron Fists, Velvet Gloves, and Diffuse Control." *Annual Review of Sociology* 37: 261–84.

Ebaugh, Helen Rose Fuchs. 1988. *Becoming an Ex: The Process of Role Exit*. Chicago: University of Chicago Press.

"Editorial: Sexuality, Suppression and the State." 2004. *Middle East Report*, no. 230: 1, 46–47.

Eickelman, Dale F., and Jon W. Anderson, eds. 2003. *New Media in the Muslim World: The Emerging Public Sphere*. Bloomington: Indiana University Press.

Eickelman, Dale F., and James Piscatori. 1996. *Muslim Politics*. Princeton, NJ: Princeton University Press.

El Khawaga, Dina. 2002. "La génération seventies en Égypte. La société civile comme répertoire d'action alternatif." In *Résistances et protestations dans les sociétés musulmanes*, ed. Mounia Bennani-Chraïbi and Olivier Fillieule, 271–92. Paris: Presses de Sciences Po.

El Shafei, Omar. 1995. "Workers, Trade Unions, and the State in Egypt: 1984–1989." *Cairo Papers in Social Science* 18 (2): 1–43.

Elshtain, Jean Bethke. 1981. *Public Man, Private Woman: Women in Social and Political Thought*. Princeton, NJ: Princeton University Press.

Emirbayer, Mustafa, and Jeff Goodwin. 1996. "Symbols, Positions, Objects: Toward a New Theory of Revolutions and Collective Action." *History and Theory* 3: 358–74.

Engel, Stephen M. 2001. *The Unfinished Revolution: Social Movement Theory and the Gay and Lesbian Movement*. Cambridge: Cambridge University Press.

Enloe, Cynthia H. 2000. *Maneuvers: The International Politics of Militarizing Women's Lives*. Berkeley: University of California Press.

Esposito, John L. 1999. *The Islamic Threat: Myth or Reality?* 3d ed. New York: Oxford University Press.

Evans, Sara. 1980. *Personal Politics: The Roots of Women's Liberation in the Civil Rights Movement and the New Left*. New York: Vintage.

Evans, Sara Margaret, and Harry C. Boyte. 1992. *Free Spaces: The Sources of Democratic Change in America*. Chicago: University of Chicago Press.

Fandy, Mamoun. 1999. *Saudi Arabia and the Politics of Dissent*. London: St Martin's Press.

Fantasia, Rick. 1988. *Cultures of Solidarity: Consciousness, Action, and Contemporary American Workers*. Berkeley: University of California Press.

Feliu, Laura. 2004. *El jardín secreto: Los defensores de los derechos humanos en Marruecos.* Madrid: Los Libros de la Catarata.

Ferree, Myra Marx, and David A. Merrill. 2004. "Hot Movements, Cold Cognition: Thinking About Social Movements in Gendered Frames." In *Rethinking Social Movements: Structure, Meaning, and Emotion,* ed. Jeff Goodwin and James M. Jasper, 247–61. Lanham, MD: Rowman & Littlefield.

Fillieule, Olivier. 1993. "Conscience politique, persuasion et mobilisation des engagements: L'exemple du syndicat des chômeurs, 1983–1989." In *Sociologie de la protestation: Les formes de l'action collective dans la France contemporaine,* ed. Olivier Fillieule, 123–55. Paris: L'Harmattan.

———. 1997. *Sociologie de la protestation: les formes de l'action collective.* Paris: L'Harmattan.

———. 1997a. *Stratégies de la rue. Les manifestations en France.* Paris: Presses de Science-Po.

———. 2005. "Requiem pour un concept: Vie et mort de la notion de structure des opportunités politiques." In *La Turquie conteste: Mobilisations sociales et régime sécuritaire,* ed. Gilles Dorronsoro, 201–18. Paris: CNRS éditions.

———, ed. 2005a. *Le désengagement militant.* Paris: Belin.

Firmo-Fontan, Victoria. 2004. "Power, NGOs, and Lebanese Television: A Case Study of Al-Manar TV and the Hezbollah Women's Association." In *Women and Media in the Middle East: Power Through Self-Expression,* ed. Naomi Sakr, 162–79. London: I. B. Tauris.

Foran, John. 1993. "Theories of Revolution Revisited: Toward a Fourth Generation?" *Sociological Theory* 1: 1–20.

Foucault, Michel. 1975. *Surveiller et punir: Naissance de la prison.* Paris: Éditions Gallimard.

———. 1990. *The History of Sexuality: An Introduction.* Vol. 1. New York: Vintage Books.

Fraser, Nancy. 1992. "Rethinking the Public Sphere: A Contribution to the Critique of Actually Existing Democracy." In *Habermas and the Public Sphere,* ed. Craig Calhoun, 109–42. Cambridge, MA: MIT Press.

Friedman, Gerald. 2009. "Is Labor Dead?" *International Labor and Working Class History* 75: 126–44.

Gaïti, Brigitte. 1994. "Les ratés de l'histoire. Une manifestation sans suites: le 17 octobre 1961 à Paris." *Sociétés contemporaines* 20: 11–37.

Gamson, William A., and David Meyer. 1996. "Framing Political Opportunity." In *Comparative Perspectives on Social Movements: Political Opportunities, Mobilizing Structures, and Cultural Framings,* ed. Doug McAdam, John D. McCarthy, and Mayer N. Zald, 275–90. Cambridge: Cambridge University Press.

Gaxie, Daniel. 1977. "Économie des partis et rétributions du militantisme." *Revue française de science politique* 27: 123–54.

————. 2005. "Rétributions du militantisme et paradoxes de l'action collective." *Revue suisse de science politique* 11: 157–88.

Geer, Benjamin. 2009. "Prophets and Priests of the Nation: Naguib Mahfouz's Karnak Café and the 1967 Crisis in Egypt." *International Journal of Middle East Studies* 41: 653–69.

Geisser, Vincent. 2001. "Les blagues populaires comme symptôme social du discrédit du régime de Ben Ali." *Forum Nokta*, October.

Geisser, Vincent, and Éric Gobe. 2006. "Des fissures dans la 'Maison Tunisie'? Le régime de Ben Ali face aux mobilisations protestataires." *L'Année du Maghreb* II: 367–74.

————. 2007. "La question de 'l'authenticité tunisienne': valeur refuge d'un régime à bout de souffle?" *L'Année du Maghreb* III: 371–408.

Geisser, Vincent, Karam Karam, and Frédéric Vairel. 2006. "Espaces du politique. Mobilisations et protestations." In *La politique dans le monde arabe*, ed. Elizabeth Picard, 193–213. Paris: Armand Colin.

Giddens, Anthony. 1984. *The Constitution of Society: Outline of the Theory of Structuration*. Cambridge: Polity Press.

Ginat, Rami. 2011. *A History of Egyptian Communism: Jews and Their Compatriots in Quest of Revolution*. Boulder, CO: Lynne Rienner Publishers.

Giugni, Marco, Marko Bandler, and Nina Eggert. 2006. "The Global Justice Movement: How Far Does the Classic Social Movement Agenda Go in Explaining Transnational Contention?" Civil Society and Social Movements Programme, paper no. 24, June, United Nations Research Institute.

Gobe, Éric. 2013. "Les avocats, un corps professionnel au cœur de la 'révolution' tunisienne?" In *Devenir révolutionnaires. Au cœur des révoltes arabes*, ed. Amin Allal and Thomas Pierret. Paris: Armand Colin/Recherches.

Goldstone, Jack A. 1980. "Theories of Revolutions: The Third Generation." *World Politics* 32: 425–53.

————. 1995. "Predicting Revolutions: Why We Could (and Should) Have Foreseen the Revolutions of 1989–1991 in the U.S.S.R. and Eastern Europe." In *Debating Revolutions*, ed. Nikki R. Keddie, 127–52. New York: New York University Press.

————. 2003. *States, Parties, and Social Movements*. Cambridge: Cambridge University Press.

Goldstone, Jack A., and Charles Tilly. 2001. "Threat (and Opportunity): Popular Action and State Response in the Dynamics of Contentious Action." In *Silence and Voice in the Study of Contentious Politics*, ed. Ronald R. Aminzade et al., 179–94. Cambridge: Cambridge University Press.

Goodwin, Jeff. 1994. "Toward a New Sociology of Revolutions." *Theory and Society* 6: 731–66.

————. 2001. "Introduction." In *Rethinking Social Movements: Structure, Meaning, and Emotion*, ed. Jeff Goodwin and James M. Jasper, vii–x. Lanham, MD: Rowman & Littlefield.

Goodwin, Jeff, and James M. Jasper. 1999. "Caught in a Winding, Snarling Vine: The Structural Bias of Political Process Theory." *Sociological Forum* 14: 27–54.

Goodwin, Jeff, James M. Jasper, and Francesca Polletta. 2004. "Introduction: Why Emotions Matter." In *Passionate Politics: Emotions and Social Movements*, ed. Jeff Goodwin, James M. Jasper, and Francesca Polletta, 1–24. Chicago: University of Chicago Press.

Gould, Roger. 1991. "Multiple Networks and Mobilization in the Paris Commune, 1871." *American Sociological Review* 56: 716–29.

Guazzone, Laura, and Daniela Pioppi, eds. 2009. *The Arab State and Neoliberal Globalization: The Restructuring of State Power in the Middle East*. Reading, UK: Ithaca Press.

Günçıkan, Berat, and Erzade Ertem, eds. 1996. *Cumartesi Anneleri*. Istanbul: İletişim.

Gurr, Ted Robert. 1970. *Why Men Rebel*. Princeton, NJ: Princeton University Press.

Habermas, Jürgen. 1996. *Between Facts and Norms: Contributions to a Discourse Theory of Law and Democracy*. Studies in Contemporary German Social Thought. Cambridge, MA: MIT Press.

Haddad, Bassam. 2012. "My 50 Minutes with Manaf." *Jadaliyya*, July 26. http://www.jadaliyya.com/pages/index/6611/my-50-minutes-with-manaf (accessed October 31, 2012).

Haenni, Patrick. 2005. "Divisions chez les Frères musulmans, la nouvelle pensée islamique des déçus de l'expérience militante." *La vie des idées*, April.

Hafez, Mohammed M. 2003. *Why Muslims Rebel: Repression and Resistance in the Islamic World*. Boulder, CO: Lynne Rienner.

———. 2004. "From Marginalization to Massacres: A Political Process Explanation of GIA Violence in Algeria." In *Islamic Activism: A Social Movement Theory Approach*, ed. Quintan Wiktorowicz, 37–60. Bloomington: Indiana University Press.

Hafez, Mohammed M., and Quintan Wiktorowicz. 2004. "Violence as Contention in the Egyptian Islamic Movement." In *Islamic Activism: A Social Movement Theory Approach*, ed. Quintan Wiktorowicz, 61–88. Bloomington: Indiana University Press.

Hale, William. 1994. *Turkish Military and Politics*. London: Routledge.

Halliday, Fred. 1974. *Arabia Without Sultans*. London: Penguin Books.

el-Hamalawy, Hossam. 2007. "Comrades and Brothers." *Middle East Report*, no. 242. http://www.merip.org/mer/mer242/hamalawy.html (accessed June 20, 2010).

Hammoudi, Abdallah. 1997. *Master and Disciple: The Cultural Foundation of Moroccan Authoritarianism*. Chicago: University of Chicago Press,

Hamzeh, Ahmad Nizar. 2004. *In the Path of Hizbullah*. Syracuse, NY: Syracuse University Press.

Hanafi, Karim, director. 2008. "Hikayat kull yawm." Cairo: New Woman Foundation.

Harb, Mona, and Reinoud Leenders. 2005. "Know Thy Enemy: Hizbullah, 'Terrorism' and the Politics of Perception." *Third World Quarterly* 26: 173–97.

Hassan, Bahey el-Din. 2006. "A Question of Human Rights Ethics: Defending the

Islamists." In *Human Rights in the Arab World: Independent Voices*, ed. Anthony Chase and Amr Hamzawy, 37–48. Philadelphia: University of Pennsylvania Press.

Henderson, Sarah L., and Alana S. Jeydel. 2007. *Participation and Protest: Women and Politics in a Global World*. New York: Oxford University Press.

Hersant, Jeanne. 2007. "Mobilisations politique, co-gouvernementalité, construction ethnique. Sociologie du nationalisme turc à travers le cas des Turcs de Thrace occidentale (Grèce, Allemagne, Turquie)." PhD dissertation, Ecole des Hautes Etudes en Sciences Sociales.

———. 2008. "'Frères Turcs' et indésirables à la fois: les migrants de Thrace grecque en Turquie." *Revue européenne des migrations internationales* 24: 129–46.

———. 2008a. "Contourner les normes européennes . . . grâce aux instruments européens. L'impératif de sécurité nationale ou les résistances à l'intégration européenne de la Grèce." *Revue internationale de politique comparée* 15: 639–52.

Hersant, Jeanne, and Alexandre Toumarkine. 2005. "Hometown Associations in Turkey: An Overview." *European Journal of Turkish Studies* 2. http://ejts.revues.org/index397 .html (accessed April 20, 2010).

Heydemann, Steven. 2002. "La question de la démocratie dans les travaux sur le monde arabe." *Critique internationale* 17: 54–62.

———. 2007. "Social Pacts and the Persistence of Authoritarianism in the Middle East." In *Debating Arab Authoritarianism: Dynamics and Durability in Nondemocratic Regimes*, ed. Oliver Schlumberger, 21–38. Stanford, CA: Stanford University Press.

———. 2007a. *Upgrading Authoritarianism in the Arab World*. Saban Center Analysis Paper, Brookings Institute, 13.

Heydemann, Steven, and Reinoud Leenders. 2012. "Authoritarian Governance in Syria and Iran: Challenged, Reconfiguring and Resilient." In *Middle East Authoritarianisms: Governance, Contestation, and Regime Resilience in Syria and Iran*, ed. Steven Heydemann and Reinoud Leenders, 1–35. Stanford, CA: Stanford University Press.

Hibou, Béatrice. 1998. "Retrait ou redéploiement de l'État?" *Critique internationale* 1: 151–68.

———. 1999. "Tunisie: le coût d'un miracle économique." *Critique internationale* 4: 48–56.

———. 2008. "Nous ne prendrons jamais le maquis. Entrepreneurs et politique en Tunisie." *Politix* 84: 115–41.

Hicks, Neil. 2006. "Transnational Human Rights Networks and Human Rights in Egypt." In *Human Rights in the Arab World: Independent Voices*, ed. Anthony Chase and Amr Hamzawy, 64–88. Philadelphia: University of Pennsylvania Press.

Hinnebusch, Raymond. 2012. "Syria: From 'Authoritarian Upgrading' to Revolution?" *International Affairs* 88: 95–113.

Hirschman, Albert O. 1982. *Shifting Involvements: Private Interest and Public Action*. Princeton, NJ: Princeton University Press.

Hmed, Choukri. 2008. "Des mouvements sociaux 'sur une tête d'épingle'? Le rôle de l'espace physique dans le processus contestataire à partir de l'exemple des mobilisations dans les foyers de travailleurs migrants." *Politix* 84: 145–65.

Holt, Maria. 1999. "Lebanese Shi'i Women and Islamism: A Response to War." In *Women and War in Lebanon*, ed. Lamia R. Shehadeh. Gainesville: University of Florida Press.

Honig, Bonnie. 1995. *Feminist Interpretations of Hannah Arendt: Re-reading the Canon.* University Park: Pennsylvania State University Press.

Hoodfar, Homa. 1997. *Between Marriage and the Market: Intimate Politics and Survival in Cairo.* Berkeley: University of California Press.

Hoover, Dean, and David Kowalewski. 1992. "Dynamic Models of Dissent and Repression." *Journal of Conflict Resolution* 36: 150–82.

Hopkins, Nicholas S. 1995. "La culture politique et l'Égypte." *Égypte/Monde Arabe* no. 24: 29–41.

Howard, Philip N. 2010. *The Digital Origins of Dictatorship and Democracy: Information Technology and Political Islam.* New York: Oxford University Press.

Howeidy, Amira. 2005. "A Chronology of Dissent." *Al-Ahram Weekly* (June): 23–29.

Hudson, Michael. 1996. "Obstacles to Democratization in the Middle East." *Contention* 5: 81–105.

Human Rights Watch. 1997. *Routine Abuse, Routine Denial: Civil Rights and the Political Crisis in Bahrain.* New York: Human Rights Watch.

———. 2004. *Morocco: Human Rights at a Crossroads.* New York: Human Rights Watch.

———. 2005. *Morocco's Truth Commission: Honoring Past Victims During an Uncertain Present.* New York: Human Rights Watch.

———. 2010. *Torture Redux: The Revival of Physical Coercion During Interrogations in Bahrain.* New York: Human Rights Watch. February.

Huntington, Samuel. 1991. *The Third Wave: Democratization in the Late Twentieth Century.* Norman: University of Oklahoma Press.

Ibaaquil, Larbi. 1999. "Les diplômés marocains de l'enseignement supérieur: une mobilité sociale en panne." In *Diplômés maghrébins d'ici et d'ailleurs*, ed. Vincent Geisser, 137–53. Paris: Éditions du CNRS.

Ibrahim, Saad Eddin. 1982. *The New Arab Social Order: A Study of the Social Impact of Oil.* Boulder, CO, and London: Westview Press and Croom-Helm.

———. 1998. "The Troubled Triangle: Populism, Islam and Civil Society in the Arab World." *International Political Science Review/Revue internationale de science politique* 19: 373–85.

———. 2003. "A Vision of the Arab World Out of 40 Years of Activism." Ibn Khaldun Center for Development Studies. http://www.eicds.org/english/publications/saadarticles/2003/visionforarabworld.htm (accessed April 9, 2007).

Ihde, Don. 2007. *Listening and Voice: Phenomenologies of Sound*, 2d ed. Albany: State University of New York Press.

Inglehart, Ronald. 1977. *The Silent Revolution: Changing Values and Political Styles Among Western Publics*. Princeton, NJ: Princeton University Press.

İnsel, Ahmet. 2008. "'Cet État n'est pas sans propriétaires!' Forces prétoriennes et autoritarisme en Turquie." In *Autoritarismes démocratiques et démocraties autoritaires au XXIème siècle*, ed. Olivier Dabène, Vincent Geisser, and Gilles Massardier, 133–53. Paris: La Découverte.

International Crisis Group. 2005. "Reforming Egypt: In Search of a Strategy." *Middle East/North Africa Report*, no. 46 (October 4).

Ion, Jacques. 1997. *La fin des militants?* Paris: Editions de l'Atelier.

Ismael, Tareq Y. 2005. *The Communist Movement in the Arab World*. London: Routledge, Curzon.

Ismael, Tareq Y., and Rif'at El-Sa'id. 1990. *The Communist Movement in Egypt, 1920–1988*. Syracuse, NY: Syracuse University Press.

Jacquemond, Richard. 2007. "Retour à Nasser des intellectuels égyptiens." *Le Monde Diplomatique*, July.

———. 2008. *Conscience of the Nation: Writers, State, and Society in Modern Egypt*. Cairo: American University in Cairo Press.

Jahoda, Marie, Paul F. Lazarsfeld, and Hans Zeisel. 1971. *Marienthal: The Sociography of an Unemployed Community*. New Brunswick, NJ: Transaction.

Jansen, Johannes J. G. 1986. *The Neglected Duty: The Creed of Sadat's Assassins and Islamic Resurgence in the Middle East*. New York: Macmillan.

Johnston, Hank. 2005. "Talking the Walk: Speech Acts and Resistance in Authoritarian Regimes." In *Repression and Mobilization*, ed. Christian Davenport, Hank Johnston, and Carol Mueller, 108–37. Minneapolis and London: University of Minnesota Press.

Jorisch, Avi. 2004. *Beacon of Hatred: Inside Hizballah's al-Manar Television*. Washington, DC: Washington Institute for Near East Policy.

Kalberg, Stephen. 1994. *Max Weber's Comparative Historical Sociology*. Cambridge: Polity Press.

Kandil, Hazem. 2012. "Why Did the Egyptian Middle Class March to Tahrir Square?" *Mediterranean Politics* 17: 197–215.

Katznelson, Ira. 1994. "The 'Bourgeois' Dimension: A Provocation About Institutions, Politics, and the Future of Labor History." *International Labor and Working Class History* 46: 7–32.

Kaya, Ayhan. 2001. "Türkiye'deki Çerkes Diyasporası ve Siyasal Katılım Stratejileri." In *21. Yüzyıl Karşısında Kent ve İnsan*, ed. Firdevs Gümüşoğlu, 201–15. Istanbul: Bağlam.

Kayılı, Erkan. 2004. "'Çıplak'İtaatsizlik Olarak 'Cumartesi Anneleri.'" In *Kamusal Alan*, ed. Meral Özbek, 349–56. Beyoğlu, Istanbul: Hil.

Keck, Margaret, and Kathryn Sikkink, eds. 1998. *Activists Beyond Borders: Advocacy Networks in International Politics*. Ithaca, NY: Cornell University Press.

Kecskemeti, Paul, ed. 1952. *Essays on the Sociology of Knowledge by Karl Mannheim.* London: Routledge and Kegan Paul.

Keenan, Alan. 2003. *Democracy in Question: Democratic Openness in a Time of Political Closure.* Stanford, CA: Stanford University Press.

Kempf, Raphaël. 2011. "Egypt: First Democracy, Then a Pay Rise." *Le Monde Diplomatique,* March.

Kertzer, David I. 1988. *Ritual, Politics and Power.* New Haven, CT, and London: Yale University Press.

Khallaf, Rania. 2005. "Change, Not Reform." *Al-Ahram Weekly,* August 11–17. http://web .archive.org/web/20070102035943/http://weekly.ahram.org.eg/2005/755/cu5.htm (accessed June 20, 2010).

Khawaga, Marwan. 1993. "Repression and Popular Collective Action: Evidence from the West Bank." *Sociological Forum* 8: 47–71.

Khiari, Sadri. 2003. *Tunisie, le délitement de la cité. Coercition, consentement, résistance.* Paris: Karthala.

———. 2012. "Tunisie: Révolution, contre-révolution et transition démocratique." *Revue marocaine des sciences politiques et sociales* 2.

Kienle, Eberhard. 2001. *A Grand Delusion: Democracy and Economic Reform in Egypt.* London: I. B. Tauris.

Knight, Lionel. 2007. *Post-privatization Impact Assessment: Final Report—A Review of 17 Companies.* Cairo: USAID.

Koçali, Filiz. 1996. "Kadınların Galatasaray'ı." *Pazartesi,* July 16.

———. 2004. "'Cumartesi Anneleri'nin İnadı." In *Kamusal Alan,* ed. Meral Özbek, 357–60. Beyoğlu, Istanbul: Hil.

Koopmans, Ruud. 1993. "The Dynamics of Protest Waves: West Germany, 1965 to 1989." *American Sociological Review* 58: 637–58.

———. 2003. "A Failed Revolution, But a Worthy Cause." *Mobilization* 8: 116–19.

———. 2003a. "Protest in Time and Space: The Evolution of Waves of Contention." In *The Blackwell Companion to Social Movements,* ed. David A. Snow, Sarah A. Soule, and Hanspeter Kriesi. Malden and Oxford, UK: Blackwell Publishing. http://www .blackwellreference.com/subscriber/uid=1079/tocnode?id=g9780631226697_chunk _g97806312266973#citation (accessed October 9, 2012)

———. 2005. "The Missing Link Between Structure and Agency: Outline of an Evolutionary Approach to Social Movements." *Mobilization: An International Journal* 10: 19–33.

———. 2007. "Protest in Time and Space: The Evolution of Waves of Contention." In *The Blackwell Companion to Social Movements,* ed. David A. Snow, Sarah A. Soule, and Hanspeter Kriesi, 19–46. London: Wiley-Blackwell.

Koopmans, Ruud, et al. 2005. *Contested Citizenship: Immigration and Cultural Diversity in Europe.* Minneapolis: University of Minnesota Press.

Kramer, Martin. 1996. *Arab Awakening and Islamic Revival: The Politics of Ideas in the Middle East*. New Brunswick, NJ: Transaction.

Krauthammer, Charles. 2005. "Syria and the New Axis of Evil." *Washington Post*, April 1.

Kriesi, Hans Pieter. 1995. "The Political Opportunity Structure of New Social Movements." In *The Politics of Social Protest*, ed. John C. Jenkins and Bert Klandermans, 167–98. London: UCL Press.

Kriesi, Hans Pieter, et al. 1995. *New Social Movements in Western Europe: A Comparative Analysis*. London: UCL Press.

Kubicek, Paul. 2002. "The Earthquake, Civil Society and Political Change in Turkey: Assessment and Comparison with Eastern Europe." *Political Studies* 50: 761–78.

Kuran, Timur. 1995. *Private Truths, Public Lies: The Social Consequences of Preference Falsification*. Cambridge, MA: Harvard University Press.

Kurzman, Charles. 1996. "Structural Opportunity and Perceived Opportunity in Social-Movement Theory: The Iranian Revolution of 1979." *American Sociological Review* 61: 153–70.

———. 2003. "The Qum Protests and the Coming of the Iranian Revolution, 1975 and 1978." *Social Science History* 27: 287–325.

———. 2004. *The Unthinkable Revolution in Iran*. Cambridge, MA: Harvard University Press.

———. 2004a. "The Poststructuralist Consensus in Social Movement Theory." In *Rethinking Social Movements: Structure, Meaning, and Emotion*, ed. Jeff Goodwin and James M. Jasper, 111–20. Lanham, MD: Rowman & Littlefield.

———. 2012. "The Arab Spring: Ideals of the Iranian Green Movement, Methods of the Iranian Revolution." *International Journal of Middle East Studies* 44: 162–65.

Lahmar, Mouldi, and Abdelkader Zghal. 1997. "'La révolte du pain' et la crise du modèle du parti unique." In *Tunisie: mouvements sociaux et modernité*, ed. Mahmoud Ben Romdhane, 151–92. Dakar: Codesria.

Lamloum, Olfa. 1999. "Janvier 84 en Tunisie ou le symbole d'une transition." In *Émeutes et mouvements sociaux au Maghreb*, ed. Didier Le Saout and Marguerite Rollinde, 231–42. Paris: Karthala.

Land Center for Human Rights. 2010. "Change Is the Demand of the Workers and the Protesting Employees. More than 700 Protests in 432 Sites Expressed the Extent of Anger in Egypt in 2009." *Economic and Social Rights Series* no. 76, March 4. http://www.lchr-eg.org/index.htm (accessed November 10, 2010).

Langohr, Vickie. 2004. "Too Much Civil Society, Too Little Politics: Egypt and Liberalizing Arab Regimes." *Comparative Politics* 36: 181–204.

Lapeyronnie, Didier. 1988. "Mouvements sociaux et action politique. Existe-t-il une théorie de la mobilisation des ressources?" *Revue française de sociologie* 29: 593–619.

Leca, Jean. 2003. "De la lumière sur la société civile." *Critique internationale* 21: 62–72.

Lecomte, Romain. 2011. "Révolution tunisienne et Internet: le rôle des médias sociaux." *L'Année du Maghreb* 7: 389–418.

Lewis, Bernard. 2004. *The Crisis of Islam: Holy War and Unholy Terror.* New York: Random House.

Lichbach, Mark Irving. 1987. "Deterrence or Escalation: The Puzzle of Aggregate Studies of Repression and Dissent." *Journal of Conflict Resolution* 31: 266–97.

Linz, Juan. J. 2000. *Totalitarian and Authoritarian Regimes.* Boulder, CO, and London: Lynne Rienner Publishers.

Longley-Alley, April. 2010. "Yemen's Multiple Crises." *Journal of Democracy* 21: 72–86.

Lust-Okar, Ellen. 2005. *Structuring Conflict in the Arab World: Incumbents, Opponents, and Institutions.* Cambridge: Cambridge University Press.

Lynch, Marc. 2006. *Voice of the New Arab Public: Iraq, al-Jazeera, and Middle East Politics Today.* New York: Columbia University Press.

———. 2007. "Young Brothers in Cyberspace." *Middle East Report,* no. 245. http://www .merip.org/mer/mer245/lynch.html (accessed January 20, 2008).

MacLeod, Hugh. 2010. "Inside Deraa," *Al-Jazeera,* April 19. http://www.aljazeera.com/in-depth/features/2011/04/201141918352728300.html (accessed October 31, 2012).

Maghraoui, Abdeslam M. 2002. "Depoliticization in Morocco." *Journal of Democracy* 13: 24–32.

Mahfouz, Afaf el Kosheri. 1972. *Socialisme et pouvoir en Égypte.* Paris: Librairie Générale de Droit et de Jurisprudence.

Mar'i, 'Afaf, Fatma Ramadan, et al. 2008. *Su'ud al-haraka al-'ummaliyya wa'l-niqabiyya al-misriya khilala 'amm 2007.* Cairo: al-Jam'iyya al-Misriyya li'l-Nuhud bi'l-Musharaka al-Mujtama'iyya.

Marteu, Elisabeth, ed. 2009. *Civil Organizations and Protest Movements in Israel: Mobilization around the Israeli-Palestinian Conflict.* New York: Palgrave Macmillan.

Martin, Deborah, and Byron Miller. 2003. "Space and Contentious Politics." *Mobilization: An International Journal* 2: 143–56.

Mason, David S. 1989. "Solidarity as a New Social Movement." *Political Science Quarterly* 104: 41–58.

Mathieu, Lilian. 2002. "Rapport au politique, dimensions cognitives et perspectives pragmatiques dans l'analyse des mouvements sociaux." *Revue française de science politique* 52: 75–100.

———. 2004. "Des mouvements sociaux à la politique contestataire: les voies tâtonnantes d'un renouvellement de perspective." *Revue française de sociologie* 45: 561–80.

———. 2007. "L'espace des mouvements sociaux." *Politix* 77: 131–51.

Matonti, Frédérique, and Franck Poupeau. 2004–5. "Le capital militant. Essai de définition." *Actes de la recherche en sciences sociales,* no. 155: 4–11.

Maurer, Sophie, and Emmanuel Pierru. 2001. "Le mouvement des chômeurs de l'hiver 1997–1998: Retour sur un 'miracle social.'" *Revue française de science politique* 51: 371–407.

McAdam, Doug. 1982. *Political Process and the Development of Black Insurgency, 1930–1970*. Chicago: University of Chicago Press.

———. 1983. "Tactical Innovation and the Pace of Insurgency." *American Sociological Review* 48: 735–54.

———. 1986. "Recruitment to High-risk Activism: The Case of Freedom Summer." *American Journal of Sociology* 92: 64–90.

———. 1988. *Freedom Summer*. New York: Oxford University Press.

———. 1988a. "Micromobilization Contexts and Recruitment to Activism." *International Social Movement Research* 1: 125–54.

———. 1995. "'Initiator' and 'Spin-off' Movements: Diffusion Processes in Protest Cycles." In *Repertoires and Cycles of Collective Action*, ed. Mark Traugott, 217–38. Durham, NC: Duke University Press.

McAdam, Doug, John D. McCarthy, and Mayer Zald. 1988. "Social Movements." In *Handbook of Sociology*, ed. Neil J. Smelser, 695–738. Newbury Park, CA: Sage.

———, eds. 1996. *Comparative Perspectives on Social Movements: Political Opportunities, Mobilizing Structures, and Cultural Framings*. Cambridge: Cambridge University Press.

McAdam, Doug, and William H. Sewell Jr. 2001. "It's About Time: Temporality in the Study of Social Movements and Revolutions." In *Silence and Voice in the Study of Contentious Politics*, ed. Ronald R. Aminzade et al., 89–125. Cambridge: Cambridge University Press.

———. 2001. "Emotions and Contentious Politics." In *Silence and Voice in the Study of Contentious Politics*, ed. Ronald R. Aminzade et al., 14–50. Cambridge: Cambridge University Press.

McAdam, Doug, Sidney Tarrow, and Charles Tilly. 2001. *Dynamics of Contention*. New York: Cambridge University Press.

———. 2007. "Toward an Integrated Perspective on Social Movements and Revolutions." In *Comparative Politics: Rationality, Culture and Structure*, ed. Mark Irving Lichbach and Alan S. Zuckerman, 142–73. Cambridge: Cambridge University Press.

McCarthy, John D., and Mayer N. Zald. 1987. "Resource Mobilization and Social Movements: A Partial Theory" and "The Trends of Social Movements in America: Professionalization and Resource Mobilization." Both in *Social Movements in an Organizational Society*, ed. John D. McCarthy and Mayer N. Zald, 15–48, 337–92. New Brunswick, NJ: Transaction.

McClymond, Michael J. 2004. *Embodying the Spirit: New Perspectives on North American Revivalism*. Baltimore, MD: Johns Hopkins University Press.

McPhail, Clark, David Schweingruber, and John McCarthy. 1998. "Policing Protest in the United States: 1960–1995." In *Policing Protest: The Control of Mass Demonstrations in Western Democracies*, ed. Donatella della Porta and Herbert Reiter, 49–69. Minneapolis: University of Minnesota Press.

Meddeb, Hamza. 2011. "L'ambivalence de la 'course à el khobza'. Obéir et se révolter en Tunisie." *Politique Africaine* 121: 35–51.

Megally, Hanny. 2006. "Human Rights in the Arab World: Reflections on the Challenges Facing Human Rights Activism." In *Human Rights in the Arab World: Independent Voices*, ed. Anthony Chase and Amr Hamzawy. Philadelphia: University of Pennsylvania Press.

Mehrez, Samia. 1991. "Experimentation and the Institution: The Case of Ida'ah 77 and Aswat." *Alif: Journal of Comparative Poetics* (Poetic Experimentation in Egypt Since the 1970s), no. 11: 115–40.

———. 2008. *Egypt's Culture Wars: Politics and Practice*. London: Routledge.

Meijer, Roel. 2002. *The Quest for Modernity: Secular Liberal and Left-Wing Political Thought in Egypt, 1945–1958*. London: Routledge, Curzon.

Mellakh, Kamal. 1999. "L'expansion scolaire et universitaire au Maroc. Aspects et enjeux." In *Diplômés maghrébins d'ici et d'ailleurs*, ed. Vincent Geisser, 92–101. Paris: Éditions du CNRS.

Melucci, Alberto. *Challenging Codes: Collective Action in the Information Age*. Cambridge: Cambridge University Press.

Menoret, Pascal. 2005. "De la rage à l'enthousiasme. Le parcours d'un jeune électeur saoudien." *Chroniques Yéménites*, no. 12. http://cy.revues.org/document188.html (accessed June 14, 2010).

———. 2008. "Fighting for the Holy Mosque: The 1979 Mecca Insurgency." In *Treading on Sacred Ground: Counterinsurgency Operations in Sacred Spaces*, ed. Christine Fair and Sumit Ganguly, 117–39. New York: Oxford University Press.

———. 2009. "Urban Unrest and Non-religious Radicalization in Saudi Arabia." In *Dying for Faith: Religiously Motivated Violence in the Contemporary World*, ed. Madawi Al-Rasheed and Marat Shterin, 123–37. London: I. B. Tauris.

———. 2009a. "Apprendre à voter? Le cas des élections municipales saoudiennes de 2005." *Genèses: Sciences sociales et Histoire*, no. 77: 51–74.

Mermier, Franck. 2012. "Le movement sudiste." In *Yémen: Le tournant révolutionnaire*, ed. Laurent Bonnefoy, Franck Mermier, and Marine Poirier, 41–66. Paris: Karthala/CEFAS.

Messadi, A., et al. 1998. "Contribution à l'étude des aspects épidémiologiques des brûlures suicidaires en Tunisie: à propos de 94 cas." *Annals of Burns and Fire Disasters* 1. http://www.medbc.com/annals (accessed May 30, 2012).

Meyer, David, and Suzanne Staggenborg. 1996. "Movements, Countermovements, and the Structure of Political Opportunity." *American Journal of Sociology* 101: 1628–60.

Meyer, John W., John Boli, George M. Thomas, and Francisco O. Ramirez. 1997. "World Society and the Nation State." *American Journal of Sociology* 102: 144–81.

al-Mirghani, Ilhami. 2008. *Ru'ya 'an ma hadatha fi 6 abril*. Cairo: Markaz Hisham Mubarak.

Mishal, Shaul, and Avraham Sela. 2002. "Participation Without Presence: Hamas, the Palestinian Authority and the Politics of Negotiated Coexistence." *Middle Eastern Studies* 38: 1–26.

Mitchell, Timothy. 1991. "The Limits of the State: Beyond Statist Approaches and their Critics." *Annual Review of Anthropology* 85: 77–96.

———. 2002. *Rule of Experts: Egypt, Techno-politics, Modernity*. Berkeley: University of California Press.

Moaddel, Mansoor. 1992. "Ideology as Episodic Discourse: The Case of the Iranian Revolution." *American Sociological Review* 57: 353–79.

———. 1993. *Class, Politics, and Ideology in the Iranian Revolution*. New York: Columbia University Press.

Moghadam, Valentine M., and Fatima Sadiqi. 2006. "Women's Activism and the Public Sphere: An Introduction and Overview." *Journal of Middle East Women's Studies* 2 (2): 1–7.

Moore, Barrington. 1966. *The Social Origins of Dictatorship and Democracy: Lord and Peasant in the Making of the Modern World*. Boston: Beacon Press.

Morris, Aldon D. 1984. *The Origins of the Civil Rights Movement: Black Communities Organizing for Change*. New York: Free Press.

———. 2004. "Reflections on Social Movement Theory: Criticism and Proposals." In *Rethinking Social Movements: Structure, Meaning and Emotion*, ed. Jeff Goodwin and James M. Jasper, 233–46. Lanham, MD: Rowman & Littlefield.

Moubayed, Sami. 2012. "Capture the Flag: What the Rebel Banner Says About Syria's Civil War," *Foreign Policy*, August 6. http://www.foreignpolicy.com/articles/2012/08/06/capture_the_flag (accessed October 31, 2012).

Mouffe, Chantal. 2005. *On the Political (Thinking in Action)*. London: Routledge.

Mu'assasat Awlad al-Ard li-Huquq al-Insan. 2011. "Hisad al-haraka al-'ummaliyya fi al-nisf al-awal min 'amm 2011." Cairo.

Munson, Ziad. 2003. "'My Life Is My Argument': Reconceptualizing Religion in Understanding Social Activism." Paper presented at seminar, Religion, Political Economy and Society, Harvard University, October 22.

Nachtwey, Jodi, and Mark Tessler. 1999. "Explaining Women's Support for Political Islam: Contributions from Feminist Theory." In *Area Studies and Social Science: Strategies for Understanding Middle East Politics*, ed. Mark Tessler, Jodi Nachtwey, and Anne Banda, 48–69. Bloomington: Indiana University Press.

Najmabadi, Afsaneh. 1997. "The Erotic *Vatan* [Homeland] as Beloved and Mother: To Love, to Possess, and to Protect." *Comparative Studies in Society and History* 39: 442–67.

Navaro-Yashin, Yael. 1998. "Uses and Abuses of 'State and Civil Society' in Contemporary Turkey." *New Perspectives on Turkey*, 18: 1–22.

———. 2002. *Faces of the State: Secularism and Public Life in Turkey*. Princeton, NJ: Princeton University Press.

Noakes, John A., and Hank Johnston. 2005. "Frames of Protest: A Road Map to A Perspective." In *Frames of Protest: Social Movements and the Framing Perspective*, ed. Hank Johnston and John A. Noakes, 1–29. Lanham, MD: Rowman & Littlefield Publishers.

Noonan, Rita K. 1995. "Women Against the State: Political Opportunities and Collective Action Frames in Chile's Transition to Democracy." *Sociological Forum* 10: 81–111.

Norman, Julie M. 2010. *The Second Palestinian Intifada: Civil Resistance.* London: Routledge.

Normand, Roger, and Sarah Zaidi. 2008. *Human Rights at the UN: The Political History of Universal Justice.* Bloomington: Indiana University Press.

Norton, Anne. 1988. *Reflections on Political Identity.* Baltimore, MD: Johns Hopkins University Press.

Norton, Augustus Richard, ed. 1995. *Civil Society in the Middle East.* 2 vols. Leiden: E. J. Brill.

Norval, Aletta J. 2007. *Aversive Democracy: Inheritance and Originality in the Democratic Tradition.* Cambridge: Cambridge University Press.

Nouaydi, Abdelaziz. 2000. "Elites and Transition to Democracy in Morocco: The Example of the Advisory Council of Human Rights." Paper presented at the annual meeting of the Middle East Studies Association, November.

Oberschall, Anthony. 1973. *Social Conflict and Social Movements.* Englewood Cliffs, NJ: Prentice-Hall.

Olson, Mancur. 1971. *The Logic of Collective Action: Public Goods and the Theory of Groups.* Cambridge, MA: Harvard University Press.

Opp, Karl-Dieter, and Wolfgang Roehl. 1990. "Repression, Micromobilization and Political Protest." *Social Forces* 69: 521–48.

Oran, Baskın. 1991. *Türk-Yunan ilişkilerinde Batı Trakya sorunu*, 2d ed. Ankara: Bilgi Yayınevi.

Osa, Maryjane. 2003. *Solidarity and Contention: Networks of Polish Opposition.* Minneapolis: University of Minnesota Press.

Oweidat, Nadia, et al. 2008. *The Kefaya Movement: A Case Study of a Grassroots Reform Initiative.* Santa Monica, CA: Rand Corporation.

Oxford Business Group. 2008. *The Report: Emerging Egypt.* London: Oxford Business Group.

Özgür-Baklacıoğlu, Nurcan. 2006. "Türkiye'nin Balkan Politikasında Rumeli ve Balkan Göçmen Dernekleri." In *Sivil Toplum ve Dış Politika: Yeni Sorunlar, Yeni Aktörler*, ed. Semra Cerit Mazlum and Erhan Doğan, 46–60. Istanbul: Bağlam Yayınları.

Parsa, Misagh. 1989. *Social Origins of the Iranian Revolution.* New Brunswick, NJ: Rutgers University Press.

Passeron, Jean-Claude. 1991. *Le raisonnement sociologique.* Paris: Nathan.

Passy, Florence, and Marco Giugni. 2001. "Social Networks and Individual Perceptions:

Explaining Differential Participation in Social Movements." *Sociological Forum* 16 (March 1): 123–53.

Pearlman, Wendy. 2011. *Violence, Nonviolence, and the Palestinian National Movement.* Cambridge: Cambridge University Press.

Peet, Richard. 2009. *Unholy Trinity: The IMF, World Bank and WTO,* 2d ed. London: Zed Books.

Pfeifer, Karen. 1999. "How Tunisia, Morocco, Jordan and Even Egypt Became IMF 'Success Stories' in the 1990s." *Middle East Report,* no. 210: 23–27.

Philbrick-Yadav, Stacey. 2010. "Segmented Publics and Islamist Women in Yemen: Rethinking Space and Activism." *Journal of Middle East Women's Studies* 6: 1–30.

———. 2011. "Antecedents of the Revolution: Intersectoral Networks and Post-Partisanship in Yemen." *Studies in Ethnicity and Nationalism* 11: 550–63.

Phillips, Sarah. 2008. *Yemen's Democracy Experiment in Regional Perspective. Patronage and Pluralized Authoritarianism.* New York: Palgrave Macmillan.

Pierskalla, Jan Hendryk. 2010. "Protest, Deterrence, and Escalation: The Strategic Calculus of Government Repression." *Journal of Conflict Resolution* 54: 117–45.

Piore, Michael, and Charles Sabel. 1984. *The Second Industrial Divide: Possibilities for Prosperity.* New York: Basic Books.

Pipes, Daniel. 1983. *In the Path of God: Islam and Political Power.* New York: Basic Books.

Planel, Vincent. 2012. "Le réveil des piémonts. Taez et la révolution yéménite." In *Yémen. Le tournant révolutionnaire,* ed. Laurent Bonnefoy, Franck Mermier, and Marine Poirier, 125–42. Paris: Karthala/CEFAS.

Poirier, Marine. 2008. "'Yémen nouveau, Futur meilleur?' Retour sur l'élection présidentielle de 2006." *Chroniques yéménites* 15: 129–59.

———. 2011. "Performing Political Domination in Yemen: Narratives and Practices of Power in the General People's Congress." *The Muslim World* 101: 202–27.

———. Forthcoming. "De la place de la Libération (al-Tahrir) à la place du Changement (al-Taghyir): Recompositions des espaces et expressions du politique au Yémen." In *Devenir révolutionnaires. Au cœur des révoltes arabes,* ed. Amin Allal and Thomas Pierret. Paris: Armand Colin/Recherches.

Pommerolle, Marie-Emmanuelle, and Frédéric Vairel. 2009. "S'engager en situation de contrainte." *Genèses: Sciences Sociales et Histoire* 77: 2–6.

Pope, Nicole, and Hugh Pope. 1997. *Turkey Unveiled: A History of Modern Turkey.* Woodstock, NY: Woodstock Press.

Posusney, Marsha Pripstein. 1997. *Labor and the State in Egypt: Workers, Unions, and Economic Restructuring, 1953–1996.* New York: Columbia University Press.

Pratt, Nicola Christine. 1998. *The Legacy of the Corporatist State: Explaining Workers' Responses to Economic Liberalisation in Egypt.* Middle East Paper, no. 60. University of Durham, Centre for Middle Eastern and Islamic Studies.

Qasim, Tal'at Fu'ad. 1996. Interview by Hisham Mubarak. In *Political Islam: Essays from*

*Middle East Report,* ed. Joel Beinin and Joe Stork, 314–26. Berkeley: University of California Press.

Radwan, Samir. 2008. "Egypt Does It Again." *Al-Ahram Weekly,* September 18–24.

Rady, Faiza. 2005. "Esco Ordeal Ends." *Al-Ahram Weekly,* June 2–8.

———. 2005a. "Twice as Dead." *Al-Ahram Weekly,* July 7–13.

Ragaru, Nadège. 2008. "ONG et enjeux minoritaires en Bulgarie. Au-delà de l' 'importation/exportation' des modèles internationaux." *Critique internationale* 40: 27–50.

Rancière, Jacques. 2006. "Democracy, Republic, and Representation." *Constellations* 13: 297–307.

al-Rasheed, Madawi. 2002. *A History of Saudi Arabia.* Cambridge: Cambridge University Press.

———. 2007. *Contesting the Saudi State: Islamic Voices from a New Generation.* Cambridge: Cambridge University Press.

Rasler, Karen. 1996. "Concessions, Repression, and Political Protest in the Iranian Revolution." *American Sociological Review* 61: 132–52.

Ricciardone, Francesca. 2008. "Gendering Worker Contestation in Egypt." Master's thesis, American University in Cairo.

Risse, Thomas, Stephen C. Ropp, and Kathryn Sikkink, eds. 1999. *The Power of Human Rights: International Norms and Domestic Change.* New York: Cambridge University Press.

Robinson, Shira. 2006. "Occupied Citizens in a Liberal State: Palestinians Under Military Rule and the Colonial Formation of Israeli Society, 1948–1966." PhD dissertation, Stanford University.

Rodley, Nigel. 2007. "Report to the UN Commission on Human Rights." UN Commission on Human Rights, Report of the Special Rapporteur on Torture and Cruel, Inhuman or Degrading Treatment or Punishment," UN Doc. E/CN.4/1994/31 (1994). http://www1.umn.edu/humanrts/commission/torture94/cat-Egypt (accessed April 17, 2007).

Rollinde, Marguerite. 2002. *Le mouvement marocain des droits de l'homme: Entre consensus national et engagement citoyen.* Paris: Editions Karthala.

Roque, Mª Àngels. 2001. *La sociedad civil en Marruecos.* Barcelona: Edicions Bellaterra.

Roussillon, Alain. 1990. "Intellectuels en crise dans l'Egypte contemporaine." In *Intellectuels et militants de l'Islam contemporain,* ed. Gilles Kepel and Yann Richard, 213–57. Paris: Le Seuil.

Roy, Olivier. 1994. *The Failure of Political Islam.* London: I. B. Tauris.

———. 2004. *Globalized Islam: The Search for a New Ummah.* New York: Columbia University Press.

Ruddick, Sara. 1989. *Maternal Thinking: Toward a Politics of Peace.* Boston: Beacon Press.

———. 1998. "Woman of Peace: A Feminist Construction." In *The Women and War Reader,* ed. Lois Ann Lorenzten, 213–27. New York: New York University Press.

Rupp, Leila J., and Verta A. Taylor. 1987. *Survival in the Doldrums: The American Women's Movements 1945 to the 1960's*. New York: Oxford University Press.

Saaf, Abdallah. 1999. *Maroc: L'espérance d'Etat moderne*. Casablanca: Éditions Afrique Orient.

Sabatier, Paul. 1998. "The Advocacy Coalition Framework: Revisions and Relevance for Europe." *Journal of European Public Policy* 5: 98–130.

Said, Mona. 2009. "The Fall and Rise of Earnings and Inequality in Egypt." In *The Egyptian Labor Market Revisited*, ed. Ragui Assaad, 53–81. Cairo: American University in Cairo Press.

al-Sa'id, Rif 'at. 1988. *Tarikh al-harakah al-shuyu 'iyya al-misriyya*. Cairo: Sharikat al-Amal.

Sakr, Naomi. 2004. "Women-Media Interaction in the Middle East: An Introductory Overview." In *Women and Media in the Middle East: Power Through Self-Expression*, ed. N. Sakr, 1–14. London: I. B. Tauris.

Salamé, Ghassan. 1994. *Democracy Without Democrats?: The Renewal of Politics in the Muslim World*. London and New York: I. B. Tauris.

Sancar, Serpil. 2001. "Türkler/Kürtler, Anneler ve Siyaset: Savaşta Çocuklarını Kaybetmiş Türk ve Kürt Anneler Üzerine Bir Yorum." *Toplum ve Bilim* 90: 22–41.

Sanders, Lynn. 1997. "Against Deliberation." *Political Theory* 25: 347–76.

al-Sayyid, Kamal Mustapha. 1995. "A Civil Society in Egypt." In *Civil Society in the Middle East*, vol. 1, ed. Augustus R. Norton, 269–93. Leiden: E. J. Brill.

Schedler, Andreas. 2002. "Elections Without Democracy: The Menu of Manipulation." *Journal of Democracy* 13: 36–50.

Scheper-Hughes, Nancy. 1998. "Maternal Thinking and the Politics of War." In *The Women and War Reader*, ed. Lois Ann Lorenzten, 227–34. New York: New York University Press.

Schlumberger, Oliver. 2000. "The Arab Middle East and the Question of Democratization: Some Critical Remarks." *Democratization* 7: 104–32.

———, ed. 2007. *Debating Arab Authoritarianism: Dynamics and Durability in Nondemocratic Regimes*. Stanford, CA: Stanford University Press.

Schrand, Irmgard. 2004. *Jews in Egypt: Communists and Citizens*. Münster: Lit.

Schwedler, Jillian. 2006. *Faith in Moderation: Islamist Parties in Jordan and Yemen*. Cambridge: Cambridge University Press.

Scott, James C. 1985. *Weapons of the Weak: Everyday Forms of Peasant Resistance*. New Haven, CT: Yale University Press.

———. 1990. *Domination and the Arts of Resistance: Hidden Transcripts*. New Haven, CT, and London: Yale University Press.

Scott, James C., and Benedict J. Kerkvliet, eds. 1986. *Everyday Forms of Peasant Resistance in South-East Asia*. London: Frank Cass.

Seddon, David. 1989. "Riot and Rebellion in North Africa: Political Responses to Economic Crisis in Tunisia, Morocco, and Sudan." In *Power and Stability in the Middle East*, ed. Berch Berberoğlu, 114–35. London: Zed.

Seddon, David, and Leo Zeilig. 2005. "Class and Protest in Africa: New Waves." *Review of African Political Economy*, no. 103: 9–27.

Selbin, Eric. 2010. *Revolution, Rebellion, Resistance: The Power of Story*. London: Zed Books.

Sewell, William H. 1992. "A Theory of Structure: Duality, Agency, and Transformation." *American Journal of Sociology* 98: 1–29.

———. 2001. "Space in Contentious Politics." In *Silence and Voice in the Study of Contentious Politics*, ed. Ronald R. Aminzade, Jack A. Goldstone, Doug McAdam, Elizabeth J. Perry, William H. Sewell, Sidney Tarrow, and Charles Tilly, 51–89. Cambridge: Cambridge University Press.

Sharabi, Hisham. 2003. "Arab Satellite Channels and Their Political Impact After the Iraq War." *al-Hayat*, July 18. www.worldpress.org/article_model.cfm?article_id=1482& dont=yes (accessed June 13, 2010).

Sharoni, Simona. 2001. "Rethinking Women's Struggles in Israel-Palestine and in the North of Ireland." In *Victims, Perpetrators or Actors? Gender, Armed Conflict and Political Violence*, ed. Carline Moser and Fiona Clark, 85–89. London: Zed Books.

Shehadeh, Lamia Rustum. 1999. "Women in the Lebanese Militias." In *Women and War in Lebanon*, ed. Lamia Rustum Shehadeh, 145–66. Gainesville: University of Florida Press.

Shukr Allah, Hala. 2006. "Min al-bayt ila mawqi' al-'amal: dirasa 'an zuruf al-'amala al-nisa'iyya fi misr." *Tiba* 8: 31–52.

Sikkink, Kathryn. 2004. *Mixed Signals: U.S. Human Rights Policy and Latin America*. Ithaca, NY: Cornell University Press.

Siméant, Johanna. 1993. "La violence d'un répertoire: les sans-papiers en grève de la faim." *Cultures et conflits* 9–10: 315–38.

Singerman, Diane. 1995. *Avenues of Participation: Family, Politics, and Networks in Urban Quarters of Cairo*. Princeton, NJ: Princeton University Press.

Skalli, Loubna H. 2006. "Communicating Gender in the Public Sphere: Women and Information Technologies in the MENA." *Journal of Middle East Women's Studies* 2: 35–59.

Skocpol, Theda. 1979. *States and Social Revolutions: A Comparative Analysis of France, Russia, and China*. Cambridge: Cambridge University Press.

Slyomovics, Susan. 2002. "Torture, Recovery, and Truth in Morocco." In *Experiments with Truth: Transitional Justice and the Processes of Truth and Reconciliation*, ed. Okwui Enwezor et al., 213–30. Kassel: Hatje Cantz.

———. 2005. *The Performance of Human Rights in Morocco*. Philadelphia: University of Pennsylvania Press.

———. 2009. "Reparations in Morocco: The Symbolic Dirham." In *Waging War and Making Peace: Reparations and Human Rights: A Report from the Reparations Task Force, the Committee for Human Rights, American Anthropological Association*, ed. Barbara Rose Johnston and Susan Slyomovics, 95–114. Walnut Creek, CA: Left Coast Press.

Smith, Jackie. 2005. "Building Bridges or Building Walls? Explaining Regionalization Among Transnational Social Movement Organizations." *Mobilization* 10: 251–69.

Snow, David A., and Robert D. Benford. 1988. "Ideology, Frame Resonance and Participant Mobilization." *International Social Movement Research* 1: 197–219.

Snow, David A., Louis A. Zurcher, and Sheldon Ekland-Olson. 1980. "Social Networks and Social Movements: A Microstructural Approach to Differential Recruitment." *American Sociological Review* 45: 787–801.

Snow, David A., et al. 1986. "Frame Alignment Processes, Micromobilization, and Movement Participation." *American Sociological Review* 51: 464–81.

Soule, Sarah A. 2007. "Diffusion Processes Within and Across Movements." In *The Blackwell Companion to Social Movements*, ed. David A. Snow, Sarah A. Soule and Hanspeter Kriesi, 294–310. London: Wiley-Blackwell.

Stacher, Joshua. 2005. "Rhetorical Acrobats and Perpetuations: Egypt's National Council for Human Rights." *Middle East Report*, no. 235: 2–7.

Stack, Liam. 2007. "Mansoura Workers Attack Factory Sale, Sit-in Reaches Day 20." *Daily Star Egypt*, May 11.

Stack, Liam, and Maram Mazen. 2007. "Striking Mahalla Workers Demand Govt. Fulfill Broken Promises." *Daily Star Egypt*, September 27.

Staggenborg, Suzanne. 1998. "Social Movement Communities and Cycles of Protest." *Social Problems* 45: 180–204.

Stagh, Marina. 1993. *The Limits of Freedom of Speech: Prose Literature and Prose Writers in Egypt Under Nasser and Sadat*. Stockholm: Almqvist & Wiksell International.

Stepan, Alfred, and Graeme B. Robertson. 2003. "An 'Arab' More Than a 'Muslim' Democracy Gap." *Journal of Democracy* 14: 30–44.

Stones, Rob. 2005. *Structuration Theory*. New York: Palgrave Macmillan.

Swidler, Ann. 1986. "Culture in Action: Symbols and Strategies." *American Sociological Review* 51: 273–86.

Tahhan, Aram. 2012. "Ticking Musical Time Bombs Are Behind the Sound of the Syrian Uprising." In *Culture in Defiance: Continuing Traditions of Satire, Art and the Struggle for Freedom in Syria*, 47–50. Amsterdam: Prince Claus Fund Gallery.

Tanrıkulu, Nimet. 2002. "Gozaltında Kayıp Yok Diyenlere Bir Yanıt." *Bianet*, May 17. http://www.bianet.org/bianet/insan-haklari/10046–gozaltinda-kayip-yok-diyenlere-bir-yanit (accessed April 14, 2010).

———. 2003. "Bizde yok!" In *Toplumsal Hareketler Konuşuyor*, ed. Leyla Sanlı, 275–92. Cağlıoğlu, Istanbul: Alan.

Taraki, Lisa. 1995. "Islam Is the Solution: Jordanian Islamists and the Dilemma of the 'Modern Woman.'" *British Journal of Political Science* 46: 643–61.

Tarrow, Sidney. 1988. "National Politics and Collective Action: Recent Theory and Research in Western Europe and the United States." *Annual Review of Sociology* 14: 421–40.

———. 1989. *Democracy and Disorder: Protest and Politics in Italy, 1965–1975.* Oxford: Oxford University Press.

———. 1990. "The Phantom at the Opera: Political Parties and Social Movements of the 1960s and the 1970s in Italy." In *Challenging the Political Order, New Social and Political Movements in Western Democracies*, ed. Russel J. Dalton and Manfred Kuechler, 251–71. Cambridge: Polity Press.

———. 1993. "Social Protest and Policy Reform: May 1968 and the *Loi d'orientation* in France." *Comparative Political Studies* 25: 579–607.

———. 1994. *Power in Movement: Social Movements and Contentious Politics.* Cambridge: Cambridge University Press.

———. 1995. "The Europeanisation of Conflict: Reflections from a Social Movement Perspective." *West European Politics* 18: 223–51.

———. 1995a. "Cycles of Collective Action: Between Moments of Madness and the Repertoire of Contention." In *Repertoires and Cycles of Collective Action*, ed. Mark Traugott, 89–114. Durham, NC: Duke University Press.

———. 1998. *Power in Movement: Social Movements and Contentious Politics*, 2d ed. Cambridge: Cambridge University Press.

———. 2000. "La contestation transnationale." *Cultures et conflits* 38–39: 187–224.

———. 2003. "Confessions of a Recovering Structuralist." *Mobilization* 8: 134–41.

———. 2011. *Power in Movement: Social Movements and Contentious Politics*, 3d ed. Cambridge: Cambridge University Press.

Tarrow, Sidney, and Charles Tilly. 2006. *Contentious Politics.* Boulder, CO: Paradigm.

Taussig, Michael T. 1997. *The Magic of the State.* New York: Routledge.

Taylor, Verta. 1989. "Social Movement Continuity: The Women's Movement in Abeyance." *American Sociological Review* 54: 761–75.

Taylor, Verta, and Nancy E. Whittier. 1992. "Collective Identity in Social Movement Communities: Lesbian Feminist Mobilization." In *Frontiers in Social Movement Theory*, ed. Aldon D. Morris and Carol McClurg Mueller, 104–26. New Haven, CT: Yale University Press.

Tekeli, Şirin. 2004. "Yeni Dalga Kadın Hareketinde Örgütlenme." *Bianet*, November 29. http://www.bianet.org/bianet/kadin/49886–yeni-dalga-kadin-hareketinde-orgutlenme—2 (accessed April 14, 2010).

Temelkuran, Ece. 2006. "Şehidiyle 'Övünmeyen' Anne: ' Çocuğum Ölmüş. Nasıl Gurur Duyayım?" *Milliyet*, September 8. http://www.milliyet.com.tr/2006/09/08/yazar/temelkuran.html (accessed April 14, 2010).

———. 2006a. "Biz de Tuzağa Düşmeyeceğiz." *Milliyet*, September 13.

Teske, Robin L., and Mary Ann Tétreault. 1999. *Feminist Approaches to Social Movements, Community, and Power.* Columbia: University of South Carolina Press.

Tilly, Charles. 1978. *From Mobilization to Revolution.* Reading, MA: Addison-Wesley.

———. 1984. "Les origines du répertoire de l'action collective contemporaine en

France et en Grande-Bretagne." *Vingtième siècle: Revue d'histoire contemporaine* 4: 89–108.

———. 1985. "European Lives." In *Reliving the Past: The Worlds of Social History*, ed. Olivier Zunz, 11–52. Chapel Hill: University of North Carolina Press.

———. 1986. *The Contentious French*. Cambridge, MA: Harvard University Press.

———. 1993. *European Revolutions: 1492–1992*. Cambridge, MA: Wiley-Blackwell.

———. 1995. "Contentious Repertoires in Great Britain, 1758–1834." In *Repertoires and Cycles of Collective Action*, ed. Mark Traugott, 15–42. Durham, NC: Duke University Press.

———. 2003. "Contention over Space and Place." *Mobilization: an International Journal* 2: 221–26.

———. 2008. *Contentious Performances*. Cambridge: Cambridge University Press.

Tilly, Charles, and Sidney Tarrow. 2007. *Contentious Politics*. Boulder, CO: Paradigm.

Tocqueville, Alexis de. 1983. *The Old Regime and the French Revolution*. New York: Anchor Books.

Toumarkine, Alexandre. 2000. "Civil Society and Nationalism: The Example of the Associations of Migrants from the Caucasus and the Balkans." In *Civil Society in the Grip of Nationalism: Studies on Political Cultures in Contemporary Turkey*, ed. Stefanos Yerasimos, Gunter Seufert, and Karin Vorhoff, 425–50. Istanbul: Orient Institut/IFEA.

Tozy, Mohamed. 1994. "Représentation/Intercession. Les enjeux de pouvoir dans les 'champs politiques désamorcés' au Maroc." In *Changements politiques au Maghreb*, ed. Michel Camau, 153–68. Paris: Éditions du CNRS.

Traugott, Mark. 1985. *Armies of the Poor*. Princeton, NJ: Princeton University Press.

———. 1995. "Recurrent Patterns of Collective Action." In *Repertoires and Cycles of Collective Action*, ed. Mark Traugott, 1–14. Durham, NC: Duke University Press.

Tunçay, Mete. 1976. "Misak-ı Millî'nin 1. Maddesi Üstüne." *Birikim* 18–19: 12–16.

Turshen, Meredeth. 2002. "Algerian Women in the Liberation Struggle and the Civil War: From Active Participants to Passive Victims?" *Social Research* 69: 889–911.

Utvik, Bjorn Olav. 2006. "Religious Revivalism in Nineteenth-Century Norway and Twentieth-Century Egypt: A Critique of Fundamentalism Studies." *Islam and Christian-Muslim Relations* 17: 143–57.

Uysal, Ayşen. 2005. "Maintien de l'ordre et risques liés aux manifestations de rue." In *La Turquie conteste. Mobilisations sociales et régime sécuritaire*, ed. Gilles Dorronsoro, 31–50. Paris: Éditions du CNRS.

Vairel, Frédéric. 2005. "Espace protestataire et autoritarisme. Nouveaux contextes de mise à l'épreuve de la notion de 'fluidité politique': l'analyse des conjonctures de basculement dans le cas du Maroc." PhD dissertation, Institut d'études politiques d'Aix-en-Provence.

———. 2005a. "L'ordre disputé du sit-in au Maroc." *Genèses*, no. 59: 47–70.

———. 2008. "Morocco: From Mobilization to Reconciliation?" *Mediterranean Politics* 13: 229–41.

Vermeren, Pierre. 2002. *École, élite et pouvoir au Maroc et en Tunisie au XXè siècle*. Rabat: Alizès.

Waltz, Susan. 1995. *Human Rights and Reform: Changing the Face of North African Politics*. Berkeley: University of California Press.

Waltz, Susan, and Lindsay Benstead. 2006. "When the Time Is Ripe: The Struggle to Create an Institutional Culture of Human Rights in Morocco." In *Human Rights in the Arab World: Independent Voices*, ed. Anthony Chase and Amr Hamzawy, 174–95. Philadelphia: University of Pennsylvania Press.

Weaver, Mary Ann. 2000. *A Portrait of Egypt: A Journey Through the World of Militant Islam*. New York: Farrar, Straus and Giroux.

Wedeen, Lisa. 1999. *Ambiguities of Dominations: Politics, Rhetorics, and Symbols in Contemporary Syria*. Chicago: University of Chicago Press.

———. 2007. "The Politics of Deliberation: *Qat* Chews as Public Spheres in Yemen." *Public Culture* 19: 59–84.

———. 2008. *Peripheral Visions: Publics, Power, and Performance in Yemen*. Chicago: Chicago University Press.

White, Jenny B. 2002. *Islamist Mobilization in Turkey: A Study in Vernacular Politics*. Seattle: University of Washington Press.

Whitman, Lois. 1990. *Destroying Ethnic Identity: The Turks in Western Thrace*. New York: Helsinki Watch Report.

Wickham, Carrie Rosefsky. 2002. *Mobilizing Islam: Religion, Activism, and Political Change in Egypt*. New York: Columbia University Press.

———. 2004. "The Path to Moderation: Strategy and Learning in the Formation of Egypt's Wasat Party." *Comparative Politics* 36: 205–28.

Wiktorowicz, Quintan, ed. 2004. *Islamic Activism: A Social Movement Theory Approach*. Bloomington: Indiana University Press.

World Bank. 2007. *Doing Business in Egypt 2008*. Washington, DC: World Bank. http://www.doingbusiness.org/documents/subnational/DB08_Subnational_Report_Egypt .pdf (accessed October 1, 2008).

———. 2007a. *Arab Republic of Egypt: A Poverty Assessment Update*. Report no. 39885–EGT. Washington, DC: World Bank.

Young, Iris Marion. 2002. *Inclusion and Democracy*. Oxford: Oxford University Press.

Yurdatapan, Şanar, and Abdurrahman Dilipak. 2003. *Opposites: Side by Side*. New York: George Braziller.

Yurtsever, Leman. 2009. "Neden Cumartesi, Neden Anneler?" *Amargi* 13: 13–14.

Zaatari, Zeina. 2003. "Women Activists of South Lebanon." PhD dissertation, University of California, Davis.

Zaki, Lamia. 2007. "Transforming the City from Below: Shantytown Dwellers and the Fight for Electricity in Casablanca." In *Subalterns and Social Protest: History from Below in the Middle East and North Africa*, ed. Stephanie Cronin, 116–37. London: Routledge.

————. 2009. "Maroc: dépendance alimentaire, radicalisation contestataire, répression autoritaire." *États des résistances dans le Sud—2009. Face à la crise alimentaire.* Centre tricontinental, Louvain la-Neuve. Paris: Cetri/Syllepse.

Zengin, Nilüfer. 2008. "Singer Bülent Ersoy's Courageous Anti-war Utterances on Live TV Have Provoked a Nationalist Backlash and an Investigation." *Bianet*, February 27. http://www.bianet.org/english/minorities/105191–nationalist-uproar-at-singer-s anti -war-stance (accessed April 14, 2010).

Zerilli, Linda M. G. 2005. *Feminism and the Abyss of Freedom.* Chicago: University of Chicago Press.

Zine, Jasmin. 2006. "Between Orientalism and Fundamentalism: The Politics of Muslim Women's Feminist Engagement." *Muslim World Journal of Human Rights* 3 (1). http://www.bepress.com/mwjhr/vol3/iss1/art5 (accessed June 13, 2010).

Zyiad, Leen. 2012. "Syria's Revolution as Carnival." In *Culture in Defiance: Continuing Traditions of Satire, Art and the Struggle for Freedom in Syria*, 39–46. Amsterdam: Prince Claus Fund Gallery.

————. 2012a. "Wall Wars." In *Culture in Defiance: Continuing Traditions of Satire, Art and the Struggle for Freedom in Syria*, 27–28. Amsterdam: Prince Claus Fund Gallery.

# INDEX

Activism: among intellectuals, 64; "de-centered," 51–52, 59–67; homosexual, 69, 107; human rights, 105–7; Islamic (*see* Islamic movements); memory, 134–38
Al-Assad, Bashar, 251–53, 257, 260
Alekry, Abdulnabi, 109–10, 112
Arab Spring, 9, 35, 255; of 2005, 8
Authoritarianism, 47, 106, 108, 120; civil society and, 36–37; of Islamic groups, 81, 85; neoliberal globalization and, 207–8; SMT and, 25–26, 206. *See also* Repression

Bahrain: human rights movements in, 110–12, 127, 128; repression in, 108–9
Ben Ali, Zine el-Abidine: "generation of," 199–200; opposition to, 21–22, 186–87, 192, 196–99; regime of, 190; support for, 194, 204
Bouazizi, Mohamed, 22, 191

Center for Trade Union and Workers Services (CTUWS), 114, 209, 217, 219, 222
Civil society, 1, 208–9; authoritarian regimes and, 36, 37, 47, 100; "awakening of," 16–19; democratization and, 36, 39, 42, 157–56, 168; human rights and, 121; media's effect on, 91; SMT and, 16–19, 169; Western model for, 87, 99, 101
Cold War, lasting political impact of, 71, 74. *See also* Communism
Collective action: culture of, 85; cycle of, 129; repertoire of, 14–15, 143
Communism, 171; collapse of, 54, 105; in Egypt, 55–67, 107, 114; and its movements in 1970s, 58
Consultative Council on Human Rights (CCDH), 119–20; Equity and Reconciliation Commission (ERC), 120, 122–24
Contentious politics, 140; actors, 15–18, 137–38; cycles of contention, 19–20, 209; repertoires of, 145–46, 247–48; spaces, 33, 48, 165
Corruption, accusations of, 43, 110, 189, 191–94, 202, 208, 232, 250–51

Demobilization, research on, 18, 27–28, 50–51, 59–60
Democracy, 35, 38, 121, 139, 158; military and, 163–65; social movements and, 150; theory of, 149–50
Democratization, 35, 115, 157, 227

Detachment, political, 131, 138–40, 147

*Diplômés chômeurs*: definition of, 129–30; mobilization of, 131, 134–37, 141, 146. *See also* Unemployment, of university graduates

Economy: Egyptian, 55, 210–12, 216–18; as motive for activism, 74

Education: and Islamic movements, 69–70, 99, 117; and unemployment, 133–38

Egypt: economic liberalization (*infitah*) in, 55, 210–11; human rights in, 107, 112–18, 127; privatization in, 216–18; social movements in, 33–34, 49–50, 105; workers in, 205–27; workers' organizations in, 208–9. *See also* Al-Jama'a al-Islamiyya; Kifaya; Muslim Brothers

Egyptian Federation of Independent Trade Unions (EFITU), 223–24

Egyptian Organization for Human Rights (EOHR), 113–18

Egyptian Trade Union Federation (ETUF), 208, 217–19, 223–26

Elites, governing, 17, 40, 47, 134, 142; criticism against, 63; formation of, 147; and protests, 147

ESCO Spinning Company, 216–17, 226

European Union (EU), 168–69; framework on human rights, 178–81; trade agreements with Egypt and Morocco, 35

Gafsa Phosphate Company (Compagnie des Phosphates de Gafsa; CPG), 188–89, 197

*Gallery 68*, 56

Gender relations, 17, 159; domestic abuse, 97–98; militarization and, 162–63, 166; neoliberal economy and female workers, 218. *See also* Women's movements

Globalization, 47, 118

Ghazl al-Mahalla, *see under* Misr Spinning and Weaving Company

Hamas, 88, 90–91

Hassan, Bahey el-Din, 113–18

Hizbullah, 18; intra-movement transformation and, 87; "Lebanization" of, 92; media and, 87, 91–92, 95–100; women and, 87, 95

Human rights, 1, 8, 16, 26–27, 35; discourse of, 14, 18, 19–20, 44, 109; framework, 105, 110–11, 117, 181; institutionalization of, 134; minority, 167–70; Sunni view on, 107; Western Thracians in Turkey, 178–81; women's, 94, 111, 149–50; workers', 42, 113–14

Human Rights Association (IHD), 124–26, 156, 157, 161

Identity formation, 15

Individualism, 85

Informality, in social movement literature, 52–53. *See also* Networks, informal

Intellectuals: and activists, 53–54, 58; changing roles of, 53, 66–67; Egyptian urban middle class, 209; lawyers, 118; leftist writers, 51, 53; secular, 66; "social fatigue" of, 66

International Monetary Fund (IMF), 20, 36, 206; Egypt and, 210; Tunisia and, 21

Iranian revolution of 1979, 4, 105

Iraq War of 2003, 20, 38, 49

Islah Party, 232–33, 236, 239–40, 242

Islam: human rights and, 116, 128; moral economy in, 208; proselytizing methods, 70; Turkish identity and, 171; victimization of, 73; women and, 101

Islamic Jihad, 115

Islamic movements, 2; in academia, 133; disengagement from, 79–82; in Egypt,

58; history of, in Bahrain, 108–11; history of, in Saudi Arabia, 69–72; human rights movements and, 116–17, 120; politicization of, 71–75; radicalization mechanisms and, 75–78; SMT and, 3–4, 28; violence in, 28. *See also* Terrorism

Islamic organizations, 149; armed, 13, 28, 115–16; organizational problems in, 79–82; structures and hierarchy in, 77–80; women in, 89

Israeli-Palestinian conflict, 38, 42–43; Intifada, Second, 37, 73, 49, 92, 209; Popular Committee in Solidarity, 209; 1967 War, 55; 1982 invasion of Lebanon, 92, 112

Al-Jama'a al-Islamiyya, 115

Jihad: Afghan, 74; Islamic rhetoric and, 73–74

Journalism, 67, 91, 122

Justice and Development Party (AKP), 107, 125, 169

Karama: party, 121, 208, 222; newspaper, 60

Karman, Tawakkul, 242–43

Al-Khawaja, Abdul-Hadi, 110–12

Kifaya ("Enough!"), 59–60, 63; formation of, 34, 49–50; in 2004, 34, 42–46; workers' movement and, 210

Kurdistan Workers' Party (PKK), 107, 124, 126, 156, 179–80

Labor, history of, 205

Literature, as resistance, 55–56

Lobby, 169, 180–81

"Lumpen intelligentsia," 1, 12, 27

Al-Manar (television station), 18, 87, 91–100, 246

March of Life, 242

Marxism: in Egypt, 55, 61, 113–14; in Morocco, 118, 136

Media: censorship of, 91; Hizbullah and diversity in, 91–92, 95–100; rise of new media, 91, 209; violence in, 99; women in, 92–93, 95–100

Migrations: to the Gulf, 71; to Turkey, 167–71

Militarism, 162–66, 175, 141; of Hizbullah, 92

Misr Spinning and Weaving Company, 210, 218–24, 226

Mobilization, 51; codification of practices and, 137–38; informal, 10–13, 70; as a resource in different sectors, 147; "semiformal," 69–70; shaping space for, 234–36. *See also* Networks

Modernization: intellectual, 54; of religious practices, 85

Moroccan Association for Human Rights (Association Marocain des Droits de l'Homme; AMDH), 44, 119, 121

Moroccan Organization for Human Rights (Organization Marocain des Droits de l'Homme; OMDH), 44, 119

Morocco: human rights and, 105–6, 118–24; National Association of Unemployed Graduates of Morocco (ANDCM), 133–45; social movements in, 33–48; unemployed university graduates in, 129–33, 135–36, 147; women's rights in, 34

Mubarak, Hosni: and labor movement, 209, 223–26; protests against, 13, 19, 21, 44, 205, 210, 221, 223–26; regime of, 43, 49, 58, 116, 208. *See also* Kifaya

Muslim Brothers, 92, 114–17; human rights and, 116–17, 128; as opposition, 37, 41, 45–46, 59, 62–6, 232, 240; in Saudi Arabia, 71, 79, 81–84; workers and, 208–9

Nasser, Gamal Abdel, 51, 56, 207

Nasserism, 55, 60, 65, 114–15, 208–9

Nationalism: Bahraini, 108; and its discourse in Egypt, 66; Turkish, 156, 163, 167, 171–72; women's organizations and, 94

Nazif, Ahmad, 211–12, 216, 218, 220–21

Neoliberalism (economic): Egyptian, 207, 210, 216–18; Moroccan, 131–32

Networks, 10–14; human rights, 105–6; informal, 11–13, 52, 67, 88, 154; intellectuals, 84–85; international groups, 109; Islamic, 4, 13, 70; local, 206, 250; militant, 181; al-Qaʻida, 78; *shilla* (cliques), 82; in Social Movement Theory, 50; student, 71–73, 57; women's, 151–52; working-class, 206–9. *See also* Mobilization

Nongovernmental organizations (NGOs), 25, 42–43, 51, 106, 122; government-controlled NGOs (GONGOs), 111; human rights, 182; labor-oriented, 209; Palestinian solidarity and, 209

Nonviolence, 5, 152; mobilization and, 196–99, 234–35, 241; silence and, 161–62

Political Opportunity Structure (POS), 6, 50, 56, 59, 106, 144, 169

Political participation, 105–8; standardization/codification of, 135–37

Political prisoners: Bahraini, 110; Moroccan, 118–21, 133–34; solidarity activism, 127

Politics, contested definition of, 49, 149, 160–61

Popular committees: in Bahrain, 112; Palestinian solidarity, 209

Post-Islamism, 83

Private sector, collective actions in, 216–18

Privatization (economic): Egyptian, 209; Moroccan, 131–32; workers' collective action and, 216–18

Public sphere: media and, 91; politicization of, 70–71, 85, 168; theories of, 158–59

Al-Qaʻida, 25, 83; structure and hierarchy, 75, 77–78

Radicalism, 17–18; definition of, 40–41; relationship with repression, 61, 69; in Saudi Arabia, 75

Rational actor model, 3

Rational Choice Theory, 50

Repression, 39–45, 50; in Bahrain, 108–9; Egyptian workers and government, 223–25; and engagement, 69, 76; in everyday life, 76–77; history of, in Saudi Arabia, 70–71; human rights and, 106–7, 109; ideological orientation and, 141; in Morocco, 119, 133; in Syria, 109; torture, 71, 107, 111, 114, 116–18, 123–24, 129, 150; in Tunisia, 190, 200–201; against women, 254; in Yemen, 235, 241. *See also* Authoritarianism

Repression/opportunity structure framework, 60–61

Resource: mismanagement of, 81, 85; social movement and, 108, 144, 206; transfer of, 141

Resource mobilization: theory of, 3, 10, 41, 50; in the 1979 Iranian Revolution, 4

Sadat, Anwar, 55–56, 210

Salafi, 71–72, 83–84, 201, 252

Salih, ʻAli ʻAbd Allah, 229–32, 238–39, 241–45

Salih, Muhammad, 243

Saudi Arabia: Islamic activism and, 68–85; regional influence of, 230, 260. *See also* Islamic movements

Secularism, Turkish, 169

Sha'ban, Buthaina, 246, 252

Shi'a, 87, 92–93, 101, 107–11, 229; Zaydi revival movement, 229, 236–37,

Social constructionism, 4

"Social fatigue," 65; definition of, 51

Social Movement Theory (SMT), 50, 86; classical, 2–4, 132, 169, 206, 247; democracy and, 149; *Dynamics of Contention* (McAdam, Tarrow, and Tilly), 2, 6–7, 14, 50, 161, 206, 247, 255; feminism and, 89; "frame bridging," 259–60; framing, 50, 88, 128, 130–31, 133, 147, 159, 248; human rights and, 105, 127–28; internal dynamics and, 88–89; mobilization and, 255; Political Process Model (PPM), 4, 6–7, 10, 14, 24, 169, 209–10; resources and, 108, 206; revised conceptual model of, 6–8, 26–27; structuralist tradition of, 6–7, 55

"Social nonmovement," 65, 70

Socialism, 42, 55, 208, 210, 212

Southern Movement (*al-Hirak al-janubi*), 229, 235, 237

Strikes, 212, 213–15 (Tables 10.1, 10.2); Egyptian union, 208, 217–19, 223–26; minimum wage, 211–12, 220, 223, 225–26; private sector, 216–18; violence in, 221, 223. *See also* Egyptian Trade Union Federation (ETUF); Misr Spinning and Weaving Company

Structuration theory, 230, 244

Student movements: Islamist, 70–75; in the 1970s, 38, 51, 55, 113–14; Moroccan, 129–33, 135–36, 140–41; Turkish, 172–73, 181

Supreme Council of the Armed Forces (SCAF), 224–25

Symbolic spaces, 52, 59, 64, 67, 175

Syria: mobilization in, 256–60; politics of contention in, 247–48; repression in, 109; revolutionary tactics in, 248–53

Tagammu' Party, 50, 52, 58–59, 63, 208

Terrorism, 1, 18, 154; bombings in Saudi Arabia, 70–71, 74; women and, 94

Tilly, Charles, 14–15, 23, 45, 50, 161, 206; notion of inclusiveness, 62

Torture, *see under* Repression

Trade unions: Egyptian, 114, 208–9, 219, 223, 226; mobilization and, 142; Tunisian, 21, 185–86, 189, 195

Tunisia: Democratic Constitutional Rally (RCD), 185, 189–90, 193–98, 202; protests in, 187–92, 195–96; youth radicalization, 199–202

Tunisian General Labor Union (Union Générale Tunisienne du Travail; UGTT), 21, 185–86, 189, 195

Turkey: application of democratic theory in, 149–50; coup (1980), 174–75; Cyprus and, 167, 171–75, 177; human rights in, 105–7, 124–27; Kurdish minority in, 107, 124, 151, 154, 165; migrants from Western Thrace, 167–74; military in, 162–66, 168, 171–72, 175; Saturday night vigils (1995–1998, 2009), 150–56; violence in, 156, 176

Unemployment, 21; mobilization of the unemployed, 108, 133, 136, 146–47; of professionals (*see* "Lumpen intelligentsia"); rates of, 132; scoring system of, 135–37; uniqueness of Moroccan unemployed graduate activist, 136; of university graduates, 129–48

Voluntarism (*tatawwu'*), 70

Western Thrace Turks Solidarity Association (Batı Trakya Türkleri Dayanışma Derneği; BTTDD), 168, 170–81; demonstrations, 175–77

Women's movements, 90–91, 150–51, 158–59; in Bahrain, 111; changing role of, 93–94; Islamic, 89; media and, 95–100; in Morocco, 122; recruitment of, 90; rhetoric of motherhood, 93, 163–65; Saturday People and the Mothers, 150–56, 160, 165

Women's rights, *see under* Human rights

Workers: "working class," definition of, 206–7; Egyptian, 205–27; mobilization of, 13; violence and, 223–25. *See also* Strikes

World Bank, 20, 36; Egypt and, 210–11, 220; Tunisia and, 188

Yemen: General People's Congress (GPC), 229–30, 232, 240–44; Joint Meeting Parties (al-Liqa' al-mushtarak), 232, 239–40, 242; mobilization in, 231–32, 234–36; repression in, 235, 241; revolutionary groups, 232, 236, 239–40

---

**Ariella Azoulay and Adi Ophir,** The One-State Condition: Occupation and Democracy in Israel/Palestine
2012

**Steven Heydemann and Reinoud Leenders, editors,** Middle East Authoritarianisms: Governance, Contestation, and Regime Resilience in Syria and Iran
2012

**Jonathan V. Marshall,** The Lebanese Connection: Corruption, Civil War, and the International Drug Traffic
2012

**Joshua Stacher,** Adaptable Autocrats: Regime Power in Egypt and Syria
2012

**Bassam Haddad,** Business Networks in Syria: The Political Economy of Authoritarian Resilience
2011

**Noah Coburn,** Bazaar Politics: Power and Pottery in an Afghan Market Town
2011

**Laura Bier,** Revolutionary Womanhood: Feminisms, Modernity, and the State in Nasser's Egypt
2011

**Samer Soliman,** *The Autumn of Dictatorship: Fiscal Crisis and Political Change in Egypt under Mubarak*
*2011*

**Rochelle A. Davis,** *Palestinian Village Histories: Geographies of the Displaced*
*2010*

**Haggai Ram,** *Iranophobia: The Logic of an Israeli Obsession*
*2009*

**John Chalcraft,** *The Invisible Cage: Syrian Migrant Workers in Lebanon*
*2008*

**Rhoda Kanaaneh,** *Surrounded: Palestinian Soldiers in the Israeli Military*
*2008*

**Asef Bayat,** *Making Islam Democratic: Social Movements and the Post-Islamist Turn*
*2007*

**Robert Vitalis,** *America's Kingdom: Mythmaking on the Saudi Oil Frontier*
*2006*

**Jessica Winegar,** *Creative Reckonings: The Politics of Art and Culture in Contemporary Egypt*
*2006*

**Joel Beinin and Rebecca L. Stein, editors,** *The Struggle for Sovereignty: Palestine and Israel, 1993–2005*
*2006*